. . . there is in such a population, of itself, no *help* at all towards reconstruction of the wreck of your Niagara plunge; of themselves they, with whatever cry of 'liberty' in their mouths, are inexorably marked as *slaves*; and not even the immortal gods could make them free,—except by making them anew . . .

Thomas Carlyle, "Shooting Niagara: And After?"

. . . there was *something*, something that his men had been unable to grasp, . . . that neither prison nor torture, nor a state of siege could put a stop to; *something* that was moving in the subsoil . . . with unpredictable manifestations. . . . It was as if the atmosphere had been changed by the addition of some impalpable pollen or hidden ferment.

Alejo Carpentier, *Reasons of State*

People have always aspired to an idyll . . . , a realm of harmony where the world does not rise up as a stranger against man nor man against other men, where the world and all its people are molded from a single stock . . . , where every man is a note in a magnificent Bach fugue and anyone who refuses his note is a mere black dot, useless and meaningless, easily caught and squashed between the fingers like an insect. . . . From the start there were people who realized they lacked the proper temperament for the idyll. . . . But since by definition an idyll is one world for all, the people who wished to emigrate were implicitly denying its validity. Instead of going abroad, they went behind bars.

Milan Kundera, *The Book of Laughter and Forgetting*

Atrocity and Amnesia

The Political Novel Since 1945

ROBERT BOYERS

New York   Oxford

OXFORD UNIVERSITY PRESS

1985

OXFORD UNIVERSITY PRESS

Oxford   New York   Toronto
Delhi   Bombay   Calcutta   Madras   Karachi
Kuala Lumpur   Singapore   Hong Kong   Tokyo
Nairobi   Dar es Salaam   Cape Town
Melbourne   Auckland

and associated companies in
Beirut   Berlin   Ibadan   Mexico City   Nicosia

Published by Oxford University Press, Inc.
200 Madison Avenue, New York, New York 10016

Library of Congress Cataloging in Publication Data
Boyers, Robert.
Atrocity and amnesia.
Bibliography: p.
Includes index.
1. Political fiction—History and criticism.
2. Fiction—20th century—History and criticism.
I. Title.
PN3448.P6B68   1985   809.3'9358   85-13745
ISBN 0-19-503620-4

Printing (last digit): 9 8 7 6 5 4 3 2 1

Printed in the United States of America

Preface

Ever since I read Irving Howe's *Politics and the Novel* twenty years ago, I have wanted to write a book of my own on the subject. Not for a moment did I wish to compete with or displace a book I continue to regard as one of the most valuable works of criticism that I know. I did, however, wish to consider for myself whether there is such a thing as the political novel and to ask why books of a certain kind generally appeal to me more than others. There was much I wanted to say about the classic works of Stendhal, Conrad, Dostoevski, Malraux, and others to whom Howe devoted such scrupulous attention in his book, but I decided in the end to write about novels published in my own lifetime. Around some of this literature a considerable body of scholarly and critical commentary has been built up, but until now there has been no sustained attempt to treat the post–World War II political novel as an important literary phenomenon. Not that the best writers of this period constitute a movement or have in common a political ideology; what is important is that a great many successful and demanding political novels have been produced in this period, a post modern era often considered resistant to the political content of art. My study testifies predominantly to the quality and variety of recent political fictions and to their capacity to alter the way we think.

I imagined when I began to work on this study that I would be very much assisted by recent developments in literary theory, and so, despite my aversion to *la nouvelle critique*, I dutifully read many of the texts so highly esteemed in the American literary academy. I found, alas, that they helped me very little and that with few exceptions my instructors continue to be the critics and thinkers who shaped my understanding of literature and culture when I was a student in the early sixties. These are critics for whom theory is a noble but not sufficient end, for whom philosophy and the history of ideas are primarily important as they enhance our ability to think, enable the critique of culture, and inform the appreciation of works of art that are the chief glory of our civilization. Those who believe that great novels are "texts" like any others, that meaning itself is a naive assumption imposed on texts by "innocent" or unscrupulous interpreters, and that politics is an epiphenomenal instancing of desire, will find little in this book that is not defiantly "elementary." Such readers may find ways of their own devising to contend with the fiction of Günter Grass, Milan Kundera, and the other major figures I engage; but I do not think they will rightly appreciate what is at stake in the works of these authors.

I am aware that my book does not cover the full range of distinguished novels that might justly have been included in such a study. One reason for the exclusions—if reasons there must be—is simply that I did not wish to write a survey of contemporary political fiction. But my reader may well wonder why an American critic should not have devoted even a single chapter of his book to an American writer. Had there been a dominant American political novel produced in the last forty years, a novel that would stand in relation to American culture in the way that *The Book of Laughter and Forgetting* stands to Czech culture, I would, of course, have included it. But, like other readers before me, I have often been struck by a provincial element in most American works devoted to political subjects. To discuss the relevant novels by Mailer, Heller, Doctorow, Coover, and others would require an extended focus on the peculiar "American-ness" of these works and direct us to matters largely unrelated to the themes of this book. I would like one day to write on the striking disjunction between political intelligence and advanced literary thinking in the United States, but that is not an issue I am about to argue here.

Not much need be said about the organization of this study. The two opening chapters present not so much a theory of the political novel as a defense of the idea that it is useful to think about certain kinds of books as if they belonged to an identifiable genre or subgenre. What makes such an enterprise useful, I argue, is the quality of the literary and political insights thereby generated. Subsequent chapters of the book dwell at length on particular writers and texts and may be judged by their success in pursuing critical issues while refining our grasp of the distinction between politics and all that may not properly be subsumed under that heading. The first of the chapters devoted to a single author—chapter 3, on V. S. Naipaul—is a good deal less demanding than the most consistently theoretical chapter—Chapter 9, on Günter Grass—, but throughout I am guided in my procedures by what I take to be the intrinsic demands of the material before me. That my readings are "interested" I would not begin to deny. I would hope that they are never less than respectful of the "otherness" inscribed in the novels they discuss.

Saratoga Springs, N.Y.   R.B.
December 1984

Acknowledgments

Parts of this book appeared originally in *Salmagundi*, *The American Scholar*, and the *Times Literary Supplement*. I am grateful to Tony Outhwaite, formerly of Oxford University Press, for encouraging me to write the book, and to William Sisler for seeing it through its final stages. Skidmore College and its Dean of Faculty, Eric Weller, provided several research grants and a sabbatical leave that eased my way. My colleague Thomas S. W. Lewis, by assisting my wife and me in the editorial production of *Salmagundi* magazine, contributed more than he knows to the relative peace of mind that allowed me—if only for brief periods—to turn my attention from the magazine.

I have incurred a great intellectual debt to a number of people. Nadine Gordimer, Larry Nachman, Regina Janes, and George Steiner read portions of the manuscript and offered valuable criticisms and suggestions. I have benefited greatly from discussions with novelists Clark Blaise and Bharati Mukherjee Blaise, who shared with me their extensive knowledge of "third world" writing and politics and often debated with me the issues at stake in contemporary political fiction generally. My dear friend Ben Belitt has continued over many years to embody a principle of aesthetic scruple and inexhaustible curiosity. My wife Peg Boyers has demonstrated again and again an impeccable sense of intellectual relevance and has continuously nurtured my sense that most serious work is, in Eliot's terms, "a raid on the inarticulate." For her friendship and love I have no adequate words of gratitude.

for my wife Peg
and for Ben Belitt

Contents

A Note on
the Major Texts

Important secondary sources are referred to in standard notes, but the novels discussed at length in the various chapters of this book are not footnoted. The major texts from which quotations are taken are as follows:

Miguel Angél Asturias, *El Señor Presidente* (New York: Atheneum, 1980; original Spanish edition, 1946).

Alejo Carpentier, *Reasons of State* (New York: Alfred A. Knopf, 1976; original Spanish edition, 1974).

Gabriel García Márquez, *The Autumn of the Patriarch* (New York: Harper & Row, 1976; original Spanish edition, 1975).

Nadine Gordimer, *Burger's Daughter* (New York: Viking Press, 1979).

Günter Grass, *The Tin Drum* (New York: Pantheon Books, 1961; original German edition, 1959).

   Cat and Mouse (New York: Harcourt Brace Jovanovich, 1963; original German edition, 1961).

   Dog Years (New York: Harcourt Brace & World, 1965; original German edition, 1963).

Graham Greene, *The Heart of the Matter* (New York: Penguin Books, 1962; originally published 1948).

   The Quiet American (New York: Penguin Books, 1962; originally published 1955).

   The Comedians (New York: Penguin Books, 1967; originally published 1966).

   The Honorary Consul (New York: Penguin Books, 1974; originally published 1973).

A Note on the Major Texts

Milan Kundera, *The Joke* (New York: Penguin Books, 1983; original Czech edition, 1967).

    The Book of Laughter and Forgetting (New York: Penguin Books, 1981; first published in France, 1979).

V. S. Naipaul, *A Bend in the River* (New York: Alfred A. Knopf, 1979).

Jorge Semprun, *The Long Voyage* (New York: Grove Press, 1964; original French edition, 1963).

    What a Beautiful Sunday! (New York: Harcourt Brace Jovanovich, 1982; original French edition, 1980).

Aleksandr Solzhenitsyn, *The First Circle* (New York: Harper & Row, 1968).

George Steiner, *The Portage to San Cristobal of A.H.* (New York: Simon & Schuster, 1982; originally published in *The Kenyon Review*, vol. I, no. 2, Spring 1979).

Atrocity and
Amnesia

1

Toward a Reading of Political Novels

To speak of the political novel one must assume first of all that it is worthwhile to distinguish between one kind of book and another. One must assume as well that the political interpretation of literary texts is best managed when the texts at hand plausibly invite that kind of approach. It may be that any novel can be profitably examined as a political document, but no one should suppose that a book's sense of itself is of no consequence in determining what it is. In fact, the tendency of many recent critics to ignore a book's sense of itself has led them also to be indifferent to what it is. Confounding the construction of a book with the book itself, they typically consign the meaning of a novel to the dustbin of epiphenomenal trash that was earlier asked to take in "naive" concepts like character, psychology, and ethical posture. The very idea that there is a political novel, and that in such a work one is characteristically invited to consider such concepts in a way not entirely possible elsewhere, should serve as a corrective to the large tendency promoted by ostensibly advanced critics in our time.

But to insist on the continued viability of "naive" concepts is not enough. The deconstructionist attack on notional or impressionistic readings of texts has made it necessary to make a case for meaning and character and ethical content that goes well beyond anything the better critics of the novel thought they were doing thirty or forty years ago. If the deconstructionists have fostered an excessive skepticism about the integrity of literary texts, they have also alerted us to problems we need to consider. If our interest in political fiction leads us to a species of genre criticism, for example, we may well ask what dangers are inherent in our approach. A deconstructionist would rightly argue that to group novels primarily on the basis of meanings or world views is unduly to privilege a dimension of our reading. Such a privileging allows us to ignore the subversions to which all meanings and views are inevitably subjected in a successful novel. The idea of the political novel as a work in which certain positions are taken or in which private experience is necessarily seen as subordinate to political activity is an idea not likely to satisfy extended inquiry, precisely because it cannot account for our actual experience of the various works we should have to include in our study. A deconstructionist insistence on the diversity of codes inscribed within a single text and on the structural discontinuities even of works that labor to conceal the competition among the several narrative paradigms they contain will usefully remind us to beware of seductive unitary schemas.

In his book *The Political Unconscious*, Fredric Jameson describes traditional genre criticism as an attempt to get at "the essence or meaning of a given genre by way of the reconstruction of an imaginary entity—the 'spirit' of comedy or tragedy, the melodramatic or epic 'world view,' the pastoral 'sensibility' or the satiric 'vision'—which is something like the generalized existential experience behind the given texts."[1] Such a criticism usually avoids the structural considerations that seek to uncover the laws and the precise limits of a kind of work. Where the novel is concerned, traditional genre criticism has always had an unpromising terrain to cover. Even Northrop Frye has been unable to do for the novel what he and others have done for our generic reading of the lyric, the epic, the folktale, and so on. To try to speak of the spirit of the novel or of the inevitable relation between character and incident is to discover almost at once that the terms are inadequate. One does better to speak of the spirit of realism in the novel, or the vision of apocalypse in the novel of a particular place and time. But, even there, attempts to encompass even a limited aspect of *the novel* in terms proposed by traditional genre criticism are not often satisfactory, and the exceptions are so eccentric as to prove the rule.[2]

Can we do any better with "the political novel"? Surely it helps to confine oneself to works written, say, between 1945 and 1980. But no sooner does one consider the different kinds of political fiction produced in these years, and the various purposes to which the individual novels may be assigned, than one despairs of generating adequate classifications. It is not just that a belated realist bearing witness to the experience of the Gulag will see himself in a way radically different from a writer who responds in his work to a less dramatic, less fundamental aspect of his society. More important is the fact that the very form of the novel is routinely called into question by its most ambitious practitioners in a degree unmatched in the other literary arts. And this is at least as true of ambitious political novelists as of any other kind. Solzhenitsyn may be in some respects an old-fashioned realist, but there is a documentary intensity in his fiction that calls into question certain formal presuppositions. Grass may work on the margins of farce, but he is as interested in preserving a recognizable ethical perspective as the bourgeois novelists his work would seem to repudiate. And Milan Kundera, for whom "a novel is a long piece of synthetic prose based on play with invented characters," defends his most various and remarkable work as "a novel about Tamina," though Tamina appears only intermittently in its pages. His reasoning? "Whenever Tamina is absent, it is a novel for Tamina. She is its main character and main audience, and all the other stories are variations on her story and come together in her life as in a mirror."[3] All of which is to say that, like it or not, the novel may assume almost any shape it pleases and continue to do what in essence a novel does. And, since Kundera's book and others like it do in fact inspire the gratitude we feel for novels less disposed to challenge formal assumptions, we are little inclined to dispute their radical claims.

If it is impossible to speak in generic terms of the form of the political novel, though our experience tells us that there is such a novel, it may yet be possible to work toward an acceptable, if fluid, definition. In his 1957 book *Politics and the Novel*, Irving Howe argues that the term *political novel* can at most "point to a dominant emphasis, a significant stress in the writer's subject or in his attitude toward it."[4] That dominant emphasis, Howe goes on to say, will have to do with the relation between political ideas and the experience of characters who take hold of those ideas. A political novel is one in which "an attempt is made to incorporate ideology into the novel's stream of sensuous impression." In the best of such works, the ideas are made to "have a kind of independent motion, so that they themselves . . . seem to become active characters in the political novel." These ideas are set in motion in such a way that they become the imperious necessity against which the human characters press. They press because they are moved also by "an apolitical temptation," because their attraction to politics and to political ideas is contaminated by their desire for gratifications that have in the end little to do with political objectives. What is for Howe the necessary "polarity and tension" of the political novel is provided by the usual novelistic opposition between the will of variously motivated individuals and the realm of impediment or necessity. That realm, a combination of external circumstance and the ideas that erect an imposing perception of circumstance, will assume in political novels a determining force rarely present in other works.

Howe is rightly uneasy about the attempt to create a theory of the political novel. He is also aware that, by selecting for study *these* novels rather than *those*, he is permitted to draw general conclusions he should otherwise wish to revise or abandon. Thus he can say that "in treating twentieth century writers I have found myself placing a greater stress upon politics and ideology as such . . . a gradual shift in approach that seemed to be required by the nature of the novels themselves." Attentive as he must be to the texts of novels he admires, respectful of their intentions in a way that must seem naive to advocates of *la nouvelle critique*, he develops a flexible approach responsive to his shifting sense of the objects at hand. No doubt Howe has noticed that since the publication of his book the major political fictions of our day compel a very different perspective. One wishes, of course, to look hard at the politics of places used as settings in the novels of V. S. Naipaul or Nadine Gordimer or, for that matter, of Gabriel García Márquez or Günter Grass. And "ideology as such" remains an important factor. But the intentions at issue are so much more various in these writers than in the early twentieth-century novelists studied by Howe that one must find new ways of discussing them. No theory of the political novel that installs Orwell or Koestler as a representative figure is likely to know what to make of *The Tin Drum* or *Autumn of the Patriarch*.

The standard test case for considerations of the modern novel as a classifiable form or genre is, of course, Joyce's *Ulysses*. Early reviewers of the book, including Eliot and Pound, denied that it was useful to think of it as a novel, and later critics have concluded that if it *is* a novel, it is a novel to end all novels, a form that consumes and exhausts the model on which it is created. But, of course, new novels continue to be read, and written, and if there is no recent work to compete with *Ulysses* in complexity or virtuosity, there are more than a few that raise comparable critical issues. Howe's reluctance to settle on a firm structural theory for the political novel, his willingness to seem flexible and impressionistic in his approaches to particular instances of political fiction, are plausible responses to a literary form that can accommodate not only *Ulysses* but *Nostromo*, Broch's *The Death of Virgil*, and others we have named. To be sure, the temptation to classify will remain, not because we seek mechanical solutions to complex problems, but because of what E. D. Hirsch calls "the temporal character of speaking and understanding." "Because words follow one another sequentially," he argues, "and because the words that will come later are not present to consciousness along with the words experienced here and now, the speaker or listener must have an anticipated sense of the whole by virtue of which the presently experienced words are understood in their capacity as parts functioning in a whole."[5]

Obviously, what Hirsch calls "an anticipated sense of the whole" is more useful in some works than in others. Often, our sense of the whole will have little to do with the type of work we are reading. It may be built up incrementally by means of clues, repetitions, extended image clusters, or metaphors woven through the given text. Frequently, particularly in the modern or postmodern novel, structural or generic anticipations are misguided. They may even prevent the reader from paying careful attention to elements in the fiction that might have satisfied his literary appetite, if only he were not so disappointed in his more usual expectations. The reader who demands a particular kind of development in a contemporary political novel because it seems closer in kind or intention to Conrad's *Under Western Eyes* than to *Pride and Prejudice* will need to beware of premature disappointment or simple confusion. If a book like *Ulysses* is bound to violate even the broadest expectations associated with the novel as a genre, how may we demand that an audacious postmodern fiction satisfy the much narrower generic expectations established for the political novel? Irving Howe's discussion of ideas and ideology in a certain kind of fiction is helpful, but it does not provide the "anticipated sense of the whole" that will serve as a reliable basis for directing us through Grass, or Márquez, or Kundera. Nor does it confront in a general way the issue raised by *Ulysses*, namely, that "at its deepest reaches" a great work "denies the validity of genres and seeks to be wholly itself."[6] But A. Walton Litz and other critics willing to grant special status to Joyce are unwilling to go as far in other cases. "One could argue," says Litz, "that all successful works of literature ultimately undergo such a transformation"—and seek, therefore, to be wholly themselves—"but I do not believe that to be true." We may need, then, to refine what we mean by *an anticipated sense of the whole*, but some such sense of generic expectation is likely to be both useful and possible in most instances.

Of course, what will seem like a refinement of perspective to one reader will sometimes seem foolishness to another. Litz reminds us that S. L. Goldberg's *The Classical Temper* (1961) sought to "save" *Ulysses* from itself by reconstructing "the novel which was botched or obscured by Joyce's persistent intellectualism and his willful parade of symbolic correspondences."[7] The authentic article salvaged by Goldberg is, quite predictably, a realistic novel containing, in Goldberg's terms, " 'probable' and significant characters, in a 'probable' and significant setting, doing and saying 'probable' and significant things."[8] Goldberg's sense of the whole is his insistent expectation that a successful novel must be, and therefore will be, a representational artifact conforming to standards taken from familiar works in the great tradition. In the same way, Q. D. Leavis proposes to account for the success of *Wuthering Heights* by cutting away parts of the original text and revealing the realistic novel clamoring to emerge.[9] Again, the critic's generic expectations instruct him to ignore or to repudiate essential aspects of the text at hand in the interests of a particular experience he takes to be the only proper sense of the whole. Such audacious critical refinements—some would call them violations—will necessarily encourage skepticism about the claims of genre criticism to represent fairly the project of the novel. Confronted even by so dexterous a critic as Mrs. Leavis, or by F. R. Leavis's efforts to extract a successful "novel" entitled *Gwendolen Harleth* from George Eliot's *Daniel Deronda*,[10] the reader may well take refuge in the idea that an important work invariably "seeks to be wholly itself."

But what does it mean to say that a novel seeks to be wholly itself? Not, certainly, that a reader will bring nothing to his encounter with the text, that he will forget what he knows and see no resemblance between the object at hand and other books he has read. Grant that *Ulysses* is finally like no other novel. Would one wish to contend on that account that in its parts it does not resemble other novels? Not to see that resemblance and to think about it would be to miss the point of the book, to ignore the way in which Joyce builds on and ultimately cannibalizes the available forms of the novel. Just so, it may be necessary to think of writers so diverse as Swift and Conrad to understand how it is that V. S. Naipaul creates something that is more or less "wholly itself." Without that very complex generic projection, one may be tempted—quite in the way that Naipaul's hostile critics have been—to read Naipaul's fiction as an extension of his journalism, to bring to bear on it the considerations and opinions typically generated by his nonfiction books on India, the Caribbean, and Islam. There is no reason to discuss one sort of work in perfect isolation from another, but it is vital to read a novel as a novel, not as an effort to take a position on an issue of current interest. If Naipaul's *A Bend in the River* is no more than that, if it does not succeed as a novel rather than as a book on African politics, then it has no long-term importance and is in no sense "wholly itself."

A work that is an achieved and unique creation, then, accomplishes its purpose by coming to terms with its nature as a thing of a certain kind and by pressing against the constraints imposed by that sense of what it is, quite as the work presses against internal constraints produced by the material it invents. To say that *Ulysses* is more wholly itself than Naipaul's *A Bend in the River* is only to say that their projects are different in their degree of formal invention and in their relative impatience with generic limitation. One means no disrespect to Naipaul's novel in saying that it is closer to its generic type than are some other ambitious novels to theirs. Just so, one may describe García Márquez's *Autumn of the Patriarch* as brilliantly original, a work that is unmistakably *sui generis*, and conclude that it is an audacious and sterile failure. No mechanical genre criticism can by itself accomplish the work of evaluation that needs inevitably to be done. To identify the nature of the constraints that operate in a kind of novel is only to begin to consider what the particular novel does with those constraints.

By concluding that "the criteria for evaluating a political novel must finally be the same as those for any other novel: how much of our life does it illuminate? how ample a moral vision does it suggest?"[11] Howe concedes in effect that exclusionary definitions are out of place. Perhaps one means by a political novel "any novel" one wishes "to treat as if it were a political novel."[12] But if that is all one can say with confidence, what does one make of the peculiar terms invoked in the discussion of that novel? One's criteria for arriving at a final evaluation may be the standard criteria, but the concern with ideas and ideology will make the course of one's reading a special experience. If there is in the political novel a more forceful and ideological projection of circumstance than one finds elsewhere, then such a work is likely to take hold of us in a way that should be distinguished from our experience of other works.

Let us accept, provisionally, the main terms of Howe's description of the political novel, including most especially the notion that ideas in such a novel will have "a kind of independent motion" and "become active characters." Let us add to this, however reluctantly, the stipulation that in such works "political intrigue is more than a backdrop for the dramas of sensibility their authors wish to unfold," and that their main characters "regard their personal fates as intimately bound up with social and political arrangements that can be controlled only by those who are capable of intrigue and calculation."[13] And let us accept also that in a political fiction there will be some attempt to project a common world that is more than a series of isolated tableaux, images, or emblems. These stipulations should serve at least to get us started in our attempt to identify the generic constraints recognized by the political novelist. And if we can make ourselves believe even provisionally in the actual existence of these significant factors, we can select pertinent passages from a representative work to help us to focus our inquiry.

We turn to a work written on a small scale, a novella by Doris Lessing entitled *The Temptation of Jack Orkney*. Is it a political novel? Surely it lacks the full complication and variety of incident we associate with most major works in the tradition, from *Nostromo* to *The First Circle*. Though it introduces us to several potentially interesting characters, only the title character is substantially developed. The setting of the fiction shifts several times, but only one of the settings may be said to allow the enactment of a political conflict, and that is perhaps the least consequent setting in the work. There are, no doubt, ideas in *Jack Orkney*, but they are decidedly fragmentary and deliberately flattened or oversimplified.

To set down these observations is to see clearly that Lessing's work is constrained first of all by the fact that it is a novella rather than a novel. Some novellas read like long stories in the sense that they are organized around a single incident and mean to develop a single idea or impression. *Jack Orkney* is organized like a novel. It depicts a crisis in the life of its protagonist by pitting him against a variety of other figures and by making him think about the pattern of his entire life. Had Lessing wished to write a novel, she might have retained the structure of *Jack Orkney* and simply developed further the characters actually presented there. Ideas would have to have been more complexly elaborated, and the view of the common world projected by the main figures made clearer, more vividly present. But Lessing has, in what exists, a kind of blueprint for that development. She has the various settings she would need and she has the materials required to complicate the action just enough to document the critical changes in character and perception more conspicuously. She writes a novella because she feels she can say best what she wants to say by means of elegant compression and suggestion. To have worked things out with novelistic fullness would have been to say more and therefore to have risked saying something quite different.

So the constraints imposed on *Jack Orkney* by Lessing's sense of it as a novella have largely to do with the degree of elaboration permitted the various elements. What is affected primarily is the focus of the work, and that focus in turn controls the range and kind of implication intended. Is the character of the work as a political fiction also affected? To say that it is affected is not to say that the fiction is any more or less a political work because it is a short novel rather than a longer novel. It is to say, rather, that the political content or meaning may in Lessing's view have required a narrow focus in order to be persuasively communicated.

Two or three excerpts from the fiction will clarify matters.[14] In each of them Jack Orkney will be seen to reflect on the political ideas and affiliations that have given his life a purpose and a direction. The perspective is that of a late-middle-aged professional activist, an "Old Guard" socialist idealist, petition signer, and journalist-adventurer whose father has just died and left him to wonder what all of his activities amount to. In the first passage, Jack returns home from the hospital on a train passing "pleasantly through England's green and pleasant land," and strikes up a conversation with an attractive young woman.

> She was not a stranger to Jack's world; that is, she was familiar with the names of people whose lives expressed concern for public affairs, public wrong and suffering, and she used the names of his friends with a proprietary air—she had, as it were, eaten them up to form herself, as he, Jack, had in his time swallowed Keir Hardie, Marx, Freud, Morris, and the rest. She, those like her, now possessed "the old Guard," their history, their opinions, their claims. To her, Walter Kenting, Bill, Mona, were like statues on plinths, each representing a degree of opinion. When the time came to give her his own name, he said it was Jack Sebastian, not Jack Orkney, for he knew he would join the pantheon of people who were her parents-in-opinion and, as he had understood, were to be criticised, like parents.
>
> The last time he had been Jack Sebastian was to get him out of a tight spot in Ecuador, during a small revolution; he had escaped prison and possible death by this means.
>
> If he told this girl about that, he knew that as he sat opposite her, she would gaze in judiciously measured admiration at a man retreating from her into history.[15]

In the next passage the reflections are associated with preparations for a rally in support of sufferers in Bangladesh whose fate was then—in 1970–1971—being decided in the war between India and Pakistan. The scene of the rally itself provides the only political action in the fiction and forces Jack to consider the rather different orientation of his children and their friends who also participate in the rally.

> These names appeared constantly together on dozens, hundreds, of letterheads, appeals, protests, petitions; if you saw one name, you could assume the others. Yet their backgrounds had been very different, of all classes, countries, even races. Some had been communists, some had fought communism. They were Labour and Liberal, vegetarian and pacifist, feeders of orphaned children, builders of villages in Africa and India, rescuers of refugees and survivors of natural and man-made calamities. They were journalists and editors, actors and writers.

. . . They sat on councils and committees and the boards of semicharitable organizations; they were Town Councillors, members of Parliament; creators of documentary film programmes. They had taken the same stands on Korea and Kenya, on Cyprus and Suez, on Hungary and the Congo, on Nigeria, the Deep South and Brazil, on South Africa and Rhodesia and Ireland and Vietnam . . . and now they were sharing opinions and emotions on the nine million refugees from Bangladesh.

Once, when they had come together to express a view, it had been a minority view, and to get what they believed publicized had sometimes been difficult or impossible. Now something had happened which not all of them had understood: when they expressed themselves about this or that, it was happening more and more often that their views were identical with conventional views put forward freely by majorities everywhere. Once they had been armed with aggressive optimistic views about society, about how to change it; now they were on the defensive. Once they had forecast utopias; now they forecast calamity, failed to prevent calamity, and then worked to minimize calamity.[16]

In our final passage Jack observes the members of the younger generation debating their respective views on Women's Liberation, Christianity, Vegetarianism, and so on. He had been "looking forward to letting the false positions of the day dissolve themselves into unimportance," but finds this impossible. His earlier, terribly unsettling experience of watching his radical son and friends behaving "like laboratory animals unable to behave in any other way than that to which they had been trained" is here repeated and exacerbated. In the earlier encounter Jack's conclusions had run to the inevitable failure of socialism as a result of the splintering to which all political movements are fated. With that splintering comes the refusal of each new generation and group to study history, "because history began with them. Exactly as history had begun with Jack and his friends."[17] But the conclusions Jack reaches in the following passage are rather more general, and more startling.

He had to stop himself saying that they sounded like a Conference of World Churches debating doctrinal differences, because he knew that if it came to dogmas, and disagreements about historical personalities, then his faith, socialism, beat them all. He looked at, listened to, his daughters, his brother's daughter, and knew that in two, three, ten years (if they were all allowed to live so long) they would be laying claim, with exactly the same possessiveness, to other creeds, faiths, attitudes.

Again he felt like a threatened building, the demolition teams at work on its base. He was seeing, like a nightmare, the world like a little ball covered over with miniscule creatures all vociferously and viciously arguing and killing each other over beliefs which they had come to hold by accident of environment, of geography.[18]

We are in a position now to consider what are the instigations and advantages to treating Lessing's work as a political fiction. First, the instigations. The fiction has at its center a man who has devoted his life to political activities. He considers himself a political figure and judges himself in terms of the ideas he has espoused and the qualities of character those ideas may be said to reveal. His view of character, in fact, is inseparable from his sense of a person's fitness for political conviction. When, at one point, he thinks of his lawyer-brother Cedric's having in his youth "defended labor agitators, conscientious objectors," and so on—"from religious conviction, not from social feeling"—he asks himself: "Well, did it make any difference why a thing was done if it was done?" This thought, he immediately decides, was "seditious of everything Jack believed. . . ."[19] Cedric is a tolerable fellow, rather more admirable, in fact, than Jack had previously been willing to grant. But his detachment from genuine political conviction marks him as someone less worthy than Jack and his colleagues of strenuous moral judgment.

It is also clear that political ideas in the novel take on "a kind of independent motion," in the sense that they are made to assume a negative significance and predictability they didn't have when they were originally engaged. What, after all, does Jack discover if not that certain ideas grow stale when they are resorted to time and again; that they serve after a while to insulate their possessors against the shock of experience, though they were originally thought to make events, persons, abuses seem more real, more immediate. In fact, the political ideas to which Jack Orkney returns over and again do become "active characters" precisely in the degree that they take the place of actual persons associated with them. When Jack thinks of his Old Guard colleagues, he thinks less and less of them as individual persons, regarding them instead as more or less interchangeable embodiments of ideas with which they are collectively identified. And he assumes that others outside their political circle will regard these people— will regard *him*—in the same way. He refuses to give his true name to the young woman he meets on the train because it would automatically make her "gaze in judiciously measured admiration at a man retreating from her into history." As a man who feels that he has lived for certain ideas, he cannot imagine anyone seeing past those ideas to the person still in doubt about himself and the point of his commitments. He sees himself as an historical figure because the ideas he embodies are now terribly familiar, if not popular, and because he sees no new way of bearing witness to them. The ideas exist, they have a reality of their own which persons associated with them can do little to alter.

The alternative to standing in that relation to one's ideas is detachment, skepticism, withdrawal. Briefly adopting that perspective, Jack sees on every human being he meets a mask of vanity, imagines that ideas have no reality at all, nor any capacity to take hold of us. If all is vanity, after all, then there is nothing but the isolate human creature, self-regarding, cut off from others because there is nothing larger than himself that he can share with them. To look at oneself and at others in this way is quickly to fall prey to the delusion that nothing is better than anything else, that all arguments or struggles are at bottom empty, without content, that human beings desire nothing more than power or command. In the terms of this delusion, ideas have no independent motion but are simply taken up for a particular purpose and set aside when they are no longer needed. If they seem conventional, that is only because they are fitted to a variety of purposes and can be easily manipulated by persons of various abilities. The most familiar ideas are those that can satisfy the greatest number of power drives.

Strangely, the one view of ideas and its alternative view come together in Lessing's novella. Both tend, in Lessing's treatment of them, to make of ideas, all ideas, a temptation that had best be avoided if one is to be in touch with oneself and one's feelings. Those who view ideas as potent, independent, active, are dominated to the extent that they behave more out of habit—or principle, as they like to call it—than out of fresh conviction. The others, who view ideas as a device or mask for getting what one wants, are either too cynical for us to care about or too depressed by their own tawdry devices to feel anything but horror at what they see. In either case, ideas, even noble ideas, are projected in this work only enough to be seen *through*. Look hard at an idea, Lessing seems to say, and you will see that it is not what it takes itself to be. Those who take it up, or are taken up by it, will in the end be sorely disappointed.

But let us also consider the condition that in political novels political intrigue will be "more than a backdrop for the dramas of sensibility their authors wish to unfold." This is a particularly challenging stipulation to consider in connection with Lessing's work. In a sense, *Jack Orkney* is a novel of sensibility. It does dwell very largely on a crisis in the life of its main character, a crisis brought on not by a political event but by the death of his father and his interactions with members of his family. More important, Lessing's tendency to treat political ideas as ultimately disappointing, no matter what their content, may bespeak a desire to use politics in general as nothing more than a backdrop for another kind of action. Is this the case? To answer, one must look closely at the depiction of political intrigue in the novel. Is it a perfunctory depiction? Is Lessing content simply to indicate that the air "out there" is charged with political turmoil and to signal that the main stakes in the various personal conflicts are elsewhere? There is reason to believe, surely, that Lessing is as interested in the psychological breakdown of Jack Orkney as in anything else; but it is difficult not to conclude that she is interested in the breakdown because it has temporarily incapacitated him for political activity. There is nothing in Jack Orkney but his politics to make him a compelling and unusual figure, and there is nothing Lessing can do with him that would justify the notion that he exists to focus a novel of sensibility. If Lessing wanted to write such a novel, she would have placed at its center a character more capable of growth or more generally impatient with his own inadequacies. Such characters may be found in *The Golden Notebook, Memoirs of a Survivor*, and other Lessing works that may more properly be described as novels of sensibility.[20]

As a novella *Jack Orkney* cannot work out the details of the relevant political intrigue as it might if it were conceived as a longer work. This we have indicated. But consider the detail Lessing does nevertheless provide. Throughout she is careful to name the causes and identify the key places. Though she does not work out the issues or allow her characters to discuss the specifics of any international conflict, she organizes the various personal conflicts so that they become political. Jack's dissatisfaction with his brother and sister has to do with their appropriating enlightened attitudes to which they are not entitled. Why not? Because their political convictions are vague, meliorist at best, and because they have done little to unsettle the life of privilege to which they are accustomed. The conflict between Jack and his son similarly involves the spirit in which views are held and the inability of people to make others understand what they have learned. Lessing invokes at one point "the famous 'generation gap,' " but the gap is here said to be "much worse because a new kind of despair had entered into the consciousness of mankind: things were too desperate, the future of humanity depended on humanity being able to achieve new forms of intelligence," and so on. These thoughts belong as much to Lessing as to Jack, we are made to feel, and the arguments between father and son move us, therefore, not because they rehearse the familiar frustration associated with generational conflict; they move us because they demonstrate how personal resistance or indisposition can turn a good man off even to a reasonable and perfectly decent political appeal. This does not amount to the playing out of an elaborate political intrigue, but it does establish a view of the ground to be covered by middle-class radicals in advanced countries for whom politics is a choice, a vocation rather than a function of mass hysteria.

So there are palpable instigations to considering *Jack Orkney* a political novel. It does not quite immerse us in the kind of intrigue for which there are obvious and immediate political consequences; it does vividly depict characters who "regard their personal fates as intimately bound up with social and political arrangements that can be controlled only by those who are capable of intrigue and calculation." And the novel does attempt to project "a common world that is more than a series of isolated tableaux, images or emblems." That common world is imagined not as it would actually take shape in Korea, or Hungary, or Bangladesh, but as the collective will-to-a-decent-future shared by a political fraternity called The Old Guard. The common world here, as in most political fictions, is a projection of hope, a movement toward a world not yet made. Often it exists only in the mind of the protagonist figure, whose absorption in the domain of the actual and in subversive intrigue encourages him at least occasionally to think of something better. In *Jack Orkney* the common world remains more or less implicit, but it is intermittently embodied in the shared memories of struggle and the planned protests to which Jack and his friends have recourse.

But what advantages are there in considering Lessing's work a political novel? The advantages, of course, are inseparable from a consideration of the operant constraints. The novel's sense of itself as one thing and not another allows it to distribute the stresses precisely, and thereby to direct our reading. When we consider for the first time Jack's meeting with the young woman on the train, we do so in light of the information provided at the beginning of the work, that Jack has been a political figure and worries that his activities have been pointless. We are constrained, by the steady introduction of political projects, memories, and ideas, from assuming that Jack's various encounters are intended primarily to dramatize his withdrawal and depression. Jack's meeting with the young woman is not just an instance of the old losing touch with the young. Lessing stresses the way in which political ideas and events are gradually domesticated, reduced to atmosphere, easy generalities, myths. And the stress we are made to acknowledge in this instance will in turn affect our reading of subsequent passages. Throughout, our anticipated sense of the whole prevents us from reading *Jack Orkney* as a psychological novel. The focus on the protagonist's inner life and confusions enables us to think about politics precisely in the way that Lessing intends. We conclude, as she wants us to, that persons committed more or less exclusively to political goals and ideals are apt in the end to be disappointed with themselves and with those in whose name they were seeking a better future. There is more to the novel than that, but not to see the crucial political dimension is to anticipate another kind of development that the work refuses to provide. The progressive elaboration of Jack Orkney's breakdown is interesting and significant because it is tied to several larger issues.

Of course, it may well be argued that there are not in novels intrinsically smaller or larger issues, that issues are significant or not by virtue of the way in which they are treated. In this sense, there is no advantage in regarding a work as a political fiction if in doing so we are simply encouraged to think personal relations trivial and political conflicts important. Nor is it legitimate to organize our responses to a work by insisting—except provisionally—on the priority of certain passages at the expense of others. The expectation that a work will conform to the pattern of a political fiction is useful only if we can also plausibly account for elements not ordinarily associated with the pattern. The advantage of a generic anticipation lies in its providing an orientation toward material that will in any case produce surprise and contradictions. As we come more and more to see Lessing's work as a political fiction, and to settle into expectations associated with that kind of work, we see that Orkney's breakdown is indeed less significant than the erosion of political hopes and attitudes he has for so long entertained. But we are alert as well to discontinuities in the work, and attend to various elements that seem not to contribute to the political perspective. In the end we demand that the novel at least attempt to reunify the various elements. Separate issues—psychological, political, ethical—must be seen to work together in the service of a determinate goal. That goal may not be fully realized or acknowledged in the work itself, but it will inevitably be seen to underlie the competing narrative codes and issues. And if the work is in fact properly designated a political novel, the determinate goal toward which the various elements tend will have something to do with ideas about community, collective action, and the distribution of power.

2

Time,
Presence, Ethics:
Imagining
a Shared Reality

Whether or not we agree that there is a political novel, we can surely agree that novels in which political ideas play a prominent role will have very pointed attitudes toward time. Those attitudes will vary in accordance with the ideological disposition of a given work, but the interest in time will always underlie the various other interests a political fiction may pursue. This is inevitable. To commit oneself to a political view is, after all, to make a judgment on the viability of a particular way of doing things, or to attach one's hopes to a future that is struggling to be born, or to seek the restoration of an earlier dispensation that the present has betrayed or abandoned. Even to ask a political question, with no sense that a determinate answer or position is available, is to begin to think about one's relation to time.

To say that a character or an author or a book has an attitude toward time is not, of course, to suggest that anyone can be for it or against it. Even those who set themselves against future time live in some sense for their own future or the future of those they care about. And those who wish to forget the past because of the suffering it has inflicted or because it no longer seems relevant to present concerns will in most cases recall with some fondness aspects of their own past they should like somehow to retrieve. One is involved in time, like it or not, and can no more succeed in escaping the past than in launching oneself directly into the future of one's dreams. It is the business of the novel generally to confront the individual with impediments to his wishes and plans, but the political novel will give an especially prominent role to worldly impediments. This will be clear to us only if we agree that a view of time is intimately connected with a view of Being itself, and that Being typically refers to those things that already exist, in contrast with other things that are imagined or imperfectly remembered.

To speak of time in this way, in connection with Being, is to see that the attitude of the political novel toward such matters is fundamental to its entire project. A novel that does not concern itself with politics may well do its best to ignore these matters. It may pay attention only to a present circumstance, treating it as if it were in no sense problematic, as if it alone constituted Reality and had no need ever to compete with any other incarnation in time or space. But a political novel is necessarily engaged in drawing comparisons and thinking out ideas whose motive is change or resistance to change. And the will to change, need we say, is a function or a consequence of an attitude toward Being. "The radical wishes to alter Being," Fredric Jameson nicely reminds us, "to change, reshape, destroy it, to leave it different from what it is; the conservative wishes to associate himself with the permanence of Being, its massive quality; to live in it and feel its stability and continuity around himself."[1] A political novel will assume an attitude toward time because it will treat Being itself as problematic. Radical or conservative in outlook, it will project Being as an arrangement of objects, persons, and institutions in a world that has undergone change and may undergo change again. It is haunted by time because it concerns itself with arrangements that it knows to be impermanent, whatever the wishes of those who would like to believe otherwise.

Most novels dwell more insistently on things as they are than on things as they might be or ought to be. Their commitment to narrative and to character is part of their concern with a world in which things assume a certain density, in which the presence of certain objects, customs, and memories may be taken for granted. Even those modernist fictions which eschew narrative and aim through other means to build up an autonomous vision of a reality all their own retain some traces of the world outside the author's imagination. But the political novel is always in some unmistakable way an engagement with the common world, and its sense of that world is communicated in the attention it pays to present things. Characters in such a work may feel contempt for everything around them, may live only for the future, but they are inevitably presented to us as belonging to a here and now that occupies us more than any vision of the future can. If political novels were not particularly good at showing how things in the world are worked on by ideas, if their sentiment of Being were not highly developed, they could not sustain an extended inquiry into the conditions of power and the ideas likely to move the world. Inevitably, radical novelists discover that too exclusive a commitment to future time compromises the sentiment of Being without which *no* novelist can generate a plausible narrative.

But there is more than the general nature of the medium to explain the absorption of the political novel in a present object world. The political novelist draws us into this densely textured world because he believes that only in or through such a world can we find our salvation. The writer who has no love for this world, no patience with its imperfection, may propose to write a novel excoriating the present. But if he does not find along the way that he is more fascinated than he supposed with the shabby arrangements he despises, then he will produce not a political novel but a polemic. The impulse to withdraw, to nourish the interior life, to tend one's garden, may be honored—it may even be represented as a superior option—but it will be seen as an option not belonging to the protagonist in a political fiction, who will live in his own present moment because he can conceive no other way to get where he wants to go. When he shuts himself off, retreats to some perspective out of time, or regards himself as man in the abstract, he may feel consoled or uplifted; but whatever he may feel, he will know that he has lost his way, and that for him there will always be a contingent common world, a present time, to turn to.

Saul Bellow's Albert Corde is a recent example of a character who is tempted to remove himself from present time and to assume the astral perspective he associates with his astronomer-wife. Bellow also seems sorely tempted on his behalf, and inscribes within his novel everything a man like Corde would need to help him see that salvation lies elsewhere than in the quotidian immediacies of "an all-but-derelict civilization." But no sooner do they—novelist *and* character—think to elude the claims of the grasping present than they are recalled. "The spirit of the times was in us by nature," Corde reflects at one point. "We all belonged."[2]

To what do we belong? To what Albert Corde calls "the material habitat" of our sense of "the way things are." This material habitat, awful though it may be, is characteristically a projection of hope. It is the basis of every serious thought we can entertain, the constantly available antidote to empty piety and false consciousness. It is, in Bellow's terms, all of the "furniture that civilization was able to install" to prevent us from flying off too readily into the cold outer space of cockeyed theories, dangerous inspirations, and compulsive protests.[3] What makes it characteristically a projection of hope is its very accessibility, the opportunity it presents to each of us to take hold of it and test ourselves against it. To the political novelist it may represent everything that thwarts a decent human aspiration, but he knows that without the steady pressure it exerts he can have no sense of the choices he can make. He welcomes impediment, the clutter of furniture that obstructs movement, because he wishes to create a world in which there is consequence, failure, purpose, possibility. His interest in politics is a reflection of his interest in the *way* things happen, in the *way* problems are overcome or stubbornly resist our efforts at amelioration. He is always, in his way, the enemy of what Bellow's character calls "the advanced modern consciousness," a "reduced" consciousness that contains only the "bare outlines" of the equipment needed to conduct human affairs in a satisfactory way. Those bare outlines are the assortment of abstractions, obvious practical judgments, and ostensibly enlightened moral standards to which "advanced" persons uniformly subscribe without being able to consider what their convictions mean or commit them to. Considered in this way, the political novel forces us to occupy a here and now because it is only by feeling ourselves chosen, laid claim to by the embodied force of a contingent universe that we can confidently know what we know. On what other basis are we entitled to hope?

We are not speaking here of a conservative vision. Though Bellow's cautionary observations and contempt for the advanced modern consciousness are often identified with a kind of political reaction, there is no reason to consider them in that way. Bellow's opinions may be conservative; he may distrust revolutionary zeal and detest liberationist rhetoric; but his views on the nature of the consciousness required to take in experience and make judgments are the views of accomplished novelists of other persuasions. Writers as different from Bellow as Kundera and Grass subscribe to his view, whether they admit it or not. It is a view of authentic novelistic time as a time present, and of politics as the attempt to engage necessity. Marxist writers speak of "the collective struggle to wrest a realm of Freedom from a realm of Necessity,"[4] and though someone like Bellow might argue with them about the meaning of Freedom, he surely knows what is customarily meant by Necessity.

But the Marxist theory of Necessity, particularly as evidenced in the works of Louis Althusser and Fredric Jameson, asks us to consider novelistic time in terms that are unfamiliar to most of us. They speak of the novel's elaboration of an "absent cause" that accounts for the material habitat though it is "nowhere empirically present as an element."[5] It is an interesting and useful idea. This absent cause is a system of social relations so various that it is impossible to describe it as a totality. When we read a novel, we attend at once to the present time in which the characters move and to the absent cause that is remote from any element we may apprehend. The absent cause may be said to be apparent only in the sense we have that nothing in the narrative's here and now can adequately explain what happens. The temptation to assign palpable causes to palpable consequences is very great, but "the billiard-ball model of cause and effect"[6] is at best an answer to local problems. Why does Günter Grass's Oskar break up a Nazi rally in *The Tin Drum*? Because he likes to play his drum and finds the only answer to mass hypnosis is subversive violence. The answer, we see, formulates a cause to explain an effect. Necessity, in these terms, is the incarnation of mass hypnosis represented by the Nazi rally. That Necessity has its extension and its force in the way in which the state's repressive norms are internalized by its citizens. Oskar stands apart from his fellows by virtue of his refusing to internalize those norms.

But there is, as we have suggested, another version of Necessity which contemporary Marxists ask us to identify with the absent cause. To think in these terms is to propose broader questions for which local answers are not appropriate. What are the general conditions required to induce mass hypnosis? Why in a given culture will a new politics succeed in unifying diverse constituencies while elsewhere it manages to bring long-standing class conflicts to a head? In what degree is a new state apparatus to be seen as independent of economic conditions? These questions can usually be addressed only with reference to an absent cause. And since it is absent, we have every right to ask about its status. Does an absent cause exist? If it is no more to be found in the past than in the present, who is to say that it has any reality at all? Isn't it customary to associate Necessity with something experienced by human beings as they move to actualize their wishes? If we believe in the absent cause, then we are, of course, required to believe that it exists, though it is "nowhere empirically present," quite as the Marxists contend. This belief will put a considerable strain on our inclination to feel that the materials of a successful novel will be adequate to the points it wishes to make. Obviously, the very notion of an absent cause indicates that while a novel may put us in touch with what we need to know, it will never fully embody that knowledge. This is not a matter of language, of the novel's failing to find the right words to say what it knows. We have an absent cause because the forces that together produce the dominant modes of behavior and of production within a society are resistant to the reductions in scale and diversity that an organized narrative will require.

We have said, all the same, that we may know the absent cause and that we are put in touch with it by major political novels; and, we may add, we can know it only by the appeal such novels may make to the political unconscious. That unconscious, a repository of narratives and of narrative schemas or codes, is brought into play, as it were, by the actual novelistic discourse.[7] The master codes or narrative paradigms are never available to us in a pure form. They are a *type* of narrative elaboration, a scheme of development or resolution of conflicts. They are unconscious in the sense that we resort to them without trying and are often unaware of how entirely we rely on them to resolve uncertainty. Present conflicts or perceptions are measured against them even when we feel we are attending only to the phenomenon at hand. Just so, in reading a work like Conrad's *Under Western Eyes*, we feel that a particular narrative paradigm will govern the unfolding of the Conradian fiction before us. As we follow the novel's developing contrast between East and West, we superimpose on our experience of the present narrative the master narrative, in terms of which mutual understanding between alien cultures is made possible by their respective efforts to get rid of outworn insular habits. The absent cause, we may say, is suggested by the refusal of the Conradian fiction to conform neatly to the proto-narrative from which it might well have drawn its impetus and its form.

But let us try this again. We have before us a text that aims to perform a narrative function. It may or may not respect the conventions of verisimilar representation. Either way, it tells a story in the course of which certain human activities are accounted for. Those activities, along with the thoughts and intentions and cultural assumptions of those who perform them, are made to seem necessary—not predictable, perhaps, but necessary. They are what they are because they can be no other. As we seek to explain them, to determine for ourselves what constitutes the source of our conviction that they can be no other, we find ourselves resorting to secondary explanations. We accept immediate and secondary causes for primary ones and thus try to believe that we have found infallible foundations for our reading. These efforts are assisted by our resorting to a variety of proto-narratives or master codes which furnish standard resolutions to the kinds of conflicts encountered in the text at hand. We resort to these proto-narratives not usually in a deliberate or systematic way, but unconsciously, as it were, reaching for them because they are orderly and familiar and do not need to be questioned closely. They are loose enough in outline to be roughly applicable to a wide range of actual texts, and they do not disturb our sense that there must be a discernible logic in the text at hand, whatever its opacity.

The procedure we have described is of course particularly evident in our experience of novels that challenge our customary perceptions of order and stability. A conventional, if accomplished, domestic novel will not typically drive us toward a variety of master codes or competing narrative paradigms because it works comfortably within a single narrative convention.[8] It does not operate on the assumption that Being itself is problematic. A political novel, though, as it is inevitably concerned with change, with the actual or threatened disappearance of established forms, will always project a narrative that is problematic. And it will, therefore, call to mind a consideration of causes and probabilities and unforeseeable consequences. As the novel needs to identify palpable causes, it will gesture at the range of available paradigms that may be said to underlie or inform this kind of material. These paradigms will compete, will overlap with one another, and will never seem fully satisfactory resolutions of the apparent conflicts unleashed in the actual text. But they will seem attractive all the same for the example they give of an orderly approach to difficult problems. Even master codes that have been repudiated by generations of writers and readers will continue to compel and seduce. Fredric Jameson speaks of the "providential histories" of Marx and Hegel, of the "catastrophic visions of history (such as that of Spengler)," and of the "cyclical or Viconian visions of history" as master codes we should know enough to resist.[9] But we know that these versions of historical development continue to operate in the political unconscious along with a wide range of other paradigms. And these historical schemas—dramatized or extended in the more specifically literary narrative paradigms we associate with the major writers whose works have become part of the air we breathe—are nowhere more potent than in the precincts of a political novel.

It is, quite clearly, a long way from the text itself to the absent cause. That cause, we have said, is a crucial aspect of our experience of political novels because in such works issues are raised that go beyond or defeat local cause-and-effect explanations. In thinking about such issues, one does not leave the text behind or suppose that the text exists only to drive us to some other source of information. The political novel at its best has the competing master codes suggested if not inscribed within it, and the reader's task is to make contact with those codes without relying on them so entirely that the surfaces of the actual text cease to matter. In working out a proper response to the text as it is, the reader will in time come to know the absent cause, which is apprehensible only in the activity of those plural and overlapping proto-narratives as they are seen to operate in the production and deciphering of actual texts. Obviously, one will want to summarize or define the absent cause as soon as one feels it has been grasped, and there is no reason not to try. But we are likely to find that, in keeping our eye perpetually on the evolving text and its shadowy master codes, we will do best simply to discuss the inadequacy of local explanations and to identify the many contradictions to which any issue will give rise.

Our sense of the absent cause will vary as we move from one kind of political novel to another. In reading Bellow's novel *The Dean's December*, we will attend to the way in which a traditional bourgeois humanism extends its grasp of mundane fact by teaching itself to look for confirmation in the domain of the physical sciences. Want to know why black people in Chicago have failed to pull themselves out of the filth and violence to which they are inured? Consider the effects of lead poisoning on the brains of generations of black children. Consider, in fact, any theory, buttressed by scientific research, that can begin to come up with possible explanations. And then consider what it is that drives a sensible and decent person to look to science in this way. Bellow's novel doesn't ask us to buy the explanation to which its protagonist is tempted, but it invests a great deal in the explanation and in the various perspectives from which it can be made to seem positively hopeless. The novel is structured, then, to entertain causes that point unmistakably to their own insufficiency and that call into question the very impulse to turn in their direction. That this is a political matter no reader of the novel will doubt. For why should a fellow like Bellow's Albert Corde look in the direction of science for answers to questions that are clearly social and political if he does not despair of addressing those questions politically? The immersion in politics, coupled with the refusal of political options (on the ground that they miss the point), produces an attitude that can only be called willful. Since the familiar political solutions have been tried, and conditions in the major cities continue to worsen, there must be some hard fact to show why the awful conditions won't respond to the generous treatment of enlightened liberals.

The prototype of this kind of fiction has to be the story of the good man who tries and tries to do good and finds that no one appreciates him, that his efforts are in any case fruitless, and that he had better mind his own business and nourish in private the thought of his nobility of spirit. Another very different prototype is the story of the mad scientist possessed by a wild and unprovable theory and willing to do anything to test and prove it. In the course of his ravings, needless to say, he loses sight of the original goal that impelled his speculation and allows the momentum of his present obsession to carry him where it will. Of course, Corde is not himself a scientist, but he is possessed by a theory produced by one, and for a while at least he seems incapable of considering the objects of his study—urban blacks—with the compassion that must originally have moved him. His affection for one or two individual blacks does not alter the more general inability to see the mass of black people apart from the horror generated by the theory of their collective deterioration. And, of course, this theory is very much embedded in the Spenglerian paradigm of a world rushing toward catastrophe.

There are other relevant paradigms, of course, and in what we have thus far said of Bellow's novel we have avoided any mention of Eastern Europe, where much of the novel is set and where very different issues are raised. But we have wanted simply to indicate that there are various paradigms that a fiction will call to mind, and that these paradigms never fit perfectly any aspect of a successful work, though they help us to see what is important to it. Bellow, like any accomplished novelist, works against the competing paradigms by resisting the full playing out of the patterns associated with them. By turning the paradigms against one another, as it were, Bellow creates an impression of an absent cause that would address the questions variously set in motion. What is that absent cause? It is the particular Necessity wherein the bourgeois humanist finds his generous sentiments irrelevant to the hard facts he confronts, though the sentiments are intrinsically as valid and as essential to his sense of himself as they ever were. And this Necessity, so conceived, becomes a political fact that is itself a part of that Necessity. For—and this is a question the novel asks over and over again—how is there to be a politics at all when persons absorbed by political issues cease to believe that the relevant causes are political? What hope is there for sustained political discourse when the very terms of that discourse seem suspect, tainted by the accumulated wishful thinking that obscures our impression of the facts in Chicago as in Eastern Europe? One might almost say that the absent cause in Bellow's novel is the will to be done with politics altogether, to be done with the frustration of investing in political solutions to problems that go on worsening and proliferating no matter what is done. But, then, Bellow makes it hard to settle on that formulation also; the novel shows how well he knows that the refusal of politics is as much a political decision as any other, and that some political remedies are more effective, in their limited way, than others.

Does it help to speak of the absent cause as we have tried to do? It helps, I think, in indicating that our sense of what is in a political novel is inevitably measured and tested against our sense of what is not in it but essential to it nonetheless. Bellow's book, like other political novels, may have a highly developed sentiment of Being, may consider the common world the only proper arena for the working out of struggles aiming at an enhancement of life for a variety of people. And, in keeping with this view, the novel sinks us steadily into a densely populated universe full of customs and assumptions and bureaucratic routines, all the elements that, taken together, constitute an intimidating embodiment of Necessity. That Necessity, we have tried to say, is at once extended and undermined by the sense we have of the various narrative paradigms that play beneath it as it unfolds in the novel. The paradigms serve, do they not, to drive our perception of the issues to a level of generality that demands the insertion of an absent cause as an operating principle. And with that principle in view, we ask the kinds of political questions that are fundamental to the novel and to our understanding of its main action. Without those political questions, without a sense of the absent cause we seek to identify, we allow the novel to slip away from us into mere personal drama. The protagonist's subjectivity then becomes the sole antidote to the material dilemmas raised, and the final effect is of a common world that exists solely to exercise the soulful reflections of an isolate, ever-so-sophisticated consciousness. That this is in fact a routine misconception of Bellow's work should come as no surprise to anyone who sees how easy it is to ignore the absent cause and to operate exclusively with causes and effects that are clearly labeled.

But, quite distinct from the idea of the absent cause, there are several other factors that focus a novel's attitude toward time and toward Being itself. There is, for example, the novel's interest in establishing an ethical basis for judgments it will make of characters and of the state apparatus. In a political novel those judgments will have to grow out of the novel's grasp of the interrelations among personal and political activities. For the novelist to represent private life as potentially out of the way of politics, utterly set apart, is to ensure that his work will lack the requisite features of a political fiction. This is not to say there can be no private life in a political novel, only that the very possibility of such a life must be seen to be a function of political arrangements that impinge on it or tolerate it. The requirements of a political novel do not, though, compromise the possibility of an ethical projection that has constant reference to the activities of individual characters. In fact, there is something like an ethical perspective even in novels that do not aim to adopt an ethical position as such, as, say, in Gabriel García Márquez's *Autumn of the Patriarch*. But how this perspective is mounted and sustained will vary from one work to another and will raise important questions about the novel's mastery of its relation to time and to Being.

Ethical thought typically projects an ideal vision of the way people ought to behave, and this is a more or less constant feature of political fiction. At a time when literary theorists of every school deny that there can be a valid ethical criticism, political novels continue to demand an ethical interpretation. This is not a simple thing to do. A novel that concerns itself with change, or the prospect of change, on a broad scale will always find it hard to underscore ethical imperatives that are generated far from the immediate scene of the novelistic action. But those ethical imperatives would seem to be the only kind of ethics to which political novelists are typically drawn. Though political novels should, given the nature of their task, prefer a situation ethics growing out of single encounters and having no binding force outside of those encounters, writers like Grass and Kundera and Alejo Carpentier are generally not embarrassed to work from more or less stable ethical presuppositions. The Marxist contempt for such presuppositions is finally of no interest, not only to so-called reactionary writers like Bellow and Solzhenitsyn, but also to their more radical colleagues. Perhaps ethical thought does project "as permanent features of human 'experience', and thus as a kind of 'wisdom' about personal life and interpersonal relations, what are in reality the historical and institutional specifics of a determinate type of group solidarity or class cohesion";[10] but the political novelist characteristically shows that certain ethical standards may be extended to other groups and classes without making them lose sight of their long-term interests, revolutionary though they may be. The idea that ethical wisdom is invariably a manipulative tool wielded by members of a dominant class has never been persuasive to the great political novelists.

But consider for a moment how an ethical thought of the sort we have begun to describe is actually projected in a political novel. First we have a concrete action, a present conflict between, say, one party or class and another. Individual actors may be represented as belonging to a particular side because they were born into it or because they have chosen to struggle on behalf of a goal they had a hand in fixing. Either way, they carry in their actions the burden of the material judgment the novel aims to make. Nietzsche regarded ethics as "the sedimented or fossilized trace of the concrete praxis of situations of domination,"[11] and there is no doubt that in the novel the concrete praxis comes first. But that is exactly why the Nietzschean and Marxist repudiation of ethics has no bearing on our experience of novels. One sees very clearly in novels how the novelist moves from praxis to ethics, and so one has not "a fossilized trace" but a transformation or translation that continues all through the pages of the work. As with translations of any kind, what you end up with is not what you began with. The ethical code that emerges is not quite the clear and unarguable reflection of the situation that called it forth; but neither is it a fossilized trace—not, that is, a code or standard which rationalizes a mode of control hidden from us. Characters in the novel may not understand how or on whose behalf they are asked to accept an ethical code. As readers attentive to the procedures by which in the novel ethical standards are made to dominate our sense of the relevant actions, we cannot be so readily taken in. We are protected, as it were, by the very nature of the fiction as an unfolding narrative. To watch the ethical standards grow, or to see them introduced into the work by the will of the novelist, is to understand a good deal about the relation between meaning and praxis.

Now the ethical codes themselves are not invariably present in a political novel in the way that other elements are present. If they are implicit, though, they are likely all the same to be unmistakable. Malraux doesn't have to tell us in so many words that for him terrorism can have no positive ethical value. A group or a faction may think it necessary to conduct a terrorist campaign, and such a campaign may help to realize certain goals, but the ethical standards of a novel like *Man's Fate* are determined not by the success of campaigns, but by the spirit in which they are conducted. It is clear that, as a resistance fighter, Malraux himself consorted with a good many terrorists, and found some of them quite admirable as men. But in his novels they cannot simply be men. They are men who perform terrorist actions and are subject to an ethical judgment whose dominant terms are taken from more or less stable convictions. In Malraux, there is the conviction that an ethical action always has an end in view, and that the actor has the capacity to respect the humanity of other persons affected by his action. The actor may in a given instance decide to take the life of an enemy, but he must have a clear sense of the gravity of his deed, and the responsibilities placed on him by his decision. These ethical presuppositions are not arguable in the terms of the novel. They are given, and the action of the novel demonstrates *that* they exist. The political novel will also show *why* they exist, and in this sense it is quite different from the sort of fiction in which stable ethical imperatives are thought to reflect a stable situation.

In conventional fictions, ethical claims are shown to emerge naturally from a situation in which every reasonable and decent person knows what they are. In Malraux, it may be that no character can say what constitutes an invariably binding ethical claim, but we as readers can, and that is because the novel is so organized as to make us feel that we have seen the dominant ethic taking shape as a concomitant of the narrative. The ethic belongs to the narrative, is finally inseparable from the narrative, even though it is not present in the narrative in the way a single idea or event may be. And though the ethic may in part be formulable as an abstraction, we know as we utter the abstract formula that it will not do, that we are not giving a satisfactory account of the novel's ethical code. That code, we must insist, is in the political novel based on stable assumptions, but it is in the end not possible truly to know it apart from its relation to the narrative.

There is, of course, no such thing as an ethical position that is characteristic of political novels. But we can say that political novels have an ethical foundation, and that the wisdom they project will reflect their sense of what ought to be "permanent features of human 'experience.' " To deconstructionists, for whom the simple question "What does it mean?" is a scandal, the question "What is its ethical posture?" is likely to seem an intolerable outrage. Both questions will seem, in fact, to rewrite or allegorize texts in terms of a master code that somehow corrupts the primary narrative material.[12] Our contention, to the contrary, is that no violation need take place, and that there need be no attempt to impose any set expectation on the narrative, which is not in any case a passive receptacle that will take anything at all the interpreter chooses to impose. To say that political novels will generate an implicit ethics in terms of which the narrative material may be understood is not to say that there is no other way of understanding it. We are also a long way from legitimizing an ethical criticism that ranks and evaluates novels on the basis of ethical presuppositions that may or may not have anything to do with the works themselves.

But it is necessary here also to distinguish between the activity of the reader and the activity of the writer. They are not, *pace* the deconstructionists, one and the same. For the novelist to suggest what ought to be permanent features of human experience is not to block all access to other experiences. Neither is it to withhold respect from points of view that do not conform to what the novelist hopes will become the dominant ethical perspective. There are always, in the political novel, several points of view in which the novelist wants us to be interested, even when he deplores most of them. And it is invariably the capacity of a major political novel to do justice to those various points of view that very largely impresses us, when we are impressed. The dominant ethical perspective will not cancel out the other perspectives generated in the work, will not make others "look bad" so as to have the field all to itself. A major novelist like Solzhenitsyn has to be able to show us how Rubin in *The First Circle* can be in some respects an admirable person and a committed Stalinist. For us to pay attention to Solzhenitsyn's ethics is not to allegorize or rewrite his novel any more than the author himself needed to do that to formulate an implicit ethics. We pay attention to the ethics of a political novel because they are relevant to the judgments it will make and because the ethics of a genuine novelist are in no way superadded to, or a distortion of, his material. If the ethics are, as the Marxist may say, timeless and therefore without exclusively rational or material foundation, they are all the same substantial in terms of the importance attributed to them by the novelist and, in turn, his reader.

The consideration of ethics in the political novel is also necessarily a consideration of its capacity to, project a sense of what an acceptable political culture might be. Most political fictions do not get around to showing us that culture. Since it nowhere exists, and since any attempt to describe it would very likely seem foolishly literal, it is usually left for readers to infer it from what is shown of the major conflicts and debates. In this sense, we may say, not only does the acceptable political culture on behalf of which the battles are fought not exist in the present time of the novel; it doesn't exist in the future time either. If we feel we know what the novelist means to project or attributes to the imagination of his characters, that is because the acceptable political culture is in essence an affair of spirit. It is something to be aimed at and talked about and used as a basis for comparison, but it will not be thought actually to exist, even as an ideal future projection, in the way that current events actually exist and may eventually be regarded as having happened. No important political novel can project an ideal culture as an actual possibility whose lineaments may be meticulously described. The most we can expect is a glimpse of a few component elements, generally given as functions of spiritual strengths associated with representative characters. What is the political culture in which Stendhal would have us live? It is a culture in which the happy few can continue to exercise their talents and in which they are not unduly corrupted by the plebeian values of the many, a world in which the San-severina and her Count Mosca will be regarded not merely as ornaments but as the very soul of what is good. This is, need we say, a world that has never existed and never will exist. But the novelistic projection of valuable, not to say central, component features of such a world serves to focus the novelist's discontent with anything less stirring, less singular than that example.

Just so, we cannot learn from Solzhenitsyn's novels what would be an acceptable and conceivably actual political culture. But we find in the circumscribed universe of the sharashka elements of community, of disciplined intelligence and of modest courage that together allow us to discern the foundations of Solzhenitsyn's hope. It is not a hope founded on any stable arrangements located in the present tense of the novel, but it is a spiritual possibility for which some version of a suitable material condition must be imagined.

Political novels that cannot gesture in the direction of that possibility, that condition of hope, are likely to seem suffocating, willful, obsessive. Such works—think of *Autumn of the Patriarch*—subvert ordinary notions of time, change, and progress. They create an unreal time, a time without end, a duration that in the main refuses to allow for growth or hope. It is, as in so many Latin American novels and European holocaust fictions, the time of the dictator or of the totalitarian state. Such works thwart all efforts to project an acceptable political culture. Committed as they are to an unnatural conception of time, they can promote no plausible sense of human agency. Characters—with the possible exception of the dictator- or commandant-figure himself—are reduced to the status of those *to* whom things are done. Events unfold with a kind of numbing predictability, eccentric though their secondary features may be. These events have not the inevitability we associate with an organically evolving circumstance. Lacking any sense of human beings as potentially autonomous agents, these novels without hope attach us to a mechanism, seek to immerse us in an artificially closed form. For such novels there is but one Being, and that is the Being of the closed form itself, of the novel-as-machine or of the artificially sealed totalitarian universe the novel is designed to reflect.

If most political novels were unable to project some sense of a vital political culture, were wholly resistant to projections of hope, we should have to revise our view of the species. In fact, political novels do a great many different things, and the absence of one characteristic or another cannot ordinarily exclude a work from consideration in these terms. But the absence of any semblance of vital human or political agency should at least call into question the status of a political fiction. To call it into question is not the first step on the way to dismissing or repudiating it, but a necessary condition of discrimination and evaluation. To paraphrase a telling cautionary remark by Kenneth Burke, you can't properly separate comparable things until you have first put them together.[13] But once you have discovered substantial grounds for separating them, separate they are likely to stay. And what more can we want, finally, than to keep them separate, to regard our theorizings and generalizings as approaches to singular works that have a life of their own? William Gass speaks of "critics who have thought they had jaws hinged like snakes, and could swallow masterpieces like small pigs . . . but Balzac and Bovary and Mann and Proust, they return alive without the benefit of the whale's belch or woodsman's ax. Slowly the swallowed systematically supplants the swallowers."[14] In the chapters that follow we shall see how the major political novels of our time defeat attempts to pin them down and invariably "return alive" in spite of the theories assiduously cast over them like so many nets full of—what else?—holes.

3

V. S. Naipaul:
From Satire and
Society to Politics

I

In 1961, V. S. Naipaul published a six-hundred-page novel called *A House for Mr. Biswas*. A number of readers thought it a masterpiece, and each of his five subsequent novels has been accorded comparable praise by critics and reviewers. This has been the case with his several books of nonfiction as well, including most especially *The Loss of El Dorado* (a strange "meditation" on the history of Naipaul's Trinidad) and the polemical travel-memoir *India: A Wounded Civilization*. His books are widely available in paperback editions, and he is frequently mentioned as a leading candidate for the Nobel Prize in Literature.

Yet it is a fact that, in the United States more than in England, Naipaul's novels have relatively few readers. Novelists far more difficult and technically demanding sell many more books, attract more sustained critical attention, and are taught more regularly in the college classroom. A cynical explanation would have it that Naipaul is too serious, too austere to appeal to most readers, that Americans especially read either to be edified or tickled, and that academics have no use for anything they cannot work at as if it were a code to be broken. Naipaul may be witty and morally bracing, he may even create memorable characters, but his novels are not likely to console anyone and have too much to do with the real world—with politics and race and personality—to appeal to readers with an appetite for exclusively "literary" fictions. They are difficult in the wrong way and for the wrong reasons. Were Naipaul a more generous man, a man more sensible of our common need for positive recommendations and moderately consoling resolutions, his books would be easier to take. Were he more hopeful about the advantages available to some of the people in the world his characters inhabit, he would seem less single-minded, less bitter and alienating.

The cynical explanation has a good deal to recommend it. In part it is accurate. It is also interesting and proposes to our attention a number of extraliterary considerations we would do well to pursue. But it is also, perhaps, a little unreasonable. For Naipaul has his fair share of readers, and more and more his work is known to represent a real alternative to the fiction that passes for "advanced" writing. His books *are* demanding and, in the main, unpleasant, and there is no reason to feel that they should appeal to everyone. More important, they bear witness to an experience that is entirely unfamiliar to Anglo-American readers at least, and invoke a version of political reality that is inimical to the humane aspirations of liberal intellectuals. For it is the constant burden of Naipaul's fiction to suggest that human beings are fundamentally unequal, and that right thinking cannot alter what are the facts of life. "The sad fact about prejudices," he has written, ". . . is that they are an accretion of observation and cannot be destroyed by simple contradiction." This attitude, more than anything else, has made him a suspicious character at a time when most serious readers like to pretend there is nothing they cannot handle.

Naipaul is our primary novelist of disorder and breakdown. Like Stendhal, he is interested in the phenomenon of revolution, though he feels that the revolutions of our time have come to nothing and justly brought to despair both adherents and opponents. In the wake of extinguished revolutionary prospects he can propose, at best, lucidity and remembrance. With no Stendhalian cult of energy to encourage him, he finds nothing to support, no party to stand by, no social class or character type to esteem. He detests privilege *and* equality, oppressors *and* oppressed. His typical protagonist-figures are negative characters, inadequate in all but their capacity to register shame or to reflect on their failures. Affection is reserved for those who struggle against things as they are without imagining that they will effect a general or enduring improvement; compassion for those who can find no suitable way to express love or allegiance and see themselves driven to loathing or betrayal. For every decent impulse in Naipaul there are three or four that express a general revulsion from life with others and from the hope of a redemptive principle on which people may depend. The most telling detail in the novels of Naipaul's maturity is the acute sensitivity to smell exhibited by the superior protagonist. "In this smell of heated sweat," Ralph Singh recalls in *The Mimic Men*, ". . . I tried to find virtue, the virtue of the poor, the laboring, the oppressed. Such is the vulgarity that mobs generate, in themselves and in their manipulators." The note of disgust, of an offended superiority, resounds through much of

Naipaul's fiction, and his attempt to master that revulsion has been the most satisfying aspect of his development as a novelist.

It is tempting to think of Naipaul as a man with a plan or a blueprint for development. He did outgrow the local color satirical novels of his youth and he has sometimes seemed to be moving deliberately toward a kind of political fiction that would set him more squarely in the tradition of Conrad and Stendhal than in the line of Caribbean and third world writers with whom he is often compared. At the same time, no writer of equivalent stature has so fiercely resisted the temptation to open up his narratives, to invite the participation of a wider range of characters, or to work with a wider range of emotions. There has been development, but it has taken the form of refinement, not enlargement of scope or feeling. The prose, from the first a sharp instrument wielded with scrupulous restraint, has nicely accommodated itself to more brutal uses but is still the rather spare and self-limiting tool it always was. The writer who could do the portrait of Mr. Biswas in 1961, a portrait alternately satirical and forgiving, has never done a richer portrait, though he has found ways of placing his characters in more complex circumstances and, therefore, of motivating them more variously. It may be, as it seems to me, that Naipaul's 1979 novel *A Bend in the River* is his best, but to speak of his development is to describe a progress both fitful and, in some fundamental way, compromised.

The early novels were promising. They seemed so when they appeared, and they seem so now. Even the straggly, episodic *Miguel Street* and *The Suffrage of Elvira* are readable and, in their way, delightful. They rely more than they should on eccentric character profiles and on quaint native dialects, but one sees from the perspective of the present moment that Naipaul was already working with his proper materials. His characteristic mode is not comedy of manners, as it was then, but the young novelist could not be expected to bring to bear on his materials the brutal clarities and discriminations he has exercised more recently. The small dramas of West Indian island life permitted Naipaul to think about the prospects of democracy and the inducements to change required in a society typically resistant to "progress." He cared enough about the issues to plot his dramas carefully, and showed at the same time that he had no way really to judge what he saw, to establish a reliable angle of vision. Anecdotes were included for no better reason than that they seemed amusing, and dialogue "exposed" characters on the simple principle that exposure is preferable to concealment. The obvious truth worked at so assiduously is that people make deals and are susceptible to the small corruptions that are so much a part of political life in advanced as well as backward societies.

The first novel, *The Mystic Masseur*, published in 1957, focuses attention on the kind of bogus social climber and briefly successful politician who in subsequent works is granted only marginal novelistic status. Why the figure should once have seemed central to Naipaul is not hard to figure out. Ganesh Ransumair seemed to him the type of the people's representative in a third world society: An opportunist, lacking in formal education but always ready to make use of advanced ideas he can but barely comprehend, he is at once a simpleton and a charlatan, something more than a perfect fool and less than a demagogue. Naipaul's narrator stresses throughout Ganesh's typicality, and goes so far as to contend that "the history of Ganesh is, in a way, the history of our times." One doesn't know quite what to make of this, but it is clear that Naipaul thought to provide an analysis of third world social institutions by studying the career of Ganesh. Were Naipaul's relation to his narrator more carefully defined, we should know better what to make of the claims advanced for Ganesh's typicality. As it is, we can say only that the narrator is himself an object of mild ridicule as well as a deftly ironical observer with a nice comic touch. Naipaul decided to place Ganesh at the center of his novel because he felt that the rise and fall of such a man would tell us what we need to know about his society without requiring a definitive or summary analysis such as a fully reliable narrator might provide. More, it is possible to laugh at the character without overlooking the fact that he is capable of great mischief. Naipaul was not yet ready to direct at his representative types the withering contempt and unforgiving severities he has since adopted. The novel succeeds as a portrait of a man who learns that it is better to make things happen than to suffer them as they occur. It fails as an attempt to show that such a person is the typical representative of his society and that the society, in effect, has in him what it deserves.

The most surprising feature of Naipaul's book, as we look ahead to its successor volumes, is the degree in which it forecasts certain problems he has had to negotiate all along. Primary among these are two: the relation between author and narrator and the detail required to bring to life a social or political setting. These we shall examine one at a time. First, the narrator. In *The Mystic Masseur* he has rather narrow terrain to cover. He is and is not a part of what he sees. In place of anger he inclines to acceptance, so that the satirical thrustings are felt not as actively corrective insights, but as colorings of a surface that might otherwise seem too uniform in its almost predictable simplicities. The author cares less about the narrator than about Ganesh and believes that the reader will work out for himself an appropriate relation to the ironies at issue. There is no illogic in the depictions, and the narrative voice is never asked to perform at a pitch that would seem to the reader unlikely or unseemly. Where the author's relation to the narrator is at all problematic, the reader necessarily hesitates to complain, since Naipaul himself seems not to care about the issues in a way that would invite—or satisfy—passionate inquiry.

In the mature fiction this is never the case. Naipaul's involvement in the issues and in the judgments that are ever present in the arrangement of his materials makes it necessary that we inquire scrupulously. Even where, as in *The Mimic Men*, he is not careful enough to differentiate his own views from the views expressed by his narrator, the matter of discrimination bears heavily on our responses to events. What do we think of the so-called colonial mentality? What can socialism amount to in a newly independent state? These are questions we can address only when we have considered what Naipaul wants us to think of them. We are, after all, looking at them as readers of particular novels, and we cannot know what to accept or resist unless we understand how things stand in those novels. It is one thing to believe, with Ralph Singh in *The Mimic Men*, that to assume political power in a Caribbean country is to enter into a tragic relation with one's constituents. It is something else to conclude that, though the view is persuasive, it is hardly what Naipaul believes and hardly what events in the novel are organized to show. It matters that, in *The Mimic Men*, Ralph Singh is in flight from active life as he narrates the events of his political career. It matters that, at forty, he seems to care about the past largely as a way to establish in the present materials adequate to sustain a contemplative life. Would Naipaul have brought Singh to his present condition if he wanted us to think him a reliable witness? Would he have made him so impressively intelligent if he wanted us to stand apart from him and to weigh his observations with the skeptical detachment we reserve for the pronouncements of others?

We want answers to these questions as we read *The Mimic Men*, and find that there is no way to come up with them. No one demands that Naipaul speak in his own voice, that he commit himself absolutely on every issue. We ask only that he furnish a point of view to which we can respond more or less consistently. If Singh were the only narrative presence in the novel, we would know how to establish a consistent relation to him. If there were an alternative presence, or several narrative sources, we should similarly decide—by playing off one stress against another—what Naipaul intended. Readers might differ with one another, but each would feel that he had been given a chance to reach a decision for himself. In effect, what Naipaul does in *The Mimic Men* is to pretend that it does not matter what the author thinks. Ralph Singh is entirely capable of speaking for himself, and we are free to accept or reject only what *he* says. Naipaul doesn't consider that the issues involved may seem to us too signally important to be left entirely in his narrator's capable hands. This will be especially true when we feel, as we do from time to time, that there is an authorial presence at work in the narrative voice, and that it wishes to withhold itself from some of the judgments spoken, though it is ever determined to stay out of sight. At such times we have to feel that Naipaul wants to have it both ways: He wants to be able to say, with Singh, that chaos is the natural and terrible order of things and that he never meant to say such awful things, that it could come only from a fellow like Singh, who had fallen so far. He wants to take credit for the hard truths and to say that he knows better than to fall for them.

The problem is most apparent in books with a first-person narrator who is an intelligent and articulate witness. By contrast, we have no problems at all with the two brilliant stories included in Naipaul's *In a Free State*. There the speakers are so obviously pathetic victims of the conditions they describe that we cannot for a moment identify them with an authorial presence. Not only their dilemmas but their speech patterns give them away, place them, as it were. We do not need to be told that the fellow who lives in the streets of Bombay in "One out of Many" cannot possibly speak for Naipaul, or that the driven creature in "Tell Me Who to Kill" harbors a kind of anger that can belong only to a man with a very low estimation of his endowments. More elusive by far is the narrator-protagonist of *A Bend in the River*, for Salim is at once shrewd and innocent, capable and adrift. From time to time he says things that make us wince, so readily can he be influenced to shift his ground. What had seemed at one moment a settled conviction is displaced rapidly by another, and for the smallest of reasons. Determined to look at a friend or antagonist in one way, he suddenly sees something that changes his mind altogether. Though he has the words to describe what he sees, and "reads" human motive with the skill of a practised novelist, he allows himself to drift into precincts of human relation he knows to be forbidding and ruinous, and is inclined to thematize experience in a way that underlines his distance from Naipaul.

At the same time—and here is the nub of the problem—even when he most resembles the student of life, the young man from the third world provinces entering the "real world" for the first time, the conclusions he draws seem to us terribly impressive. They have the ring of formulations we encounter in Naipaul's nonfiction. Even the opening lines of the novel are impressive in this way: "The world is what it is; men who are nothing, who allow themselves to become nothing, have no place in it." Or consider the narrator's response to a rather high-toned party he attends, at which he hears for the first time the sonorous protest songs of Joan Baez played on a phonograph: "It was make-believe—I never doubted that. You couldn't listen to sweet songs about injustice unless you expected justice and received it most of the time. You couldn't sing songs about the end of the world unless . . . you felt that the world was going on and you were safe in it. How easy it was, in that room, to make those assumptions." Are these the plausible reflections of a man who has had neither formal education nor a range of experience in which the habit of thought would have been strenuously encouraged? It is clear that, for the purposes of his story, Naipaul had to make Salim what he is. A more experienced man, with greater "advantages," would not have had access to the events and various human types he meets in the course of the novel. He'd have been too intelligent to take certain risks, too secure to traffic with certain kinds of people. But how does he come by his powers of analysis? To what extent are his judgments a reflection merely of a peculiar mind-set that has had only the experience of loss and retreat to furnish models of possibility? If we were more certain that Naipaul wished to establish Salim as a thoroughly adequate and reliable witness, we would have fewer incentives to close reading than the novel actually provides; but we would also feel more compelled to address the political issues themselves in place of the literary questions the novel sets in our way.*

With *Biswas* and the other third-person-omniscient narratives—including *In a Free State*, *Guerrillas*, and *Mr. Stone and the Knight's Companion*—we are on firmer, if not more fruitful, terrain. We do not always know what Naipaul would like us to feel about an issue, but we do know what the options are and we can declare precisely how much Naipaul has invested in each of them. In *Biswas* it is hard to say what Naipaul takes to be the future of the eccentric resistance and protest represented by his central character, but we do know that Biswas himself took the protest as far as he could, and that Naipaul thought it extraordinary even as he thought it hopeless and pathetic. In *Guerrillas* we are given no alternative to political turmoil and personal malaise, but it is clear that, to Naipaul, some forms of human perversity are preferable to others. We know that he can sympathize with those who struggle with their own futility, provided only that they place themselves aggressively in the eye of the disorder they oppose and covet. And we know that those—like the protagonist's mistress Jane—who play at revolution, who move easily in the knowledge of their own security, are treated with contempt and made to suffer at last what they deserve. *Guerrillas* is an ugly book. Within this kind of knowledge there is room for considerable complexity and ambivalence, and no one should suppose that Naipaul had to sacrifice doubt to achieve clarity.

Problems of point of view, of authorial presence and intention, assume significance only when they are seen to serve or to stand in the way of the novelist's emerging vision. Just so, when we have doubts about the sheer physical detail brought to bear on that vision, we assume that the vision cannot stand on the rhetorical basis provided by the author's assertions. In one novel after another, Naipaul or his protagonist-narrator will announce that in the third world the best intentions amount at last to nothing; that what has seemed "whole" or intact has seemed so only because of the power of illusion; that nothing useful can ever really be done for "the people," who betray whatever favors they receive. These and other views abound in the light comedies and in the darker works. Even in Naipaul's one "English" novel, *Mr. Stone and the Knight's Companion*, one finds attenuated versions of the familiar insights, presented from the perspective of the hardly passionate Mr. Stone. Consider: "And the further the brilliance receded the more clearly he recognized its unusual quality. It was a brilliance which was incapable of being sustained, yet a brilliance of which every diminution was a loss to be mourned, a reminder of darkness that had been lived through and a threat of the darkness that was to come." For "brilliance" here we read in the other novels "the mobilization of power"; for "darkness," "business as usual or—no business at all." Either way, Naipaul's represented view is that, whatever the ephemeral accession

---

* That it is fruitful to address the relevant literary and political questions at the same time we shall demonstrate in part II of this chapter.

to power or influence of this force or that, the briefly activated energies and enthusiasms are bound to run down. The beasts will bloody themselves and all around them in the end. Even the pacific Mr. Stone concludes on the last page of Naipaul's novel that "it was not by creation that man demonstrated his power and defied this hostile order, but by destruction, as the man who carried the possibility of the earth's destruction within him." This is a rather silly fantasy to be entertained by so settled a bourgeois as Mr. Stone, but it is fitting that even he should have ascribed to him a view that seems so menacing when it is associated with Naipaul's other characters.

The views of men like Stone, Singh, Salim, or Peter Roche of *Guerrillas* may be said to underlie, though not to constitute, the vision each work seeks to embody. For example, the fact that Roche is eager to generalize his own shame and moral doubt, and therefore to call into question the motives of others who exhibit political courage, is not enough to indicate the vision of *Guerrillas*. For that we need the kind of detail that can make us feel that Roche does truly represent the most typical kind of white liberal involvement in contemporary third world politics. We must feel that Roche has been made to test the limits of the universe in which he moves, that his failures are not determined by Naipaul's fixed view of him but by a genuine interaction with the circumstances that are said to defeat him. If we feel that Naipaul has simply insisted on a particular view of things, we can do nothing but accept or reject the view. To engage it, as we engage a vision that asks to be taken up and looked at from several angles, we must feel that the novel has created its own hard facts to negotiate. It must have pitted its own predispositions, the novelist's own yearnings and ideas, against what can only be called necessity. No doubt, one man's necessity may be another man's whim, but it is reasonable to suppose that most readers will agree on what the novel requires. Naipaul succeeds as a writer when he sets up a universe—usually political—that can significantly check his own too ready impulse to dismiss everything before it has really been given a chance.

In *Biswas* the vision, such as it is, requires not the detail we associate with political conflict, but a matrix of social relations so dense that it will be thought to restrain the protagonist's quirky individualism. So leisurely a novel is *Biswas*, so carefully does Naipaul spread before us the practices and emblems by which a traditional society is known to its constituents, that we never doubt the authority of the emergent vision. It is a vision of an orthodox communal life corrupted by its own rigidities and unable to respond—except with resentment and calumny—to the forces that would refresh it. What makes the novel so fine, so unusual, is not Naipaul's organizing of evidence to show that the modern world erodes and corrupts traditional institutions. His ambivalent support of rebellion and individualism does not entitle him to special praise or attention. Who isn't, in our time, an opponent of the blind traditionalism that stunts lives in places like India and Trinidad? *Biswas* claims our attention because it demonstrates what it is like to be provoked to rebellion and to lack the means to do it properly. Naipaul's goal is to sink Biswas so deep in the traditional life represented by Hanuman House and the Tulsi family that he has no alternative, as a man of spirit, but to scream and fight. And having put his man there, where others more or less like him spend their narrow lives, Naipaul finds also that he must allow the man one or two of the fragile victories a man of spirit would require to carry on. Biswas knows, as he struggles, that he is a defeated man, that he will sink further and further into the void occupied for so long by others in such families. But he holds before him the possibility of small pleasures, a house of his own he can retreat to in place of the communal structures that would chasten his options past the point of tolerance. What makes it all so compelling is the apparently easy accumulation of detail to make the life at issue seem inevitable, encompassing, at once human in its scale and terrible in its fixities. We are speaking here of the way food is prepared and served, the way children are praised and punished, the relative obligations of wives and husbands, the degree of self-expression prescribed for these occasions and for those, and so on, right down to the toilet arrangements that obtain in large families. Had Naipaul elevated any of these to the status of subjects in their own right, his novel would read more like a documentary history than like the story of a man. It is his great achievement to have avoided a mechanical piling on of details and yet to have planted his character amidst the objects and customs of his world in such a way that, try as he will, they remain a part of him and of all he can be.

There is no politics in *Biswas* because neither the protagonist nor anyone else in the novel has been stimulated to conceive of the future as something that can be affected by collective effort. A novel in which collective action is to be made a primary issue requires another kind of detail, and another kind of consciousness at or near the center. That consciousness will be susceptible to the fascination of ideas and to the identification with an ideological cause. Biswas has no interest in ideas or in any general view of the future they may propose. He opposes the social order out of personal necessity, not out of a conviction that grows with the growth of his thought. He learns certain things, but his capacity for abstract thought remains primitive and he conceives the future more as a dream than as an altered order of relations. Collective action would suggest to him a routine commerce with just those persons he would be least likely to trust. He is remote from any conception of political detail because his plots are in the main expressions of blind rage or immediate inspiration. What makes him so attractive as a person makes him politically hopeless.

Naipaul is often considered a political novelist, but not until *A Bend in the River* did he write a novel in the great tradition of Western political fiction. Earlier, in a work like *In a Free State*, he exhibited merely a will to political fiction and a gift for drawing people in crisis. There are ideas in the novel. People know how to think. There is even a conception of the future. But it is all atmospheric, sketched in at the level of background.

The sketches are vivid, intense, frightening. One has a sense of dangerous ideas in the air, of a politics taking shape somewhere—but out of sight, of persons touched by strong ideological currents they have not the ability to grasp or discriminate among. Political reality is given in the form of starkly isolated tableaux: a sudden glimpse of tribal prisoners in a civil war, men stripped of their newly won freedom and reduced again to their immemorial status: "Some were roped up in the traditional forest way, neck to neck, . . . as though for delivery to the slave-merchant." The image is regarded as sufficient, a sign of something ended, an emblem. Ignored are the actual programs or strategies of the captured men, the organizational difficulties of the conquering armies and their president, the relation between the frail structure of capital and the struggle for unification and independence. *In a Free State* is a moving and powerful work, but to think of it as a political novel is to suppose that such a novel can work largely at the level of symbolic gesture. What separates *In a Free State* from the political novel some readers would like it to be is the absence of appropriate detail and the related absorption in a consciousness whose counters are mostly personal and, in an unduly limiting sense, subjective.

Let us be clear about this. The central figure in the work, an Englishman named Bobby, thinks of his life as deeply implicated in the future of the African state to which he is attached as a civil servant. But his relation to the state is given at the level of personal investment alone. Here and there a particular attitude to an issue is vaguely hinted at, but the stress is on the fact that his position makes Bobby feel he belongs to something. He wants to do some good and incidentally to continue to have the homosexual adventures he craves. Ultimately, before he finally gets back to the safety of the western compound, he is detained on the road and beaten. The brief encounter with political reality teaches Bobby that his hopes for a political solution to African problems and for his own useful role in effecting that solution are misguided. But the insight may be said to have only marginal political status. How representative are the isolated events of the novel? What have men like Bobby actually done in the countries in which they serve? How is power in an African state shifted from one party to another? From what sources do Bobby and his traveling companion Linda learn to feel as they do about those they administer? To be fair, we think of such things only when we try to think of *In a Free State* as a political novel. As readers of the novel we are never tempted to think in such terms because we are content to read it as a novel of sensibility. We are interested in Bobby as we are interested in, say, a Henry James character who thinks he knows what life is all about better than he actually does. It makes no sense to say of such characters that they have no relation to politics or that they are not social beings. They are, in part, what they are because of conditions obtaining in their society; but only if the social constraints are stressed as *determinants* do we agree to call the books in question social novels. Just so can we consider *In a Free State* a political novel only if specifically political conflicts and loyalties are brought into play; and so too must characters be shown to think of themselves as political actors in a struggle for which there are definable goals and more or less suitable strategies. The fact that we cannot say what are the political objectives of the parties to the vague conflict that conditions everything in *In a Free State* determines our judgment of it as a novel of sensibility. There is nothing wrong or inferior in such a work, though it is apt to be misleading when it makes political noises that may be taken for the real thing.

Does it matter that we call one book a novel of sensibility, another a political fiction? Again, it is useful to consider the nagging question. Such designations do help us to focus our questions and to demand of a work only what it is designed to give. They are also useful when, as with Naipaul, the author involved may be said to have moved from one kind of work to another. In sheer economy and efficiency of suggestion Naipaul is not likely to surpass *In a Free State. Guerrillas*, by contrast, goes too far in fleshing out the menace without significantly extending our understanding of political circumstance or personal motive. We are treated to a hideous cruelty and perversion we were perfectly capable of imagining for ourselves in the earlier work. *A Bend in the River*, though, does enlarge our understanding without sacrificing either shapeliness or implication, and it marks Naipaul's movement to a more difficult and demanding fiction. It is a narrative rich in complication and incident, though it withholds as much as it delivers. It gets at the mechanics of power while suggesting that there is much it cannot explain or show. To speak of it as a political novel is to consider that it can handle ideas and the consciousness of ideas as well as it can handle personal motive. We conclude that it is adequate to its own purposes and to our designation of it.

II

I said earlier that the most satisfying aspect of Naipaul's development was his attempt to master his inveterate revulsions: from persons, from groups, from political action itself. That self-mastery is a function, we may say, of vision and of art. The sentiments exhibited in *A Bend in the River* are no nicer than those found in earlier books. There is no greater optimism about revolution. The African setting is as torn by senseless violence as it ever was. Yet we feel throughout that Naipaul is examining things as they are. We do not entertain the suspicion that he simply contrived to make things as bad as he could to justify his own revulsion. It may be that conditions in Africa are better, or worse, than they appear in the book, but we have reason to believe they might be this way, and we understand why an intelligent person would despair of them as he does.

In the essay "A New King for the Congo: Mobutu and the Nihilism of Africa,"[1] Naipaul had earlier taken on the themes to which he later devoted *A Bend in the River*. The essay treatment is, quite as he says in a prefatory note to the book edition, "obsessional"; moreover, in various essays examining Argentina, Trinidad, and the Congo, "the themes repeat," and so, too, do many of the supporting details: abandoned buildings at the center of what were to be impressive urban centers, vegetation running wild in what were planned as formal gardens or the tended lawns leading up to once handsome public structures, vandalized street lamps and broken sidewalks. The Congo essay, to my mind the most relentless and effective of the third world studies, raises to a new pitch the idea of mimicry that Naipaul had examined elsewhere. "Creativity itself now begins to appear as something that might be looted, brought into being by decree," Naipaul writes; or, "So the borrowed ideas—about colonialism and alienation, the consumer society and the decline of the West—are made to serve the African cult of authenticity"; or, more pointed still:

> It is with people like Simon, educated, money making, that the visitor feels himself in the presence of vulnerability, dumbness, danger. Because their resentments, which appear to contradict their ambitions, and which they can never satisfactorily explain, can at any time be converted into a wish to wipe out and undo, an African nihilism, the rage of primitive men coming to themselves and finding that they have been fooled and affronted.[2]

The ideas examined in Naipaul's essay, the prediction repeated over and again—that the bush is the enduring reality of Africa, that it alone works and ensures that vacancy, the recurring dream of the past to which the African is perpetually drawn—are everywhere present in Naipaul's African novel. Particular passages proclaim those ideas and predictions with the same kind of clarity and punishing logic that one finds in the essay. And yet, no reader of *A Bend in the River* may suppose that the novel is written simply to promote those ideas. The view of Naipaul as a writer with a relatively simple point to make and with a reflex reaction to all third world phenomena may be, mistakenly, derived from a careless reading of his essays and journalism. The complexity of his best novels should prevent anyone from assuming that he has sought simply to enforce a prediction or promote an old idea he had earlier tested in the West Indian context. Nor will a novel like *Biswas* or *A Bend in the River* permit scrupulous readers to conclude that Naipaul writes exclusively out of irrational biases. Obsessional he may be—even on such small matters as West Indian steel bands—but it should not be so hard to see that for Naipaul, as Canadian novelist Clark Blaise has said, "steel drums are the debris of colonial exploitation; they stop their practitioners at a relatively low level of conventional mimicry; they reward a pimpish desire to turn a tourist trick."[3] And if one should have no trouble in concluding, even on the basis of Naipaul's nonfiction writings, that "his commitments are impeccably liberal, even when they seem calculated to outrage third-world sympathizers,"[4] so the novels should seem even more bracing and rewarding. "We had to live in the world as it existed," says Salim in *A Bend in the River*: not as petty biases would have it, not as we would wish it to be, but as it is. And this, we feel as we read Naipaul, can be accomplished only by those who face up to their personal hatreds and are not content simply to adopt edifying postures. Though Naipaul's fiction has occasionally been weakened by producing the impression that the novelist knew before he set out exactly what he wished to find and was unwilling to discover anything else, *A Bend in the River* would seem to have evolved in another way. The ideas stated in the Congo essay, though nowhere repudiated, clearly seemed inadequate to the facts of life taking novelistic shape under the writer's hand. What the novel therefore discovers is far from identical with or reducible to the terms of the essay.

In the essay Naipaul at one point speaks of the apparently defunct university in Zaire: "But the students are bright and friendly," he writes. "They have come from the bush, but already they can talk of Stendhal and Fanon; they have the enthusiasm of people to whom everything is new." We note that the reporter wishes to be generous and admiring. He likes the students, at least for the enthusiasm which, though it "deserves a better equipped country," will be justified by their finding government jobs. To hold on to those jobs, of course, these persons will have to remain loyal Mobutists and willingly restrict the range of their intellectual inquiry. They will have to accept that simplification of the world, that official view of things that ultimately "simplifies people," which makes obedience seem the only essential prerequisite of social progress. Those who do not take readily to these requirements will experience pain, in itself a potentially ennobling experience associated with the "awakening to ideas, history, a knowledge of injustice," and so on. "But no," Naipaul concludes. Such pain, authentic, deepening, is not likely to be. A place destined to remain "trapped and static"[5] is not destined to produce that kind of authentic discovery and pain. Enthusiasm is one thing, genuine advance another.

In the novel the arc of Naipaul's falling sentiment is much harder to trace. He gives us a vivid portrait of a student named Ferdinand. From the first we feel that we know the type. He is bright, ambitious, impatient. The son of a *marchande,* or traveling retailer, named Zabeth who travels out of the bush once each month to buy the wholesale goods she will sell, he belongs to the bush in a way that makes everything he will learn seem positively new and tempting. Though in time he grows into one of the "new men" of Africa, we are never permitted to forget what he has recently been and how frail are the institutional means by which such persons are afforded an inspired view of themselves. Typical at first in his pride and in his inability to get past programmed responses to questions he hardly understands, he seems nonetheless a little enviable in his self-importance and inquisitiveness. The temptation to dismiss him as hopelessly muddled and ridiculous is regularly countered by the alternating sense that he *is* a new man of Africa, that he is anything but simple or primitive. Genuine pain and discovery might have seemed too rich for the young Africans described in Naipaul's essay, but Ferdinand eminently deserves a disillusionment and anguish that can only belong to someone who has passed far beyond the bush. Whatever Naipaul had originally thought to do with

Ferdinand, whatever ideas he may have been conceived to illustrate, the character quickly establishes a life of his own and demands that he be regarded in his own terms.

What Naipaul does with Ferdinand is important because the idea that there can be a new man of Africa is very much at issue in the novel. So, too, are the costs involved in producing a new man at issue. To be new in Africa, Naipaul suggests, is to start from nothing and rapidly make oneself free by assuming that one is entitled to good things and that good things come to those who acquire knowledge and make plausible demands. Starting from nothing ensures that one will have none of the guilts and uncertainties that inhibit those who carry a remembered past. There may be something unfair in the assumption that one deserves instant mastery of "those things that other countries and peoples had taken so long to arrive at—writing, printing, universities, books, knowledge." But to be free in Ferdinand's sense is not to worry over that kind of fairness. Neither is it to wonder how far the knowledge one has been offered may be expected to take one, or how enduringly good are the good things one hopes for. The freedom created by men like Ferdinand may be built on an elaborate hoax. Clearly there is more to developing a viable civilization than leveling the bush, building a few polytechnic institutes, and teaching an elite to regard itself as comprised of fully evolved representatives of a people laying claim to its dignity. But there is a kind of promise, even in such a hopeless enterprise, that the novel teaches us not to dismiss too lightly. Out of the dreams of the new men may come something genuinely new, a capacity to confront despair and futility that is potentially valuable beyond anything the polytechnic can teach.

A Bend in the River is no song of praise to the new man, and no sentimental tribute to the capacity for despair. Naipaul has always thought it best not to confuse suffering with anything else. Ferdinand helps the novelist sustain a tension between loss and hope that keeps the novel from sliding into an easy despair or indulging a bittersweet tragic emotion. He is a political figure insofar as he is in part the object of whatever political revolution a new African nation may be said to launch. And he does, of course, actually come to a kind of power which it is in the nature of the emergent society to betray. If *A Bend in the River* is a political novel, it must make of Ferdinand a figure in whom others can see political promise or futility. It must view him as someone conditioned by the more or less inflexible circumstance to which he belongs, and yet moving beyond the reach of that conditioning, free to fail in a way no observer can fully have anticipated. Others subject to the same circumstance may succumb more entirely, but it is not for Naipaul in this work to propose that all Africans are the same, or that the hopelessness of one is finally the same as the hopelessness of another. One need only think of the "Citizen" who has been given Salim's shop in the course of the President's nationalization program to recognize how deeply Naipaul wishes us to admire Ferdinand.

Not for Ferdinand the sodden excuses, the impulse to blame everything on "the situation" while mouthing obligatory phrases turning on empty words like *radicalize* and *compensation*. The "Citizen" is no political man, not even a *victim* of politics. He is a dumb cipher, symptom of a nullity that exists whatever the shiftings of power in an Africa that has always had more than its share of nullity. Ferdinand is the political man, wishing to take action on the basis of aims he shares with others like himself, understanding, however imperfectly, that there are difficult questions to address even as he must often pretend that nothing is too difficult. For Naipaul to have cast Ferdinand as if he were simply a more fortunate version of the "Citizen" would have been to suggest that what can be thought about Africa is self-evident and coherent. It would have been to repress the unthinkable, to opt for a strategy of containment in which the very possibility of collective praxis would have been denied.[6] To deny such a possibility would, of course, have been to deny not only the possibility of a politics, but the thought of a viable African future.

Those in the third world who have no stomach for Naipaul accuse him of having no sympathy whatever for independence movements, and argue that no real collective praxis is suggested in *A Bend in the River*. The accents of hopelessness and nullity are sounded from the opening pages of the novel, it is argued, and nothing Naipaul sees in Ferdinand or anyone else can effectively compete with those accents. They may not always ring with satisfaction, as though an airtight case for the worst had been neatly and exhaustively assembled, but they ring with the sense that the African truth is known, that no newer truth could conceivably displace it. What, after all, can the newly conscious Ferdinand do in the face of the bush? What can an occasional fellow struggling with his own disillusionment do about the inevitable reversion to primitivism in a continent that has known little else? Had Naipaul wished to propose an alternative possibility, had he been able to take seriously the prospect of revolutionary change, would he have made of Ferdinand an exemplary figure whose main virtue is his capacity to acknowledge the hopelessness of Africa? Had he wished to resist defeatism, would Naipaul have installed at the center of his novel not a new man but one who believes in nothing and is permitted to see the worst only because he is preternaturally alert to fraudulence and empty mimicry?

The assault on Naipaul is in effect not only an assault on his politics but also on his work; in *A Bend in the River*, surely the politics and the literary quality of the writing may not be separated. If the novel is credibly organized, if characters have independent rather than merely illustrative identity, if conflicts are genuinely worked out, not made up to seem like conflicts when in fact all the answers are in, then it is fair to say that the political vision of the novel warrants serious consideration. Those who reject the novel, on the grounds that it is depressing or that Naipaul would not accept any version of a revolutionary solution, impose on the work an irrelevant bias. Only if the novel is mechanically depressing—that is, made to reach depressing conclusions on the basis of nothing but the author's settled predisposition—can the one objection be taken seriously. Only if the inveterate authorial skepticism about grandiose revolutionary aims led Naipaul to violate plausibility in his depiction of the new men pursuing their collective goals would the repudiation of Naipaul as a counterrevolutionary writer have any importance in the novelistic context. But *A Bend in the River* is not what its third world critics claim.

Consider Naipaul's central character, Salim. Is he what one would call a reliable narrator? As one who has no privileged perspective to defend, no illusions to maintain, he would seem ideally suited to reporting exactly what he sees. The idea that, like everyone else, he sees what he wants to see is challenged by the fact that he sees all sorts of things. Also, he is aware from time to time of quandaries and complexities he had not anticipated, and takes no pleasure in the despairing conclusions he is led to draw. True, he begins the narrative with the words "the world is what it is; men who are nothing, who allow themselves to become nothing, have no place in it." But these words are too often taken to describe the condition of everyone in the novel, whereas it is only the narrator they describe. And what, after all, ought one to object to in the formulation? It is not fate that Salim blames for the anomic drift of certain men; only those "who allow themselves to become nothing" find that they are nothing. Just so, "the world is what it is" does not mean that no man is better or wiser than any other or that one had as well do nothing as something. Salim has an irritating way of subverting both his own generosity and his most patently hopeful enthusiasms, but he enforces critical distinctions again and again. When he sees that the youthful Ferdinand is largely indifferent to the magazines and reproductions he shows him, he concludes that really there isn't much of value in the magazines and that the paintings are really junk. But what he "wanted to say" to Ferdinand carries a good deal of novelistic weight and helps us to feel that Salim struggles against his own better instincts only because he expects to be disappointed by everything and finds no support in the surroundings he has chosen for himself. " 'Look at these magazines,' " he wants to say.

> "Nobody pays me to read them. I read them because I am the kind of person I am, because I take an interest in things, because I want to know about the world. Look at those paintings. The lady took a lot of trouble over them. She wanted to make something beautiful to hang in her house. She didn't hang it there because it was a piece of magic."

The passage contains many, if not all, of Naipaul's central themes: the belief in disinterested inquiry as a way of learning about the world and of avoiding excessive preoccupation with oneself; the satisfaction in creation itself and, more especially, in the making of beautiful things; the resistance to magic and to the expectation that things happen because one wants them to happen or because one has found magic formulas. Salim does not say these things to anyone in the novel, but they are part of what he thinks and of what we are permitted to share with him. Their potency is measured by the degree in which they are made to correct the perspectives even of characters who are ordinarily credited with a progressive or enlightened view of human affairs. The insights are also made to function in the novel as political ideas insofar as they detach Salim from the policies and projects of others. Salim is not really a political actor in *A Bend in the River*, but he is involved in the intrigues of others and driven to take an interest in what they do. If Naipaul made him chiefly an observer rather than an effectual political operator, that was not to suggest that effectual political activity is unthinkable. Salim as narrator mainly stays on the margins of the important action because only there can he be permitted to register what happens in a more or less disinterested way. In himself he says nothing about the general advisability of action or inaction, but he tells us a great deal about political intelligence and about the abuse of power by those who have no respect for the truth. Salim is not a likable man—Naipaul once or twice goes out of his way to ensure that we do not like him—but he is admirable in accomplishing the one thing he is genuinely good at: He describes the world as it appears before him, as if no good could come from representing it in any other way.

What does Salim see? In Ferdinand he sees the possibility of a great stride that can take someone from instinct to consciousness in one miraculous transformation. He never quite brings himself to believe in this transformation, but the character comes to embody it in a degree Salim could not at first have imagined. At the same time, Ferdinand is required—not by Naipaul only, but by his symptomatic status among other young men also required by their societies to demonstrate that Africa has a future—to stand for something larger than himself. He must prove that African revolutions are built not on false hopes but on sound prospects. This burden Ferdinand as a character cannot bear, and he cannot therefore be made by Naipaul to assume a central role in the novel. Since he is not in himself a failure, and since he cannot by that token alone be said accurately to represent the African experiment, the focus must be located more broadly in the African political arena. And, insofar as that arena requires for adequate novelistic representation a particular focus, Naipaul bends Salim's reflections quite naturally in the direction of the new President himself.

The resemblance between Mobutu and Naipaul's fictional President is obvious. So, too, are the attitudes Naipaul expresses in his essay on Mobutu very similar to those expressed by Salim in the novel. But the character of the President assumes in the novel almost the dimensions of a controlling intelligence, at once terrifying and impressive, arbitrary and exact. Where in the essay Naipaul had necessarily to consider the man from the perspective of the bemused and critical outsider, in the novel he is observed by persons—including Salim—who depend on him at least for some sense of order and superficial stability. He may change direction and disappoint even his close supporters, but he remains an extravagantly elusive figure, larger than anybody's criticism of this or that aspect of his program. Even at the end of the novel, when everything seems about to go to pieces, we remember one character's earlier description of the President as " 'conservative, revolutionary, everything,' " a leader who manages to honor the African past and to insist on rapid modernization. The portrait is studded from the first with compromising details, and the grandiosity of the President's design is sharply apparent to Salim if to no one else. But even Salim, with his inveterate skepticism and hostility to extravagant charades, does not quite reject what he sees. The President, he reports, "was creating a miracle that would astound the rest of the world," a town with monumental buildings and a look that owed nothing to the European suburb that had once occupied the site. In one grand gesture, Salim concludes, "he was by-passing real Africa, the difficult Africa of bush and villages. . . ." A hopeless business, perhaps, but one likely to accomplish something at least, or so Salim's account, bolstered by the more infatuate encomia delivered by other sophisticated witnesses, would have us feel. The critique of a dangerous illusion is manifest in the very language of Salim's description, but the accents of wonder and self-doubt are never completely submerged.

Admiration of the President grows, in fact, even as his demagogy is unmasked. Delivering his speeches no longer in French, he speaks now in a simple African language which he makes into "the language of the drinking booth and the street brawl, converting himself . . . into the lowest of the low." More remarkably,

> while appearing just to restate old principles, the President also acknowledged and ridiculed new criticism. . . . He made everything fit; he could suggest he knew everything. He could make it appear that everything that was happening in the country, good or bad or ordinary [from food shortages to local uprisings against his authority], was part of a bigger plan.

Reasserting his own authority by establishing in ever more convincing ways his identity with "the *petit peuple*," he puts to route the malcontents, the intellectuals with reasonable grievances, and those who have forgotten to be modest in their personal ambitions. His demagogy may signal the decline of his ideal stature as a leader, but it works so well in accomplishing what the President ardently desires—the strengthening of his absolute power—that it seems somehow impressive even to those who are likely to suffer.

The political vision of the novel is nowhere more complex than in this ambivalence toward the President. No effort is made to conceal or to explain away the deficiencies associated with his strategies. On the first page Salim had told us that many of the places he knew in the President's Africa "have closed down or are full of blood." At the end of the novel he tells us that, quite as it has always been in the African bush, "men could be destroyed for nothing," so that, for all the President's strategies, "there was no plan; there was no law." Even when one felt the President might have had some genuine control of events one felt also that no one could discipline the competing forces indefinitely, that sooner or later the massive buildings and the popular speeches would cease to satisfy. And yet, for all that, the urge to cry "Demagogue!" had never quite been allowed by anything in the novel. One knew to what extremes the President might resort to have his way, but did that mean one was required to repudiate him or his goals? He was, no doubt, the great promoter, selling to all comers an "Africa of words," in consequence of which the reality of forest and rubbish and ignorance might be harder and harder to acknowledge. But what alternative was there to the attempt to leave behind the unspeakable humiliations of the African past? It is not only Salim's wretched disillusionment with his own life and the life of others like him in London or elsewhere that attracts him to the President's glittering Domain. It is the idea that men may be driven to deny their condition, to deny even the facts of life, that attracts him. The President's Domain "was a hoax," no doubt. "But at the same time," he cannot help thinking, "it was real, because it was full of serious men (and a few women). Was there a truth outside men? Didn't men make the truth for themselves?" It is not in the charge of Naipaul's novel to provide definitive answers to these questions, but it does provide a perspective from which one will inevitably be more sympathetic not only to failure, but to certain ideas that are inherently untrustworthy.

The consequence of the sympathy one is made to feel is not an inability to accept the withdrawal of revolutionary hope. By the time Ferdinand announces, almost at novel's end, " 'Nobody's going anywhere. We're all going to hell, and every man knows this in his bones,' " we are fully prepared to accept the truth of his statement. And when, a few pages later, we hear the terrible prophecy toward which the entire novel had apparently been building, we respond not as to something unthinkable but to an eventuality all too obvious, whatever our previous reluctance to consider it. " 'They're going to kill everybody who can read and write, everybody who ever put on a jacket and tie,' " Salim is told. " 'They're going to kill and kill. They say it is the only way, to go back to the beginning before it's too late.' " This, we understand, will be the work of the President, who will have seen no other way to seize what is left of a deteriorating situation on behalf of the ignorant and forever dispossessed. No prediction as to what may follow the bloodletting is offered, but it is clear that to start from the beginning is to proceed without the legal, parliamentary, or moral designs furnished by the discredited colonialist models. So terrible is the prophecy, and so entirely are we prepared to believe that it is accurate, that it leaves nothing really to be said about the future of the African nation at issue. Salim's decision to get out is inevitable, and with that Naipaul's inquiry must come to an end. Salim continues to believe that, no matter what the carnage, those who have courage and bide their time are likely to come through. Even those who talk about the beginning soon find that they cannot do without certain goods and services and techniques that are not of the beginning. Where at once there is nothing, in time there will be something. Such thoughts are not enough to hold Salim at the bend of the river, but they seem plausible enough even to those of us who cannot banish from our minds the horror of the novel's culminating prophecy.

Of course, *A Bend in the River* is not a prophetic book but a political novel whose main business is to represent a conflict without converting its dominant counters into inert positions; neither will it propose that its dominant actors merely reflect the circumstance by which they are constrained. In this sense the novel is most in danger of failing when it makes of the central conflict an opposition between past and present, retreat and advance. What is the ever-beckoning alternative to modernization in Africa? The bush, which is to say, savagery and the belief in magic. What is the form that modernization takes in Africa? Presumption, grandiosity, pathetic mimicry. Put this way—and the novel does on occasion tempt one to believe that these are the only options Naipaul can conceive—the dominant counters do assume the rigidity of inert positions. But it is the special achievement of this novel to resist its own occasional predilections and to recommend a more generous, if not a more hopeful, reading of the situation. Not only is there Ferdinand, and the sometimes impressively commanding President—figures who are more than products of a circumstance, whatever their eventual submission—there is, as well, the steady articulation of what is at stake in the achievement of independence. This articulation is the work not primarily of Salim, who from the first feels himself one of the defeated, but of lesser characters who are implicated in the fate of the new nation. That these other figures are not Africans has nothing to do with a racialist bias. It reflects the fact that, in the initial stages of a third world revolution, even nativist rulers will wish to avail themselves of assistance from outsiders.

In fact, we are given to understand, the revolution itself was in part at least the creation of white men. This is not presented in the novel as a judgment on the revolution or on the quality of white consciousness; it is simply a fact worth dealing with in other terms. And what, after all, is one to make of the fact that a white man named Raymond nurtured in the President revolutionary ambitions and taught him how to become a leader? How does one respond finally to Raymond's idea that third world leaders are shaped by the quality of their despair, and that the last thing a successful African leader must do is "to become involved in politics as they exist" in the prerevolutionary society or "posture for Europeans and hope to pass as evolved"? In themselves, these ideas seem extraordinarily penetrating, and one sees that they did indeed have much to do with shaping the President in Naipaul's novel. But the ideas are judged, in effect, by the disastrous turn the revolution takes. The refusal to "posture for Europeans" is, we come to see, more than a matter of wearing African tunics or refusing to mouth soothing neocolonialist phrases. Insofar as there is in Raymond's advice an instigation to defy, to refuse what he takes to be the merely formal proprieties associated with parliamentary conventions and "debating societies," his ideas may be seen to encourage that ultimate flouting of civilized norms to which the President has final recourse. It was perfectly understandable that, as the country moved into a new stage of development, the President would need to banish the white man from his entourage so as not to be regarded by his people as a tool of the great powers. Such necessities are not, perhaps, pretty, but they are hardly symptomatic of any major retrogression. One suspects that, for all the disappointment Raymond might have felt, he would surely have accepted the necessity of that banishment as consistent with his own earlier ideas. One wonders, though, whether white radicals like Raymond are at all capable of appreciating the degree to which their own ideas are implicated in the return to chaos that concludes so many revolutionary experiments.[7]

Raymond is not alone in articulating the risks and dimensions of revolutionary progress in a way that is frequently compelling. Salim's Indian friend Indar is more uncertain than Raymond about himself and his role in the new society, but he is just as good at describing what is at issue. Naipaul seems more interested in him than in Raymond not only because he is a more richly ambivalent character, but because his desire to overcome his own problems as an Indian casts considerable light on the African project. A university-level teacher at the new Domain erected by the President, he is at once an eager participant in a great experiment and a wary outsider. Attracted to the bright young men like Ferdinand, he is at the same time fearful that they will settle for " 'politics and principles,' " that for all their new sophistication they will wish not to think and end up keeping the world " 'in turmoil for the next half century.' " Persuasive as he is in stating these ideas, they are brought into question by his obsessive desire to " 'trample on the past,' " his sense that since " 'the past is something in your mind alone,' " it has no reality and need have no claim on us. " 'In the beginning it is like trampling on a garden,' " he admits. " 'In the end you are just walking on ground. That is the way we have to learn to live now.' " Just so, for the African to enter the modern world he must leave the past behind completely, resolving his stubborn relation to African religion and tribal loyalties by abandoning them. To do less is, for Indar, to make oneself susceptible, to weaken one's resolve to be one's own man. To hold on even to a fragment of a past in which one (or one's kind) has been a subject creature is to allow oneself to be exploited by others who control the originary institutions. To be, potentially, a free man is to make oneself a free-floating modern with no need to be solaced by "that idea of the great men of our tribe" who can represent or fulfill the manhood of others too ready to "surrender" it as the price of "home and security."

Stirring sentiments, to be sure, and not without considerable poignance in light of the African prospect as well. But no one will suppose that Indar's are the final words on these matters, or that Salim's pitying "his exaggerations, his delusions," is anything less than a just response. Quite as Raymond had been shown to be a less reliable guide to the primary issues than he'd hoped, so Indar's insights are tainted, as it were, by his too rigid, almost hysterical commitment to certain assumptions.

If the steady articulation of promising ideas is an important part of Naipaul's resistance to inert political categories and programmatic dismissals of revolutionary fervor, why is the novel organized to subvert these ideas? This question, more than any other, disfigures most discussions of Naipaul's work. In presuming to stand above the various positions articulated or embodied in his novels—so the standard criticism would have it—Naipaul pretends to have transcended ideology and thereby to have presented things as they are. But this, as a critic like Fredric Jameson argues, is to buy into a kind of empiricism, "the mirage of an utterly non-theoretical practice."[8] Naipaul may think simply to represent competing versions of the political and historical truth, but his representation is itself a privileging of certain views at the expense of others, and only false consciousness can come of his pretending to a sublime, if severe, dispassion. So the consequence of Naipaul's ostensibly fair representation of the available options in *A Bend in the River* is the conclusion that no good can come of third world revolutions, and that Africans especially had better give up the fight before the continent drowns in blood. No matter that the novel itself refuses to draw that conclusion, or that much in the novel supports a more hopeful reading of revolution. Intention is not finally what matters here. Those convinced of Naipaul's "negative" impact on third world liberation movements see only that the native cultures are studied always in their implicit relation to the dominant hegemonic culture of the West. Since the native cultures cannot possibly accomplish what Naipaul most values in advanced Western societies, and in most cases do not wish to emulate the formerly dominant culture, the mode of judgment is transparently inappropriate. The sympathy Naipaul directs at persons who are trapped in unpromising situations, the dignity he confers on those who struggle against the burden of their inheritance, are of no consequence to those who want a more "positive" representation of the revolutionary prospect.

What also disturbs many readers is Naipaul's success in depicting the dynamics of political change as though these dynamics were responsible to particular laws and rhythms. He makes us feel that nothing in Africa just happens, that though there is much we cannot explain in the psyche of new men public decisions do follow a fairly predictable course. He takes no relish in outlining that course, but he is attentive to its smallest shifts. If the tone of the novel frequently suggests that we have been here before, there is no consequent suggestion that things could not have happened another way, or that unforeseeable surprises might not still take us unawares. To object to Naipaul's handling of political dynamics is to contend, in effect, that he stacks the odds against his revolutions. It is also to contend that the state apparatus in Naipaul's emergent societies is too entirely a semiautonomous operation dominated by a single figure or small oligarchy that can be counted on to move it in a ruinous direction. Naipaul's critics, especially those on the left, want the state apparatus in third world novels to be represented as an epiphenomenon of the economic realm.[9] The novelist would not, in that case, need to pay very much attention to the dynamics of repression or to the corruption of political discourse. The controlling assumption would then be that the repressive apparatus so central to most third world revolutions must inevitably wither away when a satisfactory stage of productivity is achieved by the new society. Only the intolerable economic pressures experienced by emergent countries, taken together with the cultural dislocations caused by new modes of production and competition, can account for the unpleasant features of their political systems: so the familiar argument goes. By paying attention to the President's control of his people and the excesses associated with the extension of political power at the local level, Naipaul grievously distorts his portrait of Africa.

No one can say for certain what effects Naipaul's work will continue to have, whether his unmasking of third world delusions will serve illiberal or counterrevolutionary purposes. There is reason to feel not only that Naipaul has told important truths about Africa—and about developing countries elsewhere—but that he has understood even what international development experts have refused to acknowledge. Consider that demodernization is very much under way in countries that achieved independence in the early nineteen-sixties and turned rapidly to modernization in the years following. Experts now increasingly urge third world populations to return to the land, after luring them to cities where work can no longer be found and where the middle classes are being destroyed by the withdrawal of foreign investment capital and intolerably high interest rates. But not only have the agricultural skills been lost, as we are routinely and properly reminded; not only is the family unit "no longer organized to sustain the previous existence" and the land no longer available; more important by far is the violation of promises, the destruction of hopes, the creation of confusion among masses of people who have no recourse but despair and a violent anger. Naipaul cannot be surprised to read:

> In Africa, populations are actually returning to the bush. Thousands of Ghanaians expelled from Nigeria . . . had no work to go back to in Ghana. They had to retire to their villages, and the world may never learn their fate. Africa today has millions of people moving across borders and within countries in a search for survival.

Nor is it any wonder that governments once considered stable are preparing "to fire on the mobs when they revolt" and looking to outside military elites in the advanced countries to protect them against the unfocused rage of constituents.[10]

But it is not finally by being "right" that Naipaul's novel convinces us. Naipaul makes us believe in the validity of his depiction, if not in its perfect accuracy or prophetic foresight, by doing what a major political novelist must invariably do. He locates the action of the novel precisely. He creates a world that imposes itself on people in particular ways. He indicates the palpable differences between one political faction and another, and the means by which people without political traditions gain and manifest real power. He shows how no economic or social relationship in an emerging society can ever be free from politics and from the corruptions wrought by imminent disorder. And he shows, finally, how ideas are twisted and betrayed by persons who have little respect for thought itself, who have too many pressing needs to look beyond immediate utility. No one of these elements is strictly necessary to a successful political fiction, but equivalent features at least are required in any work that wishes to chart the inter-section of personal and cultural necessity. In a more stable society the novelist can usually manage with fewer details, relying on his reader to know how political and economic life are structured, how threats to the polity are handled. But Naipaul is writing about societies in transition, and in the main he is not writing about them for third world readers. His ability to convince us that he knows what he evokes, that he is in control of his own feelings, is a consequence of his willingness to confront the mechanics of the real world.

Vision and compassion grow out of that encounter. Is this too obvious to say? Naipaul's vision—of men frightened and grasping and broken—is bracing and elusive because it reflects his sense that everything matters, that the past is implicated in every projection of the future, that the will is never entirely free unless it be to engineer its own destruction. In this, Naipaul's vision goes against the grain of the characteristic modern con-viction that the "liberated" will can accomplish anything, that we can make reality in the image of our desire. Naipaul's is finally the more sociable perspective, though he would decline to put it that way himself. For, as we see in *A Bend in the River*, human beings may truly meet only where there exists a common world. There may not be enough good things to go around in that world, but at least each will have some possibility of assigning values to things and of negotiating with others about plausible objectives and liabilities. A novel in which the will is at liberty to leave or to take reality may generate thrilling special effects, but it will not generate a full respect for persons as impediments to all ideologies and abstractions. It is no coincidence that, of all of Naipaul's books, *A Bend in the River* is the least colored by revulsion. It is not a hopeful book, but it takes seriously even the most extravagant ambitions of its characters. More important, it treats politics not merely as the pursuit of a mirage, but as the necessary effort of persons in despair to change their lives. What more can one legitimately ask of such a work?

4

Graham Greene: Political Virtue and the Fiction of Innocence

In an autobiographical volume entitled *Ways of Escape,* Graham Greene defends himself against critics who "have referred to a strange violent 'seedy' region of the mind . . . which they call Greeneland." Over and over again, the critics complain, in novels set in Africa or Indochina or Central America, one finds the familiar landscape of treachery and violence and a self-indulgently knowing despair. Greene responds:

> "This is Indo-China," I want to exclaim, "this is Mexico, this is Sierra Leone carefully and accurately described. I have been a newspaper correspondent as well as a novelist. I assure you that the dead child lay in the ditch in just that attitude. In the canal of Phat Diem the bodies stuck out of the water. . . ." But I know that argument is useless. They won't believe the world they haven't noticed is like that.[1]

Of course, the issue involved in the debate on "Greeneland" is not the issue the novelist chooses to engage. Few serious critics deny that awful things happen in the regions of the world that Greene visits. Few deny Greene's power to evoke with frightful clarity the dead children or the wasted lives of persons committed to struggle or indifferent to it. But readers do sometimes complain that there is in Greene's depictions of very different places a disturbing sameness. One does not on that account forget that *The Comedians* is set in Haiti, *The Honorary Consul* in Argentina,

55

or *The Quiet American* in Vietnam. One does, however, frequently feel that it little matters where these works are set, that for all their attention to particularizing detail, their true setting is a region of the mind, their object not the examination of political conflict or the testing of human possibilities but the striking of desirable attitudes or postures. These postures are viewed by the novelist as desirable not because they are edifying, but because they are not edifying, because they are worldly and cynical and touched with just the measure of bitterness and self-irony to make them seem irreproachably tough-minded. No liberal twaddle or sentimentality for Mr. Graham Greene, thank you.

Greene's appeal to experience, his pride in having been a newspaper correspondent and his consequent capacity to distinguish fact from fantasy, answers not at all the charge brought against him. It is clear, moreover, that long after the first loud criticisms of Greeneland were sounded, he continued to provide the critics with fresh ammunition. What are we to make of the statement, in *The Comedians,* that "Haiti was not an exception in a sane world: it was a small slice of everyday taken at random"? Another passage in the same novel has it that " 'the situation isn't abnormal. It belongs to human life. Cruelty's like a searchlight. It sweeps from one spot to another. We only escape it for a time.' " It is important to remind oneself that Greene himself doesn't speak in these passages, that the narrator ought not to be confused with the author, but nothing in *The Comedians* contradicts these sentiments or calls them seriously into question. Haiti may be a terrible place, unique in many ways, but it is finally, in the perspective of Greene's novel, just another seedy spot in which human beings go about their shabby ways. The local color is finally no more than local color, and Greene's contention that he well knows the difference between "Papa Doc" Duvalier and Paraguay's General Stroessner doesn't alter one's view of the various novels at all.

A more suitable reply to the critics of Greeneland would dwell on the authority with which the vision of each novel is established. It would concede that there may well be a sameness in the characteristic attitudes associated with the dominant figures in different novels, but would insist that there is more to those novels than an attitude or a posture. Perhaps for the reader it does little matter in the end whether the corruption belongs peculiarly to Haiti or to Sierra Leone. Perhaps it is true that the politicians in the one place have as litle regard for their constituents as politicians in the other, or that revolutionaries everywhere are distinguished by a more or less standard and frequently touching innocence. This does not mean that the politicians in each work are drawn with less than compelling authenticity, or that the revolutionary figures seem somehow unconvincing, their feckless ambitions more or less than we'd expect of such persons. The attack on Greeneland is valid only insofar as it can be shown to derive from a careful regard for the intention inscribed in each novel and for the effects actually achieved. Too often, objections to characteristic attitudes come from people who have no interest in literature except insofar as it may be said to reenforce their own prejudices. In this sense, the attack on Greeneland will often be the work of critics who have little patience with novels that raise unpleasant questions on matters for which "correct" answers are typically thought to be sufficient. Readers who demand a vision more tractable and more generous than Greene's are required to demonstrate that the vision is not an inevitable, organic outgrowth of the material with which he works.

To speak of the intention inscribed in Greene's novels is to recall that he did not always seem a political novelist, that even now he is widely regarded as one for whom religious issues are primary. Surely he has always been interested in politics, which is to say, in "the world," but no one will deny that the novels on which his fame for a long time rested—especially *The Power and the Glory* and *The Heart of the Matter*—are Catholic novels. They consider what it means to have faith and what is left to a man without it. Affirmation has chiefly to do with the capacity to satisfy God or to be adequate to the sense of oneself as a child of God. The Catholicism that directs the novelistic vision is never dogmatic, and characters who betray their religion are often shown to do so by what one critic calls "a pietistic over-literalism."[2] But one feels in reading Greene's Catholic novels that only the religious issues are matters of life and death. Human life itself is valuable, human relations are indispensable, love is difficult and necessary: All this is true, but it is also somehow secondary when set beside the matter of faith and one's relation to God.

The powerful disappointment one feels with *The Heart of the Matter,* in fact, has much to do with the way in which the religious intention is permitted to interfere with the proper development of the narrative. In *The Power and the Glory* one was never tempted to believe that the secular effort to end human suffering had any real importance in the novel compared with the effort to recover a sustaining faith. One might have wished for another sort of novel, but there was no question that Greene had mounted a work of a certain kind to which all the narrative materials contributed. In *The Heart of the Matter* one had reason to suppose that Greene was after various things, that his depiction of a virtuous policeman in a West African English colony during World War II was intended as a study not only of a human heart, but of the relation between sentiment and circumstance. One expected not so much a political novel as a novel about the corruption of sentiment in a setting that would necessarily defeat everything hopeful and virtuous. But necessity is betrayed in the novel, betrayed by a will to wallow in the psychology of sin. What might have been realized in the working out of a significant conflict is abandoned before the novel can really assume a momentum of its own. Instead, Greene willfully insists on the development of his central character as a pathological figure, thereby consigning to irrelevance the promising materials he'd evoked in his initial effort to establish a political and cultural climate. Why is Scobie made into a pathological figure? Because, we feel, only in this way did Greene believe he could dramatize the intensity of the religious conflict weighing on him. Only so could Scobie be made to suffer *in extremis* on behalf of the categorical knowledge every Catholic carries with him like a fate. Only so could Greene demonstrate how utterly without binding consequence are the worldly considerations that obsess the Catholic penitent even as he knows that his true problems abide in another dimension of consciousness.

One objects, of course, not to the idea of a novel devoted to the psychology of sin or the excesses of the true believer gone astray. One objects to a novel that does not know its own way, that sets in motion material to which it is unequal and which it allows the novelist to betray. One objects, in *The Heart of the Matter*, to what Elizabeth Hardwick once called the "snobbishness" of serious Catholic writers,[3] a quality one might also describe as smug or superior. How can a novelist be smug when he persistently questions the dogma to which he ostensibly owes allegiance? Greene's snobbishness emerges in the impression he sometimes allows that the petty corruptions, tyrannies, and brutalities he describes are no more than predictable, that the spirit in which man regards his fallen estate is alone worthy of his novelistic exertions. Ever resistant to pieties, Greene is yet too often a victim of religious pride, in terms of which the Catholic especially presumes to know from the start what others labor through one experience after another to discover about the meaning of life. To know in the way that Scobie knows is, of course, to be perversely incapable of living a satisfactory Christian life, and yet—so *The Heart of the Matter* would propose—is there no more to be said for the pain of an exile from grace like Scobie than for those who have never been obsessed by anything?[4] The conclusion rankles not because it bespeaks a conviction we cannot share, but because it is put forward without the novel's having been permitted to work through the ostensibly "smaller" concerns it had generated. For all its grim, inexorable pursuit of Scobie's Catholic conscience, the novel lacks the seriousness we associate with a work for which necessity is more than a fixed idea in the mind of a character or his creator.

Though it may be that the later, "political" novels lack the staying power of one or two of the earlier Catholic works, novels like *The Quiet American* (1955), *The Comedians* (1966), and *The Honorary Consul* (1973) surely deserve attention in a study of this kind. Principally, they show what may be accomplished by a political intelligence for which the idea of Freedom is always and only the freedom from destructive illusions, and collective struggle has only the validity conferred on it by participants moved by their capacity for commitment. Insofar as there is in such novels a sense of history, it operates as absent cause only in the sense that it seems vaguely responsible without anyone's being able to say precisely how or when or for how long. There is no effort in Greene's novels to imagine or embody the synchronic system of social relations in terms of which particular causes might be said to operate. There are events, and motives, and interactions, but nowhere is there an approach to a totalizing representation of the social matrix. Politics in Greene is thus a web of intrigue and ambition, but without reference to anything beyond the web itself. Those who demand a wider reference—so the novels suggest—must look beyond political motive to religion or some other kind of "solution." The novels provide no exploratory projection of what a vital political culture might be, because they can imagine no political enterprise that is not fouled by the corruption inherent in human nature. Politics is interesting not because it promises an alleviation of human misery or an extension of human capacities for cooperation and forward dreaming. It is interesting because it removes people from the tedium of settled pursuits and involves them in ways that confirm—vividly, unmistakably—what we always knew about them, about all of us. Those for whom political activity produces surprises are either innocents, in which case nothing very favorable may be said about their discoveries, or worldly types for whom the surprises come to seem less than momentous.

The most striking thing about Greene's secular novels is their undaunted creation of characters as closed monads. No matter what experiences these characters may be exposed to, they are always to be understood as translating experience into subjective terms and relativizing the insights available to them. Issues circulate freely in the novels; characters discuss political options and plan strategies. But continually we are returned to psychology, not a psychology we can share, but a psychology that belongs absolutely to this figure or to that. Here and there a marginal character may be depicted as operating out of a will or vision that is not solely his own, but typically we are positioned outside those figures quite as we are positioned outside the others. The closed monad remains an isolated "point of view" whether it is drawn as a psychological subjectivity or as a single manifestation of collective will. To such a monad or point of view, as Fredric Jameson has usefully argued, the reader can relate "morally or ironically or with identification," but never with a sense that there could conceivably exist a binding, organic social order in which human beings might discover a disalienated identity.[5] That is why Greeneland seems always a dispiriting and lonely place. It is a place in which what can be known is known, in which all are obviously and irredeemably cut off from everyone else, and in which collective activity is never more than the delusional exertion of persons who've found nothing better to do with their time.

In his late novels Greene likes to pretend that he is writing about the committed and the uncommitted, that he is genuinely interested in the difference between them, and that it is important to know where one belongs. To "be political," according to this neat dichotomy, is to believe in something and to act on its behalf. To be uncommitted, in these terms, is to know better than to believe in anything, or to be too faint of heart to risk involvement. The committed may feel ineffectual, but their capacity to feel involved depends only on their continuing to believe that some things are better or more important than others. The uncommitted may find themselves temporarily involved or at risk, may even resolve to put themselves at risk for the sake of an idea or a group, but they continue to be uncommitted so long as they do not deeply believe their actions will make a momentous difference. The uncommitted are those who can say, even after watching or participating in a violent conflict, that "there were no heights and no abysses in my world—I saw myself on a great plain, walking and walking on the interminable flats." So says the narrator of *The Comedians,* who reminds himself frequently that he cannot be "concerned," that he has learned all too well how dangerous action can be. To be concerned, he contends, is somehow to feel that one has a vocation, that one has been called away from one's own private life to look after someone else.

But, of course, Greene's representation of commitment is compromised by his inability to move beyond the perspective of the closed monad. One believes that this or that figure in Greene is committed, but the motive is typically private, a matter of psychology or of a circumstance so individual as to make it seem the possession of the one character alone. Greene may not have wished to suggest that commitment is no more than a consequence of individual psychology; he may not have wished his characters to be seen only from the perspective of the alienated witness. And yet he has done very little to avoid these impressions. Always he has been more comfortable with the uncommitted, who have nothing to prove, no convictions to live up to, and who can seem sophisticated simply by making witty remarks and saying no to the soulful appeals of their obviously more limited brethren. With the uncommitted, Greene can say that he is best suited to serving as "a painstaking and accurate diagnostician," conceiving of everyone as an essentially private sufferer. To be "truthful" is thus to avoid the sentimental and the theatrical, the grandiose and the general.[6] The committed are clearly more difficult to treat in this way, involved as they are in variously misguided attempts to raise sentiment to a principle or to prove that a meaningful alliance may be forged between the private and the general will. To represent such persons as if they were reducible to psychology is, of course, to suggest that the projects they espouse have no reality outside of their origins in the private needs of partisans. One may labor to establish the heroism or altruism of a committed character conceived as a closed monad, but one does not thereby establish the validity of the enterprise with which the figure is associated.

So Greene's dualism, committed versus uncommitted, is not finally a workable proposition for a fiction that aims to embody an actual difference. One accepts in Greene that characters are moved by different things, and that some are more inclined to act than others, but one never really accepts the reality of the determined actors, the politically committed figures alternately mocked and envied by the others. If the committed come alive at all, they do so either as types or as shadow figures with no enduring claim on our attention. Their goals are conceived either as comically implausible or so vague as to inspire little more than a dim, mostly unexamined sympathy. Third world Communists may know more or less what they are doing, and may seem to deserve our respect for refusing to trade in the corruptions mandated by the dominant imperial powers, but their activities bear little close examination and their goals seem nothing more specific than the will to subvert the present arrangement of power. Their goodness comes, we feel, from Greene's reluctance to get too close to them or to imagine what they would be like if they held power. Just so, the idealists in Greene, insofar as they are treated with affection, are never more than persons who seem to have decent motives and can be stirred to indignation by injustice. One would not take them seriously because of their vision or the rigor of their insurrectionary calculations. They emerge at best as isolated instances of persons who are on the right side, though what their commitment is worth and what the right side amounts to the novels are not equipped to indicate.

Consider what commitment amounts to in *The Honorary Consul*, "perhaps the novel I prefer to all the others," according to Greene.[7] Ostensibly a work about the ineluctable slide into commitment of a man without a belief in the future or in his own moral vocation, the novel leaves us feeling that Greene has refused to take seriously the issues for which a man like his Doctor Plarr might reasonably have given his life. Why does a resolute skeptic, scrupulously aloof ironist, and uncompromising diagnostician allow himself to become involved in a revolutionary action? He is not himself a revolutionary. He believes neither in the wisdom of his committed friends nor in the efficacy of the particular stratagem they have adopted. He may feel that life without some sort of faith is hard, that not to have faith in something is finally to be unable to love, but these are feelings that come and go and in any case have little to do with Plarr's more settled antagonism to hopeless engagements. His father was a revolutionary, of course, but the affection he feels for someone he hasn't seen in many years and who may well have been killed in a Paraguayan prison doesn't seriously tempt him to follow in his father's footsteps. Though some have said that the "very amateurishness" of the revolutionary terrorists persuades him to become involved, that he cannot but assume responsibility for persons he knows who have been caught up in the conflict, he hardly seems humane in the way that we associate with one who would risk his life for others.[8]

In fact, Doctor Plarr becomes involved because he is confused about what he is and what he wants. He never commits himself to a goal or even to a particular course of action the consequences of which he has carefully imagined. He is involved only in the sense that he strays into something he has neither the will nor the clarity of mind to get out of. His commitment is neither edifying nor significant in any other sense. It is reducible to motives that are speciously summoned to make plausible a series of gestures that would otherwise seem pointless. The character's obscure guilt for not having done honor to the memory of his father and his less obscure guilt for having seduced the wife of the honorary consul whose life is threatened by the terrorists serve only to underline the essentially private content of Plarr's commitment. To describe what Plarr does in political terms is to see at once how insubstantial are the politics at issue in the novel.

There are, of course, genuinely committed figures in *The Honorary Consul,* and one in particular surely attracted Greene's interest. An ex-priest, "Father" Leon Rivas is clearly dedicated in a way that his old schoolmate Doctor Plarr is not. For one thing, Rivas knows, as Plarr does not, that every political action may be taken as a model or as an instigation to other actions. To follow through on a plan or to refuse to follow it through is deliberately to invite consequence, and consequence is an indispensable component of all political thinking. Plarr thinks only vaguely and intermittently about consequence, and for him it is so much a matter of fated eventualities and anxiety-producing complications that his primary impulse is to dismiss the very idea as not worth his time. Rivas is more given to thinking in terms that embarrass Plarr, and his belief in revolutionary action as a means of achieving human dignity is surely central to his motives. And yet, in the end, he seems more and more a theatrical figure, a role player confused about what he wants, given up to the script he has agreed to enact and with little ability to reflect freshly on the likely consequences of his enterprise. We recall his indignation and his initial fervor, recall the way he had said, a little glibly, " 'In a wrong society . . . the criminals are honest men.' " But we think of him increasingly as a special fellow driven by his break with the church to find a substitute faith or vocation. His political motives, such as they are, recede so that they come to matter as little to him finally as to us. He is, we feel, a good man, a driven man, oddly scrupulous for one intending to kill an aging and merely symbolic enemy like the honorary consul. Greene asks us to evaluate him not on the cogency of his thought or the justness of his cause, but on the underlying decency of his private motive, however misguided. This is not promising for a work that proposes to deal not only with human nature but with a particular circumstance.

The politics of *The Honorary Consul* is a tissue of references and emblematic tableaux to which the narrative fitfully returns. Often we hear of Paraguay's General Stroessner, of the tortures inflicted on Rivas's friend Aquino, of the Americans who will continue to value and bolster third world anti-Communists no matter what brutalities the various dictators visit on their own people. Again and again we are invited, as sophisticated readers who *know*, to take in these observations with the requisite indignation and the simultaneous conviction that not much need be said to justify an oppositional stance. No effort is made to present or to think about shades of commitment or the nature of societies in which certain kinds of brutality have long seemed endemic. All is geared to establishing a neat dichotomy between the committed and uncommitted, between those who care and those—like the various "establishment" political types—who wish only to keep their hands clean and avoid "trouble." Politics in Greene's novel is not the art of the possible; it is a web of intrigue and deceit and occasional hope that has no real promise of satisfying anyone or of accomplishing any valid long-term purpose. When, near the end of the novel, the honorary consul tells a representative of the British Embassy that those who try to keep their hands clean will "never understand South America," we are moved to applaud the forthrightness of the rebuke. And then we wonder what the novel has done to further our understanding of South America or of the political prospects that continue to inspire revolutionary enthusiasm. For all the urgency of Greene's interest in commitment, we never feel that he has imagined the matrix of a political *community*—small or large, ideal or actual—that can transform singular motive into a concerted, responsible, and sustained collective action.

The most generous of Greene's political fictions is *The Comedians*. There we find several engagés who inspire in Greene more than he elsewhere allows himself to feel for such believers. The dominant tone of the book, a combination of broad satire and disenchanted wryness, ensures that even grim details be taken with the expectation that they may be turned to farce. One feels about the novel that it was written to be made at once into a popular film, in which hilariously implausible scenes would alternate with scenes of "unbearable" suspense. In such a work, if anyone at all is taken seriously, he must also be shown to be a little superior to his own sense of commitment, rather too sophisticated to be taken in by anything resembling hope. There may be, in such figures, an appealing urgency of feeling or downrightness of expression, but they are never permitted to launch an action that has a serious prospect of success. What is serious is the private motive, the depth of conviction. Politics is reduced to that which people in power do to those who are their victims. Decent people who entertain political ambitions are by nature ineffectual or so marginal in the scheme of things as to represent no more than a symbolic threat.

There are different kinds of committed figures in *The Comedians*, though finally the differences amount to very little. All seem to the narrator a little enviable, and he is even pleased to have helped to raise a stone monument to one who gave his life in an action he cannot wholeheartedly have supported. In the final page of the novel the narrator reads the last words of a friend who implores him to remember that he is a humanist and that, "if you have abandoned one faith, do not abandon all faith." In the face of a world in which, as one character earlier says, "only the nightmares are real," the greatest crime is indifference. "Catholics and Communists," he writes, may have done terrible things, "but at least they have not stood aside, like an established society." Thinking about these words, the narrator is confirmed in his sense of himself as a man without faith. He does not reflect on the fact that his friend's idea of commitment is curiously without substance. But, then, those who care in Greene are rarely reliable guides to anything, and the objects of their striving seem always less important than their idea of their own virtue.

The one guerrilla figure Greene obviously likes in *The Comedians* is a young fellow named Henri Philipot. But he likes him, it seems, because he has no real hope of overthrowing the Duvalier regime, and is inept in all of the faculties required by a revolutionary. He is attractive mainly because he is an enthusiast, even something of a naif, and because he is also disillusioned about the advantages given people of his class in Haiti. " 'In my generation we have learnt to paint,' " he says derisively. And as for his own poems, " 'they were quite melodious, weren't they, but they sang the Doctor into power.' " So earnest a disaffection from one's own labor cannot but appeal to a novelist for whom earnestness itself is credible only when it expresses disillusion and a fair measure of self-contempt.

The most wonderful creations in the novel are surely Mr. and Mrs. Smith, a couple of hopelessly dopey, eternally good-natured and well-meaning Americans who hope to change human nature through diet. Avid to open in Haiti a vegetarian health center, they are entirely unable to understand the situation of the dark republic, and mostly unwilling to accept anything they have not heard at their local tourist bureau. The fact that Mr. Smith once ran for president of the United States—he polled ten thousand votes— permits him access to Haitian government officials and glimpses of Haitian life denied to other tourists, but he learns little from what he sees and is disappointed not in the unreality of his plans but in administrators and other officials who lack the proper sympathy and insight. Greene clearly likes the Smiths, and goes so far as to have his narrator pronounce them "heroic," though they are admirable chiefly for their loyalty to one another and for their unshakable healthy-mindedness. Their presence in the novel ensures that we take nothing too seriously, and that profound sentiments like "a great love for coloured people" be taken as reflections of an innocence that is as dangerous as it is charming. Confronted with evidence of wrongdoing or of terrorist activity in Haiti, their typical re- sponse has to do with putting things "in perspective." What this amounts to for the Smiths may be summarized in the following excerpts:

"Hitler did worse, didn't he? And he was a white man. You can't blame it on their colour."

"The police are the same everywhere. It happens often enough at home."

And so on. The consequence of putting things in perspective in the way recommended by the Smiths is that specific instances of injustice are de- plored but ultimately dismissed as too familiar to require extended inquiry. Instead, a premium is placed on an ideal of decency that has no political content at all. This is not to say that an ideal of decency ought not to rate as highly as any other ideal, or that it must prove to be ineffectual in every human circumstance. But it is the case that in the world of *The Comedians* the Smiths have no power to alter social or political relations, and that those are precisely the relations that most affect the lives of people in Haiti. Mrs. Smith does—in one of the funniest "nightmare" scenes in English literature—shame a Tontons Macoute into stepping away from his victim, but her calling the man " 'a disgrace to your colour' " is hardly the sort of thing that will go very far in other comparable circumstances. Greene's decision to invest in the Smiths, as it were, has to be taken as a decision to be generous, to accredit simple goodness at whatever cost. The cost, in terms of the novel, is to appear unable to distinguish between comic and serious intentions. Is it possible, one wonders, that a man like the narrator can truly envy the Smiths or admire their kind of commitment? Can it be that, beyond the farce and the steady mockery of their ignorance and innocence, Greene wants them to appear as the incarnation of an indispensable goodness? In trying to answer such questions one soon concludes that Greene sacrificed seriousness to effect in this work, that he was content to bring the Smiths back into his novel again and again for no better reason than that they would be endlessly amusing to deal with. And they do provide the chief amusements in a novel that has other memorable characters to work with as well. That their presence compromises what might have been a more telling political inquiry into the meaning of commitment is neither here nor there. Greene gives no sustained promise elsewhere in the novel of having been up to such an inquiry.

In *Ways of Escape,* Greene briefly sketches the Haitian scene at the time of his last visit to the country, in 1963, and it is clear that *The Comedians* scrupulously recapitulates what Greene observed. What he could not have anticipated, though, is that "Papa Doc would survive to die a natural death years later" and that the Americans would soon be drawn back to tender their support for another shabby "bastion against Communism in the Caribbean."[9] One wonders why Greene himself could not have anticipated these developments. In his novel the more reliably intelligent characters are convinced that the Americans will eventually turn again to Papa Doc, that human rights violations count for nothing in the global strategy of containment to which most American policymakers are obsessively committed. Even the cynical Captain Concasseur of the Tontons regards the Communists in Haiti as no real threat, for, after all, whatever the Americans may think about irregularities in the current regime, surely they " 'would land marines if ever [the Communists] became a danger.' " This knowledge, such as it is, seems a little smug and formularized in the way that it is brought forward again and again by different characters, but all the same it has the ring of a truth that can hardly be challenged. In the same way the novel routinely reminds us that "insurgents are not always Communists until you"—meaning Americans—"make them so." The observation is useful, as far as it goes, but what anyone in the novel may be expected to do with it is never indicated. As in his treatment of commitment, Greene is content to raise various political ideas in such a way that they can seem either cogent or specious, but nowhere does he enlist them in the service of a vision that can make the insights seem fundamentally valuable. What do the insights on American involvement in Central America add up to? What are we to take from the fact that the most impressive figure in the novel is a minor character named Dr. Magiot, who considers himself a Communist and assists in a modest way the few guerrillas rallying themselves in the hills? The political knowledge contained in *The Comedians* is not worth much if it tells us only what any dutifully cynical observer already knows, namely, that the superpowers have their respective obsessions, and that well-meaning persons like Dr. Magiot will gravitate to whatever emergent forces promise resistance.

One hesitates to recommend the direction a work like *The Comedians* might have taken. Clearly, Greene made of the narrative what he could and thought the political insights generated adequate to the novelistic design and to the subject of tyranny in Central America. His interest in love and in sexual jealousy led him here, as in other works, to consider power relations among private persons as in some sense a concomitant of struggles for power in the public realm. But there is in Greene what Edmund Wilson once called "a chaos of clear ideas,"[10] so that he seems not so much unable as generally unwilling to carry through particular ideas or connections so as to make them stick. Is human love always as unreliable as Greene would seem to suggest in *The Comedians*? Are the misery and brutality that disfigure Haitian life merely a local reflection of a more general human condition? Is innocence the only real guarantor of goodness? Had Greene been willing to focus on any one of these or similar questions, or to establish a novelistic perspective in which they would be firmly linked and thereby become a part of one larger question, *The Comedians* would be a much better book. Though the novelist doesn't group the work among his admittedly lighter "entertainments," that in fact is where it belongs.

A more limited work is *The Quiet American* (1955), which is worth dwelling on as in some ways the most satisfactory of Greene's political fictions. In it Greene sets out to show something in which he clearly believes, and organizes the novel so that it progressively overcomes our resistance to the central idea as the expression of a simple prejudice. The idea reduces to the proposition that an aggressive innocence is not only distasteful but destructive, and that the prime instance of this innocence at work in the international arena is provided by the United States. So much is this idea at the heart of *The Quiet American* that many reviewers treated the book as nothing more than a bitter attack on the United States and speculated on Greene's obscure Communist sympathies as the source of his irrational prejudice.[11] Of course, Greene's novel is much more than his angrier critics were willing to admit, and irrational prejudices do not in themselves disqualify a novelist from writing persuasively about a subject he has deeply imagined. Greene did undoubtedly see his principal American character as the prime exemplar of destructive innocence, and he surely did risk turning that character into a caricature in order to make even his virtues fundamentally distasteful. But the caricatural element emerges only occasionally, and the character is himself so ready to accept his own representative status that one sees little injustice in treating him as an aggregate of more or less standard features. More to the point, the innocent American's opposite number, Fowler, is hardly a likable or wholly reliable figure. Though we accept the accuracy of his narrative insofar as the literal course of events is concerned, we are clearly not intended to share his every judgment, and he is as apt to be confused about Alden Pyle's innocence as he is about his own motives for putting an end to him. *The Quiet American* knows what it is about and sharply strikes its target. But the target is only incidentally American involvement in third world affairs, and those who are sensitive to imputations of American wrongdoing are likely to miss what is genuinely at issue.

The theme of destructive innocence surely underlies Greene's political vision in *The Quiet American,* and for once it is a vision that he is assiduous to elaborate and to test. As the embodiment of a vision, the novel may seem a little thin and one-dimensional, but the vision does not in this case pretend to do more than such a work can feasibly accomplish. A primary opposition in the novel is built around the ongoing conflict between the two main characters, Pyle and Fowler, the innocent American never more than the irritant-object of Fowler's reflections. These reflections may be described as political if by political we mean that as a working reporter who has lived for many years in Indochina Fowler is alert to the terrible things that happen all around him. The novel's setting in the waning days of the French war in Indochina ensures that an atmosphere of political futility and human waste will prevail. Even one as determined as Fowler to stand above the conflict, not to bloody his hands, cannot but be tempted to think about what might have been and what general insights may be summoned from the debris of intermingled good and bad intentions. If he is not the man to produce a theory of political action or a convincing diagnosis of long-term East-West relations, he is fully capable of recognizing what is positively useless and delusional. The political vision he enables Greene to elaborate is a vision of all *legitimate* political action as the outgrowth of an informed and *intimate* involvement in the local exigencies of the territories and persons likely to be affected by the action. Pyle represents to Fowler the ignorance not only of relevant facts, but of the very idea of political legitimacy. He is dangerous not because his intentions are bad, but because he presumes to interfere politically—which is to say, consequentially and broadly—in the lives of persons whose needs he does not understand and without that respect for cultural and political difference that no good intention can do without.

Greene's is not a moral vision. He does not make it his mission in *The Quiet American* to argue on behalf of the sanctity of the Vietnamese world view or the preservation of Eastern religion. He is not concerned with the justness of one political cause as opposed to another. The best he'll permit Fowler to say for any party to the conflict is that he cares enough to fight and die for his beliefs. The crucial value to be sustained in any political conflict is the need to keep one's real aims perpetually in view. The facts are almost always preferable to lies, and those who systematically lie to themselves to keep their collective and individual consciences clean are capable of greater evil than those who openly exploit or manipulate their subjects. No logic will "prove" the merits of this view, and no evidence will support its extension to each and every instance. A political conviction is valid, Greene would suggest, insofar as it inspires an emotional allegiance and at the same time aims at more or less feasible objectives, however misguided they may ultimately prove. Fowler has no binding conviction aside from his feeling that Pyle's destructive innocence cannot be tolerated, but his visceral aversion in effect motivates and justifies the political vision embodied in the novel. Fowler's emotional involvement in Pyle is very great, though the mixture of personal and political factors is such that he can never be more than ambivalent about the purity of his motives. Surely it is possible to say that he is committed to Pyle's removal in a way he had not seemed capable of before. Just so, though Fowler's political conviction is at best unstable, and he has no vivid sense of a future that Pyle's removal will help him or others to realize, he may be said to operate with a reasonable and limited objective: Since Pyle's activities can only do more harm than good and utterly confuse what is really at issue in Southeast Asia, it is best that he be stopped.

Those who believe that Fowler invariably speaks for Greene never adequately consider why Fowler should have been made a thoroughly unpleasant character. In addition, they conveniently overlook Fowler's confessed uncertainties, and miss the way in which Fowler's irony calls into question not only the statements of others, but his own resonant equivocations as well. Pressed at one point on whether he can believe half the things he says about the cockeyed ideas of liberty promoted by American liberals outside their own borders, he replies, " 'Probably three quarters.' " Though things are more complicated than even he is willing to admit, and though he takes a certain pleasure in going against the grain of enlightened political opinion, he is fundamentally serious in what he says, and the Pyles of the world who continue to believe that men of good will must at bottom go along with them are sorely mistaken. So Fowler gives his antagonist any number of opportunities to understand, and thus Greene conveys to us the depth of his investment in Fowler's visceral aversion. One doesn't have to like Fowler to see that he means most of what he says and that he has good reason to despise those who admit only to "higher" motives.

The evidence of Pyle's destructive potential is considerable, particularly if one considers that *The Quiet American* is a novel, not a documentary brief setting out a formal indictment. After all, it is not just that Pyle is shown to have facilitated the setting of a bomb that took many innocent lives; or that he is clearly incapable of appreciating how little political effect the explosion would have had under the best of circumstances. Nor is it only the case that Pyle continues to speak about an imaginary neutralist "Third Force" in Vietnam as if there were available in the faction-ridden country any political or military entity not utterly compromised by previous corruptions and commitments. Pyle's involvement with a General Thé is transparently misconceived as it is described in the novel, and the idea that such a character would agree to be directed by the decorums of a virtuously neutralist American policy is so idiotic as not to require detailed refutation. But, in novelistic terms, Pyle's capacity for innocent destruction is perhaps best manifested in his "principled" pursuit of his "friend" Fowler's Annamite mistress. What more suitable manifestation of Pyle's delusional propensities have we than his conviction that it is his mission to protect the girl, to give her a respectable life by introducing her to the virtues of bourgeois mediocrity? What better expresses his unwittingly cruel and destructive innocence than his insistent assumption that Fowler must somehow approve the justness of his mission and remain his friend, even as his mistress is carried off by the more dashing and youthful figure? It may be said that Greene loads the dice rather too obviously here, but the skill with which the narrative accumulates evidence while allowing us to read the evidence in several ways is singularly impressive.

No effort is made in *The Quiet American* to account authoritatively for the origins of French involvement in Vietnam or to predict what degree of subsequent American involvement may be expected. Here and there characters suggest what may or may not be usable insights. A French officer refuses to believe he is fighting in what is just another colonial war and insists that most of the time he believes the fate of Europe itself is at stake. In another breath the same officer ruefully admits that the politicians are likely in the end to conclude a treaty that will make a mockery of all the years and lives that have been sacrificed. Fowler himself cannot believe that the great powers know how to keep their filthy hands off the smaller countries, and though the French have at least the "excuse" of long years invested and French lives put on the line, none of the advanced countries would seem to realize that their "values" are inevitably beside the point in Indochina. The idea that Vietnamese peasants will fight for the abstract liberty to think for themselves is as implausible as the idea that Frenchmen or Americans will shed their own blood simply to win that liberty for them.

Several political explanations offered in the novel are compelling, but none seems underwritten by a conviction that it is necessary to know what to do in order to know what is not to be done. The shadowy Communist militant named Heng, who seems more interested in protecting the " 'good name of his people than in mobilizing battalions, tells Fowler, " 'Sooner or later . . . one has to take sides. If one is to remain human.' " But Fowler does not seem to know what taking sides would amount to in Vietnam. Is the decision to take a hand in disposing of Pyle a decision to take sides? Surely it commits Fowler to no necessary course of subsequent action. Nor does Greene intimate that a better man than Fowler would necessarily cast his lot with the Communists, or with any other force that might defeat the French and resist the Americans. The furthest reaches of Greene's political vision would seem to stipulate that acceptable political action is the province of those who are genuinely interested parties and who know all the same that their situation may well be irremediable. Implicit in this vision is an ethics of limits. To be ignorant of what is at issue for the inhabitants of a place like Vietnam and to entertain no intensive doubts about the viability or consequence of one's projected involvement is to violate the terms of any responsible political contract.

The attack on innocence in *The Quiet American* is an attack on the failure to respect limits: the limits of one's own benevolence, the limits within which conflicting parties may be expected to move in a search for compromise, the limits, finally, of political solutions applied to dilemmas that are never solely political or susceptible to rational accommodation. Greene's careful probing of the necessary limits in this novel, like his respect for the necessarily limited parameters and registers of a work so schematically conceived as *The Quiet American,* makes his book a minor classic in the genre of the modern political novel.

5

The Head of State
and the Politics
of Eternal Return
in Latin America

I

Whatever its reputation for "lo real maravilloso" and its indisputable commitment to new beginnings, the Latin American novel has never ceased to concern itself with its own origins and to take up historical and political questions as if nothing less could properly occupy a serious literary intelligence. To think of Donoso or Cortazar, of course, is not to think of politics as such, and fabulous narratives like *One Hundred Years of Solitude* are hardly describable as historical inquiries, despite their interest in the past and in the elaboration of cultural myths. But one sees even in writers so singular as Cortazar and García Márquez the makings of a vision of Latin America that is not so far removed from politics as may once have been supposed. Though politics cannot mean for a Colombian or Guatemalan or Cuban novelist precisely what it has meant to a European writer, Latin American writers have found in the new novel they have created a way to engage the central political issues of the day. Their rejection of European models—literary, parliamentary, psychological—has not issued in a rejection of the political imagination itself. If they have often spoken of the writer's need to abandon contexts altogether, most have concluded that they are stuck with them and have used the novel not so much to transcend culture as to change it. The Latin American political novel is at its best neither polemic nor lament. It is, in fact, like nothing else. But in its excesses and distortions it often does the work that the political imagination has typically assigned to the novel. It aims to do nothing less than create a view of reality as Necessity, and to pit against that Necessity the ideas and aspirations of men possessed by the will to change.

To speak in this way of politics in the Latin American novel is not to suggest that there is a single purpose to which the various writers subscribe. Neither is there any single novel which may be said to represent all the others. We know what we mean when we speak of the Latin American novel, because it has in the main flouted the decorums we associate with the well-made novels of the high-European tradition and because it has sought through hyperbole to characterize the colonial reality as an intolerable series of contradictions. But the major figures in Latin America are often divided about the goals and achievements of their contemporaries, and it is not surprising that Cabrera Infante should be given to mocking Carpentier, or that Roa Bastos should promote an idea of revolutionary literature largely inimical to the "radical" experiments of Fuentes and García Márquez. To speak of the Latin American novel is to consider something so various as to defy definition. To speak of the politics of such a novel is to compound the difficulty and to open up questions to which only a very pointed inquiry can do justice.

One plausible point of departure for such an inquiry is the dictator or patriarch figure in Latin American fiction. To be sure, there are plenty of Latin American novels that ask political questions but do not revolve about a protean head of state. One thinks of Cortazar's *A Manual for Manuel.* Even in Fuentes's *The Death of Artemio Cruz* the dictator appears only briefly. But it is fair to say that much of the political fiction of Latin America has been haunted at least by the idea, if not the actual presence, of the dictator, and that many of the important political novels do revolve about that figure. Some observers deplore the fact, but it is a fact and it does tell us something about one enduring view of politics in Latin America. In the degree that the dictator has seemed an inevitable focus for some writers, their reading of the available political options and of popular resistance to the more promising options has been unremittingly grim. Dissatisfied with this reading, several critics complain that the dictator figure is nothing but a narrative expedient and, as such, an evasion of the more complex manifestations of power in Latin America. If this is so, it is at least equally true that the dictator figure has seemed compelling to readers little interested in narrative expedients of any kind, and that the figure is rarely conceived so schematically as to banish all complexity.

One obvious test case for considerations of this sort is García Márquez's *Autumn of the Patriarch.* When it appeared in 1976, it was inevitably and unfavorably compared with *One Hundred Years of Solitude;* but it is really a very different book that deserves to be considered alongside of comparable works, namely, Carpentier's *Reasons of State,* published in the same year, and Asturias's much earlier *El Señor Presidente.* García Márquez's novel is by far the most forbidding and exotic of the three, written in a prose notable for its ripeness and florid extravagance. Like the others, it identifies the cult of the dictator as a principal source of the misery and destitution endemic in Latin America. And, also like the others, it suggests that the removal of the dictator will not in itself produce the conditions required for a sustained political revolution. It stands apart from the others in the projection of its central character as a force of nature only vaguely and intermittently subject to the ravages of time and circumstance. This, more than anything else, has made *Autumn of the Patriarch* seem dubious to readers who have wanted to see in it a serious engagement with political realities.

It seems clear, though, that García Márquez had determined from the first to engage those realities in his own way, not as a web of institutional procedures and conflicts of interest, but as a mode of perception. On the novel's first page the patriarch's countrymen tentatively enter his residence, described as "the rubble pits of the vast lair of power," only to find that "the air was thinner" there and that "things were hard to see in the decrepit light." Later in the novel, remembering the patriarch's early years, "when power was still not the shoreless bog of the fullness of his autumn but a feverish torrent that we saw gush out of its spring before our very eyes," his countrymen recall that "all he had to do was point at trees for them to bear fruit and at animals for them to grow and at men for them to prosper." In both instances—in the first, where things are hard to see; in the second, where "miracles occur before our very eyes"—the patriarch himself is conceived as a wondrous being with powers and failings that go far beyond anything previously known. After a great flood he orders the waters to recede, and they do; but he is also known for his monstrous sexual appetite and panting insufficiency. Whatever he does is customarily regarded with astonishment and awe, and though he is feared and hated, no one is quite willing to believe that he is less than the "purest incarnation of our dreams of glory." He may look like a "rusty old man"; he may fail and betray and murder; but he is, finally, in the eyes of his people, very much like the miraculous comet he observes, "his eyes overflowing with tears": a comet that "left across the world a trail radiant with star debris and dawns delayed by tarry moons and ashes from the craters of oceans previous to the origins of earth time."

It is tempting to describe this enduring impression of the patriarch as the manifestation of a collective pathology, and it may well be that García Márquez had some such notion in mind as he built his figure, but it is also possible to account for the impression in less drastic terms. The patriarch may seem so awesome, even in his decrepitude, simply because the average person in such countries understands nothing of power but its immediate effects, and routinely ascribes to unexpected events in the real world the miraculous agency of an extraterrestrial force. Or it may be, more simply yet, that the accession to power in Latin America of one despot after another makes it seem that a single figure holds sway longer than anyone can remember. Between one absolute despot and another there is usually little difference to tell, and persons accustomed to hearing of political activities only through rumor and popular legend may not be expected to perceive subtle changes even when changes have in fact taken place. If García Márquez's patriarch is said to be "at an indefinite age somewhere between 107 and 232 years," the uncertainty owes more to the way in which power is exercised and handed down in Latin America than to elementary arithmetic confusion.

The most obvious consequence of this portrait of the patriarch is his seeming to exist apart from the people he rules, on a plane inaccessible to ordinary praise or censure. Though his subjects may refer to "the inconceivable evil of a heart which had sold the sea to a foreign power," the terms of the judgment are characteristically such as to exempt him from determinate blame or punishment. His subjects may wish him dead, but typically they can imagine his removal only as the result of a miraculous, not to say divine, intervention. The patriarch himself is ever alert to plots against him and lives in constant dread of a spontaneous popular uprising that will cast him out of office. But his fears and the steps he takes to allay them serve in the main merely to insulate him from genuine contact with other persons. He is well advised to guard against plots; his fear and growing isolation keep him from considering what grounds his subjects might legitimately have for demanding reforms. When he listens to cabinet reports, he understands almost nothing of what he is told, and he is sincerely taken with "the magical idea that came to him that the trouble with this country is that the people have too much time to think on their hands." Protected as he is from all knowledge of his subjects, he becomes for them an abstraction, an elemental force they can harness no more than they can harness the tides of the sea. As an embodiment of "inconceivable evil," he is both the enemy of good and a proof that the world is what it is, no matter what anyone thinks it ought to be.

Readers of the novel who expected a committed Marxist like García Márquez to avoid turning the enemy into a force of nature had more than this to complain of. Though the patriarch is granted a certain majesty, in the end he is left with what the author would call a "shitty" grandeur. The cow that appears on the presidential balcony early in the novel inspires not contempt but shame in ordinary passersby, and the many references to the patriarch's invincibility and occult power are surely matched in emphasis and number by references to his pitiful infirmity. Compelled on the one hand to draw a larger than life-sized figure, García Márquez inclines on the other hand to describe a human, all too human, patriarch who might have done better if he'd been given more of a chance. Looked at either way, the patriarch is permitted to exist as a character in a way that makes decisive judgments difficult to summon. Such at least is the view of many readers who have deplored the novelist's handling of his central character.

The most interesting of these negative responses is that of the English critic Gerald Martin, in an essay on Roa Bastos's *Yo el Supremo*. Martin argues that García Márquez's patriarch, like Carpentier's head of state, is a nostalgic throwback to former times when "the enemy was a simple and straightforward *coronel* or *doctor* imbued with charisma and *machismo*, and not the anonymous, technocratised, neo-fascist enemy of the 1970's."[1] In such novels, which yearn for the "linear and chronological" simplicities of works "built around a central protagonist," the reader is effectively moved not toward indignation and disapproval, but toward understanding, forgiveness, and—who knows?—complicity. "It is hard to bear the thought," says Martin,

> that Chile's Pinochet will some day have a sympathetic, if supercilious book written about him to demonstrate that he was really the alienated one and not his tortured, exiled or murdered victims. Yet this is precisely what García Márquez appears to be suggesting with his portrait of an elephantine dictator condemned to solitude and absurdity. Satire is the last thing needed to deal with Latin American tyranny . . . , and fantasy seems inevitably trivial in the face of contemporary horrors. The brutal fact is that there is nothing absurd about Pinochet.[2]

Martin's response ignores several essential aspects of the patriarch. First, though he is pathetic, and in part understandable, the power he holds rests neither on his human vulnerability nor on his charismatic brilliance. He is throughout the novel neither simple nor straightforward, and the narrative exposition is sufficiently circular, oblique, and shifting in its focus as to ensure that no one will think the patriarch an easy figure to take hold of. Though one is tempted now and again to the psychological reductivism that can make of a monster a momma's boy who operates more from fear than from evil intent, the narrative is relentless in exposing the hideous cruelties and deceptions that are practised in the name of nothing but power itself. It is one thing to wonder why the author chose to dwell on the patriarch's infirmity; it is something else to claim, as Martin does, that the effect of all that is simply to create sympathy for him, no matter what atrocities he commits. There is more than one kind of understanding promised in a novel of this complexity, and it hardly seems fair to characterize a novel so resistant to straightforward chronology and so committed to plural perspectives as an exercise in nostalgic simplification. It is more plausible to say of the patriarch that, given the contradictions in his character, he is finally irrelevant as an individual, and that the author dwells on his infirmity to suggest one of the ways in which such a figure would present itself to the popular imagination. As there is no stable authorial perspective on which to rely in the novel, the patriarch's infirmity must be seen after all as a reflection of his own self-image and the natural tendency of ordinary people to project their own weaknesses even onto those more usually regarded as gods or monsters. The fact that García Márquez does not represent his insights as the fruits of analysis ought not to suggest that there is no analysis in *Autumn of the Patriarch*.

More important, Martin ignores the unmistakable continuities in the transition from the world of the patriarch to the "technocratised, neo-fascist" regimes of the present. His critique suggests that one form of domination has come to an end, with another, more efficient system taking its place. García Márquez is at some pains to show that this idea of inevitable technological advance is rather too schematic. In its own way the control exercised by the patriarch is quite as effective as anything likely to be achieved by the newer American- or Soviet-financed elites. And it is useful also to remember that the old-style dictatorships have for a long while been supported in crucial ways by one imperial power or another. García Márquez's politics makes it impossible for him to portray the imperial enemy as a Marxist power, but his constant references to American marines and solicitous American congressmen serve to indicate how thoroughly implicated in international politics is the patriarch's regime. What was apparent to Conrad when he wrote *Nostromo* cannot plausibly be represented as a revolutionary insight today. The old-style patriarch figures are not charismatic individualists any more than Pinochet or Argentina's short-term President Galtieri may be said to be.* The dictators rely on varieties of coarse manipulation, military and police power, and—where necessary—foreign assistance to keep themselves in office. To emphasize the element of technocratic control, as Martin does, is to imagine that Latin America has more in common with the United States itself than it has demonstrated. García Márquez chose to work with the patriarch because he is at once a colorful and suggestively atavistic figure and because his activities are not all that far removed from what takes place in the present. Obviously Buenos Aires is no jungle backwater, and cows are not likely to wander onto the balconies of Pinochet's executive residence. But just as obvious are the important similarities that link the patriarch's world to the world of the new elites and keep Latin American populations as far from meaningful control of their destinies as they ever were.

In fact, the very status of García Márquez's book as a serious political novel is involved in Gerald Martin's charge that it is a sympathetic portrait of an individualist dictator who has nothing going for him but a blend of his own malarkey and his author's whimsical affinity. The question at issue is not the author's support or nonsupport of bankrupt Latin American regimes. No reader of the novel can fail to see that the patriarch is a hopeless figure who can do nothing of value for his country. Nor is it possible to overlook the wanton cruelty and destruction for which he is responsible. The question is, In what degree does the novel illuminate the procedures whereby such destruction is carried out, rationalized, and tolerated by most of those who are victimized by it? More, what are the conventionally available readings of these procedures and how far is it possible to go in proposing alternatives without losing touch entirely with the world García Márquez would have us engage? If critics like Martin are

---

* The belief in the staying power of those charismatic types went out with the dashing *capitaz*, Nostromo himself.

right, then the novel may be said to do no more than play at politics and history with no intention of definitively illuminating anything, least of all the limitations inherent in its own fictional approach.

It does no good to say, as Martin does, that the dictators in works like *Autumn* and *Reasons of State* "are not historical figures, but composite and essentially imaginary ones."[3] In the first place, anyone who takes the time to study García Márquez closely and is familiar with Latin American politics will recognize a variety of authentic historical figures who have served as models for the composite portrait. There is no legitimate aesthetic or political objection to be made to composite portraits as such. A recent book on García Márquez names as models variously employed in the novel Eva Perón, Portugal's Salazar, Somoza, and others, and goes on to quote a "Nicaraguan leftist who said of the Somozas, 'There are few of us alive who remember a time when they weren't in charge.' "[4] The point of such references is not to prove that the novelistic dictators are real in a way that would be approved by an academic historian with an appetite for hard facts. Of course, the patriarch is an "essentially imaginary" figure. What matters is that, for all his creator does to make him an object of rumor, fantasy and legend, he operates in a way that does illuminate the activities of plausibly actual dictators in a world we have come to know through other Latin American novels, poems, autobiographies, newspaper dispatches, and so on.

It is also useful to consider that, for all the novel's focus on the patriarch, what we get in the interminable sentences and rapidly shifting perspectives are states of mind rather than a standard psychological portrait. Martin complains that a "total omniscience" is out of place in a novel whose central character, the dictator, is "by definition, of all men the one whose consciousness is least available to others."[5] But García Márquez enters the patriarch's consciousness more or less at will not to show that it can be encompassed and summarized in the way one associates with a psychological case study. He enters obliquely and, as it were, experimentally, routinely testing the patriarch's insights against the facts and impressions culled from other sources. The effect of this procedure is not, as Martin suggests, identification but detachment; the motive is not sympathy but criticism. The patriarch's responses to this and that are not presented for their own sake or for the sake of any interest we may have in him as a recognizable human being. We are rarely permitted to dwell on any single response without being asked also to consider some aspect of the broader situation that has made it seem inevitable. The novel's concern with shifting states of mind—the patriarch's, his accomplices', his victims'—is a function of its various characters being forced to live under conditions of maximum instability and intimidation. Though for most people life in Latin America may seem never to change or improve, all are necessarily alert to the imminence of violent upheaval and local terror. No life can seem secure, no motives entirely private or trustworthy under such circumstances. García Márquez's determination to move rapidly from one perception to another, from one angle of vision to another, is a warrant of his refusal to acquiesce in the idea of a normative self and an evolving but orderly psychology. His interest is not in interaction—that too would presuppose a self and deter-minate others—but in the constant movement of minds responding to events that are themselves less important than the circumstances that bring them into being.

No single passage of any novel can illuminate the dynamics of the work as a whole, but almost any page of *Autumn* can show in miniature what García Márquez is up to. Consider the following fragment, in which the old man steps back from a scene of carnage caused by a hurricane and is quickly invited to bless the reconstruction of the devastated city:

In the midst of the jubilant bell-ringing, the festival rockets, the music of cel-ebration with which the laying of the first stone of reconstruction was laid, and in the midst of the shouts of the multitude crowded into the main square to glorify the most worthy one who had put the hurricane dragon to flight, someone took him by the arm to lead him out onto the balcony because now more than ever the people needed his words of comfort, and before he could get away he heard the unanimous clamor which got into his innards like the wind of an evil sea, long live the stud, because ever since the first days of his regime he under-stood the unprotected state of being seen by a whole city at the same time, his words turned to stone, he understood in a flash of mortal lucidity that he did not have the courage nor would he ever have it to appear at full length before the chasm of a crowd, so on the main square we only caught sight of the usual ephemeral image, the glimpse of an ungraspable old man dressed in denim who imparted a silent blessing from the presidential balcony and immediately dis-appeared, but that fleeting vision was enough for us to sustain the confidence that he was there, watching over our waking and sleeping hours under the historic tamarinds of the suburban mansion, he was absorbed in thought in the wicker rocking chair, with the glass of lemonade untouched in his hand listening to the sound of the kernels of corn that his mother Bendicion Alvarado was drying out in the calabash gourd, watching her through the quiver of the three o'clock heat as she grabbed a barred rock hen and stuck it under her arm and twisted its neck with a kind of tenderness while she told me with a mother's voice looking into my eyes you're getting consumptive from so much thinking and not eating well, stay for dinner tonight, she begged him, trying to seduce him with the temptation of the strangled hen that she was holding with both hands so that it would not get away from her in its death throes, and he said all right, mother, I'll stay, he rested until sundown with his eyes closed in the wicker rocking chair, not sleeping, lulled by the soft smell of the hen boiling in the pot, hanging on the course of our lives, for the only thing that gave us security on earth was the certainty that he was there, invulnerable to plague and hur-ricane, invulnerable to Manuela Sanchez's trick, invulnerable to time, dedicated to the messianic happiness of thinking for us, knowing that we knew that he would not take any decision for us that did not have our measure, for he had not survived everything because of his inconceivable courage or his infinite prudence but because he was the only one among us who knew the real size of our destiny.

This fragment, which reads so much like so many other pages of the novel, is anything but a psychological portrait pure and simple. In fact, it is difficult here to know whose version of the patriarch we are getting. When, early in the passage, we come upon "the most worthy one," do we not take it that the words are merely public words, a formal affirmation of an identity that is bogus and not to be seriously accepted by any but the most credulous of the old man's partisans? And, if that is so, what can we make of the "flash of mortal lucidity" that leads him to acknowledge his own lack of courage? Does this say, in effect, that the old man knows himself and is to be congratulated at least for honestly confronting his limitations? But this would be preposterous in light of all the delusions to which he is plainly subject and his attempt to take credit for things he cannot have done. Besides, though we read that "he understood in a flash of mortal lucidity," we do not know that the patriarch did in fact understand. We may suspect instead that this is the motive attributed to him by those who observe his hasty disappearance from the presidential balcony and are disposed at that moment to interpret his action generously.

Clearly, it is not possible to conclude that the patriarch's absorption in thought is a sign that we are to consider him a thoughtful man, or that he has been deeply moved by the disaster so recently visited on his people. Just a page earlier, confronted by the sight of a "whole community of [convent] virgins drowned in their dinner places," he'd taken a definite satisfaction in the removal of at least one woman who'd tormented him, and reflected—"smugly"—"how wild God's methods are when compared to ours." The point, again, is that no fragmentary reference or tissue of references in this novel can amply body forth a standard novelistic psychology. Even passages replete with psychological detail are designed to draw attention to the circumstance that is Latin America. That circumstance, as evidenced in the novel, is a compound of disaster, mass hysteria or delirium, and a brutal ignorance that issues alternately in melancholy, violent paroxysm or avoidance. The focus is not on the patriarch as an individual or even as a symbol. It is on the degree in which he may or may not be said truly to incarnate the circumstance to which he belongs. If his anonymous subjects believe, as they say, that "he was the only one among us who knew the real size of our destiny," it is the object of the novel to inquire whether in fact that is the case.

To begin such an inquiry is to ask what role the novelist assigns to "the people" in his novel. That they play a small part in the action is undeniable. That they are ultimately despised or discounted is less obvious. Regina Janes argues that García Márquez "does not seem to expect revolutions to emerge from a massive, miraculous change in the consciousness of the people at large"; the novels invite "no fatuous expectation of a solution to the limitations of human experience through the transformation of the individual."[6] Ordinary persons in García Márquez are ordinary, whatever the irruptions of the miraculous into the domain of everyday life. The patriarch himself may entertain populist sentiments, but he knows better than to ask people to be better or wiser than they are. Enemies of the patriarch seem, if anything, less promising as leaders than he is, and their relationship to the people is surely no more edifying. One may presume that those who object to the patriarch will often have good reasons for doing so, but their revolutionary aspirations will probably look a lot like those of García Márquez, who desires only that "the whole world lives better, drinks better wine, and drives better cars."[7] One has to begin somewhere, of course, but it is hard to feel that García Márquez has looked beyond beginnings in proposing revolution and thinking about the prospects of ordinary people.

It is also possible to say that the people in *Autumn* get no more than they deserve. The patriarch may in the end actually die, never through any sleight of hand to return, but in that case, after the initial celebrations, his "children" are likely once again to feel bereft. Unable as such persons will be to create a viable order of their own, and lacking popular institutions to express their needs and authorize common exertions on their own behalf, they will inevitably turn again to ferocious despots. Only these will make them feel that someone watches over them and binds them to a world that is familiar. In this sense, if the patriarch knows "the real size" of the common destiny, then the people, through their sufferance of the patriarch, may also be said to know what they are worth. *Autumn* is an exciting and relentlessly inventive work, but an inquiry into its political vision of the people ends more or less where it begins. If García Márquez doesn't allow himself to despair of them or invite us quite to despise them, neither does he give us any reason to think of them as agents capable of directing their own destinies. The excesses and cruelties associated with the patriarch are recalled not to justify or incite a popular revolution, but to bear witness to facts of life in which all are complicit. Change, we feel, will come, but no one, least of all the novelist, wants to look too closely at what that may entail.

In some ways, the most encouraging element of the novel is the occasional attention it pays to the deposed dictators who are maintained in modest circumstances by the patriarch. Denied even a vestige of crummy dignity by the patriarch, who at once supports and condescends to them, these ghosts of a former grandeur dream "about the chimerical vessel of their second chance" and recite "the eternal formula of puerile solemnity" according to which "the justice of the people" will restore them to their rightful place. Visiting them in the remote hideaway he's devised for their final days, the patriarch sees them as "God-damned fools [who] didn't know that in this business of men if you fall, you fall" and regards himself gratefully "in the instructive mirror of their misery." It is fair to say that a substantial melancholy emerges from these pages, and that García Márquez indulges a lament not so much for the ephemerality of worldly power as for the utter waste of a power that has no object but its own perpetuation. The effect of all of this, though, is to encourage the thought that even long-lived tyrannies die, and that something better may arise to take their place. Even the references to chests of money successfully "pilfered from the public treasury" and to inevitable repetitions of the "eternal formula" by generation after generation of deposed usurper-tyrants fail to banish the thought that terrible things do in some sense come to an end. Though we read late in the novel of the transfer of immediate powers to bureaucratic ministries working out of glass office buildings separate from the presidential palace, we feel even there that a change in the palace may well produce beneficial changes in the bureaucracies. To remember the deposed dictators is to think that there may be, somehow, a better future for Latin America, though again García Márquez did not feel he could work out the details of that future in his book.

II

What there is of a politics in *Autumn* may best be apprehended by looking briefly at comparable works by Asturias and Carpentier. The Asturias novel, *El Señor Presidente,* is a more barbaric, even primitive work in which the head of state appears only intermittently. The leading character is a presidential advisor named Miguel Angel Face, who falls in love with a virtuous young woman and thereafter finds it impossible to do his master's bidding. In the course of the novel many other characters are brutally tortured or ruined as a more or less direct result of the President's evil designs, and it is routinely said by people of experience that the best way to impress the President is to commit an unspeakable outrage against defenseless people. This the great man can understand; such villains he can tolerate and control. Only those who pretend to an implausible and inflexible virtue are despised. The politics of the novel are rudimentary. There are intrigues, spies, forced confessions, assassinations, and even a few references to "privileged industries of idleness" associated with presidential patronage and ancient money-lending practices. But in the main all is conceived at the level of virtue and evil. Characters are healthy-minded or foul-minded. An implausibly naive general may be permitted to cluck indignantly about corrupt regimes, economic exploitation, and crying injustice, but his promise to foment revolution is as ill considered and insubstantial as his previous commitment to the established order had been. The political intelligence that informs this novel is such as to make García Márquez's political sophistication impressive indeed.

No doubt García Márquez knew *El Señor Presidente* when he decided to write his own novel, and no doubt Asturias's novel has taught Latin American novelists a few important lessons. And granted, too, that Latin American politics often seems quite as one-dimensional as it is made to appear in Asturias's novel, with its familiar cast of cardboard-figure generals, paid and readily disposable assassins, and cowardly husbands cringing in fear of the President's disfavor. But no one wanting to write a political novel can conceivably have found much to instruct him in Asturias. Richard J. Callan is quite right to say of the main character that "no political thought ever enters his mind" and that even the more idealistic General Canales thinks of leading an uprising only "after the dictator had unjustly turned against him."[8] When the President himself complains that "this nation is made up of 'going' people . . . 'I'm going to do this, I'm going to do that' but for lack of determination they neither do nor undo anything," we cannot but feel that he is right. In such a world all are necessarily afflicted not only by a lack of resolve, but by a general incapacity to entertain political ideas. No political ideas, no political action worthy the name— that at least would seem to be one lesson Asturias's novel can teach.

What more García Márquez can have learned from Asturias we can only surmise. It has been suggested, by the critic Gordon Brotherston and others, that he learned from Asturias the importance of the Indian in Latin American politics. That importance, often figured in negative terms, with the Indian serving as the pliant human material that the dictator, even with arthritic fingers, can knead into acquiescent shapes, is reflected not only in *El Señor Presidente* but in Asturias's equally famous *Hombres de Maiz*. Despite the obvious differences in the two Asturias novels—the one more obviously allegorical, the other more focused on the worldly consequences of the President's misdeeds—both clearly move "beyond the pale of bourgeois rationalism" and look for solutions elsewhere than in the direction of "liberal tolerance."[9] The President in Asturias is ultimately to be seen as a temporary incarnation of a supernatural being, a sort of a "Maya Quichē divinity who demanded human sacrifice," according to Asturias himself.[10] He is kept in power by primitives in thrall to the "ancestral force" represented in the deteriorating secular image of the originary deity. Novels written to expose and to protest against the perpetuation of such deities and the rituals devised to exalt them needed to find ways of dealing sympathetically with the plight of the Indian and to recommend ways of alleviating his suffering. This Asturias wished to do by repudiating probability and by making his President a truly fabulous version of Guatemalan dictator Estrada Cabrera, operating on his victim-figures with the imperious abandon of a mad god. A number of Indian characters and references to Indian myths appear in the novel, but none seems directed effectually against the rule of the President. In Asturias Indians remain the stuff of legend and the raw material with which tyrants build their shabby empires. Even in *Hombres de Maiz,* where the Indians resist the efforts of outsiders to change them in the name of progress, Asturias is driven back on the legendary power associated with an ostensibly invincible native leader whose gifts promise nothing in the way of palpable improvement for his people.

García Márquez might well have had the example of Asturias in mind when he decided to evoke the patriarch by means of references to "prehistoric" time. But he did not bother in any systematic way to associate the idea of prehistoric time with Indian legend, or to suggest any more forcefully than Asturias that native Americans have available to them an effectual way of resisting the usual political or imperialist abuses. Brotherston recommends that we consider García Márquez's General Saturno Santos, a full-blooded Indian, one of "the more powerful hidden forces in the novel," but it is a dubious proposition. "The only one canny enough to survive" the patriarch's mass assassination program at one point, his survival is said to stem from "his mysterious Indian knowledge . . . , secrets which allow him to metamorphose (into armadillo, pond, thunder)." And he is said also to have "a share in the native American voice which re-tells, with amusement and contempt, how Columbus behaved on reaching America."[11] No doubt the spirit of some of this is consistent with the spirit of resistance Asturias locates in some of his native Americans. But *The Autumn of the Patriarch* is finally much less interested in this resistance than Asturias was, and the general effect of references to prehistoric time in both *Autumn* and *El Señor Presidente* is to undercut the notion of politics altogether. Supporters of Asturias's novels typically speak of the more profound "metaphysical" intentions inscribed in his works and routinely identify him with a kind of writing that is resolutely antithetical to the European political novel, the latter conceived as a blend of literary realism and journalistic fidelity to the plain facts. García Márquez is, if anything, less committed than Asturias to the realist mode, but his references to the Indian and to prehistoric time may not be taken as a proposed corrective to anything in the real world. If Asturias had anything to teach the younger writer, it was predominantly by negative example. General Saturno Santos is a colorful figure, but he is shuffled out of sight very quickly in *Autumn*, and it is hardly plausible to think him an emblem of a long-lived native resistance. It is the patriarch, after all, who survives longest in the novel and in the world the novel represents. In the end the references to pre-historic time and to the paraphernalia of metaphysical romance serve only to ground García Márquez's work in the primordial realities of Latin Amer-ica and to indicate the kinds of mythical thinking that will have to be broken through if any palpable improvement is to be accomplished.

III

Alejo Carpentier's major novel, *Reasons of State,* is a more plausible text to place alongside *Autumn*. It asks a variety of political questions and proposes to engage them politically. Several characters in the novel en-tertain political ideas, and those ideas are made to assume a momentum of their own that even the dictator is helpless to obstruct. Like García Márquez's novel, it dwells on a head of state who has been around for a long time, but its forays into the fantastic are much more limited, its analysis of political ferment much more believable. Carpentier is much less inter-ested than García Márquez in the popular imagination and the way in which it appropriates reality for its customary purposes, and his portrayal of the dictator and of the alternatives actually available in Latin America makes us feel we understand for the first time the mixture of promise and futility in the revolutionary politics of that region. If Asturias inclined to blame everything on the President and on the total absence of political ideas in his witless victims—in other works he showed an equal interest in the depredations of the United Fruit Company—and if García Márquez chose to blame it all on the patriarch's seeming to exist as a force of nature largely exempt from ordinary judgment or censure, Carpentier attributes the chaos of Latin America to the fact that even its most inspired reformers have little to offer their countries but good intentions and noble examples. Carpentier's head of state stays in power for a long while because he knows what he wants and acts ruthlessly to hold onto it; his successors take power by appealing in the language of mass democracy to the programmed desires of the people. In the end nothing changes. The enemy, whoever that may happen to be at any given moment, remains in control. The struggle to create a satisfactory politics goes on, though no one knows what such a politics is likely in the end to resemble. The idealists know how to stir minds and hearts; they don't, apparently, know how to do anything else.

Carpentier's vision of Latin America is complicated by the presence in it of European values and European models. His dictator chooses to spend much of his time in Paris, and he is clearly incapable of thinking about his country without considering the figure it cuts in the imagination of sophisticated Europeans casting an occasional glance in his direction. He is understandably enraged when he learns that a close associate or trusted general has led an uprising and threatened his regime, but he manages to deal more or less smoothly with these situations, even when it is clear that he can never return to power and must remain in permanent exile. But he is shaken in a more substantial way when the European papers and magazines describe him as a bloodthirsty tyrant and make him seem an impossible buffoon. This treatment at the hands of the Europeans, whom he admires, leads to his being banished from good Parisian society, and this, in sum, is the worst thing he can imagine. Toward the end of the novel we see him weeping as the American consul, commiserating with him over his loss of power, confirms his worst suspicion, that he'll soon be forgotten, winning not even a small entry in Larousse.

Europe plays a large role in Carpentier's novel not simply because the author spent much of his life in Paris and was interested in the European avant-garde. Europe is significant because neither Carpentier nor his dictator can find any perspective from within Latin America itself by which to judge what happens there. It is true that Carpentier, like Asturias and like García Márquez, has prided himself on creating a new novel and denying the centrality of European culture.[12] His novels before *Reasons of State* are quintessential examples of magical realism and play with serious philosophical ideas—European ideas—only to put them down without systematically pursuing them. But Europe has always been a presence in Carpentier, and in *Reasons of State,* by all odds his greatest work, he treats it less as a menace than as the source of whatever reality the world may be said to have. The head of state himself may not know how to hold together the bits and pieces of a European education—and Carpentier is surely skeptical about the ghosts of the past his character routinely summons in his private musings and loquacious speeches—but Europe is at least *there* in a way that is not true of Latin America, which seems an arena for the enactment of empty spectacles and violent, pointless exorcisms, a land of dreams. The little we actually see of Europe in the novel hardly provides an encouraging profile of the alternative to Latin American chaos and brutality. But there is obviously a good deal more to Europe than the President or anyone in his entourage can grasp, and one feels, in any case, that Carpentier's impulse to parody European texts and ideas is born of a deep unease about what to set in their place.

Carpentier's most enterprising critic, Roberto Gonzalez Echevarría, makes much of the novelist's beginning each chapter with fragmentary quotations from Descartes. These quotations, some of them unmistakably commenting on the material presented in the relevant chapters, point to the origin of Carpentier's original Spanish title, *El recurso del método,* literally translated as "the recourse of method." The words signify, according to Echevarría, "the turning back of method onto itself" or, perhaps, "method's availing itself of itself . . . to protect itself. Either way, what the title implies is the illusory nature of discourse, in its oratorical, pedagogical, or grammatical sense. . . . It also implies the dissolution of the discursive self as the source of truth and order."[13] No doubt, Carpentier had it in mind to question the kinds of discourse associated with Descartes, but much that he quotes from Descartes is so sharply focused and trenchant that one ought not to insist that the fragments say one thing and one thing only. Nor is it legitimate to conceive of the entire novel's having been written to illustrate an idea or to make a philosophical point about the nature of discourse. If the novel demonstrates "the dissolution of the discursive self as the source of truth and order," it does so in the belief that the discursive self has been degraded in its efforts to promote an inauthentic discourse committed to confusing the relationship between truth and falsehood. Reconceive the discoursing self, and generalizations about the inevitably illusory nature of discourse are revealed as so much fashionable academic nonsense.

Carpentier would have us see that the head of state is in no sense a true Cartesian and that his abuse of rationalist thought is anything but a demonstration of the impoverishment of Western culture. In fact, it is plausible to think of him as reversing the standard Cartesian formula, replacing the familiar "I think" with "I feel"; but this cannot be a basis for making a general statement on human nature or discourse. "In Latin America," as Michael Wood has written, "the truth is often not only unavailable, it is unimaginable, and unwanted. One of the last lessons learned by García Márquez's patriarch is that 'a lie is more comfortable than doubt, more useful than love, more lasting than truth.' "[14] Just so, Carpentier's head of state is incapable of honoring thought itself, or the truth that is the object of thought at its best. He lies habitually, to himself and to others, because he believes in nothing: not in himself, or his enemies, or the country he rules. He believes that he is thinking when he is merely remembering what he has read. He occasionally comes out with an impressive observation, and he is certainly more than the perfect buffoon derided in newspaper caricatures. But his fondness for opera and admiration of Mussolini's intelligence are not sufficient to make him seem a European man of culture. He remains a *Latino* anxious chiefly to use European culture to enlarge his sense of self and to bring his own country into the mainstream of civilization. His enthusiasm for World War I on the grounds that it will distract European attention from the senseless carnage recently produced in his country indicates how far he is from being a serious man. The notion that he somehow embodies the possibilities of a European-style discourse or that Carpentier aimed in this novel to dismiss a linear or rational discourse altogether is thoroughly insupportable.

The novel does clearly show the degree to which Europe was itself in the throes of a major upheaval at the time of World War I. An idiotic French academic who hangs around the President in Paris complains bitterly about the new decadence represented by the popularity of Negro jazz musicians and the militant socialist and populist rhetoric with which so many persons were preoccupied. He prefers instead the racialist and elitist theories of Gobineau, and applauds the President as a superman type who must with other "sovereign spirits" stamp out the emergent "swarm of despicable, irresponsible and destructive insects without Souls." That Carpentier could have intended to cast the academic as a representative European, thereby to demonstrate the impoverishment of Europe, will not seem plausible to anyone who has read *Reasons of State*. If anything, the academic represents the fear of change, of republican democracy, and of the Enlightenment tradition itself, a fear that drove many Europeans, it is true, into the lunatic obsessions that created the two world wars. But it is obviously far from Carpentier's intention to claim that Europe is nothing but the sclerotic and reactionary rhetoric of the academic, on the one hand, or the mincing salon niceties of Proust's Madame Verdurin—for a while one of the President's prized Parisian contacts—on the other. No reader of the novel can fail to see that it is the Europe so detested by the academic that we are expected to prize, a Europe that is a host of contradictions and energies, with new forms perpetually jostling the old and with a commitment to liberty best exemplified by the Paris in which so much of the novel is accordingly set.

Why it is that Carpentier had to look to Europe to find a way of looking at Latin America is not all that hard to explain. It is one thing for Latin American writers to speak of inventing a new literature and of naming things for the first time, as Neruda and others have done; it is another thing to engage the political realities of one's country as though they too were part of the newly discovered flora and fauna to which names must be assigned. The political institutions of Latin America do, after all, resemble the institutions of other countries. They are managed and created and attacked by persons who in the main speak a European language. Try as they will to ignore the fact, those persons occupy a world in which the centers of power are located not in Latin America but in other places, just as the money they need to develop their resources will come from those other places. More important, the models they require to develop a historical imagination and decently responsive popular institutions are also likely to be found outside of Latin America. Europe may in some sense represent an ossified universe that has done more than its share to promote barbarism—and Carpentier does at one point in the novel insist that we remember the Europe of interminable wars and brutal ideologies—but there are in the traditions of European culture disciplined ways of standing back from those horrors and considering what they mean and how they began. History itself, it may be said, is in part a European invention, and Carpentier no doubt thought to point this out in the steady stream of references to European thinkers and theories of history.

In his book on Carpentier, Echevarría contends that the theories of Vico are used to undermine "the imperialistic centrality of thought posited by Descartes." This bears consideration, though it is worth remarking at once that one European thinker is here cited as the corrective to another. It may or may not be legitimate to find Vico at the bottom of the historical perspectives embodied in this novel, but whether it is Fichte, Spengler, Descartes, or Vico that one names, the general provenance of the central ideas is unmistakable. Much is made in the novel of the division between German *Kultur* and French Enlightenment ideas, but those who would make over Latin America are clearly obliged to consider that division and to look outside their own borders for the models they will adopt. Vico no doubt furnishes a convenient model for engaging the perpetual crises of Latin American history, the ever renewable sense of "a second beginning . . . when man begins . . . , but by himself, to remake history."[15] The spirit of the Viconian model is rather different, though, from that announced in the President's reflections. "History," he reflects, "which was his because he played a part in it, was something that repeated itself, swallowed its own tail, and never moved forwards—it made very little difference, whether the pages of the calendar were printed with 185(?), 189(?), 190(6?): it was the same procession of uniforms and frock coats." This view of a history that never moves forward belongs, of course, more to the President himself than to the novel, though it is hard to see exactly how Carpentier would refute it. The Viconian perspective insisted on by Echevarría would propose the eternal possibility of a new beginning after the cleansing flood that sweeps everything away; but apocalypse is not the characteristic mode of Latin American politics. The new beginnings conceived in Carpentier's universe seem somehow compromised by the tainting remembrance of earlier renewals brought to ruin. European ideas of progress and recursiveness transplanted to Latin America seem to lead inevitably to the easy resignation associated with the President himself, with his "words, words, words, to be or not to be, to go up or not to go up, stand up or not stand up, fall or not fall, just as a watch returns to the time it indicated yesterday when yesterday it told today's time."

Europe, then, plays so large a role in Carpentier's vision because, whatever the view of Europe or of European history one adopts, it allows one to understand what is so dispiriting in the continuing Latin American nightmare. Europe may itself be devastated in the course of its latest war; its imperial exploits abroad may be brutal and doomed to failure; but it doesn't spin in the same tracks over and over again. It is not, like Latin America, "immobilized in time." This is to say that Carpentier's Europe serves to underline the relative unreality of all that happens in Latin America, where particular events have no particular meaning but say over and over again what everyone presumably knows. In political terms, this translates into the conviction that Latin Americans must collectively learn to consider their prospects as actual prospects, must think not of the impression they make or fail to make, but of the lives their people lead and of the price to be paid for improving those lives. What is so awful about Carpentier's head of state, in spite of some amusing eccentricities, is his inability to see anything as it is, his readiness to switch sides without hesitation or embarrassment, the absence of what might be called a center. European politicians are routinely derided for bowing to expedience and committing themselves to statecraft at the expense of substance, but the Latin American despot really doesn't know on behalf of what objectives he might be struggling to stay in office. He really doesn't see, however many books he has read, that to embrace "Germanic" ideals on one day and to lead a national movement against the Germanic technological "Valkyries" on the next is to devalue the possibility of meaning altogether. And the pattern is repeated again and again, no more vividly than in the head of state's building of stately monuments to the emergent civilization even as it is in the process of coming to pieces and driving its people to despair. No wonder that the President, in one of his better moments, adopts the criticism of his bitter enemies, lamenting his own tired vocabulary and his prostitution of the language. Such insights may be said to illuminate a good deal more than Latin American politics, but they have special poignance for anyone who has studied the rhetoric of Latin America's fabulous despots.

IV

Set *The Autumn of the Patriarch* alongside of *Reasons of State* and we have some clear sense of the peculiar constraints under which both books, insofar as they are political novels, must operate. Both assume that great changes must occur if the lives of ordinary people are to be made tolerable, but neither knows how to imagine what shape those changes will take. Both are constrained by the sense that even persons unaccustomed to thinking politically will need to do so if they are to understand what they are and what is done to them. But Carpentier goes so far as to have his characters articulate political ideas, and his head of state actually is "moving in the subsoil." García Márquez's patriarch is without ideas of any kind, and the novel as a whole seems to exist at a level that has little to do with discursive reasoning. The patriarch has a sharp eye for evil omens, but he responds to his fears so brutishly, so without reflection, that the novel cannot concern itself with any kind of "manifest force" beyond the patriarch himself. Had García Márquez introduced into his novel a figure like Carpentier's student revolutionary, the figure would immediately have withdrawn into the insubstantial ether that muffles and occultizes everything in *Autumn*. Whatever the novel's unmistakable political dimensions, it resists throughout its own inclination to become a political novel. It turns away from the prospect of plausibly actual encounters, such as Carpentier invites, in the direction of an atmospheric writing that is texturally dense and full of emotional resonance. It struggles not to discriminate one idea from another or to embody a variety of alternatives entertained by thoughtful persons; its goal is unmistakably to create something new, not to reveal what everyone already presumably knows or ought to know. The point is not that Carpentier is and García Márquez is not a committed writer, whatever the intensity of their respective political convictions. The point is that, starting from roughly the same place, Carpentier chooses to write a political novel while García Márquez chooses to write a book in which politics is part of a uniform texture that subdues everything to an indivisible, undifferentiated weight and coloration.

There is no use in trying to describe *Autumn* as a novel in which certain materials—say, the political elements—are backgrounded so as to allow other elements to emerge more emphatically. There is no background, and no foreground, in *Autumn*. There are no secondary characters as such, and no issues or ideas to be examined or refuted. If it successfully mounts a view of reality as Necessity, that Necessity is conceived as so protean, so ubiquitous and endemic a force that no one can effectively project its removal or definitively penetrate to its origins. Though the patriarch does presumably operate as other dictators do, and he is more than an eccentric individualist, he is less interesting to us than he would be if he were asked to engage other characters with ideas and ambitions of their own. To the degree that the patriarch comes to be identified entirely with the circumstance he inhabits, he ceases to be a focus for the kinds of ideological debate we associate with political novels. Again, it is hard to argue with a force of nature, particularly when one feels that the manifestation in question is more a narrative expedient than a permanent feature of the landscape. One does not object to *Autumn* on the grounds that it is unreal or anachronistic in its conception of character. One objects to its adopting a totalitarian format to deal with a totalitarian, albeit primitive, Latin American society. The interminable sentences and repetitive patternings of *Autumn* serve in the end to make its reader feel that he is trapped within a system that allows for no dissent or discrimination. One is dazzled by the intricacy of the structure and the richness of the rhetorical surface; the invention of incident, however little feeling is invested in any of it, is bound to seem impressive. But one feels, finally, that the novel has manufactured too entirely the narrative constraints under which it operates. It is too satisfied with its own circular patterns and virtuosic contrivances to press against them. It too readily overcomes what might have been permitted to develop into resistant material, and moves so steadily to an appointed end that it seems never to have dealt with elements outside its own rigidly circumscribed schema.

In the end the novel neither edifies nor amuses. Its object is to bring the reader to his knees, to force him to submit. Its mode is closer at once to the sublime and the bathetic than to the satiric or tragic. It tries to be impervious to criticism by creating a reality of its own and by recommending implicitly the only proper way of receiving such a work, which is to say, mutely and with gratitude. That this is hardly consistent with the goals of a political novel one need hardly say. No one can legitimately demand that a book of a certain kind be something else. One ought to demand that an ambitious novel work with constraints beyond the single motive it is tempted to assign itself. And no evaluation of *Autumn* can be adequate that does not recognize its willful betrayal of the political content it knowingly takes up only to leave it exactly as it was found: static and unelaborated.

Carpentier's is the much greater novel not because it is a "real" political novel, but because it sets in motion a variety of narrative paradigms to which it responds not by placing one above the others, but by making each address the issues with which the work as a whole is ostensibly concerned. These competing paradigms work together so well that what emerges from their interpenetration is a resounding indictment of Latin American politics and an index of the available ways of regarding the region and its future. If no final reading of that future is offered, the novel does offer several ways of accounting for the absence of final readings, hopeful projections, and definitive analyses. The novel itself is definitive in setting out the terms of the conceptual problems with which it grapples.

The narrative paradigms inscribed within the main narrative include the Viconian, or cyclical, model of history; the Nietzschean model of the hero or superman imposed on the flux of things (a debased version of this model is also invoked in references to Gobineau) and driving the less gifted "insects" where he will; the comic model (Molière particularly is invoked) in terms of which wrongs and contradictions are exposed not with a view to correcting them for all time, but with the object of producing a state of mind capable of rising confidently above its own contradictions; the Marxist model, with its improbable offer of a predictable progress; the romantic or idealist model, represented by the inspired stone carver Miguel Estatua and the revolutionary student, in terms of which the entire novel may be read as a reflection of conditions blocking their successful emergence and as an ode to the generous possibility those figures embody; the literary model of the novel of ideas, which typically proposes that it is more important to entertain complex thoughts and to track their intellectual origins than to consider their possible application in whatever happens to be the dominant circumstance; and, finally, the political model itself, in terms of which the intrigues of persons interested in holding or wresting power are treated as if they were a key to reality itself and important beyond the temporary advantage with which most of the actors themselves are absorbed. The best thing one can say about these paradigms and the other, less critical models also contained in *Reasons of State* is that one is not compelled to choose among them. All hold sway at different times, all are affected by the others and by the novel's overarching intention to engage the problematics of political discourse and political action in Latin America. To conclude that the book is a successful political novel is to conclude that it has a focus and an emotional center at which it arrives by plausibly working through various approaches to material that can never be exclusively political any more than it can be exclusively personal or psychological or domestic. The novel's interest in politics is a function of its interest in how things take shape and in how to get beyond the rather too simple model of the dictator as origin and agent. Carpentier, we see, acquiesces in that model only to expose its insufficiency and to promote alternative views of Latin America. So does he acquiesce in a version of the Viconian model only to demonstrate how little it answers to essential aspects of the situation he details. By setting out the competing paradigms, and by taking each one seriously enough to establish it as a viable perspective, Carpentier does justice to material that routinely tempts other novelists to simplification or evasion.

The most obvious warrant of Carpentier's achievement in *Reasons of State* is the skill with which he introduces the idealist model without either cynically dismissing it or overplaying its revolutionary potential. Clearly, in a novel dominated by the head of state and by the intrigues associated with his regime, it would have been a mistake to propose idealist or revolutionary solutions in a spirit of optimistic light-headedness. Carpentier's student is an implacable revolutionary, utterly remorseless in his contempt for the established order, but he is also shrewd enough to see how far he is from having things his own way. His idealism and fervor are obviously attractive, but he is without either the wit or the majesty that distinguish the head of state even in his decline. Judged from the perspective of the comic model, the idealist is in a sense too good to be true, which is to say, too single-minded to avoid being almost too good for this world. No doubt he fails to see his future in the "success" of the more mature figure who does actually displace the head of state and who in turn becomes the student's enemy. But the novel is structured so as to judge the idealist model also and more permanently from the perspective of the political model. For the student's commitment to "a popular uprising" as the only tenable way of avoiding U.S. military intervention and of establishing genuinely popular institutions is likely in time to become a commitment to democratic institutions commanding the allegiance of ordinary persons. Powerless to go beyond sniping and, perhaps, inspiring occasional work stoppages, the idealist in a prerevolutionary setting is likely to see that to take power is to satisfy the factions that control most of the society. This insight Carpentier presents not as a stunning discovery, but in implicit recognition of the way in which competing views of reality affect and displace one another. By the end of the novel the new leader, the so-called wise man of Nueva Cordoba, defends what is to be a popular and democratic government in terms that can only disappoint idealists everywhere. He declares, eloquently, the need for opposition—provided that it is co-operative and constructive. He defends and encourages the right to strike—provided that it doesn't paralyze private enterprise. And so it goes, the new "democratic" leader demonstrating how even the most worthy goals are betrayed when ideals are translated into policies, criticism into power. The idealist model is, of course, nowhere repudiated in all of this, but it is subjected to an implicit critique that makes it seem less than the last word on the major issues.

Carpentier's novel, then, instructs and refreshes because it holds the mirror up to life without apologizing for its inspired though intermittent distortions and without forgetting that its primary business is to evoke a condition that is never as one-dimensional as partisans or antagonists want it to be. Though it is frankly baffled by some of the material it presents, and is impatient with its own occasional forays into the interior life of characters, it effectively communicates the sense that the world exists, that some things in it are more significant and more desirable than others, and that the effort to see what exists is worth making. Like other successful political novels, it grants to ideas a life of their own, whatever the efforts of various characters to control or abuse them. And though it seems sometimes to grant no more stature to good ideas than to any other lively phenomenon, it is ever alert to the way in which conditions shift and particular ideas may be seen to assert themselves with an unforeseeable tenacity. No one is likely to compare *Reasons of State* with *The Possessed* or the other handful of primary texts in the tradition of the political novel, but it is surely a major work of poised and sober intelligence. Few political novels produced in Latin America have gone so far in showing how broad may be the purposes of the so-called new novel, how adaptable "lo real maravilloso" may be to the examination of a secular world in ferment.

6

Aleksandr Solzhenitsyn: Politics and the Facts of Life

I

The critic Walter Benjamin once wrote of the special mission of "the operating" as opposed to "the informing" writer: "His mission," Benjamin contended, "is not to report but to struggle; not to play the spectator but to intervene actively."[1] The distinction seems shallow in light of what we have learned from the writings of Aleksandr Solzhenitsyn, for if struggle and intervention are wanted, no one in our time has better demonstrated how they may be accomplished. And though ambitious writers are not often thought to be content with "informing" or delivering reports, Solzhenitsyn has provided a kind of information that makes uniquely possible the struggle and intervention Benjamin valued. In so doing, he has raised troubling questions about the status of his fiction and about the ultimate aims of his intervention, but no one can doubt that he has given new meaning to the idea of the writer as an "operating" presence. Nor has Solzhenitsyn as novelist been content to work within the boundaries ordinarily associated with an activist approach to the material he engages. To describe him as a realist, or as a humanist, or even as a traditional moralist, is largely to miss what he has done. He has shown us not only how reporting may well be a precondition of struggle, he has also shown us that the affirmation of the free individual may itself be a radical gesture having as little to do with petit bourgeois pieties as with Marxist imperatives.

Well before he issued the documentary materials collected in *The Gulag Archipelago,* Solzhenitsyn had seemed in his novels to be bringing us the news that other writers had earlier thought to deliver. *One Day in the Life of Ivan Denisovich* was more than the information it contained on the Soviet prison camps, and *The First Circle* could hardly be reduced to the "information" that the entire Soviet system was a vast bureaucracy operating in the main as a terror network controlled by Joseph Stalin. But readers of those novels and of other works by Solzhenitsyn did feel that they were being told something vital for the first time. It didn't matter that twenty years earlier they had read Koestler's *Darkness at Noon,* Serge's *The Case of Comrade Tulayev,* or the autobiographical narratives of witnesses like Milosz and Spender and others who spoke of their disillusioning experiences in the Communist movement. Something in Solzhenitsyn made the critical information seem irresistible even to those who had resolved not to be moved.[2] It is too easy to say that Solzhenitsyn was simply a better novelist than those who had written of the Soviet system before, or that his every sentence seemed a reflection of his sincerity and the intensity of his feelings. Koestler and Serge were immensely skillful and convincing writers, and they surely wrote with the authority of an experience that had marked them deeply and permanently. If Solzhenitsyn seemed to bring the news as if no one else had earlier brought it, his success must have been a function of his knowing a good deal that the others didn't know. And, in the novels, that knowledge must have emerged in such a way as to seem every bit as essential to the narrative design as the intrigues that bring together otherwise unrelated characters.

What does Solzhenitsyn know? He knows that the only way to understand the Soviet mind is to dwell not primarily on an attitude or a psychology but on a situation. He knows that a situation is usually manifested in the activities and avowals of those who belong to it, but that in a totalitarian society isolated gestures and statements, no matter how predictable, often cannot accurately reflect what they come out of. One may not on that account ignore ordinary human relations or refuse to acknowledge the role that individual psychology may play in directing particular actions. But one must all the same remember that the situation in the Soviet Union constrains and colors everything in a degree that imposes special requirements on the writer, particularly if he is interested in examining the prospects for resistance.

To study the Soviet situation, then, one must construct a universe in which nothing is left to chance, in which every thought of every character will refer itself to a common terror, and in which instinct can serve only to support or to resist the given dispensation. To understand the situation in this way is, as others have noted, to study the Soviet system as if in a closed laboratory experiment. Solzhenitsyn's genius is such that he has been able to conduct these experiments, again and again, without reducing the various outcomes to mechanical inconsequence or turning his characters into helpless counters in a situation to which they can only submit. His grasp of the particular situation has enabled him at once to honor subject individuals as if they were free men and women and to indicate the degree of their enslavement.

Koestler understood the situation in an altogether different way, at least at the time he wrote *Darkness at Noon*. There he sought to uncover the very nature of Soviet Communism by reducing it to a Marxist logic that could explain and justify anything it wanted to and dismiss as reactionary sentimentality any measure of dissent or distaste. In effect, this logic served to strengthen the hand of the party apparatus and to create a brutal administrative bureaucracy staffed by persons who had nothing but the rudiments of a mechanistic logic to guide them. Conflicts within the system are therefore portrayed by Koestler as arguments conducted by interested, even impassioned antagonists who nonetheless manage to proceed with a kind of sublime impersonality. These persons are anything but bland, and Koestler is assiduous to attribute to them a variety of personal characteristics. All the same, they are presented to us in the main as apparatchiks, representatives of one generation or another of the Bolshevik administrative or revolutionary elite. Even Rubashov, Koestler's protagonist, who suffers from the kind of guilt we expect to find only in bourgeois novels, masters his guilt by recalling himself to his primary obligation, which is to think as a Communist in the recommended logical categories. Nowhere in Koestler's powerful novel is there the suggestion that this manner of working out ambiguities and conflicts is a function of the author's having chosen to work with unusually disciplined and inflexible party functionaries. Nowhere does the novel suggest that the situation is larger than the casuistical restraints self-imposed by trained revolutionaries on their own habits of thought. For Koestler, to be a Communist is to think like a Communist, precisely and without qualification. The Communist situation is simply the domination of the political sphere by persons who think like Communists. And in the Soviet Union, to think like a Communist is to be able to make a case for any directive issued by Comrade Stalin.

Now it may be argued that Koestler too rigidly identified as Communist what was a Stalinist distortion or betrayal not only of Marx but of Lenin and of the original Bolshevik design. Indeed, such arguments seemed to many readers more than feasible before the publication of Solzhenitsyn's *Gulag* and of his masterful portrayal of Lenin in *Lenin in Zurich*. But the issue for us is not Koestler's refusal, as Alan Swingewood has it, "to delineate the differences between Stalin and the left and right opposition," his desire to have us see in Rubashov "a synthesis of *all* Bolshevik trends".[3] The issue, rather, is the reduction of situation to logic. To be sure, there is also a kind of logic in the reflections of Solzhenitsyn's characters, and some of them do limit themselves largely to the familiar categorical dichotomies: ends or means, progress or reaction, supporters or enemies. But this kind of thinking is not in Solzhenitsyn to be confused with the situation, and is not therefore the object of his novelistic attentions. To say of him that he wished to inform, to report and record, that the invention of a narrative action and the creation of characters were for him finally indistinguishable from the desire to inform, is to say that the situation he aimed at was nothing less than the totality of relations in Soviet society. And if that totality could be imagined and apprehended only in a fragmentary or experimentally limited way, it was nonetheless the crucial presence informing every development in the narrative. To focus on the logic of individual, albeit representative or exemplary, characters would have been to pretend to have isolated and encompassed the elusive totality when, in fact, one could only think it as an absent cause.

To think of an absent cause in connection with the novelist's desire to report and inform is to begin to gauge the scope of Solzhenitsyn's project. For if other writers have aimed to engage the totality of relations in their respective societies, they have generally done so in the hope that a more or less representative action involving a variety of different characters would provide a satisfying account. The assigning of palpable causes to palpable effects would create the desired impression that the main issues had been mastered and suitably explained, with subsidiary issues persuasively consigned to virtual irrelevance by the logic of the narrative itself. The totality aimed at was in this sense no more than the master code or thematic orientation that made the various parts of the narrative seem to belong together and to contribute to the unified impression the reader would be grateful to receive. The novelist could afford to look on "mere" reportage or information as but one kind of raw material on the basis of which he had achieved his representative, and therefore superior, vision. If, ultimately, there was an absent cause that might be said to account not only for what happened in the narrative but for the novelist's selection of "relevant" issues, that cause would interfere very little with the reader's sense of the adequacy of the material at hand. In the degree that the work succeeded, it would appear to do what it was meant to do. Anything to which it might gesture without actually moving to engage it, the work could abandon as inconsequential or as not falling within the purview of the given work, or—more drastically—as unthinkable.

For Solzhenitsyn, though, the very notion of a representative action is problematic, for in dealing with a society that totalizes or controls all human relationships, he could not believe that the most important human possibilities could be represented by the behavior of a genuinely typical character. Neither could he believe in the validity of the antithetical hero of the bourgeois novel, who exists for us in his opposition to the social world that denies the values he upholds. Such a figure would, after all, represent the possibility of revolt or of an equally unlikely personal resilience in the face of circumstances too effectively organized to permit our taking hope on the basis of any marginally viable resistance. To create a representative action Solzhenitsyn would have to avoid the merely typical while refusing as well the temptations of the merely eccentric or heroic. He would have to bring forward an action that expressed a situation without being reducible to it or too readily transcending it. That action would in turn reflect and give rise to forms of consciousness that were not situation-specific, but were ultimately meaningful only in terms of the situation to which they were assigned. Rejecting the idea of a purely subjective experience, Solzhenitsyn managed to demonstrate how consciousness could take shape and pursue a course without submitting entirely to a context outside of which it would nevertheless cease to be what it was.

The action in Solzhenitsyn has almost invariably to do with extreme situations conceived as if they were routine, though the actions that express them are in no ways so routine as to become inert emblems that can point only in one direction. In fact, the representative action in a full-blown Solzhenitsyn novel is not a unitary phenomenon, not a reflection of some wish to contain diversity so as to underline a meaning. For all the talk of simple values and self-evident, unitary truths, in Solzhenitsyn the action is deliberately mounted to compound the insistence on those one-dimensional trophies. This is particularly true of *The First Circle*. There, the attempt to encompass the Soviet situation and to respond adequately to it leads the novelist to describe not a single action but a variety of actions, many of them contradictory. These can be made to seem necessary and inevitable only as we are made to feel that we know what Solzhenitsyn knows. We must feel, that is, that we have been given a material basis for interpreting both single actions that go against the grain of a hypostatized common sense, and contradictions in a narrative that presumes to some sort of ethical coherence.

To speak of a material basis, of course, is to recall that Solzhenitsyn's major works have always sought to bring back information from the dark side of a universe not open to most of us. The material basis for our involvement in that universe, then, can be nothing less than our sense of it as real, as compelling not in the sense that it has moved Solzhenitsyn himself or any of his characters, but that it is available to us as an object of reflection even outside our involvement in the text. The information provided by Solzhenitsyn persuades us both that he has had a certain kind of experience he wishes to share and that his experience is valid beyond the particular meanings he can assign to it. No wonder readers who like their fiction pure or nonreferential have misread the novels as a kind of documentary realism providing the sort of illustrative clarity otherwise associated with the Stalinist commissars. But the material basis in Solzhenitsyn has nothing to do with straightforward presentation of correct attitudes and unimpeachable positions. In the shorter works, particularly in *One Day*, that basis is simply the objective, detailed presentation of concentration camp routine as if it were a "permanent condition" existing at the level of "hard fact."[4] Criticism and commentary are implicit in what is shown, but the novelist's refusal to generalize or declaim contributes to our sense that we are in touch with the essentials, the bare facts of the case. The material basis of any judgments we may wish to make is both what passes for objective detail in the work and our sense of the constraints under which the novelist has agreed to operate.

In the longer and more challenging novels the material basis has more to do with the insistently represented impression that, as George Lukács has it, "the Stalinist system of rule had penetrated into all facets of everyday life."[5] The sharashka in *The First Circle* may not be an everyday locale, but one finds there the varieties of relationship and reflection that warrant our view of the system's penetration. Equally important, the more or less uniform setting allows the novelist to record what goes on there in what seems not a selective but almost an exhaustive way. To be sure, a great deal of selection is involved, but one feels in reading *The First Circle* that Solzhenitsyn has told us all there is to tell about the life of zeks under Stalin. The elaboration of technical projects, the working out of conflicts, even the handling of vagrant sexual longings—all seem to be given their due not because the narrative design demands this or because of some overarching idea that may thereby be conveyed. What seems to us a kind of completeness and sufficiency is a function of the author's sense that he is describing something that is necessarily of a piece, owing always, as it does, to the situation that is the Stalinist bureaucracy. Solzhenitsyn's passion to inform and record is consistent with his understanding of the sharashka experience as a series of facts that have the coherence of a closed system and that point beyond themselves to something equally coherent though less accessible.

George Lukács has provided what is surely the most instructive analysis of this dimension of Solzyhenitsyn's art. Invoking *The Magic Mountain* as an early instance of a similar compositional procedure, he describes a novel in which "the uniformity of the setting is made the immediate foundation of the narrative. The characters of this novel are removed from the 'natural' location of their lives and movements," so that the " 'chance' common terrain of their present existence creates new fundamental forms of their human, intellectual and moral relations with each other." In adopting this procedure, Mann is said to have aimed "to endow his characters' reactions to their new environment with a universal breadth and depth." More, their reactions reflect "the desire to become aware of and come to terms with the problems of life of which they have never been aware at home. The sanitorium is thus the factual, immediate trigger of ideological problems which were everywhere latent but which only here emerge into consciousness with all their contradictions."[6]

In the main, the procedure as described would appear to apply as well to *The First Circle* as to *The Magic Mountain*. In fact, there are critical differences that we may consider as follows:

1. "The socially invoked confrontation of man with himself in the sanitorium is a mere possibility . . . to which the characters may well react by rejecting any question of this kind." We may get, in a novel like

Mann's, "a mere release of society's potentialities" rather than a "questioning of society itself."[7]

2. ". . . when, as in Thomas Mann, the characters are only confronted spontaneously with their existence, when the only goal set is their physical recovery, then the agent of this recovery, i.e. the doctors, are only spectators of, but not necessarily in the ideological drama, which they themselves bring about."[8]

3. Questions need to be asked about the relative degree to which "characters simply submit" to their milieu or, in resisting it, manage "to achieve an awareness of and to master the crucial ideological and practical problems."[9]

In addressing these issues, it may first be said that insofar as *The First Circle* is a political novel and *The Magic Mountain* is definitely not, we should be able to articulate their differences in part by referring to the different generic constraints to which they respond. To do so is, for example, to recall that the growth of social awareness in Mann is conceived as a pure concomitant of individual growth. To become aware of oneself as a rational being with ties to other persons and with particular social obligations to meet is simply to overcome a contrary predilection whose origin lies deep in the personal unconscious and in the racial unconscious as well. The burden of a novel tracing the recovery from that predilection must be, for Mann, to embody the alternatives in such a way that each should seem compelling in its own terms without seeming to implicate its agent in a particular life choice. The individual caught between these alternatives must have the courage to confront them if he is to grow, but he is not required to work out the social or political consequences in a concrete way. He may resolve his uncertainties as Hans Castorp does, by choosing to return to the ordinary world and fight for his country, but this resolution will constitute simply a provisional termination of conflict rather than a working out of the conflict consistent with the terms in which it has been posited. As a novel of ideas, *The Magic Mountain* leads one to say about it that it is "about an age dispossessed of the very sense of definable meaning" or that it is "the *critique* of the romantic equation *la maladie c'est l'esprit*."[10] To use it to criticize specific social forms or political goals is to discover at once how rich it is and how little it is inclined to lend itself to uses of any kind. It is a great contemplative work written out of a deep critical encounter with the spirit of its own age and place, but its relation to reality is philosophic rather than political. It translates its regard for life forms and for cultural facts into ideological categories without permitting either the forms or the facts to assume a distinct political character. There is vivid and brilliant embodiment in *The Magic Mountain,* but anyone wishing to discuss its political content will necessarily be limited to general tendencies and to competing spiritual paradigms. The novel's attempt to assert a more determinant political conclusion by rationalizing Castorp's participation in World War I only serves to underline the novel's character as having nothing to do with solutions, practical or otherwise.

So, Mann shapes his narrative in accordance with the generic constraints associated with the philosophic novel, treating politics as the spirit of the age or as the unelaborated, even unknowable consequence of ideas in conflict. Solzhenitsyn, by contrast, responds to a different kind of generic constraint. He works not to embody the essence or meaning of a thing or of spiritual forces in conflict, but to get at a situation so as to make criticism not only possible but inevitable. The object of that criticism is neither a tendency nor a general inheritance nor a set of ideas, but a system. To say that ideas in general are responsible for that system is no more true than to say that human nature is responsible. For Solzhenitsyn, what matters is not the reduction of the system to general propensities or particular ideas nor the attempt to fix blame. To establish responsibility is, in his sense, to see the system as a situation that must at all costs be resisted. If, in his lectures and articles, he urges the defeat of the system, in his novels he can do no more than involve us in it in such a way as to make resistance seem compelling. This has very little to do with ideas or with the spirit of the age, whatever the inclination of Solzhenitsyn's characters to debate ideas or to reflect on the drift of their contemporaries. The horizon of *The First Circle* is the horizon of fact. Resistance can seem the only viable option only when we have accepted the embodied situation as the primary fact commanding our attention. To speak of generic constraint in Solzhenitsyn, then, is to recognize his resolute addiction to the facts that together constitute for him the reality of an intolerable situation. Though his narrative apparatus allows him to digress as much as he likes in the direction of individual encounter or psychological drama, he can pursue these opportunities only so far as they strengthen his grasp of the situation as fact.

The primary constraint under which Solzhenitsyn operates is such that he is unable to translate the characters into emblems any more than he can translate action into romance terms, the "salvational historicity"[11] of a monumental struggle between the forces of good and evil. The narrative dedicated to establishing facts will inevitably convey meanings, but those meanings are never permitted to stand forth independently, to assume a momentum or a stature of their own, for, like ideas, those meanings can be challenged, resisted, or ignored. Facts of the kind to which Solzhenitsyn is attracted may not so readily be ignored. In bearing witness to those facts, the novelist must seem at every point to be telling the truth, and the truth he tells must everywhere record what has ostensibly happened in a particular time and place while insistently posing the question: What does it mean to be human? For it is only in the context of truly imposing and unimpeachable facts that this question can be worth asking.[12]

Having said as much, we are prepared to go back to Lukács's analysis of the differences between Mann and Solzhenitsyn. In the first point cited here, he suggests that in *The First Circle* the "confrontation of man with himself " is not only "socially invoked" but literally irresistible, and that this confrontation leads to "a questioning of society itself." Why this is so will seem clear when we consider what it means to confront oneself in Solzhenitsyn. A characteristically illuminating passage is the following exchange between the youthful Ruska Doronin and Gleb Nerzhin, which begins with Ruska's ruminations on Mommsen's *History of Rome*. " 'History is so monotonous it's repulsive to read,' " he begins.

"The nobler and more honest a man is, the more despicably his compatriots treat him. . . . All history is one continuous pestilence. There is no truth and there is no illusion. There is no where to appeal and no where to go."

In the deathly blue light the quiver of skepticism on such young lips was particularly disturbing.

Nerzhin himself had planted these thoughts in Ruska, but now, as Ruska uttered them, he felt a desire to protest. Among his older comrades Gleb was used to being the iconoclast, but he felt a responsibility toward the younger prisoner.

"I want to warn you, Ruska," Nerzhin replied very softly, leaning closer to his neighbor's ear. "No matter how clever and absolute the systems of skepticism or agnosticism or pessimism, you must understand that by their very nature they doom us to a loss of will. They can't really influence human behavior because people cannot stand still. And that means they can't renounce systems which affirm something which summon them to advance in some direction."

"Even if it's into a swamp? Just to slog along?" Ruska asked angrily.

"Even that. Who the hell knows?" Gleb wavered. "Look, I personally believe that people seriously need skepticism. It's needed to split the rockheads. To choke fanatical voices. But skepticism can never provide firm ground under a man's feet. And perhaps, after all, we need firm ground." . . .

"All right!" Nerzhin replied accusingly. "You're losing sight of everything solid, of every goal. One can certainly doubt, one is obliged to doubt. But isn't it also necessary to love something?"

"Yes, yes, to love something!" Ruska took him up in a triumphant, hoarse whisper. "To love something—not history and not theory, but a woman!" He leaned over on Nerzhin's bunk and grasped him by the elbow. "What have they really deprived us of, tell me? The right to go to meetings or to subscribe to state bonds? The one way the Plowman could really hurt us was to deprive us of women. And he did it. For twenty-five years! The bastard! Who can imagine—" and he struck his fist against his chest—"what a woman means to a prisoner?"

"Watch out you don't end up insane!" said Nerzhin, trying to defend himself, but a sudden wave flooded through him at the thought of Simochka and her promise for Monday evening. "Get rid of that notion," he said. "It'll black out your brain. A Freudian simplex or complex—what the hell do they call it? Sublimation's the answer. Shift your energy into other areas. Concentrate on philosophy—you won't need bread or water or a woman's caresses for that."

The passage in effect demands that Nerzhin confront himself by responding to the peculiarly disturbing image of himself he sees in Ruska. In this way he can see what certain attitudes amount to when they are detached from their point of origin and made to seem strange. He confronts his own inveterate habits of mind almost as if they were an affectation, a form of aggression without substance or justification. His desire to protest is a desire to correct an unseemly or premature acquiescence in what can easily become a posture rather than a conviction. Nothing in the passage inclines us to believe that Nerzhin has himself held these attitudes in a spiritually false or insincere way. But his need to look at them afresh causes him to wonder what validity they can have as general truths or as instigations to easy closure in others. That "one is obliged to doubt" he can still affirm; that doubt is an answer to essential problems seems to him unlikely.

The self-confrontation is interesting in part for the way in which it emerges as an exchange. One recalls that there is little solitary reflection in *The First Circle,* little of the soul-searching so familiar in didactic novels pitting thoughtful, sensitive characters against unremittingly harsh environments. Characters in Solzhenitsyn typically work out their sense of themselves in pointed, sometimes hostile encounters with friends and antagonists. It is one thing, as Nerzhin himself acknowledges, to be content to call oneself an iconoclast; it is something else to examine, scrupulously, the effect of one's behavior on others and to have to formulate plausible alternatives to that behavior. The self in Solzhenitsyn is not conceived as noble or ignoble on the basis of an abstract ideal. Nerzhin's characteristic attitudes are more or less valid, depending on the effects they may be seen to have and the degree in which they do or do not support the Soviet system. These considerations will vary as local circumstances vary, so that what seems at one point a valid conviction will at other times be called into question. What seems good to Nerzhin, and perhaps seems noble to us, must take shape as an expression of a self that is *for others* as much as it is *for itself.* But this has little to do with a character's decision to live for others or to credit only charitable intentions toward them. The sometimes noble self in Solzhenitsyn is for others only in the sense that it is actively a part of a social universe—no matter how constricted and impoverished—and cannot but evaluate its goals and attitudes in the context of the common fate.

To conceive a self in Solzhenitsyn is to recognize that one lives in a world made by human beings. In such a world it is impossible for moderately thoughtful persons not to confront themselves. Since they are everywhere challenged by the facts of a suffering clearly inflicted by some individuals on others, it is inevitable that they should consider where they stand in relation to that suffering. Some Solzhenitsyn characters are content simply to identify with the victims, others with those in power. The character Spiridon describes the difference between guilt and innocence as "sheep dogs are right and cannibals are wrong." But this grasp of the essential facts cannot constitute the process of self-confrontation on which the novel depends. We may not be able to improve on Spiridon's terse formulation, but Solzhenitsyn clearly intends it as a kind of innocent folk wisdom to which modern men and women may not plausibly aspire. To do so would be to affect a simple grasp of fundamentals while ignoring the fact that human beings are not really sheep dogs and that it is often helpful to discuss human problems in detail. To associate Solzhenitsyn's wisdom with Spiridon's is to jettison entirely the main weight of the novel, with its emphasis on strenuous self-examination and careful penetration of the situation that is the common fate. That common fate in *The First Circle* is the world that human beings have made for purposes that are no longer present to them. Nerzhin's exchange with Ruska indicates, among other things, how gradually one may lose touch with the roots and with the palpable consequences even of one's primary attitudes or allegiances. The sharp confrontation with the self is required if we are to repossess what belongs to us.

To repossess what belongs to us will, if Lukács is right, also involve "a questioning of society itself." This may not be the case for the inhabitants of Mann's Magic Mountain, but it is surely so for the zeks imprisoned in the sharashka. Nerzhin would seem, in the passage we have quoted, to repossess his own attitudes and, consequently, his sense of himself not only by confronting Ruska's version of those attitudes, but by having to confront the idea of physical love—love of particular women—which he wishes to dismiss as inessential. In effect, the exchange with Ruska forces Nerzhin to consider the very fragility of his convictions, the possibility that they are no more than a defense against feelings of loss, permanent estrangement, inconsequence. He can still bring himself to say that it is necessary to doubt; that it is equally important to believe in something, most especially in one's own powers of resistance, if one is not to do what must not be done; and, finally, that one must live for ideas if one is to survive in circumstances that deny one the right to live for anything else. These truths Nerzhin reaffirms. But he finds himself distracted from these truths—which he will not and must not repudiate—by Ruska's simple declaration that to love something is not finally to love ideas; it is to love a woman. Nerzhin tries "to defend himself" against this other truth to the point of lecturing his young friend in the accents of a therapeutic manual. But the theory of sublimation to which he clings seems feeble when set against the thought of a woman. This does not amount, in Solzhenitsyn, to a glib dismissal of mind or a belief in the primacy of lust. The exchange, taken as a whole, plainly recommends that ideas be measured against the circumstances they are meant to address. *Skepticism, sublimation, resistance:* These words may be said to mean something only insofar as those using them continue to see themselves as concrete actors in a social world that compels and deforms their every project. To think, however briefly, of what he has been denied is for Nerzhin to be temporarily alienated from the ideology of passive resistance and sublimation to which he has subscribed. He may, of necessity, return to the posture associated with that ideology, but in doing so he will see more vividly than before what he has lost and why he must continue to deal with his suffering as he does.

In this, Nerzhin's respect for reality will also have been strengthened—that is, he will understand better than before what oppresses him and what are the consequences of that oppression. To be without women is a condition that may well be managed by turning one's attention to other things; certainly it is easy enough to believe that one can handle longing or disappointment in this way. But to see oneself as a person who is less and less apt to think about what he misses—and what others miss—is to confront another and more terrifying consequence of oppression routinized and rationalized. Not by making do, nor by cultivating an idea of his spiritual superiority, but by thinking again and again of what is done to him and to others like him does Nerzhin survive as a full human being. This is to say that, for Solzhenitsyn, to be aware of oneself is to be aware of one's situation not as an inert fact, but as a process to which one responds by remembering how one came to be the person one is. In repossessing one's characteristic attitudes and freshly imagining the ground of one's behavior, one questions the society that threatens to separate persons not only from what they love but from the sense of their own vital agency.

To question society itself, then, is not in this case to ask what right the society has to do this thing or that. It is not to engage in legal arguments. It is to ask, simply, sometimes feverishly, what can be done. If nothing can be done, then one is bound to throw up one's hands and declare the situation intolerable. If a little can be done, then one is bound to wonder why it should not seem enough. Solzhenitsyn's zeks are occasionally given to reflecting on their good fortune. Permitted to use their minds rather than to do back-breaking physical labor, decently fed and reasonably well clothed, they may well feel they have little reason to complain. In fact, though they never grow indifferent to their advantages, they are often bitter about the system in which they serve. They question society itself by dwelling on what a person must do to get by. They see that choices are available to all, but that the range of options is very limited and that there seems no way to sustain more than a marginal self-respect. Where every action is defined by the social purpose to which it clearly and inevitably refers, nothing like an autonomous deed—a deed performed freely and intensely for its own sake—is possible. So, desperate wagers are undertaken, as when Nerzhin insists, almost to the point of hysteria, on claiming from one of his tormentors a book that had been confiscated. In the situation he occupies there is no other way of asserting a right and denying, hopelessly, pathetically, his domination by those for whom he is nothing.

Lukács had contended, we recall, that in *The Magic Mountain* the local authority-figures—that is to say, the doctors—were "only spectators of, but not necessarily actors in the ideological drama." The point is more important than it seems, indicating how by contrast *The First Circle* implicates everyone unmistakably in the ideological drama. Not only are Solzhenitsyn's local authority-figures—the camp guards and administrators—complicit in the crimes committed by the state, but they are made to seem responsible by virtue of the way in which they pass on to their subordinates and victims precisely what the Soviet system demands. Terror is the primary ideological principle regulating the system,[13] and terror is at once the cause and the product of the actions typically performed by bureaucrats and plebeian functionaries in the camps. In the shadow of this terror some persons manage to behave as if they were not entirely controlled by the great fear, but their behavior can be evaluated only as it is set alongside the more usual responses of others. When the zek Bobynin refuses to cringe like a whipped cur before the minister of state security, he explains the differences between himself and others very bluntly. One— "They have too much in life they're afraid of losing." Two—". . . a person you've taken *everything* from is no longer in your power. He's free all over again." But Bobynin is more remarkable than these explanations suggest. Many persons in his place find ways of deluding themselves about the advantages to be gained by doing what they are told and succumbing to the pervading terror. Bobynin can rise above his tormentor because the minister sees himself as a product of the system who can act only the part he is assigned and learns readily enough to be good for nothing else. Bobynin may try also to understand himself as a product of the system, a free man in spite of himself, but next to the minister he must seem more to us than an actor in someone else's play. The ideological drama in Solzhenitsyn is focused by the way in which characters do or do not belong to, or identify with, the apparatus in which they necessarily participate. No one can be a spectator, no one can escape judgment.

We can appreciate that judgment is no easy matter as we try to talk about the meaning or the quality of resistance. Nerzhin resists dehumanization in part by repossessing his sense of himself and by freshly confronting the fact of the situation he is in. Bobynin resists by refusing to cringe or grovel and by contemptuously reciting the facts so as to articulate his conviction that they deny every standard of decency and ordinary sense. And the character Volodin, outside the sharashka, resists by risking his own safety in order to warn someone else of the danger he is in. In these instances, and others like them, we are invited to agree that something good and necessary has been done. We are tempted, in arriving at positive judgments, to resort to terms like *conscience* and *decency* and *truthfulness*— to what are, in other words, "*ideological* concepts" in their own right, "historically relative and constantly changing their content according to current historical needs," as Marxist critics particularly are given to reminding us.[14] We may not be willing at any stage in our thinking to dispense with these terms or to accept that they are *merely* "relative," but we may well agree with Lukács that a crucial component of any judgment we reach will have to do with the quality of resistance demonstrated by the various actors. Does a particular act of resistance reflect "an awareness," let alone mastery, "of the crucial ideological and practical problem"? Or does the question itself betray an unworthy desire to complicate matters that are simpler than a Lukács would like to believe?

Obviously, when we consider such questions, we are apt to come on others just as important and no less elusive. Does an awareness of ideological and practical problems necessarily entail a resolve to do something about them? Is it possible to regard the crucial questions as having been answered at a level that has nothing to do with politics and still to think politically? Insofar as available judgment terms are relative, no matter how strenuously we insist that we do not mean them to be, is it fair to say that political deliberations should always address immediate, rather than long-term, issues? And in that sense, mightn't there be a persuasive case to be made for moral intransigence as an especially valid species of political thinking, focused as it will often be on the injury done to human beings in particular circumstances? To read Solzhenitsyn is to see, as we have intimated, that the recovery of fact and the construction of situation are at the very center of his enterprise. But it is the spirit of resistance conceived as moral intransigence that is his motive. To those who would deny that such a motive can be the primary element in a politics that is more than visionary mystification, Solzhenitsyn's novel will pose the major challenge of our time.[15]

II

In searching for a reliable way to approach Solzhenitsyn, we have thus far avoided a frontal examination of what we take to be his most successful and characteristic work of fiction. We have treated *The First Circle,* in fact, as a sort of a document—a fiction, to be sure, but a work attesting to certain convictions and aversions almost as if it were not a novel. Continual references to "facts" and "truths" and "systems" contribute, perhaps, to the impression that we are interested in *The First Circle* much in the way that we are interested in the first-person "factual" accounts of the Gulag issued by writers who are not literary artists. And, in candor, it may not be denied that Solzhenitsyn has for all of us, including those who most admire his artistry, that sort of appeal. But it may also be said that Solzhenitsyn's preeminence is the consequence not of his courage or candor, but of his narrative mastery. To speak of his moral vision, of his political cunning, of his psychological penetration is at the same time to acknowledge the literary tact with which he puts us permanently in touch with a landscape we would as soon forget. And if we are to legitimize the provisional ideas and descriptions we have posited up to now, we shall have to see more clearly how they grow out of so unorthodox a novel as *The First Circle.*

When it appeared in 1968, the novel received the kind of sympathetic and detailed attention that most other writers wait a lifetime to receive. Much of this attention was useful: Not only did it bring favorable attention to Solzhenitsyn and make it possible for him to reach greater numbers of readers than would otherwise have been possible, it also provided readings of the novel that would prove to be profoundly constructive, in spite of the issues that were overlooked or misconceived. Some commentators stressed the author's achievement in creating a character "who is not an ideological vehicle but a fully realized human being."[16] Others praised the novel's revelation of "the unexpected and even joyous strength of man at the limits of life"[17] or its surprisingly original renewal of the Tolstoyan project.[18] For many, what mattered most was the evenhandedness of Solzhenitsyn's characterization, his willingness to deal compassionately even with so unrepentant a Stalinist as Lev Rubin. Even Lukács—whose career was a series of inventive and often appalling compromises—was moved to speak of the "refusal to compromise in all human and social essentials" as forming "a prerequisite for anyone wishing to remain fully human in the camps."[19] More recently it has seemed necessary to read *The First Circle* in light of Solzhenitsyn's subsequent nonfiction works, discovering in it a milder and more circumscribed version of the devastating critique he has leveled not only at Stalin and the Gulag, but at halfhearted liberals and fellow travelers in the West. These weak-kneed types do not appear in *The First Circle*—given the novel's setting, how could they?—but they are all the same implicated in the portrait of those who refuse to understand what anyone should be able to see. The early treatment of *The First Circle* as a humanist document with a political content that rarely rose to explicit statement or tendentious sermonizing has been revised to account for the fact that Solzhenitsyn had already written a good deal of *The Gulag* when he decided to write the novel.

At stake in all of this is more than an ephemeral impression of a book that has in some respects been superceded by its successors. If *The First Circle* is a great novel, it must be seen to do a particular job of work that a documentary project cannot accomplish. And if it is a great political novel, it must be seen to operate politically in a way that does not compromise the other functions assigned to it by the literary imagination. It is, to be sure, the book hailed by most of its early readers, and it does in part launch the critique attributed to it by readers of *The Gulag*. But it is more and does more than has yet been indicated.

In Part I of this chapter we spoke of Solzhenitsyn's interest in fact. We said there that to honor fact was for him to show how the Soviet bureaucratic apparatus had imposed itself on and tainted every aspect of life. To this we might have added the fact that even "positive" figures were in a grave sense compromised; that it was impossible for even a minimally educated and thoughtful person to get by comfortably in Soviet society without becoming a dishonorable person; and that the system itself was so transparently dedicated to nothing but its own perpetuation that to defend it was by definition to be either a fool, a degenerate, or a hypocrite. No reliance is placed on such epithets in *The First Circle,* and one may wish in general to deny any validity to categorical denunciations. But it is in the nature of the novel to establish its facts in such a way that, in thinking to resist evil, we know precisely what and whom to resist or to spurn. If a dialectical work is one in which ideas are brought into steady opposition and conclusions or resolutions are challenged or undermined as soon as they are formulated, then Solzhenitsyn's is a dialectical novel. But there are facts—and this cannot be repeated too often—there are facts more fundamental than ideas or impressions. To be aware of those facts is to know something that, though it cannot banish conflict or doubt or terminate the cultivation of ideas, will nonetheless strengthen the capacity to judge. It is the business of *The First Circle* to empower judgment.

The novel moves about from one knot of characters to another, focusing most often on pairs or groups of zeks, but extending its reach to private homes, ministry offices, and even to the chambers of Joseph Stalin himself. Readers are often tempted (and I am no exception) to place the character Nerzhin at the book's center, to make of him a "protagonist" and to see everything else as supporting or complicating—but never repudiating—the humane perspective associated with him. From this point of view we are introduced to Stalin because in him we see the sum total of what Nerzhin hates. Rubin exists in effect to toughen Nerzhin's mind, to present him with an immediate obstacle to his intellectual designs. And Spiridon is useful to teach Nerzhin what he cannot learn for himself. External characters who do not directly influence Nerzhin are justified in a similar way. We are to be interested in Volodin as one who, in his own way, makes a decision that ratifies Nerzhin's choices. Prosecutor Makarygin degrades his own intelligence in a way that would have seemed shameful and incredible to Nerzhin even when he was twelve and couldn't believe what he read in *Izvestia*. And so on.

But to read the novel in this way is to conclude not only that Nerzhin knows everything that Solzhenitsyn knows—that is not, after all, inconceivable—but that coherence itself is a product of a unitary perspective. This *The First Circle* would seem to deny. It dwells too insistently on characters only marginally connected with the zeks to impress us with an ordinary structural coherence. Its narrative mode is too discontinuous to make us feel that it aims throughout at the same ideological or human or political target. And it carefully poses Nerzhin's situation in such a way that he cannot be thought to address adequately, let alone rectify, the variety of circumstances we are shown. He does represent a legitimate option, and that option is surely ratified by Volodin and by other zeks, but to see Nerzhin as the unmistakable center of such a book is to make of him more than he can be in a situation so broad. It is one thing to speak of totalitarian society as a one-dimensional universe dominated by a ferociously centralizing apparatus; it is another thing to pretend that a prisoner like Nerzhin can be the sufficient emblem and integrating focus of such a world.

If Nerzhin is not a protagonist-figure but simply the most attractive character in a various cast, what is the source of the book's coherence? We have spoken of the facts and of the situation that Solzhenitsyn wishes to construct, but to understand its coherence it is necessary to consider the polyphonic character of the book. *The First Circle* is a novel about competing and interacting voices, perspectives, ideas. It is not, as has often been supposed, a work that uses many characters and shifts its focus in an erratic way simply to underscore a simple notion that remains constant throughout its shiftings. If the novel has an idea, it is not that evil is this one thing and nothing else, or that a good man is good and faithful no matter what is done to him. *The First Circle* remains a compelling work because it knows many different things at different times and with different degrees of certainty. Its polyphonic structure is means *and* end. In refusing to treat Nerzhin as hero, or even as primary focus, it says in effect that the work as a whole must know more than any character can know, and more in that sense than its author can know. He can describe his goals as simply to write "a novel without a main hero" and say that the author "must understand every character and motivate his actions."[20] But the polyphonic novel will mean more to us than that, and the consequence of the message is clearly momentous in ways that so single-minded a man as Solzhenitsyn cannot have anticipated.

The idea of *The First Circle* as a polyphonic work has been pursued by many critics, and clearly it is an idea that can be put to effective use. In summary, it contends that the author "expresses himself . . . not so much through one character or another, but chiefly through the structure of the novel";[21] that in place of "a description of the social reality of his heroes" the author provides "a presentation of their world views," in general requiring a focus on articulate persons and "men of ideas"; and that "whereas in a monological novel . . . ideas usually constitute either its premises or conclusions, or else serve as a means of characterization, in a polyphonic novel ideas themselves become objects for portrayal." Thus polyphonic novels are "ideological novels," that is, "novels about ideas *as they are* embodied in people."[22]

The troubling thing in all of this is the suggestion that novels about ideas don't need the facts associated with "social reality." And, in fact, even so astute a scholar as Vladislav Krasnov will argue that "unlike *One Day* which is concerned mainly with the physical aspect of the Stalinist hell, *The First Circle* focuses on its metaphysical, or ideological, content."[23] We note the way in which ideological content is here assimilated to the domain of metaphysics, with the consequence that the novel itself is read predominantly as a philosophical and religious inquiry conducted along the lines of a Socratic dialogue. No doubt religious feeling played an important part in forming a mind like Solzhenitsyn's, but religious ideas as such are no more a determining presence in *The First Circle* than metaphysical disputes on the nature of reality. To speak of the novel as a polyphonic work must not be to deny that as an ideological novel its primary business is to indicate what ideas can and cannot do and how they can be evaluated in terms of the facts that we must ask them to address. *The First Circle* does not concern itself with the physical objects or with visual impressions of the world it studies. It is similarly not interested in family backgrounds or local influences that may in high-realist sociological novels account for the ideas or the conduct of characters. But its interest in social facts is unmistakable, if by social facts we mean the fundamental condition under which persons live in the Soviet Union. Polyphony in Solzhenitsyn reflects his desire to compel a particular response—the determination to resist—by recording the facts of the situation as truthfully as he can. In Solzhenitsyn, polyphony doesn't relativize the facts; rather, it demonstrates that no matter how valid different ideas may be in their own terms, no matter how intensely individuals may believe in this view or that of social and political reality, the essential facts—political, social, human—are available to all.

A substantial section of *The First Circle* is devoted to Joseph Stalin himself, and it is surely the most audacious feature of the novel. For one thing, it inevitably invites us to compare its portrayal with other portraits of the man, and thereby introduces into our reading of the novel a concern with documentary accuracy that we may not always think appropriate. Moreover, and this has often been remarked, the technique of inner monologue that is used to portray Stalin is willfully compromised by the bitter irony and undisguised hatred that figure in the presentation. This might not seem objectionable were it not that Solzhenitsyn scrupulously avoids this sort of presentation elsewhere. Even more objectionable in the view of some critics is the attempt "to capture, in the character and ambiance of a single human being, the sense and spirit of a particular age."[24] Though Stalin surely dominated the Soviet scene for many years, it is not clear that his thinking or his psychology were representative of those he dominated, and the attention paid precisely to his psychology might well lead one to wonder what Solzhenitsyn intended.[25]

Even briefly to examine fragments of the Stalin chapters is to see how misguided are the various critical objections that have surfaced. References to Tito and Hitler and Churchill abound, to be sure. Standard biographical information on Stalin is similarly brought forward. But none of this is presented as documentation. It is part of the *fictional* portrait of a tyrant who is known to us chiefly by the way he thinks and the fear he is shown to inspire in others. It is legitimate to compare the portrait with other portraits of the man, but the only thing one could legitimately find objectionable in Solzhenitsyn's characterization would be a violation of probability or a willful distortion of the historical record to support a trivial or adventitious interpretation. When we read that "he had trusted one person, one only, in a life filled with mistrust" and that "that man was Adolf Hitler," we cannot worry about some scholar's angrily coming forward to tell us of Stalin's having trusted several other figures as well. For it is plausible in terms of the portrait generally that Stalin should have trusted only Hitler. And, moreover, it is largely Stalin's own reading of the "fact" that we are given in the passage, transparent though Solzhenitsyn's view of that reading is at this point and elsewhere in these chapters. Finally, the "fact" is made believable and important by its relation to other comparable details Solzhenitsyn provides, as in the following reflection on the minister Abakumov: "Stalin knew all about Abakumov's secret wealth. But he was in no hurry to punish him. Stalin liked the fact that Abakumov was that kind of person. Self-seeking people are easier to understand and easier to manage. Most of all, Stalin was wary of people committed to staying poor, like Bukharin. He did not understand their motives." Just so, we may say, Stalin would have felt he understood the motives of a Hitler, with whom he could so largely identify. Only such a person would have been worthy of his trust.

Objections to the absence of fairness or "neutrality" in the portrait of Stalin are likewise based on a serious misunderstanding. For though Solzhenitsyn is generous to other characters, including those whose views he can only deplore, he is hardly neutral. He doesn't have to tell us what to think of Rubin's ideas because he has Nerzhin or Sologdin to argue against them. He doesn't have to tell us in so many words that Ruska made a fatal error in believing he could maintain his dignity while agreeing to serve as an informer. The organization of incident and the novel's emphasis on what are clearly superior traits of character instruct us in how we are to understand Ruska's behavior—charitably, and without forgiveness. Just so, the portrait of Stalin is not implausibly black or one-dimensional, and though it lacks some of the ambiguity we find elsewhere in the novel, it is not implausibly harsh. Stalin was brutal—fact. He inspired fear in others and encouraged them to be brutal to others in turn—fact. He was prisoner of his own manias and insecurities, and increasingly of his need to justify somehow what had definitively passed beyond any prospect of reasonable justification. Worse, looked at from a more or less innocent perspective, Stalin might well have been viewed as a pathetic, isolated, desperate, and lonely old man still—after so many years in power—concerned about his image and compelled to strike intimidating poses. This perspective especially Solzhenitsyn is determined to disallow, inviting it ever so briefly only to make it seem wholly untenable. When, in a final glimpse of Stalin, Solzhenitsyn describes him as old and failing and filled "with helpless terror," he does so not to make him pitiful, but so as to conclude with the sentence "Death had already made its nest in him, and he refused to believe it." Fact: Stalin too would die. Fact: As he could not bring himself to believe that, so he could not believe in other, comparable facts equally true and, from another perspective, obvious. (" 'So you believe there is still dissatisfaction among the people?' " Stalin at one point asks his minister, assuring himself that the malcontents constitute between five and eight percent of the population, unable as he is to see what anyone else would be expected to.) To object to unfairness in the portrait of Stalin is in effect to argue that in fairness one should be able to find evidence of a compensating humanity in the man. But, of course, it is precisely the facts that make it impossible to discover a basis on which to be fair to Stalin in the desired way. And when we speak of the facts here, we refer not only to the official Western, or adversary, version of the facts; we refer to the fact of the portrait itself, to its integrity and its ability to support the reading of the situation offered by the novel. To be fair to Stalin in the way some have recommended would be to suppose that the contemptuous irony and outright derision, directed not simply at Stalin's psychological aberrance but at his intellectual and philosophical pretensions, were somehow extraneous to a proper grasp of the figure.

Which takes us, of course, to the notion that Stalin does not in himself represent what he must for Solzhenitsyn's critique of the system to be persuasive. In fact, no conceivable person can represent the combination of mediocrity and brutality that is the Soviet system, though Solzhenitsyn's Stalin comes as close to the ideal as most of us can imagine. Critics of the novel want, apparently, a more typical figure, one whose everyday activities somehow stand for the activities of all those who make the system work. But, of course, there are several perfectly average functionaries or flunkies in the novel to accomplish this purpose, while Stalin's role is obviously different. He is not a functionary, not an average product of the system. He is, as Solzhenitsyn shows, obsessed with his own personal safety and with strengthening both his power and the prestige of his office. But he is not just a petty official or careerist trying to stay afloat; he is a leader who takes command of virtually everything he can grasp. His understanding of the problems he addresses may be poor, his solutions may reflect nothing more than his belief in the infallibility of his own brutal instincts, but he is, in Solzhenitsyn's portrait, a man whose capacity to do terrible things is large enough to justify our sense of him as an extraordinary figure. He is not impressive, he is not in any sense a world-historical figure like the magnificently calculating Lenin captured in the pages of Solzhenitsyn's *Lenin in Zurich*. He is, however, loathsome, commanding, and undistinguished in just the ways required to make him seem the right man to preside over an awesomely shabby apparatus like the Soviet bureaucracy.

What Solzhenitsyn had to avoid was any suggestion that Stalin was simply a replaceable bureaucrat who just happened to achieve power. It is not Solzhenitsyn's task in the novel to account for Stalin's emergence—that would be the subject of other works he would issue—but to show that "just as King Midas turned everything to gold, Stalin turned everything to mediocrity." The reason? Stalin "hated thoroughly successful performance because he saw in it a diminution of his own uniqueness." The consequence? "So even when he seemed to be straining in harness, Abakumov was pulling at half-strength—and so was everyone else." This is not in itself an adequate explanation or account of mediocrity, but it does serve to erect a presiding spirit that may be said to dominate the age. Solzhenitsyn's Stalin is a successful portrait because it persuasively establishes a range of facts that constitute the foundation of that spirit. The portrait is memorable not least for its demonstration that great power can be plausibly exercised by a very small man, provided only that he reflect his age and the main aspirations of his subjects.[26]

The chapters on Stalin in *The First Circle* support an idea of the Soviet situation as the more or less unchecked spread of a bureaucratic terror network. They also develop an idea of power that is essential to the novel. Always in debates on Communism the relation between ends and means has been a focal point. One sees this in Koestler's novel, as also in Merleau-Ponty's response to Koestler, entitled *Humanism and Terror*. These and hundreds of other works of various persuasions proceed from the assumption that only the immediate aim of a great political movement is power, that though evil is often done in the pursuit of that end, it is committed in the main by dedicated, or at least decent, persons who hope eventually to make a better world. Not all will agree that the world envisioned is truly better than the one that had to be destroyed, but all will find it comforting to suppose that there are ends beyond the execution of orders and the perpetuation of business as usual. In revolutionary periods this comforting belief is relatively easy to sustain. In an age of consolidation and administration it is more difficult, though not impossible, to keep alive. The exercise of power may not please those who are thwarted by it, but even victims are given to imagining the benevolent intentions of those who injure or oppress them, ostensibly for their own good.

Solzhenitsyn's Stalin is in no sense a benevolent despot, though he tells himself that he acts "for the sake of humanity" so as "to lead humanity to happiness." In fact, no matter what he tells himself, he is as close to an embodiment of pure power lust as we have had outside the antiutopian fictions of George Orwell and others working in that mode. It should not be hard to imagine Stalin, had he lived just a little longer, getting past the stale rationalizations and delivering the famous speech of Orwell's O'Brien in *1984:* "The party seeks power for its own sake," O'Brien begins. "We are not interested in the good of others. . . . One does not establish a dictatorship in order to safeguard a revolution; one makes a revolution in order to establish a dictatorship. The object of persecution is persecution. The object of torture is torture. The object of power is power." *The First Circle* is not an antiutopian fiction, which is to say, not a work that in order to sound a warning deliberately flouts realistic expectations as to what goes on in the world. But its portrait of Stalin reflects an analysis of totalitarian power that is quite as extreme as anything we associate with *1984*.[27] That we should now find such a portrait plausible, and believe as we do that *The First Circle* can accurately describe the Soviet conception of power in this way, is testimony to how far we have come in our comprehension of the facts Solzhenitsyn presents.

In this sense, to say that polyphony is both means and end in *The First Circle* is to avow its vital connection with the spirit of resistance that informs the novel and its function as antidote to the unmistakable facts. There is no denying that the authority Solzhenitsyn can attribute to the idea of resistance will derive in part from the facts that his resisters confront. Stalin is an imposing aspect of those facts. The Soviet apparatus, as an extension of Stalin's will and of the ideological principles that originally rationalized such a tyranny, is yet more imposing in the way that it is shown to affect everything. To accept the validity of a resistance conceived as moral intransigence one must accept that the facts utterly forbid practical political solutions. This does not entail a refusal to think politically, to try to understand the essential issues as having grown out of political conflicts. It does entail a willingness to see that the situation has passed beyond the likelihood that it can be remedied by a concerted political action undertaken by persons of courage and good will. Polyphony is conceived and projected as an end because it reflects a regard for various persons and points of view as valuable in themselves and for the dynamic relations they enable. It implicitly repudiates the idea that persons are instrumentalities, valuable for the extrinsic ends they can be made to serve. No doubt, it would be nice to think of polyphonic structure as a reflection of an open political system encouraging reasonable conflict and the hope of amicable, if provisional, resolutions. But polyphony in Solzhenitsyn is an ideal, a narrative embodiment of a response that can have no political expression or counterpart in the real world—the Soviet society—it addresses. The pluralism that seems so much a part of *The First Circle* is less the projection of a wish than the creation of an alternative universe that exists outside the political constraints that are everywhere present in Soviet society. The theorist Mikhail Bakhtin, who is credited with the invention of polyphony as a literary theory, described Dostoevski's pluralism as the image of "a church as a communion of non-confluent souls where the sinners and the righteous meet,"[28] and this is surely applicable to Solzhenitsyn as well. But Soviet society as portrayed in *The First Circle* will not allow an open meeting of these "non-confluent souls," and will insist that the communion they enjoy issue in nothing like a solidarity that could have political consequence. The commingling of earnest spirits may be considered valid and moving in its own terms, but it will necessarily seem insubstantial and disappointing in the context of all it cannot achieve.

Of course, it is tempting to argue that as the sharashka is a part of Soviet society, so the communion that takes shape there is genuinely a kind of political response to the attempted brutalization of the prisoners, many of whom resist the pervasive corruption to which they are exposed. But we shall have arrived at a very peculiar conception of politics when we conclude that the capacity of prisoners to exchange ideas and to honor diversity within the walls of a prison is a political response to the totalitarian exercise of power. Nerzhin and some of the other comrades speak occasionally of their having become stronger and wiser as a result of their prison experience. At times, says Nerzhin, he forgets that "I haven't had any real life for many years. . . . I'm weightless, suspended, disembodied." And he goes on to quote from "the book of the Sankhya" the line "For those who understand, human happiness is suffering." But the very terms of the wisdom brought forward here make it impossible to think of the sharashka experience as enabling a political response. Those who are weightless or disembodied are not in a position to take power or to move others to give it up or modify their plans. If polyphony in *The First Circle* is an end, it is an end that neither transcends nor addresses the political issues set in motion. It is an end that affirms the value of something that may be said to exist in spite of the extent to which it can be extinguished by commissars and bureaucrats. But the marginal existence of a threatened human capacity cannot be a sufficient end in a work that concerns itself, as this one does, with politics.

Outside of polyphony—conceived as means and end and therefore as, in some sense, the meaning of *The First Circle*—and outside of the survivalist humanitarianism that distinguishes some sharashka inmates, what might the novel offer in the way of a political vision? Or is it enough that the novel impresses on us the grimness of a situation that is the product of a political vision and that is maintained by a political system? Not many would think to hold Solzhenitsyn responsible for a positive vision that would show a way out of the situation he describes. It might reasonably be argued that *The First Circle* treats the Stalinist system ahistorically, as an unchanging phenomenon, thereby in effect "proving" an apolitical thesis: that no development or improvement is possible in a totalitarian order, and that no political resistance is likely to be effectual. But it is not Solzhenitsyn's intention to provide a definitive historical analysis of Stalinism, and he was clearly aware of tensions that might conceivably lead to important changes. Stalin himself is shown to think about crucial turning points in the consolidation of his power, and though it sometimes seems that there is no good reason to hope for improvement, characters do continue intermittently to hope, if only for the passing of the Stalin era itself. That Solzhenitsyn would have provided a more accurate reading of the situation by stressing the succession of political structures within the broadly continuous Bolshevik institutional framework says nothing of his grasp of the hard realities confronting Soviet citizens.[29] In this ultimately critical regard the novel is neither misleading nor a reflection of a disabling ignorance. The facts with which Solzhenitsyn is concerned are made palpable and credible in the novel, and the failure of his characters to invent political solutions is similarly a credible political fact.

Lukács, on the other hand, objects not to the absence of viable solutions but to the absence of a properly political perspective. Such a perspective would grow out of a historical emphasis on the individual as belonging to a group or class with changing interests and strategies. He recognizes that some periods give "honest critics and reformers no opportunity to act," and that such persons "must succumb to a certain social and personal alienation." But in Solzhenitsyn, Lukács argues, "the leap into action does not even appear as something that was once possible, even if problematic."[30] The situation is conceived in political terms, the facts are accurately and soberly marshaled, the effects movingly detailed. What we miss is a sense of continuing political concern, the attempt to see individual growth as blocked by the failure to translate personal initiative into collective purpose. To think in terms of collective purpose, to recall or envision the possibility of action is not, Lukács concedes, necessarily to act; it is to struggle for a perspective that will be adequate to the facts.

The key to the problem, according to Lukács, is Solzhenitsyn's fondness for "crotchety eccentricity." The character Sologdin is a case in point.

What do his various principles amount to, Lukács asks, "but a whim of an eccentric"? Of what serious use is "his over-anxious avoidance of all words of foreign origin, which he . . . believes to be pretentious"? We may admire Sologdin, but we are forced to regard his finally trivial principles as his purely personal attempt to deny "certain forms of the society in which he is forced to live." This denial is managed "in such a way that his inner integrity . . . remains intact," but the price he pays is that "he must remain enmeshed in a more or less abstractly distorted inwardness."[31] What is more, other characters conduct themselves in the same way and are similarly made to seem admirable by an author who cares more for moral inflexibility than for a determination to act on the sources of one's discontent.

What Lukács will not see, of course, is that eccentricity is not always a product of distortion but of a will to resist that has penetrated to the very foundations of character. Is this neurotic or unhealthy? Sologdin's insistence on certain things that do not seem important to others is no proof of his alienation from reality. On the contrary, he remains viable as a person because he has attached himself to convictions that enable resistance. He is incorruptible because he has taken possession of himself in a way that prevents others from controlling him as they would like. His way is not the way of revolutionary or even of collectivist politics, and he is bound to seem merely eccentric to anyone for whom rational behavior is simply the capacity to engage in viable political activity. But Sologdin is more than his various whims, and though Solzhenitsyn clearly does not think him a definitive answer to the problems he confronts, to define him simply as an eccentric is to underestimate the potential political significance of a will to resist that is vested so deeply in every aspect of a personality.

More important for our purposes is the distinction Lukács draws between a "plebeian" and a "communist" perspective. This distinction extends the critique of eccentricity and focuses for Lukács the major theoretical deficiency in *The First Circle*. For if figures like Sologdin and Rubin seem in the end nothing but eccentrics, even the more reliable Nerzhin identifies what objective hope there is in the peasant Spiridon and thereby certifies his own addiction to an eccentric perspective that distorts his relation to the facts. Or so Lukács argues. Why? Because a man like Nerzhin, understanding as he does the objective components of the Soviet situation, cannot willfully adopt a plebeian perspective without distorting what he knows and denying himself the possibility of an action based on his knowledge. It is legitimate to see in Spiridon an embodiment of "the people," but he is that embodiment "precisely because [his] life, abundantly filled with blows of fate, again and again gives rise to the questions which cannot be answered by his view of life." One may justly credit the "genuineness" and even the goodness of his "simple peasant instincts," but one must also consider that a man who can first become "a victim of the new collective farm system" and shortly afterwards "eagerly" assist in its establishment ought not to be accepted as a model of wisdom. Nerzhin is to be admired for seeing Spiridon's "ignorant perfection." He is to be criticized for failing to see that peasant wisdom "neither provides a foundation for nor enlarges his mental world," and that the ignorance of the people must be "overcome" if they are to be moved toward "revolutionary re-birth."[32] And if Nerzhin is to be criticized, so must Solzhenitsyn be, for his seeming to acquiesce in Nerzhin's eccentric appropriation of Spiridon.

This reading of the novel is illuminating, of course, and it has the special virtue of demanding a clear definition of Solzhenitsyn's politics; but it has the defect of refusing to consider where Solzhenitsyn stands in relation to his characters. We have said that the polyphonic novel embodies an ideal that can have no political expression or counterpart in the real world it addresses. If this is so, then the question to be asked is: How aware is the novelist of the limitations inherent in his narrative procedure and in the ideological objectives associated with that procedure? Lukács routinely identifies Solzhenitsyn with Nerzhin and assumes that the horizon of the novelist's vision is the horizon of the character's reflections on Spiridon. That this is misleading is best demonstrated by seeing (1) how much more complex is Nerzhin's relationship to peasant wisdom than Lukács reports, and (2) how Solzhenitsyn indicates throughout the novel his desire for a politics that the situation will not allow him to imagine concretely or pursue.

The clearest account of Nerzhin's relationship to "the people" is given in Chapter 61, entitled "Going to the People." There, what is celebrated is not Nerzhin's identification with Spiridon, but his ability to go to him in search of a wisdom both Rubin and Sologdin spurn, possessed as they are by an "absolute truth" that blinds them to anything else. Nerzhin does not in fact buy the image of ignorant perfection presented with "swooning . . . compassion" in nineteenth-century Russian literature. His intimacy with ordinary people allows him to see that they "were of no greater stature than he. They did not endure hunger and thirst any more stoically . . . they were no more foresighted or adroit than he . . . they were blinder and more trusting about informers. They were more prone to believe the crude deception of the bosses . . . and they were also greedier for petty things." Conclusion? "What was lacking in most of them was that personal *point of view* which becomes more precious than life itself." To be one of "the people" is not, then, to hope to be like Spiridon or like any other ignorant person. One could seek inspiration from a Spiridon not in order to imitate him, but to enhance capacities that were fundamentally one's own. The more one worked "to temper, to cut, to polish one's soul so as to become *a human being*," the more one would realize what was precious in one's self. In that way alone might one hope to become "a tiny particle of one's own people."

What has this to do with politics? In the first place, it demonstrates that, insofar as Nerzhin is thought to be the central figure in the novel, the point of view promoted cannot be called plebeian. Second, it points to the way in which Nerzhin's detachment from the plebeian perspective is in part empowered by his political insight, so that "the crude deception of the bosses" will necessarily figure in his evaluation of those to whom he is attracted. This is no occasional concern in Nerzhin, and it is extended in the exchanges and reflections of other characters so as to become the dominant concern of the novel. No wonder the Spiridon chapters (61–63) are followed by a chapter called "Clenched Fists," in which Rubin and Sologdin ferociously debate the political and practical implications of the higher morality. Though hardly a pointed elaboration of what it means to become "a tiny particle of one's own people," the chapter does deliberately provide another set of terms by which to define *"a human being"* and the political responsibilities of those whose souls have been amply polished.

But the more elusive issue has to do, again, with Solzhenitsyn's desire for a politics that the situation will not allow him to imagine concretely or pursue. It is an elusive issue because it tempts one to conclude that in the end Solzhenitsyn has no politics. That is to say, his attraction to categorical moral postures and affection for traditional Christian virtues like resignation and endurance[33] may allow him to think he can do without a politics. Though this is not in itself a reason to condemn a work, some would argue that novels that set in motion political conflicts must think the issues through in the relevant political terms. *The First Circle* is in this sense a political novel whether or not Solzhenitsyn wished to think of it in that way, and he is responsible to his material regardless of the other ostensibly "higher" responsibilities he may have thought to fulfill. This seems to me a convincing argument, and it stipulates the grounds on which a case must be made for the success of Solzhenitsyn's work. *The First Circle* is a convincing novel because it does not evade the responsibility assigned by the material itself. It has a politics—not a political ideology, but a political vision of that which human beings require, minimally, to live decently with one another. The vision is political because it insists again and again that what human beings need is denied to them by a political system, and that until that system is changed, the situation cannot improve. The novel is not a lamentation or a pious celebration of saints who turn away from the world to seek a personal salvation. The situation presented matters to us because, as Solzhenitsyn presents it, it cannot be transcended or ignored. When Nerzhin thinks of the "inviolable decision" that "took root in him: to learn and understand! To learn and understand!," the context of that decision is the political reality that will necessarily affect everything he can learn.

Possibly the most significant, though also the most disturbing, political reflection in *The First Circle* occurs in the chapters excluded from the first edition so as to permit the book to get through the Soviet censors.[34] Nothing contained in these chapters should surprise a reader who has followed carefully the arguments presented elsewhere in the standard English-language edition, though it is fair to say that certain conclusions are presented more emphatically in the missing chapters. The "new" Chapter 44, for example, follows Innokenti Volodin on a trip to the countryside with his sister-in-law, Klara Makarygin. What they discover and together reflect on is, in the words of Stephen Carter, "the squalor of Russian rural life," a pervasive "ugliness," "the lies of the press, destruction of churches, degradation of peasant life," and so on: In sum, all that, taken together with other facts powerfully set before us in the novel, can prepare us for the terrifying ruminations of Nerzhin in "missing" Chapter 90.

What Nerzhin comes to is the thought that, since no revolt against the Soviet system is likely to be successful; since most Soviet citizens have been in any case spiritually destroyed in the course of efforts to get by in intolerable circumstances; and since no help can come—as Carter has it— "from the appeasement-minded west or from the USA," the Russian people will have to enter a new era if they are to be reborn. That new era is envisaged as part of an "apocalyptic and mysterious prediction," namely, that nothing less than a nuclear war is likely to bring into being a decent society in the Soviet Union. Nerzhin doesn't espouse such a war—how could he, given that he is resistant even to the limited violence proposed in the same chapter by Gerasimovich?—but he does yield vaguely to the messianic apocalyptism that is a sure component of an "optimism" predicated on nuclear holocaust.

Does the fact that Nerzhin entertains such a vision discredit retrospectively everything he has previously said in the novel? Does it warrant our concluding that he has nothing to offer us but moral sentiments and the example of personal courage? We come back to the idea of polyphony, to our conviction that Nerzhin is not the hero of *The First Circle,* and that in any case we cannot simply sum him up by pinning to him the horrific speculations he delivers in a single chapter. Just so, if Nerzhin cannot so readily be defined and dismissed, neither can we identify Solzhenitsyn's politics with speculations or recommendations isolated in a given chapter. What we find in *The First Circle* is a will-to-politics embodied in the ardent theorizings and explicit proposals brought forward by the various characters. This will-to-politics is tested, continuously, against the situation out of which everything is made to emerge and to which it in turn refers. Another way of describing polyphony here is given in the words *contradiction* and *correction.* This is to say that, as in other great novels, characters and formulated attitudes are exposed to the implicit criticism of the whole novelistic context. Especially a positive figure like Nerzhin must be intermittently exposed to contradiction or made to utter what he cannot entirely support or understand. Why? Precisely to demonstrate the distortions and excesses to which the situation condemns even those who are most equipped to deal with it. It is Solzhenitsyn's political grasp of the Soviet reality that determines his rejection of a unitary perspective from which comforting answers to intractable dilemmas may be made to issue. So, try though he will to make Nerzhin more or less equal to the fate he has chosen, Solzhenitsyn must impress on us the terrible price Nerzhin will pay for whatever spiritual and intellectual satisfaction he may achieve. The inability of a politically sophisticated and courageous man to conceive a political strategy that might conceivably be worth pursuing is itself a political fact of primary importance in *The First Circle*. And what better measure is there than this of the control exercised by totalitarian systems?

What we are left with is not a truth or message that can be isolated and made to take the place of the novel. Individual utterances—one thinks of Sologdin's statement that *"the higher the ends, the higher must be the means! Dishonest means destroy the ends themselves"*—may in themselves seem unobjectionable and stirring, but the novel is not concerned with utterances in themselves. Attitudes, in fact, are developed, challenged, and reformulated in waves of alternating intensity. What emerges is not a single attitude, some *result* of all that has gone before, but a sense that certain things are real, that one had better understand what they are, and that true wisdom at present consists in resisting, as best one can, what is mandated by the established political power to which one will in any case succumb. Is this an instance of a misconceived tragic humanism? The sheer weight of political fact, detail, and argument should indicate how hard Solzhenitsyn has worked to establish the basis on which believable characters can plausibly have arrived at the various convictions they hold. Only if the Soviet system had been observed abstractly, the available alternatives regarded from the predictable perspective of a superior, disillusioned resignation, would the epithet *tragic humanism* serve to indict what Solzhenitsyn has done. As it is, there is nothing factitious in the spirited hopelessness that permeates *The First Circle*. If it is not enough to engage a fully imagined political circumstance with all of the diversity and cunning we expect of a great novelist, without suggesting that the last word has been found, what *will* seem enough?

7

Nadine Gordimer: Public and Private

There is a kind of imagination for which personal relations can seem meaningful only when they are touched or threatened by a turmoil associated with the political realm. Such an imagination ordinarily concerns itself with the will to power and with the lengths to which individuals may go to leave a scar on the map. Even when it likes to believe it is interested in persons, it does all it can to make us feel that persons are in fact actors in what they themselves take to be an ongoing historical drama that determines the judgments they are inclined to make. The actors may not wish to devalue the personal relations in which they engage, but the imagination that controls them cannot but insist that those relations are at most a cover for the more significant activity in which those very actors participate, or ought to participate. It is not that political activity invariably enables an otherwise shabby or mediocre existence—most often it is shown to have quite the opposite effect—but the imagination I am describing finds in political activity a way of coming to terms with the promise and limitations of the self-as-agent that is thought to confer meaning as no merely intimate exchange can do. Political actors may, it is true, speak of more than strategies and programs and enemies; they may quarrel about infidelity in marriage or about household finances, but they know when they do so that they are straying from the main business to which even ordinary persons are called. They may take their time getting back to that business, or may stay out of the way of political temptation altogether, but they will inevitably pay a price for what will seem a resistance to reality itself. The very intimacies they sought as a refuge from the chaos of the public realm will more and more appear to them as petty, narrow, humanly diminishing.

Nadine Gordimer is the most accomplished of all of the novelists who have operated with something like the imaginative disposition I have cited. She is also the most innovative, having revised our sense of what a work operating in such terms can do. She has, in fact, reconceived the very idea of private experience and created a form that can accommodate microscopic details of individual behavior and sentiment without suggesting for a moment that individuals are cut off from the collective consciousness and political situations characteristic of their societies. To compare what she has done with the novels of André Malraux, for example, is to see how much more interested she is in human motive conceived not simply as instinct, but as the product of all that makes a person different from any other while clearly responsive to ordinary human pressures. And this complication of motive in Gordimer has the further merit of relegating the will to power to the status of a second-order phenomenon, dependent as it must be on other factors if it is to figure prominently in the lives of cultivated persons. To compare is also to see how much more liberty she grants her characters to behave in ways not expected of figures situated as they are, whatever the power of political determinants that may account in part for the choices they make. What Malraux gains in dramatic urgency by identifying characters unmistakably with particular positions or imperatives and pitting them against one another, Gordimer gains by casting long shadows of doubt over everything while insisting that the object of an equivocation stand forth as vividly as the object of a straightforward assertion. Less disposed than Malraux to translate political conflicts into conflicts of will, she is more patient even with characters she doesn't like and less inclined to view complex moral issues as minor when placed alongside of issues more readily resolved by intelligence and persistence.

Political novels almost invariably tend to make one feel that private life is, if not quite inferior to public life, then less interesting. Writers like Malraux will occasionally enter the bedrooms of characters to show that they do in fact have private lives, but what is enacted in those bedrooms is destined to emphasize perspectives more significantly associated with the "larger life" of those characters. We learn little from Ferral's transactions with his mistress in *Man's Fate* that cannot be made clear in his dealings with subordinates in the course of an ordinary workday. The episodes involving Ferral's mistress are effective as narrative, but they serve principally to point us toward a view of Ferral as exploiter cum capitalist. Just so, Malraux has his hero Kyo confront his wife's casual sexual infidelity not because he considers marital relations interesting in themselves, but because they indicate how elusive a goal is the freedom these people demand.

Gordimer is, by contrast, as interested in persons and their relationships as in the idea of power, and much that she writes calls into question the notion that a person is nothing but the position he occupies in a given political spectrum. Mehring, the protagonist and central consciousness of Gordimer's 1974 novel *The Conservationist,* is a pig-iron dealer whose relation to blacks is entirely typical of other affluent South African whites. But one never feels that Gordimer pursues him simply to make a case against apartheid or to say that the activities of third world capitalists inevitably coarsen their powers of moral discrimination. Mehring is more than what he may be said to represent because his comings and goings, among blacks and whites, for purposes of pain and purposes of pleasure, are invariably interesting to Gordimer in themselves. They are interesting as discernible empirical facts in a world of other comparable facts. They are interesting in the sense that attention to them forces one also to engage the very texture of a man's thoughts and feelings.

But though everything that happens in *The Conservationist* is deeply implicated in the standard social and political schemes that dominate South African society, the book is not properly described as a political novel. Political ideas in the novel are rarely granted the independent life and force they assume in political novels. Mehring is aware of the familiar objections to the way he lives. He reads magazines and newspapers and even thinks twice before saying certain unpleasant things to blacks who live on his farm. Now and again he debates with his mistress the real meaning and intent of his industrial and entrepreneurial activity. But nothing like a fully embodied, autonomous political idea emerges from all of this. Mehring doesn't finally operate in terms of an ideology; neither does he pride himself especially on managing to do without one. It seems not to occur to him to justify what he does or thinks by articulating a position that is more or less coherent and, in that sense at least, defensible. He is intelligent, but he lacks the ability to confront with genuine lucidity what Gordimer calls "the conglomeration of circumstances and inherited attitudes that make up the inner personality."[1] This is to say that, for Mehring, personal life is conceivable only as a refuge from and an alternative to public life, and that by making him the center of consciousness in her novel, Gordimer has here decided not to write a political novel as such. Throughout, the novel elaborates an implicit critique of Mehring's false consciousness, but the critique remains implicit and politics remains very much a background, a climate rather than a system of power relations, ideologies, and institutions that might be addressed in some determinate way.

Now, it is not necessary for a novel to take a firm position on the issues it raises to operate as a political novel. It must, though, raise those issues in such a way that they seem unmistakably to be political issues. The personal dimension inserted in the work may be no less interesting or critical to our sense of what matters, but we must be made to feel that the personal dimension is conceived on the same plane as the political events. The intensity we associate with political conflict saturates everything in a political novel, and the consciousness of central figures is never very far removed from political issues. Though characters may not understand perfectly what is happening around them, the novel itself must work to discern a historical pattern and to project the future shape of events. Trotsky was far too doctrinaire in attacking Malraux for the absence in his work of "a scientific mind [that can] foresee the general direction of the [historical] process,"[2] but he was certainly right to demand that a political novel conduct its inquiries into human events as if there were a discernible historical process and some prospect of identifying a "general direction."

Gordimer's novels—all of them—are remarkable for their conviction that characters are inevitably caught up in a process that carries them in particular directions without altogether controlling what they become. Even in her early works it was possible to see the cogency of her statement that "politics is character—in South Africa,"[3] though it was not always clear that Gordimer wished to write political novels as such. By the time she wrote *The Conservationist* one could conclude that her classically straightforward political novel, *A Guest of Honour* (1970), was no occasional experiment, but it was far from certain that she would go on to write what is by every measure one of the best political novels of our period, namely, *Burger's Daughter* (1979). To speak of *The Conservationist* as another kind of book is not to deny its interest in public affairs or its effective portrayal of Mehring as a representative South African white. But there is no use in contending, as more than one critic has done, that "the fundamental questions of the novel" are: "Who shall inherit Africa? How shall it be conserved?"[4] These questions are, to be sure, a part of the novel's design; they are decidedly *not* fundamental to the reader's unfolding experience of the novel. To assert their prominence is to privilege message or interpretation over *fabula* in the case of a novel whose message is never certain and whose interest in the pinning down of its subject, of its own narrative focus, is very much the center of the work. What makes *The Conservationist* so rich a novel is its ambivalent relation to the material it examines, its commitment to the "unknown signs" it discovers in the material and to its own tentative reading of those signs. Part of the ambivalence is reflected in the novel's intermittent reflection on palpable political issues and in its allowing those issues to be submerged again and again beneath the screen of semiconscious rumination that is here the primary narrative medium. The question "Who shall inherit Africa?" is important, of course, but it cannot be said to be fundamental unless it can be made now and then to stand clear of the fragmentary consciousness that occasionally entertains it in the work. What is fundamental in *The Conservationist* is the process by means of which Mehring continually persuades himself that the private sphere he occupies is his to shape and to dominate. It is a novel of consciousness, not a novel of ideas. It engages necessity not primarily as an effect of circumstance, but as a function of its protagonist's relentless self-deception. The novel knows ever so much more than Mehring knows, but its knowledge is kept implicit in deference to its fundamental object, which is the examination of a false consciousness that is endemic in a situation like Mehring's. Exactly what makes that false consciousness endemic the novel intimates but does not choose to examine frontally. It is preoccupied more with the analysis of the phenomenon than with the reconstitution of its ostensive cause.

The novel *Burger's Daughter*, another study in consciousness, demonstrates how such a work may at the same time be conceived as a political novel. It shows, too, how the relation between public and private issues can be handled so as to privilege neither the one nor the other, though public issues are made to dominate the lives even of persons who think they've achieved a separate peace. Most of all, it proves that a great novel, in seeking to accommodate various purposes, trying to be absolutely itself and like no other, doesn't deny the validity of its own generic limitations so much as it extends our sense of the relevant genre. *The Conservationist* doesn't really belong to the tradition of the political novel, though it may be said to incorporate in its narrative system paradigms we associate with that kind of work. *Burger's Daughter* is a political novel in the sense that its most fully elaborated narrative situations are destined to engage political questions. One may say that it is a novel of consciousness, but the statement must be modified to include the fact that the central consciousness is very largely preoccupied with public issues. One may say that it is a novel of generational conflict and reconciliation, but the conflict has largely to do with competing ways of bearing witness to one's sense of the public world. More, the novel's achieved reconciliation takes the form of a political affirmation so definite as almost to assume the shape of a contract. Finally, one may describe *Burger's Daughter* as a retrospective homage to generations past, a kind of historical novel without the fancy-dress apparatus and worked-up documentary cast that often characterizes such works; but then one must also say of the novel that its retrospection is rarely valedictory, that its interest in the past is colored by its continuing desire to make sense of and participate more effectively in the present, and that its focus on a consciousness unfolding in time undercuts whatever interest it might have in isolating or memorializing a particular time past. The dominant mode of *Burger's Daughter* is finally progressive rather than retrospective. In its movement toward reconciliation and affirmation it is a novel of growth, with that growth conceived as the achievement of a combined personal and political maturity. In the universe created by *Burger's Daughter*, to come to terms with oneself is to confront without illusion the circumstance one has inherited and in which one must live. One may not always do the right thing, whatever one's intentions, and one may fail to understand what seems apparent, but one will know there can be no such thing as a separate peace for those who opt for growth as it is recommended in the novel. This is a kind of knowledge that is encompassed as well in *The Conservationist*, though there the observation is more oblique, the motives more ambiguous, the figured consequences more strictly personal. *Burger's Daughter* is the greater work in knowing more entirely what it wishes to do without compromising its commitment to a variety of secondary purposes. It is, like the other work, a "book of unknown signs," but it is rather more willing than the earlier book to consider the origins of those signs and to propose a system for considering not only what they mean, but to what effect they operate in the novel.

The primary unknown sign in *Burger's Daughter* is, surely, Rosa Burger's resistance to all that her recently deceased father represents. We are entitled to describe this as a kind of unknown sign because it means more than Rosa or her creator are willing at any point to say. To be sure, there are plausible reasons offered for such a daughter's refusal to follow in the footsteps even of so patently admirable and lovable a man as Lionel Burger. An intelligent young woman, she obviously wishes to make choices for herself and to discover what she is most suited to do. More, there is something distasteful in the way in which her father's associates—"the faithful"—routinely say and do exactly what one would have expected of them and thereby make it possible to think of most of them collectively rather than as individuals. Their "example" frightens Rosa. Finally, there is the forbidding spectacle of her parents' imprisonment and their consequent untimely demise. No inspiring meaning attached to the manner of their lives and deaths can make their fates seem attractive to someone anxious to enlarge the scope of her experience and to know pleasure as something other than the satisfaction of having done "the right thing."

The unknown sign, then, is here a function of Rosa's seeming to resist her father's example for reasons that go beyond those offered in the novel. In the same way, Rosa's eventual decision to abandon the "separate peace" she is about to achieve in Europe operates as another unknown sign. One wonders what can possibly have moved Rosa to return to South Africa when everything she has heard and thought would indicate the futility of such a reversal. The unknown sign is not in either case simply an open or unanswered question, it is a crux that compels us to wonder about the relation between politics and character. It invites a reading of events that points to the insufficiency of the reading itself and of the assumptions on which such readings are founded. For if Rosa's critical decisions—to leave South Africa and the world of her father, to return to South Africa and, in effect, to take her father's place in prison—are crucial to the design of this novel, then they are crucial also in focusing what are the main assumptions both of characters and of readers. Those assumptions, we shall see, have more to do with the relation between public and private than most readers are willing to concede.

We begin, as we must, with Lionel Burger, who dominates the novel. He dominates because Rosa Burger cannot help thinking of him and measuring what she does by his example. He dominates because he embodies a principle of order that is made to seem imposing, even authoritative, though in fact he has no actual authority by means of which to enforce his idea of order. Lionel Burger is the representative of a transcendent order that serves in the novel to challenge the legitimacy of other kinds of order. He challenges the order of the earthly powers, those political leaders who have mandated and supported the intolerable system that is South African apartheid; and he challenges what may be called the popular order, the order that belongs to those who live private lives and are content to cultivate the intimacies that are part of ordinary domestic experience.[5] He challenges these alternative and obviously more familiar kinds of order by living a life that is both coherent and clearly responsive to "a standard of justice referring to an order beyond that already realized in existing institutions."[6] The power of his example is in part a function of his operating in a world which has no persuasive standard of justice, whatever the academic rigors of the so-called legal system. His exemplary power is also a function of the way in which private life has come to be conceived in the modern world as the routine privilege of an entirely autonomous person beholden to nothing but his own satisfaction and largely unaware of civic obligation. Lionel Burger serves as a presiding presence in the sense that he represents the possibility of an authority that is neither reducible to power nor an expression of contempt for what is ameliorative and ordinary. But he is also distinctive in serving more by virtue of what he is than of what he accomplishes. The key to Gordimer's political vision lies in the ideal of character that evolves from Rosa Burger's efforts to make peace with her father's example.

Lionel Burger is at once an activist and a patriarch, a sower of the seeds of disorder and a stable center around which numbers of people gather to discover where they are to go. He is, or seems to be, that most tiresome of radicals: a genuinely good man who believes in what he is doing and forgives even those who betray him. We have virtually no sense of him outside of Rosa's memories and reflections, but we accept without any hesitation that he was what his daughter remembers. Now and then, unsavory doubts on the subject of his perfect virtue are raised, but we are ready to defend that virtue even when we learn how without qualm he could use people in the service of his cause. His political enemies are, of course, afraid of him and deplore his ambitions, but they too must grudgingly admit that he is an impressive and admirable man. They do not, of course, see what his daughter can see in him, and they are in any case too busy trying to throw a net over him and his associates to stop and consider his actual merits. For a "commie," though, he certainly seems to his fellow Afrikaaners a solid man, and many are said to lament his radicalism as a loss to the community. Had Lionel Burger chosen differently, he'd have become a first-rate prime minister.

To portray a character in this way is necessarily to risk making him seem a sort of overgrown boy scout, and were it not for Gordimer's fine irony and constantly shifting perspectives, that is indeed what Lionel might seem. He is almost too good, too right, to be true. But then one reflects on what the man has actually done, and one concludes that his daring and steadfastness are really quite plausible. What he does, in effect, is to insist that South African blacks and whites together make a revolution based, apparently, not on terrorist activities but on strikes, fellowship meetings, and open refusal to honor the color barrier. The image one has of him is of a kindly patriarch cooking wieners over an open fire and serving them up to a chummy collection of black and white radicals, their sprawling families, and a number of slightly queasy though enthusiastic fellow travelers. Or one sees him addressing a crowded court room, eloquently attacking feudal social forms and capitalist exploitation, lucidly reciting the Marxist litany of revolution even as he is about to be carried away for a term of life imprisonment. What makes these images moving and believable is the freshness and the obliquity with which they are presented, the way in which they are undercut or threatened by the wand of irony that passes, not always lightly, over everything in this novel. For though Rosa Burger is very much in thrall to the typical images of her patriarch father inspiring his followers, she is also sensitive to the view of him as quaint, maybe even absurd or a little monstrous in his imperturbable conviction. She is as amused by the idea of him as "God's man" as by the opposition's idea of him as "a devil . . . destroying Christian civilization." Like those who follow him, he is "good . . . in spite of the [occasional] sanctimony." And though there is inevitably something absurd about people so single-minded as Lionel and his comrades—they are described at their Sunday barbecue gatherings as "revolutionaries at play, a sight like the secret meeting of whales"*—they are invariably forgiven their excesses. Lionel emerges as not only steadfast and true, but as reasonably sensible; not a fanatic, but a man who will proceed patiently to accomplish what ought not to be an impossible vision.

The problem in all of this is that in making Lionel good and in accrediting the transparent rightness of his course, Gordimer has neglected to demonstrate how a man like Burger operates in the political world outside his Sunday backyard gatherings and courtroom trials—that is, she has decided not to go into the unpleasant side of Burger's activities. Are we to believe there is none? Is it reasonable to suggest, or to allow one's reader to infer, that a Marxist revolutionary can keep his hands clean as he goes about the business of fomenting revolutionary unrest? So modest are the "depravities" Lionel commits that one might almost be expected to think them amiable, or cute, at worst a little sly. So he asks his daughter to pretend to be engaged to a young man in prison in order that she be allowed to visit him and pass secrets back and forth between them. No real harm seems to be done here, and anyone even modestly committed to the revolution will consider this sort of thing a worthy deception.

In the same way, we are told of how Lionel got others to practice deceptions, presumably playing skillfully on their insecurities, their guilts, their desire to do "the right thing" despite their unwillingness to endanger their lives by making openly radical avowals. But we are never permitted actually to witness Lionel's skillful operations. Nothing approaching an

---

* The words belong to the drifter Conrad, not Rosa, but there is a sense in which Rosa also sees the revolutionaries as remote and exotic.

unsavory spectacle is ever shown us.* In fact, we are told, there wasn't much of that nature to show. Whatever we may think of Communists generally ought not to be applied here. The South African Communists of Lionel's generation "made a Communism for 'local conditions,' " Rosa reflects. "The political activities and attitudes of that house came from the inside outwards." Not ideological purity and narrow-mindedness but character made Lionel the man he was and moved others to follow his lead. His opposite number, an "enlightened" Afrikaaner apologist for apartheid, speaks of Lionel's addiction to the Marxist principle, to "the notion of the historically immutable solution," but Gordimer asks us to understand this in other terms. To describe him as a Marxist is not adequately to see Lionel Burger.[7]

We must remember in all of this that it is Rosa Burger who tells us most of what we know of Lionel. But Rosa's consciousness is an exacting and subtle instrument, and it incorporates a variety of thoughts and perspectives that do not so much belong to her as pass through her on the way to some tentative resolution. The most telling of these antithetical perspectives is associated with a young man named Conrad, to whom parts of the novel are addressed and who assumes the guise of an alter ego, alternately drawing Rosa out and challenging her version of things. His contributions to the narrative, generally obliquely presented as a part of Rosa's stream of consciousness, help us to see Lionel more clearly than Rosa wants to. She listens carefully to what Conrad says, has obviously absorbed the ironies and criticisms directed at her father, and is at last affected by them in a deep and permanent way. But she has a habit of deflecting the main point of the criticism in a way that Gordimer is assiduous to expose. For all her impressive grasp of the meaning of Lionel's life, there are things that Rosa does not see.

Conrad comes to his ambivalent affection for the Burger enterprise from the outside. Neither a radical nor a radical sympathizer, he is nonetheless driven to penetrate to the secret wellspring of radical enthusiasm. His exploratory forays are often shrewd, and though his sympathies are never definitively enlarged, he does correctly identify what apparently is missing in the South African Communist. This is, to put it boldly, a properly developed historical sense that can temper present enthusiasms and raise doubts about some current objectives. More specifically, Conrad invokes the Moscow purge trials, the abortive Prague spring of 1968, and other memorable disasters on the way to concluding that "Communists are the last optimists." Opposition to apartheid is one thing, he suggests, a so-called worker's state is another. Belief in oneself may be misguided, but

---

* In a letter sent to me by Nadine Gordimer on January 23, 1983, I am urged to remember that Lionel's modest depravities may "mean involving in great risk those whom he has charmed." The substantiating details are fully persuasive, as also the statement that "whether or not one considers such recruitments 'an unsavory spectacle' depends on one's attitude to oppression, and to revolution as the necessary means of overthrowing it."

it is surely more promising than belief in a future in which social conflict has been eliminated once and for all. That way lies delusion and fanaticism. And it is precisely those who pretend to have studied history to come up with an account of its laws who seem most inclined to ignore what recent history at least so clearly shows.

Now, it is true that, so far as we can tell, Lionel and his associates never really think about the Moscow trials or the Prague spring. But it is also likely that, had they considered these at all, they would have decided that such events were the consequences of situations drastically different from theirs and therefore not strictly applicable. In South Africa, at least, the enemy was unmistakable; the need for solidarity against exploitative whites bent on maintaining apartheid was beyond question. To bear witness on behalf of one's conviction that blacks could not be maintained as an inferior and dependent population had nothing to do with Soviet tanks. And one's hope for an eventual socialist state could not be darkened by thoughts of what such hopes had come to elsewhere. There was too much to do in the present to allow oneself to be distracted by spectral possibilities.

There are other examples of Communist parties or groups that set themselves apart from the international movement or simply pursued their objectives in more or less blithe disregard of other developments occurring in the name of their creed, but none of these have been evoked with quite the cozy insularity more or less insisted on in Gordimer's narrative. Though Gordimer underscores the limitations and inaccuracies of such a perspective, her characters seem not fully to grasp what their view of themselves entails. Even Rosa falls short of fully understanding. The key to this failure is located in Conrad's observation that "being brought up in a house like your father's is growing up in a devout family. . . . It was all taken in with your breakfast cornflakes." And the key is further identified in Rosa's reflection that "we belonged to other people" or that the vital "connection" among radical militants was very much like "the memory of childhood warmth for me." All of which is to say that the main figures in this novel avoid thinking of themselves simply as Communists with blood on their hands by usefully dwelling on immediate objectives and feeling that they belong to a close-knit extended family with obligations not unlike those agreed on by close relations. Rosa affirms this vision even as she laments her inability to remain within the bosom of the family. Her instinct to escape from the suffocating family embrace is countered by the constant tribute she pays them as "the ones who matter" and by her sense of their supportive, nurturant warmth.

The image of Lionel as beneficent patriarch, then, has much to do with the sense of family that permeates the novel. In an important way it might be said that *Burger's Daughter* is a novel about familial bonds and the way in which they inform a certain kind of political vision. That vision of politics is pitted against another view in this novel, and out of that conflict comes what we may take to be a larger view that encompasses the others without presuming to banish or transcend them. But the central view, the view to which the novel accords its greatest affection and attention, if not the full measure of respect one might have expected, is the view associated with Lionel. That view of politics as the concerted activity of an extended though intimate family is based on a conception of the necessary interpenetration of public and private in the quest for a better world. This amounts to a conviction that, in making a revolution, one is in part at least living the sort of life one would wish others eventually to lead. In thinking constantly about social justice, in working to create responsive political institutions, and in reaching out to different kinds of persons without regard to their status or color, Lionel Burger enacts the objective possibility he envisions. One never feels about him or his associates what Malraux feels about his principal revolutionary characters, namely, that they can exist only in a revolutionary context, that they would find it impossible to live meaningful lives under settled conditions. Whatever the routine to which they have become inured, Lionel's people never fail to remember that they are men and women with children to care for and other simply human obligations to fulfill. Their political goals always have more to do with making a better world in which to live than with securing power. They know that black workers especially must be mobilized to wrest power from their white masters, but they seem as much involved in cultivating fellow feeling as in devising subversive strategies.

The belief in what we have called "the necessary interpenetration of public and private" has been subjected to severe criticism in the writings of prominent thinkers like Hannah Arendt, most notably in Arendt's book *The Human Condition* (1951). There Arendt argues that "the social" includes activities and relationships that are by nature "private" and not to be confused with the political or public realms. The private, in Arendt's sense, includes not only love and sex, but family relations, household arrangements, and ordinary working conditions.[8] These are matters best kept out of the political arena, which is contaminated by efforts to use it for what are in effect merely personal ends. It is hard to imagine what Arendt would have said about Lionel Burger, but there is no doubt that she would have deplored the tendency she criticized in all varieties of Marxism, specifically, the belief in politics as broadly ameliorative and dependent on economic and social forces.

Gordimer's character would surely have received a more sympathetic reading from the critic Roland Barthes, who wrote that "one must naturally understand *political* in its deeper meaning, as describing the whole of human relations in their real social structure, in their power of making the world."[9] Sheldon Wolin extends this definition in a statement that seems almost to have originated as a description of Lionel Burger's activities. "The political emerges," Wolin says, "in the literal sense, as a 'culture,' that is, a cultivating, a tending, a taking care of beings and things."[10] Lionel Burger and his friends create, in fact, a political culture that is a reflection and extension of their own familial and domestic instincts. The primary mode of their political activity is nurturant and, in the best sense, personal.

They lead and inspire by example. Always apparent in what they do is the primacy of character, the force of personal conviction, the absence of petty jealousy or internecine rivalry. Not all families can operate so beneficently, but most families surely aspire to achieve the kind of comfortable solidarity we find here. And if very few political networks or organizations may be said to operate along such lines, that is no reason for any particular group to refrain from perceiving itself in that way. Arendt's critique of the merging of public and private notwithstanding, Lionel Burger's politics certainly seem an attractive combination.

But Gordimer's novel, we remember, pits against Lionel's example another kind of politics, and is so constructed as to make Rosa's consciousness the battleground for this conflict. Rosa, we recall, for all her devotion to Lionel and her willingness to do his bidding while he lives, determines to pursue a different sort of life once her father is gone, and goes so far as to obtain a passport to leave South Africa for an extended "vacation." Her behavior, we said, was an aspect of that unknown sign it is the business of the novel to provide, and that unknown sign inevitably leads us to consider the limitations of the political mode associated with Rosa's father. We have spoken of the plausible reasons for Rosa's extended defection from "the faithful" and their course. We have not spoken in this context of that "power of making the world" which seemed essential to Barthes in his summary definition of politics. And is it not the case that, for all of Rosa's scrupulous reflection on the meaning of Lionel's life and the justice of his cause, she fails to consider the remarkable absence of any real alternative to power and what it typically does to persons who exercise it? Rosa maintains respect for her father by dwelling on his personal attributes and refusing to think about what it would take to make a successful revolution in South Africa. She performs the concrete tasks assigned to her and applauds the steadfastness of others performing their own smaller or larger tasks, but she cannot confront the failure of these more or less small-scale subversive activities to accomplish the larger task at hand. Her conception of politics is inadequate to comprehend the requirements that have to do with the exercise of power and the application of force. Her father's exemplary personal qualities blind her to the failure of the politics he represents to accomplish its purposes. Lionel's primary commitment to politics as a mode of experience rather than as a mode of taking and exercising power is bound to be confronted by another kind of commitment in which personal sympathy and familial bonding are perceived very differently or ignored altogether.

Strangely, Rosa finds another version of familial bonding in her meetings with Brandt Vermeulen, the sophisticated Afrikaaner nationalist who is her father's opposite number. Rosa visits Vermeulen to persuade him to use his influence to get her a passport, something routinely denied her as Lionel's daughter. She chooses him more or less as the consequence of an intuition that he would wish to help her, if only out of a desire to feel that he stood above petty enmities and irrational fears. Vermeulen doesn't disappoint her, but he does say a number of things that lead Rosa to compare him with Lionel. Both are the products of a determinate historical circumstance; both are prominent spokesmen for the respective positions they embrace, and have apparently won a measure of grudging respect even from members of the opposition; and both, finally, conceive of what they do in terms of a social allegiance that has some of the marks of a familial bonding. Vermeulen laments Lionel Burger's defection from "his people." The tragedy, as he sees it, is that Lionel "didn't trust us: his own people; himself." Solidarity with one's own kind, in Vermeulen's terms, not only ennobles, but builds hope. To insist on a view of things that is abstract or that comes from outside of one's own inherited parameters is to betray one's heritage and to go against the grain of one's nature. One may be as cosmopolitan as one likes; one may, like Brandt Vermeulen himself, travel widely, read eclectically, and hold "modern" or enlightened views; but one is required at last to pledge a fundamental allegiance to the *Volk*, to one's natural confreres. One bears witness to this allegiance in one's own way, but fiercely and unambivalently.

Between Lionel's version of solidarity and Vermeulen's there is an enormous gap, to be sure, and Gordimer is assiduous to expose this gap by making Rosa's encounters with Brandt the occasion for a merciless dissection. So relentless is this dissection, in fact, that it is worthy of comparison with Proust's depiction of the Verdurin circle in *Swann's Way*. And that comparison, in turn, calls to mind the critic René Girard's analysis of Proust in *Deceit, Desire and the Novel*.[11] There, Girard argues the validity of a distinction between two different kinds of nexal bonding. One operates in terms of a positive conception according to which one achieves membership in a group by affirming belief in a supreme being or in a set of values genuinely thought to be good. The denizens of Proust's Combray may not satisfy all of the demands of so positive a conception—they are, after all, terribly deluded about themselves—but they are unmistakably preferable to the Verdurins, who are caught up in a much more terrible "organic falsehood." But the positive conception of a nexal bond does clearly apply to Lionel Burger and his friends, and distinguishes them from Brandt Vermeulen quite as the Verdurins are played off against the people at Combray.

Vermeulen speaks for a connection that is fiercely defended despite the absence of a sacred center. That connection is less "a way of feeling and seeing," in Girard's terms, than "a closed culture" dedicated to keeping out or eliminating "foreign" elements. Its mode is predominantly negative in the sense that group membership is confirmed not by believing in something, but by agreeing to keep out others who by conventional definition are unacceptable. For all of Brandt Vermeulen's invoking his people, the "rites of union" he celebrates are—again in Girard's terms—"rites of separation." The Verdurins are less sure of themselves than Gordimer's Afrikaaner gentry and do not understand as fully as Brandt Vermeulen what their ritual enactments entail. But though Vermeulen is very knowing and very shrewd, he is finally deluded about his highly rated "broad sympathies" and his casual aplomb, and he is as ripe for the picking as Madame Verdurin. Listening to his ostensibly disinterested analysis of her father, Rosa is said to keep "the considering face of one who respects a scholarly approach. Of course, sentiment was too shallow an emotion for someone of her background." With that last remarkable sentence, Gordimer contemptuously identifies as the basis of Vermeulen's poise and amiability an assumption of exclusiveness, of a superiority utterly empty and utterly dependent on the willingness of persons like Rosa and himself to lay claim to it. That this has little in common with the positive conception of group identity Rosa witnessed at home with her parents is certainly obvious, whatever the superficial similarities.

But the relation between public and private, political and social, is not illuminated in a particularly helpful way in the pages devoted to Brandt Vermeulen. Those pages do not, for example, seek to explain why Rosa can be at once nauseated by Brandt and also determined to get away from her father's associates. We take Rosa's implicit judgment of Brandt to be just, and we are sympathetic toward her desire to escape. We accept that Lionel and Brandt are in limited ways comparable figures, and we go on to conclude that, finally, their differences are more important than their similarities. But the novel is not at this point interested in what makes Brandt's private or social instincts a *necessary* function of his politics. Clearly, the novel shows us, there are many ways of supporting apartheid and justifying what ones does in the name of the *Volk* or the nation or the economy or the Communist menace. One doesn't have to share Brandt's expressed feeling for "the people," which is to say, for the "loyal" white people of his society, to feel that blacks ought not to receive the entitlements they claim. With Lionel it was possible to conclude that private instincts and political posture were one. The man's attachment to family and community was simply enlarged to encompass a much larger nexal unit that could be maintained only by means of a politics designed to protect and legitimize it. Brandt, on the contrary, cultivates a wide range of "sympathies" only to dress up his continuing allegiance to a community that is conceived in the narrow sort of way familiarly associated with *Volkish* and racialist nationalism. Though Rosa has never before met anyone like Brandt, she knows him at once, readily identifying his predilections and delusions precisely because they are an outgrowth of the standard supremacist assumptions she has known about all her life. His politics, such as they are, can produce no real surprises since they can have but a single aim, namely, the maintaining of certain privileges for those who know best how to use their political advantage.

In a sense it might even be said that politics is not the issue where Brandt is concerned, though others wishing to subvert the system he represents will need to adopt political measures if they are to be successful. If we say that politics is not the issue for Brandt, that he is not a political figure as such, that is because he has what he takes to be definitive views of the

questions he considers. The issues are not for him debatable. He partici-
pates in panel discussions and debates, we are told—he is "the invariable
choice of white liberals to contribute views fascinatingly awful to them"—
but he and others like him operate from a debased sense of politics as
nothing but administration. A real politics, we may say—and here I follow
closely the writings of Hannah Arendt—is conducted by persons who have
a genuine respect for what can come out of the clash of different views
when they are made to compete with one another. "Public debate," Arendt
has said, "can only deal with things which . . . we cannot figure out with
certainty."[12] Persons who feel that they have all the answers and see public
life simply as an arena for administering solutions and enforcing them on
resistant constituents are outside the political in any meaningful sense.
Though Brandt Vermeulen may enter into debate on serious issues, he
does so in the spirit of one administering a standard solution to a problem
that he and others like him have mastered and that is not in any case open
to question by properly enlightened persons.

It might also be said that Lionel and his comrades sometimes fail to meet
the standard of political activity we have cited here. Consider Rosa's unhappy confrontation with Clare Terblanche, the daughter of her late father's closest associates. Shortly before this awful confrontation Rosa had
marveled, probably for the hundredth time, at the incredible optimism and
enthusiasm of the Terblanches, at their living for "no less than the future."
And she marveled, also, at her "need to get away as from something
obscene"—something not merely suffocating in its rightness but mechanical
in its degree of blithe certitude and definition. "*The* Future is coming,"
she reflects. "The only one that's ever existed for them, according to
documentation." And what is the central text providing for that "documentation"? A theoretical blueprint, a diagram and program for socialist
revolution, with its stages and its "inevitable" successes. No less than
Brandt Vermeulen are the Terblanches certain that what they know is all
they need to know and what they do is justified absolutely by the conditions
under which they live. And if this is obvious to Rosa as she observes the
parental generation, how much more striking is it to see the rigid certainties
and mechanical routines adopted by the children of her own generation.
Clare Terblanche asks Rosa for help not in the spirit of one who questions
what she is doing or imagines that Rosa might have misgivings. She is doing
what her parents have always routinely done, and what Rosa would presumably expect of her as well. The issue is small—the unauthorized use
of an office copier to run off forbidden political documents—but the implications of Clare's request go well beyond the immediate stakes.*

Why does Rosa refuse? Not, certainly, because she is afraid of getting

---

* Again I am reminded, in Nadine Gordimer's letter of January 23, 1983, that the immediate
stakes might potentially be very large, so that "what Clare was, indeed, asking of Rosa was
a return, through taking a strong risk, to revolutionary activism. That is the 'objective' strand
running through a situation, between the two girls, braided with the subjective questions. . . ."

caught and dismissed from what is in any case not a particularly rewarding office job. And not, either, because she entertains some ethical conflict with respect to the correctness of her behavior and the possible violation of her employer's trust. She refuses because Clare makes her request in what seems to Rosa a degrading way that demeans her and her objectives. She refuses, or so it would seem, because the political itself as a realm of action is demeaned in the unimpassioned, unimaginative plainness of Clare's request. Not individual purpose strengthened by calculation and collective design is apparent in Clare's activity, but the carrying out of a standard assignment in a standard way. "She did not know how to make me feel demeaned by my refusal," Rosa reports, and with that, she moves to express exactly what is on her mind in repudiating "conformist" children who experience none of the turmoil occasioned by generational conflict and youthful doubt but go on to behave just as their parents had. She repudiates, in effect, all public activity from which significant choice is exempt. Her desire to leave South Africa, to withdraw from the public realm altogether, is at least in part a response to the debasement of politics in the activities even of those she has most admired.

Significantly, though, Clare is given what amounts to the last word in this exchange, and no one can doubt that she speaks also for what is best in Rosa. Conceding that people like them were not as children given a choice, Clare adds: "But no! Rosa! What choice? Rosa? In this country, under this system, looking at the way blacks live—what has the choice to do with parents? What else could you choose?" In putting things this way, Clare leaves little for Rosa to say by way of refutation, and Gordimer surely knew that her reader would likewise have little to object to in that stalwart formulation. If the realm of the political, in Arendt's sense of it, is demeaned by a form of activity that is essentially administrative or routine, proceeding as it does from a kind of certainty that resists questions about ultimate things, then it may be necessary to say that *the political* in Arendt's sense can only be preserved when conditions are not intolerable. Under intolerable circumstances political actors, no matter which side they are on, are likely to operate in a way that would seem to Arendt "impure" and unsavory. And it is possible, moreover, that a political realm characterized by that sort of activity, and therefore guided predominantly by material or selfish interest, will never be able to sustain a politics in the true sense. Disinterested competition on behalf of conflicting political ideas may belong, of necessity, only to countries without a long history of fundamental human rights violations on a grand scale.

Of course, no one can read *Burger's Daughter* and conclude, simply, that the main characters are mindless organization men and women working within what are essentially conformist bureaucratic modes. To compare a Terblanche to Brandt Vermeulen is not to say that the palpable differences are insignificant or that either is quite so stock a figure as Rosa sometimes feels. Neither is it to deny that Lionel Burger is ever so much more impressive a figure than the typical party-line Communist. The key point here is that Rosa learns to be true to her father's example and to become a responsible agent in the best sense only by temporarily rejecting Lionel's example and discovering the meaning of political commitment for herself, as if for the first time. This she can do only by living for a while in a dimension outside of politics and by feeling herself drawn back into the political matrix, as it were, against her will. Strangely, it is that experience of being compelled by something fiercely resisted that enables Rosa to feel at last that she can truly lay claim to something that has long lain in wait to claim her. Politics here is understood simultaneously as a choice and a vocation, a fate and an ambitiously forbidding object of desire. The evolution of Rosa's relations with family, opponents, and others is finally the record of a political development in which the idea of a fully enlightened and disinterested politics comes to seem more palpable as the prospects for actualizing such a politics seem increasingly grim.

Of course, the actual circumstances of South African politics have much to do with Rosa's evolution. *Burger's Daughter* is in a sense a response to two crucial events, namely, Sharpeville and Soweto. The first, dating from March of 1960, occurred when Rosa was only twelve. The demonstration mounted on that occasion, and the carnage that followed, obviously had a great impact on the Burger family, though Rosa recalls that she "didn't understand what it meant, the difference if you were hit in the back or chest."[13] Her lover and interlocutor Conrad can't see that Sharpeville affected him at all, but it is obvious to us that persons involved in South African politics were moved by the incident more than they might earlier have supposed. Of course, there were other demonstrations and work stoppages of a similar nature going on at the same time—in Capetown, Durban, and other locations—but the level of police violence unleashed at Sharpeville had to make it the focus of a new sort of attention. And the government's subsequent response to reports documenting the horrors made it clearer than ever that few gains might be expected by those whose politics did not extend beyond peaceful demonstrations and orderly challenges to the legal system.[14]

So Sharpeville figures in *Burger's Daughter* as an instigation and as a kind of a proof or test case. It is incidental to the main narrative, more a point of reference than an actual topic or crux, but it is part of the air the Burgers breathe. It is important to them not simply as vivid substantiation of their conviction that the system is terrible and must be changed. It is important also as a warrant of their own growing separation from the kinds of feeling necessarily aroused in the radical black community with which they have heretofore worked so closely. For though Lionel Burger and his friends were surely moved to furious protest on behalf of those massacred at Sharpeville, their response is consistent with the general feeling of indignation and radical enthusiasm they have maintained all along. As people with a vision of a better future and the patience to wait out the reversals to which any radical enterprise is subject, they can go on with their usual radical politics even after Sharpeville. Their resolve may be toughened, their anger may be temporarily heightened, but finally they are what they were before. Gordimer doesn't have to document this response in a literal way for us to grasp what it amounts to in characters we come to know so well.

For the blacks, though, Sharpeville is something else entirely. To them it dramatizes more plainly than ever before how hopeless their situation is. It points up the utter bankruptcy of the legal system and forecasts the miserable fate of blacks inspired by well-meaning white leaders intent on raising black consciousness and organizing people to make political demands. Again, Gordimer doesn't have to spell out all of these things to communicate to us the process by which young blacks especially are newly disillusioned and radicalized beyond anything Lionel could have envisioned. She needs only to show them to us in their resplendent anger, intolerance, and impatience. Most convincing—not in the sense that one is persuaded by the logic or justice of what they say, but that one believes in the depth of their determination—is their contemptuous dismissal even of revolutionary white activists who can know Sharpeville only from outside, as one event among others. Lionel may have felt a perfect kinship with blacks, but he could not know how far from sharing the truly relevant sentiments of blacks he was. The radical white man is through in South Africa, as one particularly articulate black activist explains: "He doesn't live black, what does he know what a black man needs?" True, the white man may, like Lionel, go to jail to protest against the treatment of blacks, but, as Dhadhla says, "he goes for his ideas about me, I go for my ideas about myself." To speak of common goals is nonsense in a country where whites rule not as "a ruling class" but as "a colour." To fight for equality with whites is to accept the Marxist reading of class conflict and to ignore the primary fact of South African society, which is color. Whites who want to abolish color as a primary fact shut their eyes to the reality in which they are involved, like it or not. Sharpeville is important, or so it seems to articulate blacks, because it forces them to see that their interests lie in the growing ability of blacks to defend themselves against whites.

Gordimer is extraordinarily generous in permitting her black characters to say at considerable length what only a small proportion of South African blacks can be ready as yet to conclude. Or, it might be said, she is obviously so taken with what they say, so horrified at the terrible momentum building in their words, that she cannot but pay them the fascinated attention due any natural disaster. That we are to attend with something less than full reverence we know by the fact that Rosa is made now and again to detach herself from what she hears, to reflect ironically on the playacting that is a part of the rhetorical display, and to dismiss much of the familiar political language as all too familiar: The phrases at one point are said to have "jingled like a bunch of keys fingered in a pocket." White or black, political radicals striving to *épater* not only *les bourgeois*, but the assortment of liberal fellow travelers and their own milder constituents hanging on at the margins of political movements, are apt to brutalize the language and create a stirring impression. "Dhadhla had the air of having his back turned even to those people he was facing," Rosa shrewdly observes at one point. And anything he says thereafter will inevitably be colored for us by that observation of the man's bitterness, contempt, and inability to deal equably with what he is feeling. Gordimer would not have us on that account dismiss the origins of that pain or refuse to accord the man the pity he deserves. But his subsequent statements are bound nonetheless to seem "personal" in a way that may not have been so apparent before.

Burger's Daughter does not attempt to solve the questions raised by angry blacks. It cannot decide that blacks ought or ought not to go on working with whites like Lionel Burger for the better future they project, each group perhaps in its own special way. Neither can it conclude that "the white man's way of life is"—or is not—"best for blacks." The judgments it makes are implicit judgments, and they have more to do with exposing pretensions to perfect clarity and candor than with settling basic conflicts. When Dhadhla says that "we can't be tricked to lose ourselves in some kind of colourless . . . shapeless . . . 'humanity,' " we are prepared to credit the cogency of his remark. But we are less impressed by his proclaiming, in the name of "the black people," that "we don't accept anything from anybody. We take." The man may go far, indeed, with such determination, but Gordimer refuses to make him seem an appealing figure. He may represent the immediate future, but his accession to power will surely be the result of terrible failures rather than of choices carefully and soberly made. Gordimer's judgment of him and the solution he presents is conveyed in the resistance that comes not just from Rosa but from other blacks. He can speak amiably of "re-educating" resistant blacks, but every reader is expected to know what reeducation in revolutionary societies ordinarily amounts to. "We're bringing you the news that *you're* the black people, *Baba*," he says to an older black companion. But the exchanges are carefully structured to make us notice the absence of a substantive program around which a new black consciousness might order itself. What we have, finally, is insult and anger translated into a rhetoric of pride and separatist violence. The comforting humanitarian and socialist credos won't serve any longer to shift the direction of this process, but the process need hardly seem attractive or edifying simply because it seems more and more inevitable.

Sharpeville, then, may be regarded as an emblematic background for developments dramatized in *Burger's Daughter*. Its main effects are not shown to have been immediate, but were clearly felt over a period of several years in the course of which the position associated with Lionel eroded. Lionel did not live to see himself discounted and repudiated by those he had worked for, but his daughter has to deal with that rejection in his place. In part, this repudiation of Lionel Burger is personal. It amounts to a statement that individual persons are not what great political actions are all about. Rosa's childhood companion Baasie, now a militant radical with nothing but contempt for Rosa and her family, asserts, "I know plenty blacks like Burger," meaning not that blacks think Lionel's thoughts or entertain similar conflicts, but that they also suffer. This similarity alone is enough to warrant Baasie's dismissing the idea of Lionel as a special case, an unusually good, interesting, complex man. The perspective is conferred, in effect, by the experience of Sharpeville, of utter victimization and defeat. All that can matter hereafter is the will to take what is wanted and to avoid subsequent defeat or humiliation. "Whatever you whites touch, it's a takeover," he cries to Rosa. No matter that Lionel lived all his life without any real power; that what influence he wielded was a function of character rather than of his own desire to lead; or that he was suited by virtue of his intelligence and his wisdom to advise persons less able and less educated on how to conduct a revolution without sacrificing too much too soon. All of this comes under the heading of "takeover" in the vocabulary of black pride that is to reeducate the black masses after Sharpeville.

The repudiation of Lionel Burger, then, is personal in the very broadest sense. It is a repudiation of the special and distinguished person and of the individual qualities of heart and mind he represents. It is a function of an incipient politics that is based not on sympathy but on rage, not on respect for human diversity but on an exclusive commitment to what one black calls "group attitudes and group politics." The novel doesn't show us what the new politics will look like in practice, but it indicates very clearly what is the status of its main ideas. In their determination to banish private virtues, certainly to isolate them from the ostensibly valid public virtues—refusal to be coopted by whites; resistance to meliorist, bourgeois, and humanitarian appeals; unambivalent commitment to black solidarity at any cost—the new radicals seek to affirm an idea of politics that found articulate exposition in the writings of Franz Fanon.[15] It is the idea of politics as the collective assertion of the will to power. It has little to do with consciousness except insofar as consciousness may be said to inhere in the assertion of identity as color. Though the manifestation of such an idea will surely be a public fact, the idea itself has no conception of a public realm apart from the acting out of the collective ritual whereby rudimentary group solidarity is repeatedly affirmed. Fanon himself spoke of the phases through which a black revolution would necessarily pass, and had some sense that the more brutish ritual elements would give way to another kind of politics. But Gordimer's black characters are possessed by their rudimentary political ideas in a way that makes those ideas seem obsessive, if not permanent, and Rosa Burger's confusion about the staying power of those ideas is in its way exemplary. Unable to refute the ideas, and with nothing but a somewhat shopworn ideology inherited from her father as an alternative model, she has to rethink the connection between public and private for herself.

A considerable portion of *Burger's Daughter* is set outside of South Africa, in a comfortable European setting among persons for whom politics is an occasional topic of conversation rather than a matter of life and death.

Nothing can better point up the meaning of politics than the absence of politics Rosa confronts in France. Her primary impression is of people "careless of privacy, in their abundance: letting be." Caught up in a crowd, she considers herself "enclosed in this amiable press of strangers, not a mob because they were not brought together by hostility or enthusiasm, but by mild curiosity and a willingness to be entertained." Though she is accosted by a pickpocket in the crowd, she can be amused by one companion's statement that there "you can live the way you like" and another's promise that "nobody expects you to be more than you are." Her father's charming ex-wife, Madame Bagnelli, can plausibly speak of another of her husbands as having been "in his life as a fish in water." We are aware as we register all this that other Frenchmen have a rather more strenuous relation to reality than most of those we meet. And there are references to May 1968 and the propensity to political violence apparently legitimized for most people by the heady occurrences of that month. But the dominant notes are continually sounded by Madame Bagnelli, who frequently recalls, with a mixture of mild contempt and wry amusement, the excesses of the South African faithful, with their boring virtues, predictable meetings, and undeviating commitment to one thing only. Those remembrances are undercut by Rosa's current observations of fashionable Parisian hippies "drinking wine in the clothes of guerrillas surviving in the bush on a cup of water a day," but the effect of these juxtapositions is not so much to certify the one or the other perspective as to establish Rosa's detachment from the new world she is avid to experience. No matter how deeply she is moved by the spectacle of decent persons out to take their pleasures without apology or needless greed, she remains an observer, marginal, not critical but storing up impressions for judgments to come.

Gordimer's decision to set a quarter of her novel in Europe is crucial to the business of *Burger's Daughter* as a political novel. For politics, as Rosa comes more and more to see, is more than an action and more, certainly, than a will to power. It is, she understands finally on her European "vacation," a way of life, a habit of mind and feeling, a function of a general inability to separate public from private. It is the concerted activity of persons for whom life may not be taken for granted, for whom nothing is utterly careless and curiosity is rarely mild. In terms of this vision of politics, to feel "you can live the way you like" is not to be free but to settle for the easy assumptions of privilege and privacy held by persons unable to consider what their privilege rests on. Gordimer's object is not to despise the modest vanities and easy deceptions of the comfortable bourgeois/bohemian types she draws, but to make it clear that Rosa cannot long remain among them. Their accommodations are charming, it is true, and they do not—most of them—aim to hurt anyone or to deny others their share of the affluent spoils. But they are, it seems, weightless persons, shifting about in an ambience without pressure, without the gravitational pull of a universe in which consequence is what cannot be amended or evaded. What Rosa misses in this universe, what Gordimer's political vision thrives on, is the texture of necessity, the sense that one must be armed with ideas and convictions to make one's way through what is a forbidding landscape. Even the intimate conversations Rosa has with her French lover are made to show how complex feelings and circumstances are routinely cut down to modest size in a universe built on the assumption that anything can be managed or accommodated. "I live among my wife and children— not with them," says this sincere and attractive man who wants Rosa as his permanent mistress, a regular part of a life also spent with the familial others. There are no problems, he seems to say. Nothing that a little good will and strategy can't accomplish.

The absence of an abiding political dimension in the European landscape Rosa visits forces her to acknowledge the degree to which she is a political person. This Gordimer would seem to have intended from the first in constructing her novel. But it was the series of incidents at Soweto in 1976 that finally determined the direction that Rosa would take.[16] Indeed, Gordimer has gone so far as to say that, though "Rosa would have come back to South Africa" in any case, "there would have been a different ending . . . without the Soweto riots."[17] Soweto, it seems fair to say, confirms Rosa's decision, puts the seal on her sense of herself as her father's daughter. If she could not find a place to stand in the arguments between black radicals and black liberals, she could not feel any more secure opting out of the struggle altogether and mingling with others accustomed to living without enthusiasm or hostility. She may not have her father's "sublime lucidity" or his sense of determinate purpose, but she knows that she is called to bear witness to her sense that there is no public or personal virtue that is not charged with political meaning. To give a name to that political meaning, to see what actually connects it to the private lives of persons with whom one is necessarily associated, is an activity worthy of the father whose name Rosa carries.

The political meaning Rosa discovers—a meaning brought into permanent focus by Soweto—is intimated at least in the culminating incident that drives Rosa out of South Africa. Driving one day along an unmapped road, she sees an old black man brutally beating the donkey pulling his cart. As she watches, frozen to her seat in the car, she sees that "the infliction of pain [has] broken away from the will that creates it . . . torture without the torturer, rampage, pure cruelty gone beyond control of the humans who have spent thousands of years devising it." And this spectacle of pain and infinite pointless suffering calls to her mind, in a way that miraculously escapes the aspect of a merely literary free association, "the camps, concentration, labour, resettlement, the Siberias of snow or sun, the lives of Mandela, Sisulu, Mbeki, Kathrada, Kgosana, gull-picked on the island, Lionel propped wasting to his skull between two warders," and so on. But though Rosa sees the horror of this punishment inflicted needlessly on the dumb beast, and is appalled as well that others, even children, are compelled to look on, she can do nothing about it. Or at least she feels that she cannot intervene, "with my knowledge of how to deliver them over to the police, to have him prosecuted as he deserved and should be . . . I could formulate everything they were . . . —the final meaning of a day they had lived I had no knowledge of, a day of other appalling things." She knows what the man deserves, but not what is required for a situation in which the deed (like other comparable deeds) is "broken away from the will that creates it." She doesn't know, at last, what she most needs to know: "at what point to intercede makes sense, for me." For to intercede here is to take on herself the responsibility for an action that implicates not a single agent, but an entire system of social and political relations. "I drove on," she recalls, "because the horrible drunk was black, poor and brutalized. If somebody's going to be brought to account, I am accountable for him, to him, as he is for the donkey." Rosa leaves South Africa, she concludes, because "I don't know how to live in Lionel's country."

Not to know how to live in South Africa is more than a matter of experiencing a vague collective guilt for which there is no available relief, and it is more than the sense that people are willing to be oppressed if they can oppress others. Rosa's despair comes from her feeling that the lives of most people are finally resistant to political solutions. Looking at the man beating the donkey as at an immemorial emblematic tableau, and simultaneously regarding herself as "the white woman" representing an immemorial "white authority," she responds not to a public event that is the probable consequence of specific social and political arrangements but to a fact of life only heroes and blind optimists may hope to alter. She surely knows better than to believe that poor blacks will go on eternally beating other dumb brutes to compensate for their own misery, or that white persons must inevitably behave in the ordinary ways expected of whites. But so paralyzed is Rosa by the contradictions she observes in the society around her that she cannot move beyond the boundaries of her own reflexive consciousness. She doesn't know how to live in South Africa because it has come to seem a place of nightmare and irremediable suffering.

The political meaning Rosa must discover in all of this is that her perception of contradiction and conflict in her society is but a preliminary observation. It is preliminary to a further perception of social arrangements as causally linked to assumptions that keep those arrangements in place. It is one thing for Rosa to be reminded of all the related political horrors when she observes the donkey being beaten. It is another thing for her to think politically about those horrors. The free association, intensely registered though it is, is an affair of passing sentiment. The analogies are raised only to be acknowledged momentarily as facts of life. In recognizing necessity as that which eludes definition and does not allow for an adequate response, Rosa in effect places herself at the service of that necessity. For all her sophisticated readings of social and political conditions, her sense of how each detail of every domestic life is a function of arrangements that have made things what they are, she is unable to arrive at the conclusive political meaning staring her in the face. She agrees to leave South Africa in the spirit of one for whom politics is a series of unspeakable public events which have their counterpart and their consequence in the private sphere. To save oneself, in this view, is to move into a private sphere that is more or less self-enclosed and that refuses to recognize its relations with the public realm as anything but transient and superficial.

The conclusive and corrective political meaning demonstrated in the beating of the donkey, as, later on, in the riots at Soweto, is that intercession need never be conceived as a final or adequate gesture. Intercession is at best an expression of involvement in something that goes beyond one's immediate interest. It is a way as much as an end, though to lose sight of the projected end is to betray the meaning and the value of one's involvement. This is not an idealist or existentialist reading of politics, in terms of which one acts principally to valorize the self and affirm abstract humanitarian or egalitarian values. Gordimer builds her novel, as she must, around concrete incidents that supply particular motives for every projected action. The intercession Rosa fails to make in the incident with the donkey is a failure to do a concrete something—something that ought to have been done—on the grounds that it would not alter anything in the long run. Her failure is seen in the perspective of the novel as a failure of political vision precisely because it is a refusal of personal enactment and involvement. To view oneself simply as an object of historical forces is to make oneself a victim, and victims are notoriously subject to the kind of self-doubt and self-pity that erode the capacity to act.

To think politically, Gordimer suggests, is to think of yourself as acting on behalf of whatever needs to be done. It is not to lose oneself in a convulsive action, but to discover perpetually what one can do by *interceding* wherever one can. The meaning of Soweto, in this respect, is that South African society is moving into a volatile prerevolutionary stage in which anything can happen, for good or ill. To refrain from participating in the unfolding political process on the grounds that one cannot tell for certain where it will lead is to pretend that it is better to preserve the self *in potentia* than to take a chance in doing good. "You can't be afraid to do good in case evil results," Rosa decides. Soweto may well lead to a general uprising in which blacks will take what they want and all whites will be treated with the same vengeful hand. But that is not certain, and it is more than recklessness or altruism that can bring a white woman like Rosa Burger to join the struggle and go to jail with the thousands of nameless others who have made a similar choice.

The private virtues, then, insofar as they are here made to seem an indissoluble component of political virtues, are not simply virtues of the heart.[18] They are also intellectual virtues having to do with the capacity to remember the past and honor those aspects of the past that live on in oneself. Daniel Bell reminds us that "the greatest risk of memory is sentimentality,"[19] and it is no doubt tempting for a young woman remembering martyred parents to succumb to familiar sentimental pieties. But Gordimer's vision insists that remembrance be tempered by involvement in present circumstance. Rosa Burger cannot fall into sentimentality because, finally, the predominent shaping elements in her continuing encounter with the past are the current vicissitudes with which she grapples. She avoids the attrition to which fond, informing memories are often subject by refusing to turn Lionel into an icon; but she identifies with the kinds of activities that gave purpose to his life. Her politics are conceived not as a formal commitment to an ideology, but as a participation in a struggle that must be adopted though its outcome is unforeseeable. She operates not as a scientific Marxist responding to the laws of class conflict, but as one who has entered a causal nexus without knowing quite how to identify the connections exactly. She abjures the need for exactitude in the interests of a value she considers essential to politics, namely, the value assigned an obviously necessary action confirmed and accredited by the sacrifices made on its behalf by a revered ancestral generation. That the ancestral generation in Rosa's case is so close, is an immediate biological fact, is sufficient warrant for its seeming so important here. Rosa's politics emerge neither as an instinctual reflex of filial piety nor as an adventurist plunge into dangerous waters. They are an authorization in the deepest and most valuable sense, strenuously legitimizing a sense of indebtedness to those who have gone before and ratifying the sense of irreducible particularity that must inform authentic transactions in the present. In drawing on personal or private virtues—which is to say, in remembering and reconstructing her relationship with her father—Rosa demonstrates one of the primary motives in the shaping of a mature political imagination.

8

Political Holocaust Fiction

I. THE VOYAGE OF JORGE SEMPRUN

The term *holocaust fiction* has come to signify a growing body of work dealing with the disaster that befell European civilization in the years between 1933 and 1945. In the main, the focus of this literature has been Hitler's war against the Jews, most especially the sufferings experienced by Jews who were exterminated or by other Jews who survived and were forced to consider the meaning of their survival. The best of this literature is rich in philosophical implication and in the grave precision of its historical reconstruction. Several notable holocaust works also ask questions that go beyond the specific causes and immediate consequences of the Nazi period, and several go so far as to dwell reflexively on the inadequacy of fiction and of language itself to do justice to the subject.

It is common, in fact, for writers with more than a passing interest in the holocaust to argue that no work of literature can hope to address it adequately. The critic Alvin Rosenfeld, for example, has emphasized the peculiar and powerful conditions under which holocaust writers must work. Following the lead of Elie Wiesel, who wrote that "at Auschwitz, not only man died but also the idea of man," Rosenfeld characterizes the holocaust writer as one who inevitably addresses "the death of the idea of man in order to sustain that idea." Like others who write often on this subject,

Rosenfeld routinely distinguishes between what he calls "authentic" and "inauthentic responses to the holocaust" not as a way of establishing literary value, but as a way of determining what does and does not belong in the holocaust canon. Denying that there is a canon, he yet dismisses from his study works that are not "specifically and overwhelmingly" focused on " 'the war against the Jews' " and identifies as one of the "abiding laws" the stipulation that "there are no metaphors for Auschwitz, just as Auschwitz is not a metaphor for anything else."[1]

In a similar way, the Viennese essayist Jean Amery bitterly deplores efforts to study Bolshevism and Nazism as in any sense comparable phenomena, and insists that the Nazi experience should always be treated in its incomparable singularity. "What happened in Germany between 1933 and 1945, so they will teach and say, could have occurred anywhere else under similar circumstances, and no one will insist any further on the trifle that it did happen precisely in Germany and not somewhere else."[2] Not only, it would seem, is the holocaust finally resistant to literary treatments that purport to explain or compare it, it is also resistant to those who view evil as deviance and have no stomach for the specific assignment of responsibility.

Jorge Semprun first addressed the holocaust in *The Long Voyage*,[3] a novel that told of his deportation to Buchenwald and reflected on his experience of the camps and on his postwar efforts to think about the future. Though several readers of the novel early complained that "it produces abundantly the sense of *déjà vu*," that "every one of its episodes is reminiscent of something that has already been written,"[4] it has seemed to others one of the truly authentic holocaust fictions, and a work of considerable literary merit as well.

In fact, the praise heaped on the novel by holocaust scholars is really quite remarkable in light of the following facts: It deals in the main with the experience of resistance fighters like Semprun himself, rather than with the fate of Jews; it routinely affirms the ambition of Semprun and his comrades not to die what is called "a Jew's death," the death of those, in other words, who see themselves as victims and cannot summon the will to resist their fate; it proposes to remove the problems of which the Nazi state is the prime example by "quite simply . . . instituting a classless society," that is, by realizing the aims of those for whom the future is a Communist future and for whom terrorism is an acceptable strategy even when it becomes, as it does so often, a way of life. That *The Long Voyage* has continued to seem authentic even to those for whom many of its views are anathema can only be accounted for by the fact that its views are relatively incidental to its success as a novel.

The most peculiar item in *The Long Voyage* is Semprun's carefully articulated conviction that it is worthless and that he will have to tell his story again when he has forgotten the voyage to Buchenwald and the frame of mind in which he made sense of the holocaust as a young man. This confession of inadequacy, which seemed somehow conventional, even hollow, to readers who were impressed and instructed by the novel, has now another kind of significance. For Semprun has published another version of his story, entitled *What a Beautiful Sunday!*,[5] and if it is not so entirely a holocaust novel as the earlier work, it is nonetheless a more compelling and original book. *The Long Voyage* contains valuable episodes and observations that could not be accommodated in the later work. It has an obsessive integrity and a capacity for clear-eyed judgment that make it a model for other writers concerned with material that resists ordinary stratagems. But its successor is at once more artful and more discursive, more various, and ultimately more serious. In place of naked sincerity and more or less direct narration, Semprun has discovered a perspective that is predominantly reflective and intellectual. Sacrificing immediacy for ideas, he has succeeded all the same in building emotion by dramatizing the steady erosion of his own original views and asking us to consider what evil in history can mean when we have neither inflexible convictions nor particular goals to guide us.

To speak of the differences between the two works is to see that *What a Beautiful Sunday!* was conceived distinctly as a political novel, while the other engaged political questions at most as background to events that are compelling apart from any ideological insights that may be derived from them. The political intelligence displayed in *The Long Voyage* can be amply indicated in vivid formulations like the following: "there are those who arrest and those who are arrested"; or, "their 'krautness' is like an essence that no human act will ever be able to reach"; or, "But there is no point trying to understand the SS; it suffices to exterminate them." Striking though such observations may be, they are put forward predominantly as a means of characterizing the protagonist, of letting us know how and what he thinks. There is little effort to argue on behalf of these observations or to construct the narrative in such a way that they will seem irresistible. Plausible they do seem, and perhaps also essential to anyone wishing to confront the material for the first time, but what there is in the way of ideological conviction seems almost entirely extraneous to the concrete observations and narrative developments that constitute the heart of the novel. Semprun remembers whatever he can about Buchenwald and about the Nazi period generally because he wishes to put it all behind him. Compelled to remember, to bear witness, he continues to imagine that it will be possible eventually to do justice to the central truths of the holocaust experience without rehearsing over and over, for all time, the particular events and components of that experience. The political is, in *The Long Voyage*, not so much a way of understanding the key events as an incidental reminder that there may be a future beyond them.

By contrast, *What a Beautiful Sunday!* has more to do with establishing ideological perspectives and working through issues, as though the events on the basis of which ideas might be sought were too familiar to require steady narrative elaboration. The discoursing voice is, in consequence, not only given more to argument and summary, it is also more clearly concerned with the political function served by the novel. If the camp experience was here again to be a major aspect of the novel, Semprun did not wish again to present that experience for itself, as though direct presentation of principal events could conceivably provide anything like adequate knowledge. Like the earlier novel, the later work "complicates memory by making it an act of *anticipation* as well as recollection, thus adding to the familiar 'remembrance of things past' a seemingly impossible 'remembrance of things to come.' "[6] But in *What a Beautiful Sunday!* the "things to come" serve not so much to underline the singularity of the holocaust as to make it seem at once enduringly important and part of a larger history. It is one thing to think about the holocaust as events that happened and that stick in the memory; it is quite another to argue that subsequent events and intellectual discoveries have made one's original experience of the holocaust irrecoverable. It is the burden of Semprun's later novel to indicate that the Nazi campaign to exterminate the Jews may well have been like nothing else in Western history, but that attempts to isolate it from other comparable events are in a sense innocent and misguided: innocent in the sense that one is not then required to see how widespread are instances of extreme inhumanity in recent history and how precarious are the humane solutions we rely on; misguided in the sense that efforts to understand are not compromised, but enhanced, when particular situations are studied alongside of other comparable situations, the chief effect of such juxtaposition usually amounting to a sharp appreciation of crucial differences.

Semprun, of course, was from the first aware of the dangers inherent in adopting too broadly humanistic or general a perspective on these matters. In *The Long Voyage* he reports on a surprise visit he made to the house of a woman who lived just outside the margins of Buchenwald. The time is shortly after his release from the camp. Clearly frightened by his persistent, simple questions (" 'In the evening, when the flames shot up behind the crematorium chimney, could you see the flames?' "), she tells him that both of her sons were killed in the war. "She takes refuge," as Semprun has it, behind the sorry facts. "She's trying to make me believe that all suffering is the same, that all the dead weigh the same." This Semprun refuses to believe, and he manages to resist the thought by insisting that he is happy the woman's sons are dead. He feels no need to explain this satisfaction to the woman or to us. He can "understand her sorrow," but he respects principally the difference between her suffering and the suffering of those who were reduced to smoke and ashes. In a similar way, he is firmly reminded by a Jewish survivor that he has no right to speak of the times when he regretted not being a Jew. " 'You don't know what you're saying,' " she is compelled to tell him. For between the Jewish victim who can truly say, " 'No one has ever helped me,' " and a sympathetic comrade who guesses, " 'Maybe I was lucky,' " there is a gap that no humanitarian fellowship can bridge.

Aware of fundamental distinctions, however tempted to abandon them in the interests of a consolatory broad-mindedness, Semprun nevertheless returned to the holocaust not to speak again of its irreducible singularity, but to consider it in the light of very different experiences. Chiefly, *What a Beautiful Sunday!*—though structured around Buchenwald Sunday routines—tells of Semprun's break with the Communist party and his efforts to understand what made him a credulous partisan. It is a story he had previously told in an enthralling memoir, entitled *The Autobiography of Federico Sanchez and the Communist Underground in Spain*.[7] But the novel is even more intriguing by virtue of the greater variety of themes it pursues, and by virtue of the central connection between the Nazi and Stalinist camps it is assiduous to establish. To some readers it may well seem that Semprun loses in focus and in depth of understanding what he gains in variety and ingenuity of suggestion. Scholars like H. Stuart Hughes have long contended, after all, that discussions of totalitarianism founded on a common treatment of Nazism and Stalinism inevitably sacrifice all grasp of "underlying social realities" and attend instead to "techniques of control—the horrifying surface of life."[8] But Semprun was never chiefly interested in "underlying social realities," if by that is meant the complex of historical, national, cultural, and sociological factors that might have produced a given system and the character types that could live comfortably within it. Neither was Semprun very much interested in "techniques of control," if by that is meant an analysis of stratagems worked out by camp administrators and higher-echelon bureaucrats to terrorize their subject populations. The term *techniques of control* surely has more to do with the works of Arthur Koestler, for example, than with the work of Semprun.

Semprun's very ambitious novel recalls the Nazi camp experience in the light of subsequent encounters with the testimony of Soviet dissidents, as also in the light of his own long tenure in the Communist movement, because what matters most to him is a political vision of the future that will truly know what it has to contend with. The memory of Buchenwald has in this sense to be illuminated by "the blinding light of the searchlights of the Kolyma camps." It is not that Kolyma, or the unforgettable testimony of the Kolyma writer Varlam Shalamov, can tell us anything new about Buchenwald itself.[9] But "the desperate certainty of the simultaneous existence of the Russian camps" instructs us in how to think politically about facts that might otherwise inspire only mute horror or bitter denunciation. Semprun appreciates the value of denunciation, and he brings to bear on everything a severe moral scruple, but his political instincts are best exercised—which is to say, most fruitfully extended—when he forces himself to move beyond thoughts of simple retributive justice. To do this it was required that he cease to think so largely as he had in terms of good and evil. To accomplish this he needed not to abandon values as such, but to look at the available facts to which experience had exposed him without a fixed mask of rectitude. Strong feelings and good will were not any longer to be thought sufficient to guide anyone through the modern world. Appeals to conscience and to the future were to be submitted to the exertions of judgment as surely as appeals to class hatred. For Semprun, if his final holocaust novel was to do justice to his experience of inhumanity, it would have to pay attention both to continuities and disjunctions, to the meanings of events and to their particular contingency.

Semprun's aim in *What a Beautiful Sunday!* is not to account for the holocaust or for the willing complicity of persons like himself in the crimes of Stalin and his successors. Neither is it to evoke suffering or to apologize or get even. His aim is to show how a man endowed with great intelligence and passion can think about something for many years without feeling that he has accounted for it and without abandoning the belief that politics is an indispensable aspect of our capacity to deal with our condition. Nothing is so exemplary in Semprun's novel as his continuing to resort to political analysis after referring, again and again, to the consequences of political illusion. Unwilling to provide a conventionally satisfying representation either of camp life or of the left-wing activist's familiar routines, he opts for the sharp glimpse and the vivid tableau in place of the realist's totalizing portrayal of the individual set within a commanding social world. Out of these marginal glimpses and occasional narrative forays he builds a sense of a virtual world and its various settings without permitting us to feel that we have ourselves inhabited those settings. Always our attention is drawn to the shiftings of Semprun's restless intelligence. Principally important is his attempt to formulate political responses to experiences he can but barely summon before being called away to other instigations, other reflections. The politics that emerge from these reflections are not an ideological program but a way of seeing that is finally resistant to visionary projects. In Semprun we have a politics conceived as a mode of continuous discourse, so that the surface of the novel is in the main a sequence of open-ended arguments that proceed in fits and starts without presuming to arrive at permanently binding conclusions. Politics, in fact, is here represented as the impulse to oppose "the natural order of history" by thinking so rigorously as to betray all class allegiances and to court disorder. The politics, so-called, of those who cultivate correct thoughts are therefore viewed as a violation of the very idea of politics and a form of submission to the reigning zeitgeist. To perceive politics as discourse, to construct an entire novel as a mode of anxious if fragmentary discourse, is for Semprun to oppose with his entire being the submission of persons to the ostensive facts.

Though Semprun leaves behind him the specific convictions that informed his career as a professional Communist intellectual, he remains an oppositionist, a man who thinks inveterately against the grain. No frivolous paradoxalist, he is nonetheless attracted to pressing an insight so hard that it rapidly comes to look like something else.* The arguments are remarkable not so much for the originality of the insights as for the way in which they unfold habits of thought that are everywhere present in the novel and impress us with their quality of ambitious, self-correcting animation.

Semprun's capacity to take delight in the processes of his own thinking and to communicate that fervor to others is a function of a feeling he has never lost, namely, that something can always be done to improve a situation. This may seem shallow to anyone contemplating the consignment of countless Jewish bodies to the ovens of the Nazi camps, and yet Semprun successfully persuades us that even in the camps it was not infeasible to think politically, to conspire and plan as if one actually had a future. Like others who have studied the efforts of holocaust victims to die as men and women, Semprun dwells obsessively on this subject. His cattle-car companion in *The Long Voyage*, for example, is indignant at the spectacle of prisoners who allow themselves to be stripped and mocked and humiliated for the edification of German civilians in a circumstance less dire than others. Knowing "how to behave" is invoked as a standard of judgment even in the camps.

But Semprun is typically more interested in forms of political resistance, such as are examined throughout the later novel.** Here Semprun can speak of the insufficiency and tawdriness of political motives while demonstrating the value of an informed political orientation. He condemns the plan of the German Democratic Republic to build a heroic memorial— "something educational, political"—on the site of the camp as showing "bad taste," but we learn that this characteristic judgment is closely related to Semprun's political morality. Many years after the war, for example, Semprun had looked up a former camp comrade who had made a successful career in a ruling Communist state apparatus, and concluded that "to have

* Thinking about anti-Semitic comrades among Communist "politicals" imprisoned with him at Buchenwald, Semprun agrees with a friend's contention many years later that in the Soviet Union a Jew is "nothing" and can become "something only by creating for [himself] a nation, that is to say, by being a Zionist." For Jews generally, in fact, Israel "is absolutely necessary on the historical plane, to be defended [by all men!] absolutely against all attacks, one of the few places in the world where no compromise is acceptable." And yet, he goes on to reflect, compelled not so much by the intrinsic logic of the argument as by the characteristic momentum of his oppositional imagination, Israel represents for Jews "a fatal danger . . . on the metaphysical plane," so that we conclude at last that they are "caught up in a contradiction that is their essence and their greatness." For, if the Jews are not "a chosen people, which is unthinkable," they are "at least a reading people: the people of the Book," and they cannot survive as Jews and yet "become a people like any other."
** In *The Long Voyage* Semprun had often spoken of making life "habitable" by fighting for a better future in which persons would not feel subservient to "overwhelming 'facts,' " but most of these observations seemed unanchored. In the same way he could briefly remember a Resistance comrade who exposed himself to danger in order to kill a known informer. Though the novel ratifies the action, and Semprun is clearly moved by it, we have little sense that the questions raised are conceived politically. Semprun is bearing witness to forms of personal courage that inspire him to believe that even simple people ought to be able to resist terrible things. To have made this sentiment political would have been to think generally about what is involved in resistance and how personal costs might reasonably be tallied.

a successful career in East Berlin . . . one really had to be ready for anything . . . for every kind of baseness, every kind of rotten compromise." Not content with this resonant observation, Semprun goes on to depict the comrade in his baseness, pitifully mouthing the empty formulas to which his "unconditional submission" had accustomed him. Everywhere he turns in his travels through the Communist bureaucracies, most especially in the Soviet Union, he finds instances of "the appalling political level, the dull, petty mental world." More terrible, in recalling Buchenwald he discovers that the Russian prisoners "did not seem at all out of place . . . , as if the social world from which they came had prepared them. . . ." Semprun responds in these several instances to the betrayal of politics and of political intelligence by persons whose "lack of fidelity to what really matters" can seem fully appalling only to one not inveterately disposed to repudiate all political objectives. Semprun despises the Communist version of politics because he understands how the party functionaries despise their misguided intellectuals and desire only to create "a true specimen of the new man," which is to say, a "hate-filled robot of correct thought."

Semprun's sympathy is directed not exclusively at victims, but also at those who struggle. To struggle in the camps is not just to preserve some vestige of humanity, but to continue to make distinctions that may permit one to resist. This has nothing to do with attempting to give intellectual coherence to the ideas and prejudices in the name of which one has been imprisoned. To resist in Semprun's sense is to decide, for example, which inmates are more valuable than others and to work collectively to protect as well as possible the most valuable.* These decisions must be made not on the basis of personal or arbitrary sentiments, but by considering what the future will require—assuming that there is a future—and what camp life is likely to do to particular survivors. Semprun's involvement in these questions, both as prisoner and, later, as novelist, never leads him to assume that there is any satisfactory way of resolving them. But he is alert to particulars and driven to think perpetually about the means to ends of which he is typically uncertain. Without denying the personal dimension of the various tactical decisions he considers, he convinces us regularly that there are kinds of persons who inhabit certain kinds of situations and invite us to apply to them certain kinds of political intelligence. There are no textbook typologies in Semprun's novels and no pedantic arrangements of material to enforce properly dialectical conclusions. But there is a dialectical rigor that refuses to conceive of social phenomena as merely individual any more than they are merely typical. He is quite obviously concerned with the real suffering of real people, but he knows better than to regard the sufferers simply as victims "objectively" subject to conditions of which

---

* The most valuable, of course, include those who are not only likely to survive the camps, but those who can respect the necessity for group cohesion. That the most favored prisoners among Semprun's comrades tended to be party operatives with fraternal feelings toward one another should come as no surprise. For a disciplined relation to Necessity, few prisoners were likely to outdo trained CP operatives.

they are the necessary and "final" product. His commitment to struggle as a first principle of existence is what makes him a political man even in circumstances that conspire to reduce the idea of struggle to the tasks of elementary survival.

It is appropriate, in fact, to describe Semprun as one whose sensibility was shaped not only by the camps and by his work as a CP functionary, but also by his early years in the anti-Fascist Resistance. There, as I have previously argued, "intellectuals came to feel that they had a working model for a society of the future," that ideological differences among them were insignificant, and that one could tolerate deprivation so long as life seemed to have an "elementary simplicity" and "one belonged to something greater than oneself and more important than anything one was likely to accomplish by oneself. Private virtue was, in this sense, indistinguishable from a capacity to maintain a feeling of solidarity with one's comrades."[10] The drama coursing through Semprun's discourse is thus a reflection of his continuing passionate attachment to the kind of solidarity that is ratified by a sense of common purpose. That attachment, of course, is maintained in spite of the disillusioning experiences of Resistance intellectuals who learned, almost to a man, that the postwar world thwarted every extravagant expectation they had shared. Less and less can Semprun say with conviction what he hopes to see in the future for which he has lived, but there remains the conviction that if there is no longer a party of the just, there is nonetheless more virtue in struggling among others than by oneself. What emerges as a kind of compulsive irony in the discourse measures not only Semprun's disaffection from the goals he'd rapturously embraced, but what George Lukács calls a "deep certainty . . . that through not-desiring-to-know and not-being-able-to-know he has truly encountered, glimpsed and grasped the ultimate, true substance."[11] Unable to formulate his ultimate purposes, unable to grasp historical and social reality as a totality, Semprun makes the most of a strenuous political impulse by reminding himself that the impulse is at once a form of romantic excess and a necessary concomitant of hope. Satisfied with the task of keeping memory alive so as to restrain his surging will, he treats every element in his fiction as though only causal explanation could recommend it to our attention and as if no cause were sufficient to explain it.[12]

In the intermittence and fragmentariness of its evocation, *What a Beautiful Sunday!* confirms the loss of the unity once conferred by Semprun's belief in a state of harmonious presence at the end of history. This loss is felt so deeply and recapitulated so insistently because it is felt to affect not just the quality of Semprun's representations, but the reality of the events that define him as surely as he interprets them. The self that lived through Buchenwald and that sought in *The Long Voyage* to create an impression sufficient to its memory appears in its later incarnation less secure about the adequacy of its recapitulation and so less securely the self constituted by the enactments of memory. Buchenwald, in this later perspective, seems, if anything, more terrible than it had before not because more of the particulars are dredged up, but because the physical reality of suffering is displaced in its primacy by reflections on ideological thinking. By the time we read in Semprun's novel that Stalin was "like an ideological gas chamber, like a Crematorium of Correct Thought," we accept that ideology itself is largely responsible for what happened in Germany as also in the Soviet Union. This is not as obvious a notion as some may still suppose. A good many students of the Nazi period continue to treat the SS, for example, simply as pathological brutes and sadists rather than as persons who routinely carried out orders[13] and were pleased to participate in what they took to be a new order. Semprun's emphasis on the clichés and slogans and glib assumptions by which he had been misled creates no retrospective sympathy for those who carried out Hitler's orders; it does make Buchenwald seem more a product of mythical thinking and slavish acquiescence in the dictates of the ideological zeitgeist than an eruption of the demonic.

To get at the holocaust, then, to see it freshly in the light of Kolyma and the several betrayals associated with Prague and Budapest and the patent imbecilities of fashionable Parisian intellectuals, is for Semprun to accept the gaps in his own representation. These gaps have to do, first, with the intention to tell a story and the simultaneous recognition that the story lacks definitive shape and reliable closure. Partial and palpably argumentative representations inevitably complicate the "original" events and put their historical status in question. But the more important gap has to do with the incommensurability between suggestions that root causes are unknowable and suggestions that political formulas and ideological rigidities can account for much that matters.

To address these gaps without pretending to banish them, Semprun incorporates in the novel three "historical" figures who comment, sometimes implausibly, on the material. From the first, Goethe and Eckermann, whose favorite tree adorned the Buchenwald grounds, are summoned to witness current events and finally made to comment on things they cannot from their perspective adequately comprehend. Just so, Léon Blum, formerly prime minister of France, author of a book on Goethe and Eckermann, and an inmate in an elite Buchenwald facility in 1943, is made to cast intelligent though inadequate reflections on the contemporary situation. These audacious discursive interpolations surely are the chief wonders of the novel. But they succeed more especially not because they are intrinsically eloquent or colorful, but because they demonstrate how intelligence itself is invariably self-limiting. We see in the efforts of Goethe and Blum to enlighten us how even their resistance to historically conditioned categories is itself shaped by their personal limitations. These observations are not brought forward as part of a nihilistic project to deny the validity of reasoned reflection. Some intellects are clearly better equipped to instruct us than others, just as some ideas surely explain more than others. In this respect, the contrast between Semprun's Goethe and his Eckermann could not be greater, and Blum's idea of equality—it was "the scrupulous respect of variety and, consequently, of natural inequality"—is surely more cogent than that of any other character. But it is also obvious that precisely Goethe's wise disinterestedness prevents him from opposing Hitler, as Blum's socialist humanitarianism in its vague healthymindedness lacks the "internal dynamism" required—the judgment is uttered by Goethe—to "make an epoch." The Blum who thinks so comfortably, even in his imprisonment, of "natural inequalities" and of filling gaps in his knowledge cannot imagine what such preoccupations look like to those with a different experience of the world.

Semprun once or twice reflects in *What a Beautiful Sunday!* on the relation between reality and fiction in his work. Defending his right to invent where he likes, he claims for his novel the status of History, which is "a perpetual, ever-renewable reinvention." His object is nothing less than the truth. What, then, is the truth of the holocaust as Semprun has finally come to know it? It is that the most important things can only be understood, imperfectly, by those who refuse to be innocent, who refuse to believe that the antithesis of horror and immorality is a "disalienated society" and an accomplished moral universe. The distinction of his novel is a function of his knowing all too well that this truth is far from doing authoritative justice to the holocaust. But like others who have confronted this most important of subjects, he has quite reasonably concluded that his own fragmentary perspective can become a vital part of the historical and imaginative record and serve the truth more honestly than less modest efforts to embrace the holocaust in its entirety.

II. GEORGE STEINER'S HOLOCAUST: POLITICS AND THEOLOGY

The temptation to treat the holocaust as an event like no other in Western history has grown in recent years. Even holocaust scholars like Lucy Dawidowicz contend that "with each passing year the murder by Hitler's Germany of 6 million Jews . . . becomes increasingly harder to comprehend."[14] For Dawidowicz, of course, the murder of the Jews seems "harder to comprehend" largely because she has mastered so much material on the holocaust that she can no longer trust the easy generalizations lavished on the subject even by persons of good will and scholarly instinct. If the Jews were hunted and killed in countries as different as Poland and Hungary, or France and Austria, how can it be that simple formulas like "the banality of evil" or "Jewish self-hate" should suffice to explain what happened? If, in Hungary, the Jews were for a long time protected only by conservative aristocrats—themselves often anti-Semitic—who eventually lost control of events,[15] and in Poland the Jews were violently attacked by Catholic priests whose counterparts in other countries did much to protest the killings,[16] what kinds of political generalization can seem acceptable?

Scholars like Dawidowicz respond to the difficulty of understanding by exploring everything they can in the historical record. Others content themselves with emphasizing what they take to be characteristic episodes in the evolution of the Final Solution, and consequently regard exceptions to the emergent "rules" as marginal cases. Thus, Polish anti-Semitism is still "explained" by the "fact" that many Jews were members of the Communist party and thus perceived as a threat to Polish traditions, this in spite of the fact that only a small number of Polish Jews were actually party members and, more important, that nothing Polish Jews *did* or *didn't* do had anything to do with the fear and loathing they inspired.[17] Students of the holocaust intent on demonstrating how ideological conflict lay at the root of European anti-Semitism have little patience with intractably irrational materials that would seem to defeat such an approach.

Since the end of the war, and even for some years before 1945, many writers have thought about the holocaust in metaphysical terms that do not so much account for what happened as place the major events in an edifying philosophical perspective. These efforts have been supported by theologians and strengthened by poets and novelists who regard the holocaust as an instigation to ask what survival means in a universe that has negated all that was formerly considered sacred. Such writers may avail themselves of the massive documentary evidence collected by scholars, but typically they write as witnesses of the terrible events or as those for whom "the black mystery of what happened in Europe is . . . indivisible from [their] own identity."[18] They write, that is to say, so as to reflect on the holocaust as if it alone contained the key to their own experience and to the mystery of a suffering without purpose or the prospect of redemption.

Few have written more eloquently than George Steiner on the burden of Jewish identity in our time, and no one has gone so far as he does in his recent novel to consider the effect of the holocaust on our understanding of the relation between good and evil. Equally important, no one has demonstrated so well that a metaphysical and theological investigation of the holocaust must be informed by a deeply sophisticated political interpretation of the constituent events if it is to do justice to them. *The Portage to San Cristobal of A.H.* has offended a great many people, as George Steiner surely knew it would, but it has seemed offensive largely because of the very broad speculations it makes on the death camps as "a disease of civilization itself " and on the Jews as somehow responsible for the concept of a chosen people which inspired "the Nazi racial doctrine of 'Nordic' superiority." If such speculative assaults on a variety of established assumptions have provoked controversy in the past, they now seem to some "an upsetting and misleading" species of "anti-Jewish propaganda".[19] Conceding the purely novelistic virtues of *The Portage,* many commentators have gone on to argue that its presentation of patently dangerous ideas exempts it from serious consideration, either as art or as document.

The most sustained and intermittently informative attack on the novel thus far was written by Hyam Maccoby, librarian of Leo Baeck College in London and a scholarly authority on Jewish issues. Maccoby's attack on the novel has in common with others the deeply troubled suspicions aroused by Hitler's long speech of self-justification which concludes the work. Why, many have asked, should Hitler be given the final word? Why, moreover, should his Jewish captors in the South American swamp be given nothing effectual to say in reply? And why should Hitler's speech contain a wealth of "fine-spun theological arguments" that make it anything but the "embittered paean of hate against the Jews" that the historical record would lead us to expect? Why embody "the principle of evil" in such a way that it will have more than its fair "measure of cosmic dignity"?[20]

Maccoby seeks to answer these questions by attributing a variety of motives to Steiner and by studying the origins of the novel's leading ideas in Steiner's earlier nonfiction works, particularly *In Bluebeard's Castle*. What he consistently refuses to do is to read the novel. He refuses, that is, to consider the structure of the narrative, the way in which certain characters are so placed as to challenge, or at least implicitly compromise, the assertions of others, the way in which irony works—in the various panels devoted to French, German, British, Soviet, and American on-lookers—to frame and set a limit to the dizzier philosophical ruminations that otherwise dominate the novel. The ideas expressed in *The Portage* are not, after all, what they would be, what indeed they are, in the pages of various critical and philosophical works. They are not espoused but pre-sented as a part of the material the novelist wishes to bring before us. We take the ideas in *The Portage* seriously because they enhance the narrative design and are compellingly presented as a telling index to the attitudes and the character of particular figures with whom they are associated. Nowhere does the novel forget that it is a novel, and nowhere does it instruct us to read as if the ideas were themselves both object and motive of the narrative. By failing to read *The Portage* as a novel, Maccoby not only does a grave injustice to Steiner, whose intentions he very largely misreads, but he also misses what is central to *The Portage*, specifically, the determinedly political character even of the most philosophically ab-struse reflections with which the principal figures torment or entertain themselves. The absence or violation of literary perspective in Maccoby produces—as in so many essays on *The Portage* or other topically "sen-sitive" works—a distortion so great that the critic can confidently ignore even central components of the novel at issue.

But what was Steiner's intention in *The Portage*, and why did it seem necessary to give Hitler the final word? This we can begin to answer only by considering what materials are encompassed in the novel and how they are organized. *The Portage* is a short work, containing seventeen chapters of varying length and focus. The main action of the novel involves the capture of a ninety-year-old Adolf Hitler by a team of Nazi-hunters who attempt to deliver him from the recesses of his jungle lair back to "civi-lization." Seven chapters of the novel are focused on the struggles of the Nazi-hunters to accomplish their mission and to come to terms with the magnitude of their responsibility. What there is of physical activity in the work is mostly concentrated in these sections, which are made to alternate with others that enhance our understanding of their importance. The Nazi-hunters themselves are unified by their common purpose, but by no means constitute a uniform representation of a familiar type. In a very few pages Steiner manages, for example, to differentiate the intellectual among them from the rabbi as well as from the youngster who understands rather less than his companions how manifold the motives of their joint occupation may be. In these chapters Steiner is not so interested in the variety of characters themselves as he is in making us accept that the mission itself is plausible and difficult and necessary. This he can accomplish only by placing Hitler in the hands of men each of whom wants the captive in his own way. This precisely—in Steiner's account of it—is what Hitler must be seen to be: a figure who will mean different things to different people, but who nonetheless has a reality and a meaning that no merely personal or national or religious bias may be permitted to cover over.

Five chapters of the novel focus on influential or otherwise concerned persons representing whatever claim to Hitler may be staked out by the English, the Soviets, the Germans, the French, and the Americans. Steiner doesn't presume in these chapters to do justice to the complex and competing interests in Hitler that might conceivably be entertained by various citizens from different walks of life. He attempts, instead, incisive portraits of individuals each of whom approximates to a national type and whose reflections on the imminent delivery of Hitler permit us to consider who really is suited to judge what Hitler did. To say of these sections that they introduce more forcefully than any others the political dimension of the central issues is not to suggest that they stand apart from the rest of the novel. By placing them strategically all through the work Steiner makes us feel that they provide a perspective that is never really absent, no matter how insistently the Nazi-hunters may dwell on theological or ethical conundrums. If Chapter Three gives us a Nazi-hunter named Simeon who worries over "the true obstacle, each of them carrying it inside himself like hidden leprosy"—which is to say, "Indifference. Common sense with its fine sharp bite"—it gives us as well the politics of the holocaust legacy, the attempt of the postwar Poles—one example only—to make of the Auschwitz museum a memorial to "the heroic Polish combatants against Fascism." But the political perspective, the violation of historical memory and meaning by political cunning, is more securely brought before us in Chapter Four, with the studied evasions, the methodically ordered intimidations, the "flat and servile" nullity of the Soviet characters. *The Portage* needs Chapter Four not because we need to know that the Soviets in particular process and respond to the news of Hitler's capture in the way that they routinely handle everything. This we might have supposed on the basis of other, more extensive and detailed accounts of the Soviet bureaucracy. Chapter Four serves to underline—what the novel will brilliantly convey in various other ways—how attitudes toward Hitler inevitably reflect the circumstances in which those attitudes take shape. This might be trivial were it not for the fact that the attitudes are portrayed, dissected, with a precision that makes them seem at once terrible, familiar, and irredeemable. More important, Chapter Four serves to make Simeon's special, mostly private obsessions in Chapter Three seem necessary beyond anything his reflections themselves might suggest. Is there nothing more than hysteria and a lamentably theatrical bravado in the final paragraph of Chapter Three, with Simeon's "-AUFSTEHN. LOS" directed at Hitler, echoing the haunting commands of the Nazi S.S. to their Jewish victims? Is the following declaration—"I have a warrant here. Born April 20, 1889. In the name of man. For crimes herewith listed. In the face of God. AUFSTEHN"—nothing but the author's specious working up of an improbable encounter? Chapter Four convinces us that, in the context of political reality, of that specious Necessity which consigns historical memory to inconsequence, which makes of the past something to be altered or ignored without the prospect of punishment, only the passion to *avoid* at all costs flatness, servility, kitsch, common sense, and self-righteousness may justly be honored. The exertions of the Nazi-hunters may be properly understood only by observing what men and women, in the Soviet Union and elsewhere, typically do with the burden of the past.

There is nothing like a standard format for the chapters of *The Portage* devoted to representations of the various "concerned" nations. The French perspective is presented by means of diary entries ostensibly written by a *"Sous-sĕcrétaire d' état"* in a "Political Intelligence Section" of the government. These entries reflect concern for protocol, for French participation in whatever may ensue, and for an avoidance of the "ridiculous" or "farcical" so often attendant on grand public spectacles. Chiefly, though, what is expressed is the desire not to have opened up once again for broad public discussion the matter of Vichy as "a structure out of the heart of French history, out of an agrarian, clerical, patriarchal France which has never accepted the Revolution, which loathes the Jew and the Mason. . . ." This fear—that the world will think of Hitler increasingly as not much worse than the Frenchmen who created Vichy—is not taken to be a definitive account of a French *position* on the holocaust, but is offered as the reflection of one intelligent Frenchman who obviously has these fears in common with other Frenchmen. Just so, his thought, that if the Americans get their hands on Hitler, "the psychologists will have their day," is not the final word on American attitudes to evil but a plausible suggestion about what is surely a characteristic tendency in American culture.

The most interesting, one might almost say the most inspired, marginal character in *The Portage* is the German jurist Gervinus Röthling. The chapter devoted to him opens with his reflections on music as "a specific assertion of freedom [in/from time] so absolute as to dwarf other pretenses at liberty be they political, private, orgiastic." Indeed, Röthling's addiction to the absolute is closely related to his detestation of pretense and, consequently, to his impatience with the varieties of compromise and ordinariness that make up most of human experience. Dissatisfied with his daughter's mild virtues and solid competencies, he thinks of her as a typical young German fearful of risk, above all guilty with the burden of their parents' past. "Are they afraid it will happen again and think it best to go by the back-stairs softly?" he wonders. To the modest deceptions of the present generation he opposes the experience of those who, in the Hitler years, "heard Gieseking play the *Waldstein* in Munich, almost at the end," when "smoke hung in the concert hall and an odour of fire and burst mains blew in through the gilt and stucco foyer." Teutonic drivel? It is the achievement of Steiner's Chapter Eleven to portray Röthling as one still susceptible to a kind of nostalgic hysteria ("Would it have been better to miss the long holiday in Hell?" or "I Gervinus Röthling have emptied life not from a glass but from a magnum.") and yet somehow impressive in his implacable commitment to absolutes. His daughter confesses not to know what one might say to Hitler were he suddenly to appear, and Röthling's youthful adjunct quite reasonably argues that a Hitler "stands outside the norms of law" and therefore poses problems that can only be dealt with in imaginatively novel ways. To these credible, if finally ineffectual, responses Röthling offers what are incomparably richer, if also somewhat dubious, assertions. These are intrinsically interesting in their philosophic subtlety, and convince moreover in seeming to come out of everything that Röthling has seen and felt over many years. But they are signally important, too, in providing an alternative perspective on what occurs in the climactic chapters of the novel, in the course of which the Jewish Nazi-hunters put Hitler on trial at the edge of a swamp with no one to witness their deed but an Indian "savage" named Teku.

Röthling contends, in fact, that "either the law is an ontological totality both central in human institutions and capable by internal logic of extension to all human phenomena or it is merely and inevitably a corpus of local ordinance, an ephemeral fiat in this or that corner of history." So, "if the codex does not apply to Herr Hitler, *Junge*, then he was absolutely right in claiming that he stood above the law, that the law is a bundle of mouse-eaten parchment with no authority over the superman or the will of the Volk." Thorny questions of special circumstance, of the way in which popular support may be harnessed in totalitarian societies, of how responsibility for vast misdeeds may be localized, are swept aside by the logic of so convinced an absolutist as Röthling. And there is, to be sure, much to be said for what he proposes, tempted though one is by the idea of the exceptional and the imaginative and the insoluble. When he refers, with an articulate brilliance unmatched by his antagonists, to "the concept of the *corpus mysticum* of the ruler" in terms of which "the earthly is joined to the transcendent in a perfect *incorporation* at once mystical and down to earth," one wants to assent even as one is quite properly skeptical of a "mystic carnality of statehood" that can be used to defend the implicit Necessity even of unspeakable things. But when, finally, Röthling tells his earnest adjunct what again is so consistent with his sense of things, that he "can't help wondering whether it [the Nazi period] was very important," we understand that Röthling's fullness of life and intellectual energy have brought him no nearer than others less gifted than he to an appreciation of elemental realities. His absorption in the law and in what he takes to

be the transcendent possibilities inherent in absolutist supratemporal institutions has blinded him to the obvious, including the obviously important
murder of six million Jews.[21]

The chapter devoted to Röthling is a bravura performance from start to
finish, and though there are other things in the novel that command greater
attention, it is surely useful to ask what in the end the chapter accomplishes.
Would the novel stand without it? It would stand, no doubt, though it
would seem a lesser thing without the explosion of manic articulacy and
the vivid evocation of a sojourn in hell recalled with a kind of suppressed,
though still lurid, hysteria chastened only by Röthling's self-conscious irony
and disdain. The texture of *The Portage* is obviously made by the voices,
the intricately rendered thought-patterns of the various intensely articulate
characters who appear in its pages. But the essential contribution of Röthling's chapter is its demonstration of a thesis that Steiner has long wondered
over in essays and books: that the Final Solution was masterminded by
highly sophisticated, even deeply civilized persons in whom the capacity for
evil was not in most instances a predominant disposition. Röthling's participation in the Nazi regime is not specified in any detail, and Steiner
surely did not intend to suggest that he was personally responsible for
atrocities or in a position to do much about them. The portrait serves,
nonetheless, to indicate that politics itself is more than the calculations of
technicians or bureaucrats with master plans or orders to follow. It may
also be the appeal to those for whom the decent options seem sterile, for
whom the prospect of a long and cautious life seems mean and pinched.
We know, or feel we know, what Röthling means when he declares, "God
how we lived! Each terrible year like a hundred ordinary years, like a
thousand. He was true to his word. A thousand-year Reich inside each of
us, a millenium of remembered life." This is not, to be sure, the language
in which we should today wish to discuss the holocaust, but it is a language
fraught with political meaning and human significance. Does it not indicate
where ordinary attempts to encompass the holocaust go wrong? Does it
not point up the insufficiency of arguments that indict members of the SS
as psychopaths or describe the camp commandants as invariably obsessive
anti-Semites with an insatiable appetite for killing?[22] Röthling is a representative of but one kind of former Nazi, but he enlarges our sense of
political motive in a way that goes far beyond his eccentricities.

So, too, does Rodriguez Kulken represent a dimension of politics that
is often ignored in treatments of the holocaust. Three chapters of *The
Portage* are focused on Kulken and on an American adventurer-emissary
named Marvin Crownbacker. The American finds Kulken in San Cristobal
working to lure the Nazi-hunters and their prey to him on the shortwave
radio he commandeers at the behest of British intelligence. What emerges
in these chapters is the combination of ferocity, shabby opportunism, and
sheer gnawing *ressentiment* as index to a potent sort of political inspiration.
The Portage needs Kulken not only because someone is needed to lure in
the prize and to decipher the faint, sometimes mystifying radio messages

emanating from the jungle. It needs him because he is just the kind of slimy little beast who might have sold himself to Jew-killers had he been given half a chance. A man without conviction, he thinks of Jews, casually, as "the snot of the human race," but imagines that he feels no particular hatred of them and wonders why anyone would have bothered to exterminate them. But he is more given to reflecting on his own worldliness and savvy than on larger questions. He prides himself on knowing "the only real truths that men have set down: time-tables, shipping registers, customs regulations," and so on, "sharp-edged monads of exact wisdom." His desire to know what is worth knowing is fueled by his sense of "occasions" in the making, possibilities that might just conceivably materialize to extricate him from the make-do stratagems by which he has kept himself afloat. He is, he tells himself, a man of his time, "the century of the borrowed skin," one of "the long-legged" who can "make a bundle of their shadows," belonging nowhere, attached only to the next opportunity. He knows little enough about politics, but supposes in his customary way that he knows quite enough, thank you; specifically, that it has always to do with the efforts of "the lean ones with the tight gray skins and the talcum powder. With accents like an open razor and a lemon in their teeth" to make use of those like Kulken who can be bought and, once they have been properly buggered, scratched off "like a dry scab."

There is in Kulken a sour *ressentiment* that makes him frightening enough, though he seems even more terrifying in his unstable alliance with the American opportunist, whose "grating banality—loud, caricatural, inescapable"—nonetheless seems to Kulken to carry with it an enigmatic, unaccountable air of "authority." Crownbacker may indeed seem a caricature, and as such not quite a match for the richer figures drawn in the novel, but he is a plausible caricature, his head filled with just the kinds of things impressed on those on the climb in the lower-echelon business schools and media organizations so central to the American way of life. He gives to Kulken what Kulken alone had lacked, namely, a sense of sheer commercial avidity and exploitative cunning unmixed with more abstractly grandiose or unfocused ambitions. His grating banality includes a particular respect for "contracts, agent's release forms . . . , subsidiary and other rights, newspaper and magazine serialization," and so on.

Without being an important character in himself, Crownbacker brings to the novel that dimension of brash and sleazy vulgarity that must figure in calculations of what Hitler can be made to mean. Crownbacker is the fitting middleman for the mass audience that will wish to consume Hitler as it consumes other novelties. He is, moreover, the embodiment of the vague fears intermittently expressed by the Nazi-hunters, who know in what degree each of us has been penetrated by the imagery of commercial films and other manifestations of mass culture. They fear not only that Hitler will be taken from them and made into an empty spectacle; they fear also that the scenario they themselves enact is ridden with clichés, that their fantasies of retribution are intolerably theatrical and false to what is most vital in their mission, that the entire premise under which they operate—that justice can be done, accounts settled—is based on a cheap literary idea of closure. It is Crownbacker's world that triumphs in the patently stirring images conjured up by the Nazi-hunter who wants to make a film about the adventure. "At the end," he forecasts, "we'll be seen staggering out of the jungle, bearded, limping, almost delirious, and a great crowd will surge towards us. I'll use a zooming lens to show a sea of faces, ecstatic, unbelieving. . . . Press helicopters overhead, painted bright yellow, cameras looking at my camera. But I'll never show Hitler's face, not full-on." Etc. The incapacity here demonstrated to think outside the terms of cinematic convention and strategy is the mark of that crowning danger that invests every aspect of the effort to make an object lesson of Adolf Hitler. In the end the Nazi-hunters are by no means made to succumb to commercial temptation or to seem unduly implicated in the view of things that they guard against. But that view—of all things as at bottom nothing more than objects of use—is a powerful one as it emerges again and again in *The Portage*. It is, after all, the view that largely directs political activity and shapes the political imagination of all but the "sacred" characters in Steiner's narrative.

Insofar as politics—often regarded in its alliance with commerce and image-manipulation—may be said to be a part of the holocaust issue generally, it is, for Steiner, obviously a challenge to the idea of the sacred. But no one who reads *The Portage* will suppose that the sacred is somehow subordinated to the political or made to seem somehow ineffectual. The chapters devoted to the Nazi-hunters contain deeply stirring passages on the meaning of Jewish history, the mystery of the Jewish quest for the Messiah, and the possibility of an error in the transcription of Torah that might somehow explain the horrors visited again and again on the Jewish people. These are not occasional interjections or manifestations of local color, but the very heart of the sections devoted to the Jewish characters in *The Portage*. When Elie Barach recalls that his own master, "Shelomoh Bartov, said to us that the unfathomable error, the breath through which evil has rushed on man was the word *and* in Leviticus 10, V," we are moved not as by the eccentricity of a curious particular but with a sense of the magnitude of small things, the importance even of remote possibility for those who are possessed by a sense of the sacred and cannot think of meaning as that which may be altered by individual whim or circumstance. If political actors typically think of nothing but circumstance and believe in adjustment or compromise as an appropriate response to Necessity, "sacred" characters make it their mission to work through circumstance so as to repudiate the comforts associated with compromise. It is not in the repertoire of possibility for a well-adjusted political man to dwell overmuch on the significance of the word *tempt* as Elie does when he recalls that "the most learned Isaac of Saragossa declared that the error was in Genesis 22, i. God would command an old man to slay his child but not *tempt* him to do so. Temptation is vile, like a memory of blue air and open sea here in the cauldron of the swamp." It is one of the great wonders of *The Portage* that it should make such demanding considerations seem exigent and immediate for us even as we attend so readily to the dexterous political maneuverings of the more contemporaneously familiar figures.

But the central chapters of the book are surely Chapters Six and Seventeen. In the first, Emmanuel Lieber, a Jewish survivor of Hitler and an aged director of many Nazi-hunts, instructs the members of his search party on what they are about in their attempt to bring Hitler out of the jungle. The hunters are, as Steiner has it, "the animate embers of his calm, just madness. Of a will so single, so inviolate to any other claim of life, that its thread went through Lieber's sleep producing one incessant dream. That of this capture." That inviolate will produces in the discourse of Chapter Six "a precise register of exclamation and lamentation that simultaneously records and mourns, coldly enumerates yet carries an immense effect."[23] The discourse begins as a warning to those directly in contact with Hitler:

> You must not let him speak, or only few words. To say his needs. . . . Gag him if necessary, or stop your ears as did the sailor. . . . As it is written in the learned Nathaniel of Mainz: there shall come upon the earth in the time of night a man surpassing eloquent. All that is God's, hallowed be His name, must have its counterpart, its backside of evil and negation. . . . When he made the Word, God made possible also its contrary. . . . He created on the nightside of language a speech for hell. Whose words mean hatred and vomit of life . . . there shall come a man whose mouth shall be as a furnace and whose tongue as a sword laying waste. He will know the grammar of hell and teach it to others. He will know the sounds of madness and loathing and make them seem music.

To Hyam Maccoby, such accounts serve simply "to dignify Hitler by elevating him into a metaphysical principle," and Steiner's attempt to portray Hitler as the "Black Messiah or Antichrist" is no more than a "poetic" conceit.[24] The fact that it is Lieber who portrays Hitler in these terms is of no consequence to Maccoby, who ignores entirely the existence of characters and the conflicts they set in motion. Concerned only with views and positions, Maccoby has no feeling at all for the suggestive richness of Lieber's speculations or for their critical role in justifying what most disturbs him in Steiner's novel.

Neither does Maccoby pay any attention to what is surely the most harrowing part of Lieber's discourse, the sacred litany in which he intones in faltering voice a partial record of those destroyed. To have paid attention to this litany, of course, would have required of Maccoby—given his inability to distinguish between the author and his characters—that he attribute the eloquent recitation and remembrance to Steiner himself; this would in turn have required that he renounce his willfully obtuse reading of Steiner's intentions. What, after all, would the author of "anti-Jewish propaganda" be doing with the following words?

You will not forget. O I know you will never forget. Remember for Jacob.
. . . That he almost drove us from the face of the earth. . . . Come in, Nimrud.
Tell me that you remember. The garden in Salonika, where Mordecai Zathsmar,
the cantor's youngest child, ate excrement, the Hoofstraat in Arnheim where
they took Leah Burstein and made her watch while her father . . . , Nowy Swiat
XI, where Jakov Kaplan, author of *The History of Algebraic Thought in Eastern
Europe 1280–1655,* had to dance over the body of, in White Springs, Ohio,
Rahel Nadelmann who wakes each night, sweat in her mouth because thirty-
one years earlier . . . , can you hear me, unimaginable because innumerable,
in one corner of Treblinka seven hundred thousand bodies, I will count them
now, Aaron, Aaronowitch, Aaronson, Abilech, Abraham, I will count seven
hundred thousand names and you must listen . . . , I will say Kaddish to the
end of time and when time ceases shall not have reached the millionth name.

Maccoby pays no attention either to that part of Lieber's discourse in
which he remembers that Hitler

could not have done it alone. . . . Not without the helpers and the indifferent,
not without the hooligans who laughed and the soft men who took over the
shops and moved into the houses. . . . Not without D. initialling a memo to B-
W. at Printing House Square: *no more atrocity stories. Probably overplayed.* Or
Foggy Bottom offering 75 visas above the quota when one hundred thousand
children could have been saved.

To have considered even briefly this brief passage would perhaps have
tempted Maccoby to acknowledge the existence in *The Portage* of the various chapters devoted to Soviet and French and English and American
politics. But how, in the light of such an acknowledgment, could Maccoby
have argued that the novel "goes on to make the holocaust into a cosmic,
rather than a terrestrial catastrophe . . . , to hypostatise it into a metaphysical manifestation of an ineluctable fate"? By ignoring the novel itself,
by refuting instead a series of statements extracted from the book without
any sense of their place or function, Maccoby is permitted to strike edifying
postures and to prattle comfortably about "the effort to prevent it [the
holocaust] from ever happening again."[25]

But if Maccoby and others have misread or willfully ignored the various
aspects of the chapter devoted to Lieber, all have understandably paid
major attention to the final chapter, in which Hitler himself speaks. As he
speaks, we think inevitably not only of what he says, or of why he speaks
with such conviction, but of Lieber's earlier discourse, as of the fevered
reflections of Elie Barach. We think of these earlier passages because it is
obvious to us that Hitler's speech is at least implicitly a response to them,
because we recall that Lieber had introduced some of the very terms subsequently elaborated by Hitler, and because in a novel so obsessed as this
one is with founding words and grammars of hell and names themselves
as bearers of sacred truth, Hitler's eloquence must be pitted against that
alternative eloquence sounded by his Jewish antagonists. To fail to do this

is to suppose that the final words spoken in the novel are intended to cancel all earlier words, that the character we have been so assiduously warned against, who "will know the sounds of madness and loathing and make them seem music," is to be taken as the bearer of ultimate truths.

What Hitler says may not in the end be so important as the fact that he is given the final words in *The Portage*. But there is no doubt that had he been given more credibly Hitlerian things to say, no one would object in so strenuous a way to the novel's organization. Alvin Rosenfeld quite rightly argues that "the name Hitler is not a literary fabrication and, at least at this point in history, cannot be reduced solely to the fictive." As a consequence, one expects to hear from the character a language we associate with the actual "Führer of the German Third Reich."[26] That Steiner's Hitler has at his command an arsenal of theological and metaphysical references that go beyond the language of the German Führer's speeches and writings cannot be denied. That he is permitted to say things in his defense that had earlier seemed to many persons plausible, if not perfectly acceptable, is also true. "Would Palestine have become Israel . . . were it not for the Holocaust?" A difficult and troubling question. The fact that it is clearly irrelevant to any reasonable consideration of Hitler's guilt seems not to have occurred to commentators like Maccoby any more than it occurred to them that Steiner demands that we register this irrelevance. Did the Nazis kill nearly so many innocent people as Comrade Stalin? An important question, no doubt, but of little consequence to a focused inquiry into the crimes against humanity ordered by Hitler and perpetrated in his name. Again, Hitler's eloquence never persuades us that his arithmetic standards are finally acceptable or in moral terms consequential. Is there "the smell of blood" in the Jewish holy books, a smell that had much to do with the concept of a "chosen people" and "the setting apart of the race," with the will to chastise or destroy "the unclean, amid the welter of nations," to "slaughter a city because of an idea"? And is not this idea of "One Israel, one *Volk*, one leader" the origin—as Hitler claims—of the dream of a master race, Hitler's racism no more than "a parody" or "hungry imitation"? The suggestions are provocative, to be sure, and the fact that they are not carefully taken up and repudiated by other characters in *The Portage* is meant to be troubling. But no one who has read *The Portage* as a novel, alert to its various tensions and counterweights, can suppose that Steiner intended us to believe that Hitler was correct: that Judaism is a racialist doctrine like the Nazi religion, "that the Israelite massacre of the Canaanites should be put in the same category as the Nazi massacre of the Jews," or that events that "took place in vastly different societies,"[27] thirty-five hundred years apart and with entirely different objectives and features, should be considered in the same terms. The fact that the historical Hitler would not have been likely to say the things we find in *The Portage* should not be taken to indicate that Steiner went out of his way to support them, whatever violations of credibility the procedure might have demanded of him. Hitler is made to offer his various "inspired" suggestions in *The Portage* because some are just plausible enough to give pause to his immediate auditors, as to us, and because only by placing such suggestions in Hitler's mouth can Steiner embody in his character the potential for radical transvaluation, hence radical evil, which it is the novelist's obligation to confront.

Here we arrive at the heart of Steiner's enterprise, and at the main thrust of the objections leveled at *The Portage* even by deeply scrupulous readers like Alvin Rosenfeld. Even as Maccoby is infuriated by Hitler's closing speech, Rosenfeld is disturbed to find that Steiner's Hitler sounds more like George Steiner than like the historical figure: "To carry over not only the thinking but the distinctive idiom of one's earlier writing and ascribe it to Hitler is . . . something strongly unsettling," Rosenfeld writes.

> Steiner has argued speculatively in the past that Nazism was a travesty of Judaism, that the Jews as the embodiment of conscience became intolerable to a Christian Europe that remained pagan at heart, that by introducing God, Jesus, and Marx into the world the Jews pressed upon a reluctant mankind a 'blackmail of transcendence' that it could not abide and finally threw over in . . . the holocaust. . . . What baffles in this instance, though, are not Steiner's ideas but their transference virtually verbatim into the mouth of Hitler, as if Steiner's understanding of Hitler were identical with the latter's self-understanding.[28]

Where Maccoby dismisses *The Portage* in its entirety on the basis of Hitler's closing speech, Rosenfeld concludes that though Steiner was temporarily seduced by the "eloquence of negation," his book still brings "to a climactic moment of clarification and justification the whole Jewish obsession with the holocaust."[29]

But more is required to come to terms with *The Portage* than the conclusion that Hitler's speech marks Steiner's unfortunate lapse into "the seductive eloquence of negation." The ideas expressed in the speech had previously seemed to some of Steiner's readers unduly conjectural, quite as Rosenfeld says; other readers had found them strikingly original and fertile. But no one, to my knowledge, had spoken of them as morally objectionable. They had seemed, in Steiner's books and essays, speculative forays or probes that indicated the persistence of Steiner's absorption in questions for which there are no satisfying answers. Insofar as Steiner suggested that Nazism was a parody or travesty of Judaism, he intended not to demonstrate their fundamental similarities, but to uncover the roots of the Nazis' perilous fascination with the Jew and their simultaneous attraction to an idea of a chosen people. The spirit of the inquiry was always such as to prevent anyone from concluding that Steiner intended a definitive historical analysis. On the contrary, in his writings on the holocaust as on other subjects, Steiner has consistently challenged readers to refute his speculations and thereby arrive at more hopeful or more conclusive conjectures. The Hyam Maccobys in the readership have little interest in conjecture, of course, and are particularly impatient with anything that might give aid and comfort to anti-Semites, whatever its intention or primary effects. Maccoby is convinced by a theory of his own which he regards as definitive and unanswerable, namely, that the Jews are the collective scapegoat cum executioner required by a culture that requires a "shifting of moral responsibility" from its own constituents to others who are clearly *not* responsible for the awful deeds that worry the conscience of the faithful. Willfully blind to the fact that there is much in Steiner's speculations to support his view, he "answers" Hitler's speech in *The Portage* by arguing that Judaism is a moral religion—whereas "it is characteristic of Christianity to stress the *impossibility* of the moral life"[30]—and by insisting that there are fundamental contradictions in Hitler's speech.

That Maccoby's remarks, interesting and intermittently instructive though they may be, are largely irrelevant not only to *The Portage* but to the very ideas ostensibly engaged, should be obvious once one has seen that Steiner's primary conjectures are nowhere put to route by the "evidence" Maccoby summons. Nothing the critic says to the effect that Hitler did not really bring about the Jewish state, or that there is no good reason to dwell on the blackmail of transcendence as an essentially Jewish invention, can dispel the fact that these thoughts have occurred, in various ways and under contrary auspices, to many people. Steiner has in the past brought forward these ideas as part of a vigorous inquiry into the barbarism that has so often emerged in Western culture. He has asked, again and again, why so many of the most brilliant writers and thinkers have been attracted to ideas that are very much a part of their vision but that seem on careful inspection decidedly unworthy of them. For a Hyam Maccoby to imagine that his careful description of Judaism as a concept "far less exclusivist" than Christianity will successfully banish the disquiet felt even by many Jews about the idea of the chosen people is to misunderstand the way that ideas take hold even of intelligent people. The critic and historian of ideas is not at his best primarily obsessed with distinguishing correct ideas from incorrect ideas, but with studying the appropriation of ideas by consciousness and the role of particular ideas in the history of feeling.

In *The Portage*, of course, Steiner operates not so much as critic or as historian, but as novelist. His object is embodiment rather than analysis, though he may not be averse to analysis so long as it is compatible with embodiment. Hitler's speech in *The Portage* is not a formal presentation of ideas; it is an elaborate self-defense mounted by a *character* who aptly describes himself as "a man of my time," a "master of human moods," and one "inspired . . . with a certain . . . nose for the supreme political possibility." The speech should disappoint only those who expect Hitler to sound like the standard Hitler who addressed mass rallies; those who imagine that the man Lieber describes as "surpassing eloquent" will know only one language, or that the grammar of hell will sound on his "hundred-forked" tongue like anyone's idea of the grammar of hell. If Lieber's evocation of the character as one who can make the sounds of madness and loathing seem music is even marginally credible, how can one object to Hitler's wielding an appropriately plausible argument in his own defense? Is it not the very point of Steiner's portrait to suggest that the power of transvaluation embodied in the historical figure can be understood only by seeing it as a radical power of rhetorical persuasion allied with an utterly ruthless disregard of historical fact and theological or moral scruple? "Steiner's Hitler is involved in the devil's game of language subversion, a game that his historical prototype brought to a kind of deadly perfection," writes Alvin Rosenfeld. "The deadliness lies in appropriating a vocabulary of sacred terminology and inverting it so that words are evacuated of their customary meaning and made to take on a reverse signification."[31]

Looked at in this way, Hitler's grammar of hell, as brought before us in a living language, should be able to appropriate and invert any sacred terminology, including one originally invented—by Steiner himself, in previous essays and books—to express a combination of horror, guilt, inadequacy, and sheer driven disquietude in the face of a historical event that remains "indivisible" from his own identity. *The Portage* had to end with Hitler's speech because it is the object of the novel to show what the power of transvaluation is all about. The final speech demonstrates that a Hitler can appropriate a Steiner for his purposes by willfully ignoring, and thus violating, the spirit and intent of Steiner's original utterances and turning them to totally alien purposes. To accuse Steiner of perversity in this case is to suppose that Steiner acquiesces in the perversion of his survivor's vocabulary as practised by one who sought to incinerate those with whom Steiner is inalienably identified. If he fails in *The Portage* to invent for Hitler's auditors a suitable conclusory response, that is only because that suitable response is implicit—deliberately and only implicit—in the shape of the novel, in the way that it builds to Hitler's speech, in the way that the earlier speeches of Elie Barach and especially of Lieber prepare us to receive Hitler with the fear and loathing and mistrust he inevitably inspires. Apparently plausible some of his ideas may seem, but the spirit in which those ideas are presented will ensure that all will resist the fatal allure of a specious self-exoneration cleverly tricked out with those ideas.

If it is Steiner's aim to embody in an audaciously original way the powers associated wtih Adolf Hitler—powers that in part account for the awful "successes" of the Final Solution—is it reasonable to describe *The Portage* as hypostatizing the holocaust "into a metaphysical manifestation of an ineluctable fate"?[32] One has only to consider the relation between Hitler's final speech and the various alternative appropriations of the holocaust by ostensibly "normal" persons in France, England, the Soviet Union, and so on to conclude that the fate of the Jews under Hitler was not the consequence of an ineluctable or otherwise divinely inspired plan. The politics of the holocaust is ever a part of Steiner's vision and as such figures prominently both in retrospective accounts of major events and in the contemporary meanings assigned by various constituencies to those events. The holocaust—so *The Portage* proposes in its juxtaposition of competing though fully coherent perspectives—was the work of human beings acting alone or in concert with others to deny or more aggressively subvert the fact of massive suffering and destruction to which their actions variously contributed. *"Men are accomplices to that which leaves them indifferent,"* Steiner wrote years ago in "A Kind of Survivor."[33] So, it might be added, are men accomplices to that which inspires in them only the desire to discover political "solutions" designed to evade the critical issues. It is not the aim of *The Portage* to fix blame, as if the score could ever be settled, final responsibilities tallied, and punishments neatly meted out; but the aura of complicity is established as a fact that cannot be denied in *The Portage*. Steiner doesn't need to cast his government officials and soft men as murderers or even as villains to warrant our considering that Hitler could not have gone so far without them. Hitler can rave all he wants about the blackmail of transcendence and the Jew's addiction to a "rational Eden." His ravings are necessarily to be studied in the context of the more mundane and approachable perspectives that also claim our attention in Steiner's novel. Are not the briefly depicted maneuvers of petty and well-placed bureaucrats thirty years after Hitler's ostensive demise a fitting display of the politics that led the British Foreign Office in 1943 to refuse the way of emigration to seventy thousand Rumanian Jews, who would surely have been saved, on the grounds that there were "difficulties of disposing of any considerable number of Jews" (translate: the Arabs would have been unhappy with Jewish émigrés to Palestine, and severe embarrassment would have resulted from attempts to place the refugees elsewhere)?[34]

In the aftermath of the holocaust, the state of Israel came into being, and with it the determination of a people never again to be "the passive recipients of [their] fate."[35] But it is not the Jews who emerge from *The Portage* as the passive victims of an ineluctable fate. In effect, the Jewish characters are given in the novel an opportunity to exert their will and to affirm their existence in their own chosen terms. Those who emerge more particularly as "passive recipients" are the other political actors, winners and losers all. It is they who continually take refuge in circumstantiality, who are unable to imagine the past or any present possibility that is not dominated by a Necessity conceived as determinate and therefore sufficient. Politics for these worldly men of action is a way of life requiring above all accommodation and the "realism" of those for whom it is possible even to kill Jews without for a moment hating or fearing them. Even Hitler emerges from *The Portage* as one who has learned—in the many years since the defeat of his armies, if not before—that there is use in attributing one's own motives to others, in claiming to be an imitator rather than a creator, a man of one's time rather than a transcendentally inspired deliverer. A messiah he may take himself to be, but a messiah with the vision of Zion as the place of warriors rather than the "vacuous" refuge of dreamers. Like others, whose share of blame is in no way commensurate with his, he is made to seem responsible both for what he has done and for what he has allowed or encouraged others to do or to think. The political imagination itself is targeted in *The Portage*, quite as much as the political deeds or omissions practised under its auspices. That imagination is not by definition degraded or incapable of achieving a proper reverence for essential facts; but there is a kind of political imagination that can operate only by assuming that all human affairs fall under the heading of business as usual. And business as usual always means to this kind of imagination the need to realize in every human encounter maximum partisan advantage. The very idea that such an outlook might be narrow, or that ordinary assumptions are out of place in dealing with events like the holocaust, is ruled out by a political imagination for which special events represent at most procedural obstacles to be overcome by tact and strategy quite in the way that other obstacles are overcome.

The Portage, then, is a political novel in the sense that it takes seriously the existence of political objectives and demonstrates the way that even degraded political ideas have the capacity to take hold of people and to direct their activities. More, the central action of the novel is conducted by persons who operate often from collective purposes, no matter how misguided, and who believe that they participate in something larger than themselves, no matter in what degree that participation is predicated on the hope of personal advantage.

But *The Portage* is also a very unusual political novel. It is concerned not with change or the future, but with coming to terms with the past. Though the procedures envisioned by Emmanuel Lieber and executed by his minions in the jungle may lead to some future consequence, they are not chiefly interested in the prospect. The cause that may be said to move Lieber may be present in the person of Adolf Hitler, but the novel amply shows that he is hardly a sufficient or final cause. Like other distinguished political novels, *The Portage* gestures vigorously at what can only be an absent cause, that is, at the totality of human motives and relations that made possible the holocaust but must remain permanently unavailable to the representational enterprise. Where *The Portage* differs, again, from most other political novels is in its conviction that, though the cause is ever worth pursuing and must ever be sought in the precincts of human motives, ideas, and institutions, it is likely to be elsewhere, in a precinct unamenable to common sense or careful literary design.

9

Günter Grass: Negativity and the Subversion of Paradigms

I

In a recent book on "Postrealist" fiction, Philip Stevick invokes Günter Grass as one who has taught us to appreciate writing that is "intricately and seriously superficial." Working from the idea of "satire without an object," Stevick assimilates Grass to a "tradition" characterized by "free invention" and "bizarre extravagance," in which "there is the grotesque without the vision of a perfection of form, irrationality without the possibility of reason, bad taste without the possibility of good taste." Exemplary in this "tradition" are writers like Nabokov and Donald Barthelme, who are said to disavow "moral purpose" and even the implicit assertion of "standards of decency."[1] Günter Grass may pretend to concern himself with consequential matters; he may allude to moral postures and reasonable alternatives. Ultimately, though, he neither believes in those alternatives nor has in him that depth of contempt for the grotesque and banal that could take his writing beyond the level of the brilliant put-on. So Stevick and others routinely contend.

To many postmodern writers and critics, of course, Grass can seem a major figure largely because he resists unitary readings of objects and situations. Conceding his interest in history and politics, formalistically inclined enthusiasts applaud instead his demythologizing of standard interpretations and his resistance to bourgeois solutions. Though he poses conflicts in such a way as to put us in mind of humane interests, actual persons, and plausible objectives, he is often said to be committed primarily to the advantages of risk and vertigo, to "the unclean promiscuity of everything which touches, invests and penetrates without resistance."[2] The Grass protagonist often retreats from the world to the relative security of the asylum or an out-of-the-way mine shaft, but he belongs, ultimately, to the world he loathes and contains within himself the very contradictions by which he is beset. In no sense a clinical type, neither paranoid nor schizophrenic, he experiences nevertheless some of the terror "proper to the schizophrenic": "open to everything, in spite of himself, living in the greatest confusion . . . himself obscene, the obscene prey of the world's obscenity. . . . It is the end of interiority and intimacy, the overexposure and transparence of the world which traverses him without obstacle. He can no longer produce the limits of his own being. . . ."[3] For such a character, and for his author, there can be no determinate purpose, no ordering principle adequate to hold off or master the encroaching chaos. Grass, or so this reading would have him, is in love with his creations precisely because they promise nothing in the way of ultimately disillusioning resolutions or satisfactions. He is an amiable *mensch* who just happens also to be in love with the bottomless pit and the alternately up- and down-swirling figures who circulate colorfully in its nether reaches.

That all of this amounts to a somewhat misleading profile of Grass will come as no surprise to his more scrupulous readers. A postmodern writer, to be sure, Grass is in his novels the most committed member of that heterodox fraternity. Fascinated by the bizarre extravagance of his own imagination, he is also compulsively addicted to setting limits and proposing judgment terms. Alert to the world's obscenity and resistant to the easy satisfactions of a pious indignance, his work is clearly informed by moral purposes and saturated with contempt both for the bourgeois banal and the accommodatingly outré wit of the superficial put-on. His interest in politics and history looks here and there like a justification for elegiac commemoration and dismissive irony, but in the main he aims to criticize and to reclaim the reality nearest to him.

Grass has never issued an uninteresting book, and he is never far from politics no matter in what direction he turns, but it would seem at present that his fame and his stature are likely to rest chiefly on the Danzig trilogy. There, he gives the lie to the familiar view of him as in essence a virtuoso fabulist and engages reality as if politics had everything to do with the sense we make of it. Never one to impose narrow generic limitations on his work, Grass moved from the first to confound description, and the various parts of his trilogy are as different from one another as they are together different from the later novels. No one content to think of *The Tin Drum* as satire was likely at once to see that it was also a parody of the satiric mode. And no one disappointed in the absence of an elaborated political vision was equipped to see that the books were primarily devoted to examining that very absence. The works in the Danzig trilogy have commanded international attention for more than twenty years because, more than any other novels of our time, they pose questions for which the inevitable solutions recommended seem as much a part of the problem as an alternative to it. Capricious, whimsical, intermittently mean-spirited, Grass's imagination neither forgives nor condones, and insofar as the novels give pleasure, they do so by insisting on the extravagant rightness of a savage intemperateness or a defeated self-interrogation. Grass may well be the most ebulliently inventive writer around. He is also a devastating social critic whose missionary fervor approaches the more single-minded exertions of a writer like Solzhenitsyn.

If it was not clear at first that the novels of the Danzig trilogy were to be thought of as political novels, it was not clear either that they were to be studied together. But since Grass's decision to have them issued as *The Danzig Trilogy* some years ago, it has seemed useful to try to put them together before setting them apart. This procedure seems relatively easy to follow so long as one thinks of them primarily as inquiries into the Nazi period and its consequences or as a portrait of Danzig as emblematic lost city. These are not the only ways to think of the novels, but the various other ways are more or less compatible with them and, in any case, no single perspective can seem definitive for works of such complexity. The obvious advantage in thinking about a trilogy is the opportunity afforded to chart connections and discover whatever vision might be said to underlie the several manifestations of Grass's genius. The obvious disadvantage is that even the more patent connections are apt to be misleading, and that one will be tempted to overlook major structural discontinuities by focusing on thematic or ideological similarities.

In actuality, the problems inherent in a reading of the trilogy are not grave. The works are so utterly unlike one another in their methods of narration and in their principal motivic elements that one is rarely inclined to think of them as a coherent unit. Any spurious coherence temporarily attributed to the trilogy is inevitably subverted by the reader's simply asking, "How does this work?" rather than "What does all of this add up to?" The fact that things *don't* generally add up in Grass doesn't mean that we are not tempted to arrive at totals, but Grass's relentless estrangement of particulars from their ordinary relations with other particulars ensures that we will be insecure with anything but contradiction. Unlike others in the emergent "tradition" of postrealist fiction, Grass always makes at least implicit reference to the world outside the created novelistic universe, and so demands more than a purely formal response. Distortion, misapplication, and contradiction in Grass are evaluated in terms of the recognized deviation from a worldly standard that is taken to exist apart from anything the words on the page can establish. To think about the vision underlying a Danzig trilogy and informing its determined repudiation of naive literary unities is not to acquiesce in the privileging of content over form, or depth in place of surface. Such categorical dichotomies have no validity for Grass. The trilogy exists as a provisional unity because it has a vision and creates—or remembers—a common world. To seek to find in the trilogy the unity we associate with, say, George Eliot or Thomas Mann is to suppose that there is for Grass a retrievable, enchanted center from which all outward movement seems but a temporary defection.

In these terms, the ostensive center of the trilogy would be the city of Danzig itself, and Grass's aim would be to recapture the enchanted city of his childhood. The contrast between the degraded Danzig of 1939 and the "true" Danzig of an earlier time would then serve to structure Grass's project. The trouble with this schema, of course, is that there is for Grass no enchanted city. The inhabitants of Danzig behave in the war years quite as one might have supposed they would on the basis of their earlier record. What exists in the way of civic tradition is a grotesque parody of the idea of community. Those, like two or three of Grass's narrators who invoke lower-middle-class life in Danzig as a kind of idyll, a *bürgerlich* dream of cozy domesticity and burgeoning larders, are not finally the dupes of the dream, but its dark deniers. They summon memory not to satisfy desire, but to set out the grounds of their disaffection. Danzig may once have been alive with promise. The streets may have teemed not with comfortable sleepwalkers, but with irritable and unpredictably venturesome individuals. But memory cannot furnish even a summary transcript of that hypothetical former state. Memory has to content itself not with the myth of an unfortunate fall, but with the evocation of a long dying only intermittently sweetened by traces of genuine feeling.

To compare Grass's Danzig with Joyce's Dublin is to see at once how peculiar and grim is Grass's allegiance to his city. Not for him the celebration of this or that remaining trophy in some putative arsenal rich in civic achievements. Not for him the attenuated or wan eloquence of a language "hung with pleasing wraiths of former materials," as the poet William Carlos Williams once spoke of Joyce's language.[4] If Joyce's Dublin sleepwalkers could speak "with continual racy unexpectedness,"[5] Grass's swollen burghers succumb almost entirely to the drearily conventional or turn themselves into monsters to escape the numbing tedium of their lives. Joyce loves what Dublin was; Grass is occasionally nostalgic for what Danzig might have been. Joyce hears the impressive "crackle" of "cadence and image"[6] in the milling street voices and barroom jousts of Dublin; Grass hears a kind of menace even in the good-natured cluckings of respectable shopkeepers and devoted family men.

Hugh Kenner argues that "Flaubert, nauseated by *la betise,* catalogued intellectual junk in a kind of ecstasy of disgust, contemplating a society of empty dolls conducting their lives in clichés." But, he goes on, "Dublin was less dessicated and Joyce was more humane; he was interested in clichés for their verve as locutions, not their nullity as doctrines."[7] The distinction between Flaubert and Joyce is instructive. Though one would hardly think to use the word *dessicated* to describe Grass's Danzig, his attitude to the city surely has more in common with Flaubert's view than with Joyce's. Grass is less interested than Flaubert in discovering clichés so as to exercise a confident disdain. There is in Grass not quite an ecstasy of disgust, but an unabashed cultivation of all that can provoke disgust. This wallowing in the sty of banal ordinariness has as object not the transformation of the awful into the wonderful, but simply the recovery of a landscape on the basis of which plausible hopes or criticisms may be entertained. There is no point in considering whether Grass is more or less humane than Flaubert or Joyce, but surely he is interested in the "nullity of doctrines" and unwilling to take heart by dwelling on the "verve" of trite locutions. If Danzig is for Grass a dead city, it is because the city has in fact disappeared as a nominal and cultural entity and because the nullity that was always a part of the prevailing "bourgeois smug" made it possible for the average Danzig citizen to countenance every kind of terror and indecency. The Danzig trilogy gives us neither a city of words nor a blueprint for the resurrection of a lost metropolis, neither an homage to a vanished civility nor a singular display of an almost vanished eloquence. Grass's Danzig stands for us because it is a definitive negation not of dreams but of the city itself, of the idea of the city as a habitation fit for human beings.

It is not as a political critic that Grass speaks of Danzig. One doesn't draw from the trilogy an attack on this or that isolated aspect of public policy. There is no formulated theory of public action or of civic responsibility. What there is of political analysis has little to do with a commanding view of the way in which institutions take shape, break down, or reassert themselves. Political ideas as such emerge fitfully, with little sense that they may be interesting or instructive in themselves. They express, at most, someone's effort to understand events that are likely to be understood better without ideas. To think politically in Grass is in general not to be tempted by political ideas and not, therefore, to be distracted by any fashionable jargon of inauthenticity. One must be familiar with the ideas only so as not to be manipulated by them or by those who wield them.

But if Grass refuses to adopt in his trilogy the voice or the posture of the professional political critic, he does nonetheless project a vision that is everywhere political. Grass's Danzig is the place at which the nullity of doctrines may be seen in its effect on every aspect of public and private life. This is not a matter of Grass's taking up now this, then that reflection of some ostensibly primary cause. What we often experience in Grass as a kind of textural all-overness, a filling of the canvas to the point of bursting the hypothetical frame, is a function of his having come at his material with the intention that it everywhere seems to be of a piece with everything else. That this is no reductive enterprise is clear to any reader who has tried to come to terms with the incredible variety of Grass's forms and concerns. But underlying this variety is the seething linguistic matrix to which every particular and every inflection of discourse owes its existence. *This* is the basis as it is the reflection of all that is meant by politics in the trilogy.

It has become a commonplace of literary discourse to remind readers that novels are made of words. In this respect there is no difference between a political novel and any other kind of novel. But to consider the linguistic matrix in Grass is to think about words in a rather special sense. It is, in fact, to be reminded that the most ordinary words may be put to extraordinary uses and that nullity is the place where no center holds, where all meanings are possible and nothing true, where words are routinely violated not in the spirit of play, but on behalf of deception and terror. Grass's Danzig, whatever the crass or brutish vitality of its inhabitants, is a nullity in the sense that it is the embodiment of an empty promiscuity. There it is possible to say one thing and mean another without knowing that any meaning or intention has been subverted. There it is usual to turn guilt into an opportunity for the arousal and gratification of collective desire. And there it is possible to adopt as many father figures or brother figures as one likes, with no thought of betrayal as a possibility to which one's several attachments might lead. Language here permits one to deny the significance of the experience in which one is enwombed, and politics is the submission to fantasies of power without thought of achievable objects or consequences.

To immerse us in language is for Grass to demonstrate the way in which thought itself is subverted by its own means. Even those who, in Grass, see what is happening around them find that the language available to them has been corrupted by the uses to which it has been put. They express, in what is sometimes an injured eloquence, the inadequacy of words and of their own efforts to acknowledge horror. The focus is not on language as such, but on the telling of tales, remembering, misremembering. But it is language that now and again compels our attention and reminds us that it is involved in all that Grass wishes to examine. It is not the primary cause of corruption or indeed the only means by which political control is exercised; it is at most a principal symptom of a process that may not be reduced to simple formulas like "The Big Lie." And if that process can never be encompassed in any single manifestation or activity, neither is it to be definitively identified with any single character.

That this is so we can acknowledge by recalling how even Grass's more or less positive protagonists embody the possibilities from which they are in flight. What is Oskar in *The Tin Drum* if not a "satanic" figure, as he often tells us? What is he in the postwar period if not a cynical exploiter and profiteer? Of course, he is also the victim of more entirely diabolical characters and currents, as he is the archenemy and satirist of his fellow Germans. That combination of attributes can in no way be grasped by positing elementary symbolic oppositions, as Oskar himself is tempted frequently to do. The character is much more complex, for example, than the playful opposition and intermingling of Goethe and Rasputin can suggest. And though it is amusing to see how Grass develops the color oppositions intimated in the novel's opening paragraph (the brown eye of Bruno "can never see through a blue-eyed type" like Oskar), it is obviously misleading in suggesting that persons belong either to the one or the other category. Grass's goal in the trilogy is in part to propose versions of the truth which carry in them the bad conscience of their own inadequacy. But rather than succumbing to that bad conscience, the characters themselves determine to make the most of the words and narrative constructions to which they are tempted. Their commitment to speaking itself is a way of bearing witness to experience without pretending to have effectually distanced themselves from it.

Oskar Matzerath is, of course, an ideal vehicle for establishing the radical instability of language and of the narratives we gamefully construct. By calling everything he says into question, by mistrusting even the facts of his own life and acknowledging the whimsy that can gratuitously distort his versions of important events, he ensures that his reader will be alert to doubleness and perversity in his every utterance. From the moment he tells us, on the novel's first page, that his hospital bed "has become a norm and standard," we are prepared for anything. Insofar as norms and standards have meant something to us in the past, they must henceforth mean something very different. And insofar as the bed may be described on the same page as "goal," "consolation," and "faith," it is clear that no assumption as to meaning or priority in life is any longer secure. This has nothing to do with the commonplace literary contention that words are rich in connotative possibility or that great writers expand the limits of meaning. Grass demonstrates the elasticity of language not to marvel at creative possibilities, but to get at the corrosive effects of a circumstance in which nothing has determinate meaning. To invoke norms and standards without being able to take seriously the idea that there are such things— as customarily understood—is to be set adrift on a sea that has no shore.

In *Dog Years* we find much the same sort of thing. Open to almost any page of the novel and examples will abound. In Book Two, Harry Liebenau describes Eddi Amsel's opinion of sparrows as follows: "In his opinion they were all individualists that had camouflaged themselves as a mass society." This is more than a fleeting irony, though clearly one will know fully what can be done with the formulation only by putting it together with other comparable ones studding the narrative. Surely the word *individualist* can never quite be what it was after being made to assume its place in Grass's sentence. That seems certain. Nor can the word *productive* retain its innocence once we have read, on the same page of *Dog Years*, that Eddi built scarecrows because "at the most he wished to convince a dangerously productive environment of his own productivity."

But these are random examples of a phenomenon that is intrinsic to Grass's way of writing and thinking. In our readerly experience of the trilogy we are likely to take in such items with the sense that Grass's narrators little understand the linguistic subversions that are the marrow of their utterance. They are aware of doubleness and perversity as of a menace without name or contour. As it is everywhere and everything, so it is nowhere and, in a sense, nothing. When they respond to the menace, they do so without knowing that their response is or is not adequate, which is to say, focused and properly adversarial. Their words express, rather than control, the promiscuous possibilities of a terror without limit. Just so, Eddi Amsel's scarecrows, though "built with no adversary in mind," as Liebenau says, terrify and astonish; and Oskar's drum, taken up in a spirit of childish play and exuberance, becomes alternately a weapon and a defense against the vicissitudes of life and of feeling. The very idea of expression in the trilogy is compromised by our sense that the artist figures and narrators are complicit in the corruption of their chosen medium.

When Grass mounts a focused assault on language under the Nazis, he has in mind no single class of German citizens nor any particular city or region. He is concerned less with the responsibility of intellectuals than with the penetration of language by a suspect ontological jargon. Heidegger is a principal villain of *Dog Years*, appearing now and again as the embodiment of a false transcendence and obscurantist idealism. He it is whose jargon infects the language of ordinary discourse, so that "underdone potatoes in their jackets . . . were called 'spuds forgetful of Being' " and a most ordinary tech sergeant can be heard to mutter, "After all, the essence of being—there is its existence." This is no cheap parody or easy put-down. In using Heidegger as he does, over and over again and in the most various of contexts, Grass proposes to purge German of its legacy of the transcendent, to deidealize the traditions of German culture and to strip away all possibility of false heroics and glamorized triviality. The German problem, as Grass sees it, is not a matter of bad ideas or devilish führers. It is a matter of indulgent inauthenticity, an inability to live in the quotidian, a propensity toward monstrous inflation and deformation of the ordinary. The verbal acrobatics performed by Grass's several narrators in the trilogy serve to underline the consequences of a reality denied, betrayed, and violated.

Grass is unwilling to opt for any theory of a German national character that might account for what happened in the Nazi period. He is skeptical of all theories, whether plausible or not, and resists the various colorful generalizations that often attract students of the period. Charles de Gaulle once wrote that the Germans were " 'Knights of the Blue Flowers who vomit their beer,' thus deriding both their romanticism and their coarseness."[8] Others have sought the key in the German understanding of a *Volksgemeinschaft* not as a genuine community, but as a soulful albeit will-less and amorphous mass in thrall to a properly inspiring authority-figure. None of these observations is definitely repudiated in Grass, but then he is not concerned with definitive responses to ideas. There is little in the trilogy to make one feel that Hitler's Germany was a decent society, but the reader is rarely tempted to think of it in clinical terms, as a sick society, or to account for what happened to the language in that way.[9] Neither is the by now familiar notion of the banality of evil sufficient to summarize Grass's view of Nazi Germany. It is not ordinariness as such that is found wanting so much as the inability to live with tedium and the mundane demands of ordinary life. Monstrous deformations of language and betrayals of meaning are not a routine function of ordinariness, but a denial of the quotidian reality in which most persons usually manage to live tolerably decent, if uninspired, lives.

So Grass is committed in the trilogy to a critique of ordinariness as also to a critique of the language that subverts any ordinary apprehension of reality. In this it might even be said that the works contain an autocritique. Linguistic virtuosity serves as much to obscure as to penetrate reality. Those who use language to assert their literary mastery participate in procedures that are endemic in the German language community generally. Literary virtuoso or shopkeeper, the speaker in Grass is most likely to reveal the reality of his time by demonstrating the breakdown of language, its obscenely promiscuous elasticity. What distinguishes the artist-figure from anyone else is his conscious adoption of the mode of self-parody as a way of distancing himself, however provisionally, from the community to which he belongs. Grass himself refuses to stand above or apart from the universe he creates. He is at once the scourge of his people and their codefendant, though when called to defend himself he has nothing to offer but a record of atrocities committed in the name of *Verwandlung*, which is to say, a spurious transformation and regeneration.[10]

What there is of a larger or more generous vision in these novels can be glimpsed only very imperfectly by considering them collectively, as a trilogy. They do, all of them, have something to do with Danzig, to be sure, and they do collectively ask what is entailed in the attempt to record what the mind can never hope to fathom. They do, together, argue on behalf of the inextricable relationship between art and politics, between the play impulse (*Spieltrieb*) and the didactic impulse (*Pedanterie*). And they do insistently demonstrate how a major work always creates its own myths, whatever the artist's ambition to demythologize the experience he examines and the popular attitudes that have grown up around that experience. But Grass works through particulars in a way that once led him to speak of his object mania. Finally one understands the novels not by enumerating their broad ambitions, but by registering the many intimations of vision that are inseparable from individual characters and contexts. With a work of controlled understatement, like Heinrich Böll's *Billiards at Half-past Nine*, it is possible to summarize the action and the author's attack on the complacency of the German middle classes and to feel that one has done justice to the enterprise. With Grass, who through literary cunning and main-force gets inside the very fabric of the ordinary life, nothing less than an attempt to get inside the fabric of the fiction would seem adequate. And this one cannot do by dwelling too confidently on the broad continuities in the trilogy.

II

The Tin Drum is rightly described as a political novel. Though by its very variety and originality it would seek to deny the validity of genre designations, it asks again and again the standard questions that we associate with fictions of a certain kind. More important, in subjecting to parody virtually every posture and emblem available to writers of high seriousness, it puts us in mind of so many narrative codes and paradigmatic "solutions" as to make the status of things in the world seem deeply problematic. This problematic dimension we attribute to the fact that political novels are always necessarily concerned with change or the prospect of change. The intense pressure exerted by competing narrative paradigms we attribute to the fact that complex political fictions always seek in some sense to demystify earlier sacred emblems or paradigms while working also to recapture some idea at least of an organic social order that has been destroyed. *The Tin Drum* is at once the least conventional and—in its capacity to make us think about the unavailable totality of relations in German society—the most satisfyingly complete of political novels.

In saying of *The Tin Drum* that it is a "complete" political novel, one must concede, as we have earlier suggested, that political ideas as such do not interest Grass and have no independent life of their own in the fiction. The effect of this on the novel is that no conflict is ever made to succumb to an ideological resolution. The operant narrative principle is one of constant opposition and provisional displacement, whereby many different things occur over and over again, each time with apparently different meanings and effects. One commentator speaks acutely of a "repetitive circularity" and of "an aggressively monotonous round": For Grass, "eras may change, but wars, catastrophes and new beginnings recur mechanically."[11] Though one is tempted at almost any point to privilege some passing reference to an idea or some apparently primary narrative focus, the novel teaches us to expect that no center will hold, that there is no primary focus any more than there is a primary emblem or interpretation we must adopt. No sooner do we begin to think of the protagonist-figure as the incarnation of an innocent *Spieltrieb* than we are forced to think of him as a hideous little incubus. No sooner are we instructed to assimilate his activities to the perspective of "innocence beset by banal mendacity and corruption" than we are made to see the patent insufficiency of that paradigm. To be disabused of one's commitment to a paradigm is, however, not to see it permanently banished. Like everything else in *The Tin Drum,* it will return, in a somewhat different guise, perhaps, but recognizably similar.

The literary importance of this procedure lies in the fact that the competing paradigms are deliberately built into the fiction. They do not simply emerge in us as provoked responses to material that would otherwise seem incomplete or ideologically wayward. Grass anticipates the full range of possible coded responses to his material and incorporates them in the fiction as elaborated paradigms. In a sense, Grass's fiction may be described as a succession of fragmentarily elaborated paradigms that subvert (without definitively displacing) one another. Though each paradigm is eventually abandoned, it continues to play a role in asserting the instability of all narrative codes. And, given the obsessively circular quality of the work, even demonstrably untenable paradigmatic resolutions are likely to reappear again and again, each time renewing their implicit claim to clarify what is at issue in the narrative.

The political importance of Grass's procedure has to do with the fact that, though the main issues are largely political, the paradigms usually direct us beyond politics or to a dimension that is decidedly prepolitical. They tempt us, that is, to conclude that human behavior had best be evaluated by standards that have nothing to do with political systems or ideologies. A fellow like Oskar's father, Alfred Matzerath, may decide that it is expedient to wear a Nazi party pin and to attend Nazi rallies, but he is to be understood as a victim not of ideology, but of a bourgeois conformism that has only an incidental political component. So we often feel as we make our way through *The Tin Drum*. The consequences of Alfred's conformist behavior may under particular circumstances assume an overtly political character, but he is not conceived predominantly as a political actor. In the same way, though Grass relentlessly parodies Nazism as a grotesque state religion for which the presiding presence is "the gas-man," the paradigm invoked has more to do with the misappropriation of Christian ideals than with the correction of a political policy.

Under these conditions, it is well to ask where the political content of the novel may be found. In *The Tin Drum* it is found chiefly in the inter-section of the various competing paradigms as they together point to their own insufficiency and put us in mind of alternative perspectives. Consider Oskar and the range of proto-narratives that may be said to be opened up in presenting his story. It is, in one very important sense, the story of the artist confronted by an insensitive philistine society. To be sure, Oskar is no common artist or musician. He is a cruel parody of the artist, always ready to acknowledge the absurdity of the pretentious superiority attributed to creative types. And yet, the portrait does open up or tap into the more flattering proto-narrative associated with the artist type, and calls to mind what the historian Fritz Stern calls "an old and powerful German myth":

> That art was the highest good of a society, that it had a sublimity and timelessness . . . , that it could soar to the highest form of truth, and that it should be a teacher of man and a guide to morality . . . no theme is more characteristic of modern German literature than the struggle between the artist and the Philistine.[12]

The proto-narrative associated with Oskar as artist, then, would have to do with an examination and celebration of the vicissitudes suffered by one who was called to plumb the depths, to read the secrets of the universe, and yet affirm the resilience and basic sanity of his species.

Obviously, as Oskar is a parody of the artist-figure, so conceived, he is also the negation of that figure. As an inmate of a mental hospital, he is hardly an exemplar of basic sanity. Though he understands that he is surrounded by persons in the grip of a massive collective pathology, he is never an entirely reliable witness. Moreover, as we have indicated, he is so much a part of the scene he records that it is not possible completely to exempt him from the criticism we level at other grotesque manifestations of Nazi culture. The proto-narrative of the inspired artist is invested in Oskar only insofar as he is able, however intermittently, to subvert the philistine order. The subversion may not have any overt political intention, but it is nonetheless an element that may eventually be taken up into a political paradigm that we shall hope to define, once the more palpable narrative codes are identified.

It is not as an artist-figure that Oskar beats his drum under the rostrum at a Nazi party rally early in *The Tin Drum*. Though he subverts the established order of the moment, breaking up the rally by challenging the dominant "rectilinear march music" and introducing waltz rhythms, he sees himself quite rightly neither as artist nor as resistance fighter, but as a modest eccentric. Again, this is not to say that the invoked proto-narrative does not have to do with a standard opposition between the artist and his society, or that a related proto-narrative involving the artist engagé is not also invoked. Grass is perfectly willing to bring into play as many of these standard possibilities as he can, not merely to make fun of them, but because they have—all of them—something to tell us about the imagination's way of evaluating the human response to terror. At one level all that Oskar does under the rostrum is to behave like a naughty child and thereby introduce a saving disorder into a situation that is all too orderly. At another level he is invoking or creating his own bond with "the people," as he fondly refers to them here, demonstrating that they can respond as heartily to "The Blue Danube" ("they were hopping about merrily, they had it in their legs") as to triumphal displays of military organization. What this amounts to is not easy to say. Oskar is not one of "the people" any more than he is a portrait of the oppositionist artist-figure pure and simple. His desire to align himself with those who are moved by his drumming is no more than a passing whim. His insistence on the ability of his art to disrupt Nazi meetings testifies not to the enduring importance of his art—he refers to those successes as "historical, old stuff, dead as a doornail"—but to its use as a tool of protest. The youth who "rejected the cut and color of the uniforms" was moved to create "a bit of protest on an instrument that was a mere toy."

Protest, so conceived, is not quite the stuff of grand political conspiracies, yet there is in it an element of innocent, energetic mischief that does surely appeal to the novelist as a vital component of grass roots resistance to tyranny. Not for nothing does he have Oskar shout, "Gone were law and order," or identify Oskar's growing disillusionment with the party with an intolerance of uniformed "symmetry." Oskar's responses may be, and remain, resolutely prepolitical; they may proceed from visceral reactions that are founded, in turn, on intuitive aesthetic discriminations; yet without such discriminations and intuitions, Grass would seem to suggest, most persons would lack the initiative to lift a finger against a well-organized political apparatus. There may be in this sort of elaborated insight no trace of an established political paradigm, but it might be said, in effect, that it has the makings of a new or prophetic model. When one considers the advent of youth protest and Merry Pranksterish politics in the 1960s, one might almost suspect that Oskar did indeed become a kind of minor presiding presence in European culture, and much beyond anything he could assign to himself from the vantage point of a mental hospital.

But the question of competing and overlapping narrative paradigms remains to be examined. As yet we have considered only the activation of the obvious proto-narratives involving the artist-figure, who may be made to assume any one of several different postures. Of these, the one least apt to be claimed by Oskar is that of the artist engagé. This is so in spite of his attraction to the midget impressario and performer Bebra, who cautions him against private life. " 'Our kind has no place in the audience' " he informs him. " 'We must perform, we must run the show. If we don't, it's the others that run us. And they don't do it with kid gloves.' " But this stirring advice, complemented by vivid evocations of horrific "torchlight parades," cannot distract Oskar from his essentially ironic and critical posture. A page later Oskar transforms the encounter with evil conjured by Bebra into "the most sinister of all confrontations": a staring match between Hitler and Beethoven, whose portraits hang facing one another in the Matzerath household. " 'Neither of them was very happy about it,' " Oskar reports.

But it is more than deflationary irony that accounts for Oskar's resistance to the aggressive engagement preached by Bebra. At some level Oskar understands that the paradigm invoked therein has little to do with the image of the underdog fighting gamely against overwhelming odds simply to survive. That paradigm, too, has its day in the pages of *The Tin Drum*, but Bebra is not characteristically identified with it, despite his diminutive stature. Bebra's advice, after all, would seem to justify not mischief or subversion so much as the quest for power and influence. To seek to climb up on the rostrum and run the show in a place like Nazi Germany is a very special ambition. Insofar as the principle of engagement is herein involved, the role of onlooker or spectator or modest sniper repudiated, it is a principle of engagement on behalf of the regime. One may not wish to put it this way, but that is what it is. And one is not therefore surprised to learn, two hundred pages farther on in the novel, that Bebra—still a kind of mentor figure, though no longer very appealing—"was close to the Reich Propaganda Ministry" and "frequented . . . the privy chambers of Messrs. Goebbels and Goering." Nor is Oskar so inveterately ironical a figure as to be unable to describe this as "corrupt behavior." "He would go on," Oskar tells us, "to speak of the hard times, of the weak who must temporarily incline, of the resistance that thrives in concealment, in short, the words 'inward emigration' cropped up, and for Oskar that was the parting of the ways." What Oskar rejects is the strenuous, though finally hollow, effort at self-justification. As a kind of inner émigré himself, he knows all too well that the choices confronting even vigorous spirits like Bebra were not pleasant, and that weakness itself is ultimately forgivable. But "inward emigration" in the mouth of an accomplice in terror can have none of the flavor of secret resistance that many Germans after the war wanted it to have.[13]

The paradigm of the artist engagé, then, is invoked and subsequently traduced in various ways, including Oskar's parody of resistance by means of a mischief-making toy, and Bebra's version of engagement as a commitment to "inward emigration" or survival at any price. But at least as important for our sense of Grass's vision is the way in which the many other paradigms are simultaneously brought into play. At certain points in the larger narrative, for example, a vagrant passage covering only a few lines may remind us of other patterns and purposes that are at work. Oskar is not merely the creator or the resistance fighter or child; he is also the recorder, the historian. In the midst of all the tumult set loose by his wayward drumming, Oskar notes that

> the more culture-minded element repaired to the Hindenburg-Allee, where trees had first been planted in the 18th century, where these same trees had been cut down in 1807 when the city was being besieged by Napoleon's troops, and a fresh set had been planted in 1810 in honor of Napoleon. On this historic ground, the dancers were still able to benefit by my music.

No one will miss the derision conveyed by the words "the more culture-minded element" applied to those who were quite ready a short while earlier to be moved by the standard Nazi speeches. But the main thrust of this passage has to do with Oskar's remembering the history, as it were, of the Hindenburg-Allee. This is interesting to us not because we need to know the particulars in this instance—surely they tell us nothing important about the *present* event enacted on that ground; but we *are* interested, not least because Oskar bothers to remember. And his remembering instructs us in how to regard what we are shown. We are reading, after all, about the decimation, in spirit at least, of a city. Is it not useful to be reminded that the city *has* a history, that certain things *did* actually happen there, and that someone bothered to record them so that others would think of them? Nor were these things that happened *any* things. They involved a world-historical figure, and they included rapid reversals in the relations between that figure and the inhabitants of the besieged city. Is it not reasonable for Oskar to expect that some such reversal, sooner or later, will occur in the relation between twentieth-century Danzig and Adolf Hitler?

The paradigm here invoked has to do with the view of history as a sequence of sieges and "new" beginnings that are never really new. One knows that what one fears most has already happened before and that the past has already betrayed one's fondest hopes. Oskar, of course, does not hope for much, but he knows that the ground he walks on is and always has been contested. By the novel's end he can drum for Victor Weluhn

"Poland is not lost" and recall, again, that there *is* a Polish history, however ignominious. But this has nothing to do with resolving any problem or even with discovering a definitive novelistic closure. The overarching historical paradigm simply insists, over and over, that though events in time resemble one another, they are different. Only an idiot is likely to be consoled by the thought that the same kinds of things happen again and again. One learns from the past, to be sure, but one knows better than to expect that the past is gone for good and all. Just so, the impression that nothing is really new is routinely tempered in the novel by the sense that certain things are so awful that they can *never* have occurred before. Analogies are illuminating, but it is important not to be so absorbed in charting connections as to ignore what is unique in the present moment.

The historical paradigm serves, then, to remind us that more than the survival of individuals is at stake in Nazi Germany. So, too, is there more at stake than the survival of a particular city. Also at issue is the preservation of memory, the sense that things matter if only because they happened. This idea may be taken to absurd extremes, to be sure, and Grass is happy to subject it to parody when he can. But it is, at bottom, a serious and venerable idea. To be able to recall the history of trees on the Hindenburg-Allee is no small feat, after all. All through *The Tin Drum* we are made to think of what is entailed in remembering, though, as other readers have noted, Oskar is "conscious of the reader's appetite for variety, [his] dislike of excessive repetition." Of special interest is the way that "Oskar encourages our memories by distributing compliments when we recognize echoes of previous chapters," as with phrases like "as you have doubtless noticed by now" or "as the most attentive among you will have noted."[14] The purpose of this remembering and of this invoking of the idea of memory is not to thematize the novelistic materials in accordance with some Hegelian schema. Historical perspective in Grass is not a way of allowing what can be thought to seem internally coherent; it is not a way of making what happens seem inevitable or necessary. It is, on the contrary, a way of signaling that what matters is available to us only in a fragmentary or illusory way. We may refer to the past, but its totality is simply "not available for representation, any more than it is accessible in the form of some ultimate truth."[15] The paradigm that is history remembered functions in *The Tin Drum* as one of several limit-fictions to call into question the reliability and validity of all narrative approaches to truth.

To gather together the various paradigms actually invoked in Grass's novel—and we have mentioned only a few—is to aim at an arrangement that the reader knows in advance to be a fiction of his own making. It is, in effect, to assign to the novel an argument that its many different parts were presumably designed to promote. Each paradigm, accordingly, would contribute to the argument either by embodying an aspect of the overarching novelistic vision or by ridiculing our efforts to resolve novelistic ambiguities by privileging certain paradigms and minimizing others. Of course, the approach to *The Tin Drum* as a political novel ensures that one will be tempted to treat certain paradigms more seriously than others. One will, moreover, hope to conclude in examining Oskar's sexual exploits or his relations with his mother that these are significant only because they have something to contribute to the central argument, which has quite obviously to do with politics. If we fail to discover in the novel any overtly political major paradigm that is not subverted as it is invoked, that is only because Grass is committed to subversion and ironic deflection. So we shall wish also to conclude.

In fact, Grass *is* committed to subversion, as we have indicated. He is also committed to recording a major historical event and to enabling judgments and discriminations. If the narrative version of that event points to its own fictive nature and to the insufficiency of the several paradigms invoked in its behalf, Grass's purpose is not therefore to consign the idea of necessary judgment to irrelevance. In this novel the paradigms exist, as it were, because the mind is typically appeased by explanatory myths and because the appeasement of mind is central to Grass's subject. Other novels invite us more or less conventionally or matter-of-factly to reach for paradigmatic explanations. There it is plausible to speak of the operation of the political unconscious as a repository of master codes that may or may not be drawn on as we attend to the unfolding of a text. In Grass nothing is left to the unconscious. If we read the novels properly, we read them as persons acutely conscious of the tactics of the mind which cannot bear too much reality and therefore grasps always for the consolations of master codes that banish all sense of the inchoate and unthinkable. To speak of Grass, as many have done, as a writer who appeals more to the senses than to the intellect is clearly to miss the point of his exertions. His decision to raise all paradigms to the level of consciousness is a decision to make them objects of reflection and, ultimately, of judgment. Though we may rightly be uneasy about reducing the novel to an argument or about privileging one kind of paradigm at the expense of others, the novel instructs us in what are its intentions by dwelling even to excess on the exigencies and liabilities of narrative itself.

We have said that the appeasement of mind is central to Grass's subject. May we say that the argument of the novel proposes to account for that which is entailed in this appeasement? And if we agree to this, will the argument we recite contain a political truth that warrants our particular approach to the work? To pose these questions is to see how unsatisfactory will be our efforts to answer them. Obviously, so many things are entailed in the appeasement of mind that Grass parodies, describes, and laments that no accounting may be thought definitive. And if this is so, no argument—which is to say, no rigorously persuasive or didactic organization of details—is likely to be discovered. What is more, though judgments are enabled, that is, made possible, in *The Tin Drum,* they do not issue from a central political truth that may be identified as the purpose of the novel. Politics in *The Tin Drum* is not a background against which private lives are conducted; it is not a series of compelling ideas or a concerted action mounted by persons endowed with a collective purpose. It is, rather, the various ways in which the mind grapples with the failure or absence of collective vision or purpose. Put this way, politics for Grass would seem to be a possibility that is realized or abandoned or betrayed, and this is not far from the mark. By this token, a people may be judged in terms of their realization of a collective potential that circumstances may require them to acknowledge. In Nazi Germany, the failure to acknowledge collective potential or to act on it was tantamount to a defection from ordinariness itself, to a betrayal of the minimal decencies that are constitutive of a tolerable ordinariness. The betrayal of politics in this sense Grass identifies with the absence of an organized adversary response to the total domination of ordinary life. That domination is achieved by wringing popular consent from those who are conceived in the novel not as interchangeable ciphers, but as differentiable persons alienated from all sense of their own vital agency. And without the conviction of agency, so the novel would suggest, no idea of politics is possible.

Oskar, of course, is intermittently given to thinking of himself as an agent, and as the manipulator and recorder of the various paradigms, he is surely alert to the possibility of a political orientation. But his ironically oppositionist conception of the available paradigms is based on a peculiar misapprehension. Though concerned with self-expression and identity, he cannot see that political structures may be thought of as "institutionalized means of self-expression and self-creation"[16] and that therefore it is in the interest of individuals to erect political structures they can use.

Oppositionist irony and eccentric subjectivism are not adequate responses to the nullity of Nazi institutions or the doctrines that support them. This Grass has no way of stating in *The Tin Drum*, nor any need to state, given that it emerges unequivocally as an inferential insight in one passage after another of the novel. Neither has he any need to tell us in so many words that, as one "committed to the notion that he must not only assert, but create, himself," Oskar should also be "pre-committed to a future in which he will be other than he is now."[17] The retrospective character of the narration in the novel cannot account really for the fact that Oskar has no sense of "a future in which he will be other than he is." Had Grass wanted Oskar to be able to imagine a better future, his narrative means would surely have been adequate to the purpose. Instead, Grass wished to show that for Oskar, as for most other Germans of his time, what simply could not be imagined was the revolutionary paradigm. Though Germans lived in a world undergoing rapid material and political change, they could not see that they were themselves responsible for directing that change and creating the spiritual auspices under which it might be evaluated as a felt reality. Even one so essentially different from other citizens as Oskar finds himself obsessed with paradigms that "serve the function of controlling and interpreting experience rather than creating it."[18] Not a conservative bent on "erecting the paradigm[s] into timeless unassailability," Oskar may be seen as a kind of romantic who "characteristically places himself at that moment in time in which the existing institutions . . . are seen as no longer creating or even expressing the self . . . and therefore as malignantly hostile to the self's authenticity."[19] And yet there is no sustained effort to transform the self [20] or to reconstruct the conditions under which other selves might have been created.

The inability to imagine or to invest with genuine credibility a revolutionary paradigm marks the absence of an acceptable politics in the universe of *The Tin Drum*. This condition we associate with the submission of ego to brute fact, so that even subversion is conceivable only as a series of isolated behaviors having no capacity to disturb in any serious way the facts to which they respond. To be able to operate in the terms of a revolutionary paradigm, the actor must feel that the assertion of ego or of individual identity may be associated with a conception of self as *political* man. Such a conception includes the idea that when one is persistently confronted by an "alien structure" of paradigms that deny one's identity and the reality of one's own lived experience, then one is required and permitted to rebel against them by imagining an alternative paradigm. In this sense to be a political man is to think politically, and to think politically is to have access to a revolutionary paradigm that *makes thinkable*, even if it does not overtly potentiate, the individual's deliberate participation in a collective effort to direct change. To think of the paradigm as "less a happening than an institution: a reference point within the structure of consciousness"[21] is nonetheless to see how critical is the capacity to summon a wide repertoire of available options.

It is reasonable at this point to ask how attentive Grass was to the issue of politics generally,[22] and how absorbed he was in indicating, however obliquely, the absence of a revolutionary paradigm in the conceptual realm of his novel. To do this we might first consider what the revolutionary paradigm might conceivably have looked like had Grass been willing to embody it as an actual referent in *The Tin Drum*. It would surely not have taken the form of a scenario in which a small band of weak but feisty eccentrics, most or all of them children, conspire to overthrow the Nazi regime and successfully distract it from its business. There were instances of popular opposition to Hitler, even in the thirties, but Grass cannot have seen this as anything but marginal and eccentric opposition. Revolutionary opposition seemed possible only for those on the left, who were early murdered or silenced or driven into exile. Occasional references to an authentic leftist opposition in the novel indicate how remote this sort of thing appeared to Oskar as to other Germans. The average citizen continued to admire Hitler until the last months of the war. Those who criticized the Nazi regime usually exempted Hitler from all charges, and even those who were not enthusiastic about the war were stirred by Hitler's military victories. The very absence of sustained criticism and militant opposition made the average German feel how entirely his fate was bound up with the fate of Hitler. Grass doesn't dwell in *The Tin Drum* on true believers, but one understands in reading the novel how, for many Germans, the prospect of destroying Hitler meant destroying themselves. Grass cannot construct a revolutionary paradigm that would go against the grain of reality as it appeared to most persons in Nazi Germany. Hitler himself, in a speech to the generals delivered in January 1944, admitted that "values that do not exist cannot be mobilized. It is therefore impossible to make of the Volk something other than is already present in its values. . . ."[23]

If "the Volk" could not be thought of in activist or subversive terms, it might still have been possible to conceive a resistance role for it. Grass might well have shown, to a far greater degree than he chose to, how in refusing to do small things ordinary citizens managed to hold on to some shred of self-respect. Spontaneous local rebellions against particular edicts may after all involve very little danger for their participants, and even persons without a plan may be moved now and then to say no to an order simply because they cannot bring themselves to follow it. Such persons may lapse back into docility the next day, but there is no sense in discounting the effects even of local, temporary, and disorganized resistance. In choosing largely to ignore such manifestations of popular resistance as did exist, Grass obviously decided that they did not seriously affect the evaluation of German character and politics that he wished to make. More important than an intermittent, inchoate, or ineffectually "tacit" resistance—so Grass obviously felt—was the presence or absence of a true resistance spirit. This spirit may have nothing to do with the effectual mobilization of a countervailing political power or with armed struggle. Rather, it may have to do simply with the courage of persons to say no decisively to those who demand that they commit indecencies. In the context of Hitler's Germany, to resist the reign of terror would obviously have meant at the very least a refusal to comply with the most awful requirements, even if this entailed the end of one's hopes for professional advancement or financial reward. In this sense, the resistance spirit was manifestly *not* present in the German masses, nor even in the more educated sections of the population. If resistance is measured not in sophisticated political activity but simply by how well ordinary persons hold onto their humanity under conditions of oppression or grievous injustice, then clearly Grass had little basis for constructing a model of popular opposition.[24]

Of course, in trying to imagine a basis or a structure for the missing revolutionary paradigm, we are inevitably involved in the subject of civil disobedience, for that is what we mean when we speak of otherwise law-abiding persons who feel they have the right to refuse or violate unjust laws. Grass as novelist is not disposed to debate the fine points of a theory of civil disobedience, and *The Tin Drum* would seem again and again to demonstrate how irrelevant such fine points would be in a consideration of the German problem. Why they would seem irrelevant to Grass we can say when we remember that for his Germans change is brought about by leaders who move the inspired people in the desired direction. Civil disobedience, however, is conceivable only for persons who can sustain in an enduring tension the desire to belong to a community and the will to change that community through their own initiatives and exertions. The capacity to sustain that tension was not a part of the German character as Grass saw it. Nor was civil disobedience more than an eccentric option even for erratic individualists like Oskar. For, as various theorists have argued, "civil disobedience is not primarily an action directed *against* a person or a group. Rather, it reflects a belief in the commonality between those who engage in civil disobedience and the rest of the community. . . . Going along with this belief in a commonality . . . is a concern with one's own moral development."[25] But for a resister to believe in a commonality with other, nonresisting members of the German community would require that he view Hitler as an aberrant manifestation of German culture. From this point of view the resister would also have to believe in a "better self" to which the average German might be recalled. Any serious concern with his own moral development would also require that the resister regard the events around him with unequivocal horror rather than with the combination of fascination and playful irony that we associate with Oskar. There is no genuine sense of commonality in *The Tin Drum* because, in effect, the German community has no moral or spiritual center on the basis of which articulable beliefs can be decently shared. Any impulse toward civil disobedience would necessarily have to be directed *against* almost every German because it would entail repudiation not of an onerous policy but of the entire society that had consented to be governed by persons with no respect for ordinary tenets of law or moral conduct.

An authentic revolutionary paradigm based on the idea of resistance is summoned only once in *The Tin Drum*, in two chapters of Book Two devoted to the dusters. For our purposes, the key facts presented in these chapters are the following:

1. The dusters are all children, and their eventual willingness to be led in 1944 by Oskar (who is nearly twenty) has to do with his imaginative precocity and his assuming the role of a latter-day mock-diabolic Jesus.
2. The dusters do succeed in creating small-scale disorder, stripping soldiers of their medals and insignia, stealing "arms, ammunition and gasoline . . . , looting party treasuries, stealing food cards . . . or a membership list of the Hitler Youth Patrol."
3. The dusters "were against everything," or, as the gang's "cynic and theoretician" puts it, "against our parents and all other grownups, regardless of what they may be for or against."
4. The dusters "were not interested in politics" and can as soon occupy themselves with black masses and parodies of "Christmas plays" as with more incendiary subversions. When adult shipyard workers "with Communist affiliations" try to turn them "into a Red underground movement," only the apprentice figures in the gang are tempted, and eventually break away from the others, including Oskar, who continue to proclaim their independence of all parties.

The episodes involving the dusters have been subjected to considerable commentary, most of it focused on Oskar's mock-heroic antics and his determined identification with Jesus in spite of his not believing in him. Little has been made of the abortive political dimension embodied in the episodes. To be sure, the urge to demystify false heroics is an important part of these chapters, as of other chapters in the novel, and Oskar's flirtation with Christian sentiment and with the idea of spiritual authority is a vital component of his character. But Grass would seem here also to be testing another idea, namely, that in mass societies that have fallen under totalitarian domination resistance may be expressed only in the form of a polymorphous negativism. Another way of putting this is that insofar as the entire society is perceived as intolerable, the resisting individual must set himself up as in principle refusing everything. If he is not to be seduced by this incentive or that, his happiness must consist in the more or less indiscriminate refusal of every compromise. To think politically is, by this standard, a betrayal tantamount to casting oneself in the role of goal-oriented compromiser. To think in practical terms and commit oneself to a movement with a future is in itself to capitulate to a system that encourages everyone to feel that he belongs to something greater than himself and to a future that can redeem both the ordinariness and the brutality of his present hours. The dusters reject politics because they reject the standard habits of thought without which there can be no practical politics and, consequently, no organized mass movements.

But if the revolutionary paradigm is here presented by Grass only as a shadow of what it might have been, these chapters do nonetheless contain an implicit critique of the polymorphous negativity associated with the dusters and do therefore put us in mind of alternative postures. The trouble with the dusters is not that they are passive or ineffectual—they do succeed for a while in creating a disorder on the basis of which large-scale dislocations might well have been attempted. The problem is that the dusters are infantile and that their rebellion is prematurely self-limiting. They conceive of what they are doing not as an enlargement of human possibility, but as an effort to achieve gratification without any prospect of disappointment or unfulfilled desire. Their ambition is not to improve anything, least of all themselves, but to liberate the primary energies associated with revolutionary activity without having to locate objects on behalf of which those energies might be focused and sustained. The dusters burn themselves out because, like other countercultural rebels, they have no sense of having been chosen to perform this activity rather than that. They do not know what to do with the freedom they claim and can view political alternatives only as ways of working within the "objective" conditions ratified by those who deny the very idea of freedom.

But there is a basis for a genuine politics in *The Tin Drum*. Whatever the novel's emphasis on role playing and infantilism, on irony and dissociation, it is plainly not designed to thwart any conception of a political perspective. Obviously, the novel revels in its own multiplicities of tone and color and in what one critic calls "its constantly shifting pattern of comedy, parody, tragedy, lament, description, protest," and so on; and it does aim to show how sincere convictions especially may be part of a "false, escapist indulgence in sentimentality and empty gesturing."[26] Still, one notes an emerging political paradigm in the combination of protest and lament that underlies everything else in the novel. As soon as we ask why Oskar is as he is, we are forced to consider the nature of the society from which he would escape. In the same way, when we consider other characters in the novel we see that there is at least an implicit political dimension in Grass's view of them. Maria Matzerath, Oskar's "former mistress," has no politics to speak of, but it is the failure of her relation with Oskar that subverts his claim to sovereign independence and drives him farther toward a consuming guilt that implicates him in the holocaust scene more surely than anything else. Mariusz Fajngold is a solicitous and kindly neighbor who has no views worth discussing, but he is also remembered as "disinfector in Treblinka Concentration Camp" who "sprinkled Lysol on the camp streets, over the barracks, the shower rooms, the cremating furnaces, the bundles of clothing, over those who were waiting to shower, over those who lay recumbent after their showers, over all that came out of the ovens and all who were about to go in." Will any reader argue that the pages describing Fajngold's activities, including the names of several disinfected victims, do not stick in the memory in a way that other pages do not? Will any reader deny that Fajngold's participation in the camp scene, however modest and "innocent," is intended by Grass to be a fact worth considering as a part of the politics of the novel? Oskar's very words ("why bother with figures; he had sprinkled dead men and dead women with Lysol and that was that") attest at once to Oskar's impatience with focused inquiries and his knowing the essentials on the basis of which judgments can be made.

The political perspective of *The Tin Drum*, then, we identify with the protest and lament that inform even the most wildly irreverent passages. Again and again we are impressed by Grass's refusal to elaborate a formal political response or to tease out the ideological implications of his material. But we are impressed as well with what we take to be the unmistakably political character of virtually everything in the novel. This we may not attribute to the fact that anything involving the Nazi period is likely to be underwritten by a political vision. In the first place, this isn't true, as many works on the Nazi period amply demonstrate. In the second place, political vision is ever so much more than vague protest or hand-wringing sentiment in Grass. The political character of the material we must attribute to the fact that Grass wishes to make possible a political response that is more than unfocused sentiment or corrective reasonableness. To accomplish this he installs at the heart of his work what we have called the principle of negation, in terms of which nothing can long remain what it seems. Negation operates in the novel not merely as a tactical device. It is a way of seeing designed to focus attention on itself. Negation is not only means but end, a species of political vision as much as a warrant of metamorphic fluency in the narrative.

To speak of politics as negation in *The Tin Drum* is to come to grips with Grass's conception of Germany as a repressive society under Hitler *and* under the succeeding bourgeois-democratic regime. The Adenauer years are not strictly comparable to the years between 1933 and 1945, Grass suggests, except insofar as it is ludicrous to think of either period as having a decent answer to the important problems. In both periods ordinary persons were encouraged to practice the Power of Positive Thinking in terms of which activities can be made to justify themselves by virtue of the avidity with which they are performed. This justification applies as well to burning synagogues as to the collective expressions of shame that Oskar associates with postwar crocodile tears.[27] Grass is less concerned with the specific values proclaimed in modern Germany than with the context in which values are defined. He mocks everything because even such values as inner strength and the capacity to experience guilt or admit grievous errors are routinely transformed into occasions for self-approval and profit-making "reform." If in the postwar years Oskar becomes a cult figure who can cure "loss of memory," his appeal has mostly to do with teaching people how to make the best of a bad rap. He knows better than to believe in "Oskarism," understanding all too well its therapeutic and fundamentally evasive character.

Negation is so central to the political vision of *The Tin Drum* because only in an encompassing negativity can Grass resist the reader's inevitable efforts to use the book as a cathartic or as yet another expression of the easy guilt animating so many soulful German intellectuals. The spirit of negation is deployed so as to deny the validity of the "higher self" to which so many Germans were recalling one another. Committed in this novel to a determinedly "lower self" named Oskar, who embraces all manner of vulgar or corporeal satisfaction, Grass demonstrates how the standard dichotomies dominating German consciousness fail to do justice to what actually occurs. Negativity in *The Tin Drum* is the critique not only of totalitarian domination and of the progressive ideology of a recovered market economy, but of the standard affirmation of spiritual, or "higher," values that functions as an ostensive corrective to these "degraded" cultural forms. Grass refuses to permit his reader the easy consolation that, with the right attitudes, the German citizen can achieve the higher values "within the very [cultural] conditions which betray them."[28] Negation is for Grass the guarantor of seriousness insofar as it consistently undercuts the premature satisfactions associated with private comforts and modest social freedoms. These satisfactions, available to many persons even under totalitarian auspices, are viewed as tranquilizing and as encouraging withdrawal from politics.

Of course, as we have indicated, negation may itself be dangerously counterproductive. Herbert Marcuse often warned against "the negative which is only the reverse of the affirmative—not its qualitative opposite."[29]

In these terms, to mock the Nazis in order to have fun would be a shoddy exploit worthy only of the essentially escapist character of the average German who would never have dared to mock his superiors. That Oskar is avowedly confused about the the difference "between self-indulgence and liberation, between clownery and irony"—the words are Marcuse's—should indicate how complicated a business negation is apt to be. In a society that encourages a grossly self-indulgent sentimentality, other forms of escapist self-indulgence can have no permanent political effect, however shocking or disruptive they may seem. *The Tin Drum* is itself a radical political gesture by virtue of its attempt to "*invalidate* the ordinary language, the '*prose du monde*' "[30] by which we enter all too readily into the politics of compliance, whatever the shibboleths we profess to abjure. Grass is alert to the difference between genuine and sham negation because his own parodic gifts are such as to tempt him to settle for strikingly original effects and reversals. His genius lies in the strategies he devises to resist the ever-present temptation.

So the revolutionary paradigm embodied in *The Tin Drum* is the constantly operant principle of negation. One assumes that the negative, as invoked again and again, is part of a project of counterintegration, according to which something better than what exists in the material domain of German society may be imagined. Oskar conjures up no consoling image of such a better world, but he is sufficiently in touch with the values and habits of thought that would inform a putative future to make us feel that it is a political objective worth trying to imagine for ourselves. In refusing to permit his reader any kind of passivity, in refusing to suggest that disintegrative literary subversions are their own adequate reason for being, Grass seeks to negate not this or that behavior in particular but the whole complex of forces that is German society. This he accomplishes, in effect, by demonstrating throughout Oskar's capacity to cut through the obfuscations and myriad false paradigms in which he is nonetheless enmeshed. In a liturgical chapter of *The Tin Drum* entitled "Faith, Hope, Love," for example, Oskar comes firmly to grips with the salvational ruses perpetuated by the established churches and by the average German himself. But the goal of the chapter is not simply to mock or demystify or deny. It is to point, through mourning and the compulsive repetition of unavoidable facts, to the inadequacy of facts to get at reality itself. No more than concepts in an imperfect world can identify their true objects or referents can the facts as such signify what they ought to mean outside the paradigms with which they are inevitably associated. The power of the negative as operant principle governing the entire novelistic context is a function of its denying the ability of the standard paradigms to control thought altogether.

When, in "Faith, Hope, Love," Oskar sees various women handing out religious tracts and waving a banner with a religious inscription, his impulse is to play with the words "as a juggler plays with bottles." But he refuses to be distracted by his own play or by the compelling pieties, and returns to the facts that matter, principally to some version of the words: "There was once a toy merchant, his name was Markus, and he took all the toys in the world away with him out of this world." What these words signify in themselves is that goodness and innocence and other qualities identified with children may be eradicated, or that the culturally sanctioned murder of the Jew (Markus) marks in some sense the death of our belief in an elemental virtue. What they signify in their enforced relation with the other litany Oskar intones—some version of the words "There was once a musician; his name was Meyn and he played the trumpet too beautifully for words"—is that neither art nor discipline saves, and that the good are destroyed not merely by the wicked but by those who are themselves "innocent," which is to say, not endowed with the ironic consciousness that underwrites negative thinking. The political vision of the novel is implicated in its utopian critique of the prevailing circumstance that is German culture and character. This utopian critique is based on an ironic insistence that German society be true to its concept of itself. By everywhere underscoring the fact that German society has a concept of itself that is far from the degraded reflections it actually casts, Grass engages in what Marcuse's one-time colleague Theodor Adorno calls *nonidentity thinking* or *negative dialectic*.

What does it mean to say that German society has a concept of itself? Simply, that there is a "conceptuality prevailing in the object itself,"[31] apart from any idea that may be attributed to the object—in this case, German society—by this or that ordinary German. Grass knows that society as an object of his critique is also a concept possessing various ideal properties that are not to be found in the particulars of the actual society he examines. But he does not therefore conclude that those properties are in consequence merely ideal or inactual or, more drastically, not any longer to be regarded as properties of any living society. German society does not fulfill its concept, but it is possible all the same to insist on what it "would like to be," as Adorno has it. The goal of a rational politics in this sense is to make the actual society identical with its concept. This the writer by himself cannot practically accomplish. His political vocation, however, is realized in his attempt to make the real—which is to say, our very sense of what is enduringly real—*conceptual*. We call this kind of political vision "utopian" not because it is optimistic or focused on the distant future, but because it always confronts present society with what it truly is by comparing it "with the condition of its rational identity." The focus in any utopian critique based on negative dialectic is "the non-identity in the relation between the concept and the object,"[32] but the implicit and unmistakable goal of the critique is always the condition of rational identity. Grass's politics are everywhere presented to us in *The Tin Drum* as the will to negate what he sees, not by transforming it through acts of literary prestidigitation but by instructing us in the habits of mind essential to denial and negation.

For Grass, the beginning of a true politics as of vital thinking is the refusal to acquiesce in the paradigmatic mode, which is to say, the refusal to comfortably associate the objects of our reflection with the concepts attached to them, as it were, "from outside."[33] Oskar's stature as a political figure is measured by his capacity to play among the paradigms which he unmasks simply by acknowledging them as inauthentic constructs. The oppositional revolutionary paradigm he thereby helps to embody is in this sense *theoretical*, but that is no reason to imagine that it is without force or potential staying power. Politics in Grass is the attempt to recall the fallen or degraded object from its identity by insisting on the conceptual reality of the object's nonidentity. Political vision is not translated into programs for resistance or ideological rehabilitation, but it is inherent in the practice of negative dialectic as an encompassing alternative paradigm. The critique of paradigms in *The Tin Drum* is thus carried out on behalf of an oppositional paradigm whose primacy is established by the novel's field of action rather than by an appeal to an antecedent or external value imposed on the work and posited as the novel's final truth.

III

There is little in the way of insurrection in *Cat and Mouse*, and almost nothing in the way of collective struggle. Though it is the middle work in a trilogy that has much to do with language and with the practice of negative dialectic, it has rarely tempted anyone to speak of it in philosophic or political terms. Saturated as it is with references to Danzig in the war years, it is in the main a simple narrative of betrayal and guilt. To think of it as a political novel is to make more of the relentlessly privatized events than they can support. A moral parable *Cat and Mouse* may be; a political novel it is not.

John Reddick has done his best to argue that "the War is at the very least the unfailing backdrop to the action" and that "the minds of the various characters . . . are shown as being imbued with the spirit of the war." He also argues persuasively that the variously depicted Danzig social institutions—churches, families, schools—fully represent and encourage the aims of the Nazi political-military apparatus.[34] But even Reddick is forced to conclude that the "larger perspective" in this work is "non-specific" and "fable like": Grass's protagonist, Joachim Mahlke, "is first and last an archetypal victim, like Abel or the crucified Christ; a 'mouse' that falls prey to the eternal 'cat.' "[35] In thinking of the trilogy as a whole, we may wish to conclude that *this* mouse would not have seemed so much a victim had he not fallen prey to the spirit of the age. But Grass is so uncertain about the actual status of his mouse and about the causes of his disaffection that the age itself seems merely a collateral, rather than primary, factor.

Whatever tendency there may be to consider *Cat and Mouse* as a political novel will necessarily rely on the concreteness of Grass's social observation. The field of action is vividly and deliberately portrayed. Each character occupies a recognizably distinct position in the social scale, though none serves a merely emblematic or purely typical function. Even Klohse, the school principal who embodies so much that Grass obviously despises in the German scene, is more than a representative *Nazi* or *bourgeois* or banal *party functionary*. The portrait makes him seem real, which is to say, fully plausible, without making him seem gratuitously complex or psychologically richer than such a figure ought to be. Similarly specific, without being too complicated for the purposes of an essentially modest narrative, is the delineation of the forces operating in a person like Klohse, who is conceived as neither dupe nor victim. To have conceived of him as a victim, Grass would have needed to represent him as one for whom no alternative options were available and who writhed uncomfortably in the face of the necessity to which he succumbed. To have drawn him as a standard stalwart idealogue would have been to stress the specifically *blut und boden* character of his enthusiasms. In fact, Klohse is a tedious and tepid fellow whose "thosewhocomeafterus" and "pureofheart" speeches stir no one. Hardly an inspirational figure, he is "stiff and formal," altogether *correct* in what are the prosaic requirements mandated by the spirit of the age. But he is not a one-dimensional creation of the Nazi period. He is a well-bred, officious little man who can do his duty and rise only very modestly to the larger occasions in which he is implicated. No one will wish to construct grand political conspiracies or theories that rely to excess on such a person.

To speak of the social forces that operate on a Klohse is to indicate how intent Grass is on demonstrating the interconnectedness of the various institutional orders in Nazi Germany. It is natural in this novelistic universe that local war heroes returned from the front should be invited to address schoolchildren in their former schools, and that military virtues should be presented as continuous with other homelier virtues. But it is not Grass's intention here to suggest that the concentration of social forces thus achieved is a special feature of Nazi Germany, or that the standards upheld are invariably odious. Though Pilenz, the narrator of *Cat and Mouse*, is not up to reflecting on the matter, Klohse's definitive and *principled* rejection of Mahlke as one unfit to address children at the school from which he'd been ignominiously expelled is based on a sound and decent principle. Mahlke's adult military exploits may not indeed warrant the principal's overlooking the embarrassment Mahlke's earlier prank had caused the school. In any case, the standard invoked is not in any way peculiarly linked to a Nazi principle of honor or opprobrium. Though one is tempted to repudiate Klohse's behavior on the grounds that a Nazi sympathizer has no right to invoke ordinary principles of decorum, it is not as a Nazi but as an officious little martinet that Klohse rejects Mahlke. The political point, if any there be, is blunted in Grass's presentation of the motives operant in a fellow like the principal. This is no status-hungry would-be Eichmann eager to climb into the upper ranks of the party bureaucracy and rub elbows with the brass so as to feel important. Klohse is, much more simply, a dim, unimaginatively decorous person who deserves to be where he is and believes, so far as we can tell, in the drivel he expresses. He is nothing like a programmatic exemplar of the banality of evil, and to accuse him of simple hypocrisy is not finally to say anything about the quality of his politics. That he responds to social forces is obvious; that *Cat and Mouse* is conceived as a critique of those social forces or of the political organization of those forces is not nearly so certain.

Many have remarked on Grass's decision to include in his first paragraph the statement "the crematorium between the United Cemeteries and the Engineering School was operating." But this is hardly an adequate indication of a broad political intention in *Cat and Mouse*. Little attention is subsequently directed at the crematorium or at the particular consequences of any Nazi policy. No one in the novel thinks for a moment of organizing any serious resistance, and insofar as characters are aware at all of a political situation different from what they'd previously known, they regard it almost as if it were a fact of nature: Certain things are done, certain people are required to do them. When Mahlke refuses to applaud the war hero's speech, he refuses not from political conviction but from an entirely personal discomfort and disaffection. When, later, he deserts his military command, he has no thought of encouraging others to do the same or of trying to justify his decision in political terms. The words "I've just had enough" refer not to any particular excesses committed by the Nazis, but to the sort of exhaustion and sense of futility that any soldier fighting on the losing side might experience. In the same way, Pilenz's "I thought I would take violin lessons . . . but we were enrolled as Air Force auxiliaries and today it is probably too late" is obviously not a comment on totalitarianism but on the disruption endemic in any society at war. No one in this novel— not Pilenz and not Mahlke—ever becomes so alert to what is actually taking place in Nazi Germany as to arrive at a genuine political insight. Critics can speak all they like about Mahlke's experiencing "that same kind of existential fear that increasingly possessed Oskar Matzerath,"[36] but Oskar's political sophistication is nowhere matched in the characters of *Cat and Mouse*. As narrator, Pilenz does now and again dwell on what Reddick calls the "deadly sameness and conventionality" of the suffocating milieu, but it is the critic rather than character or novelist who wishes to pursue a potential "correlation between sterile banality in social living, and the soured, poisonous spirit vented through National Socialism."[37] Nor would it suffice for Grass simply to gesture at that "poisonous spirit" as an ample token of the political content in which it issued. Grass succeeds in *Cat and Mouse* because he does not pretend to be writing a political novel.

There is no question, however, that *Cat and Mouse* belongs in the Danzig trilogy. Though it is in no sense a culmination of anything set forth in *The Tin Drum* or a pointed preparation for anything to come in *Dog Years*, it functions as a kind of ground on the basis of which several provisional conclusions may be tested. The most general of these is that a society may be brought to total ruin when self-deception has been, as it were, authorized at the highest levels and permitted to become a way of life for everyone else. This is not presented as a political revelation in *Cat and Mouse*, but it is surely at the root of political reflections that emerge insistently in *Dog Years*. The focus of the idea of self-deception in *Cat and Mouse* is, of course, Pilenz, an "equivocating narrator" if ever there was one.[38] Why he equivocates is hard to explain beyond the statement that he is in perpetual bad faith and is ridden by guilt over his fatal mistreatment of Mahlke. All efforts to leap from this statement to some general conclusion about what Pilenz couldn't bear in the figure he admired more than any other, or about what Mahlke should mean to us as one who couldn't survive in Nazi Germany, inevitably come to nothing, and the clues that Grass liberally deposits like so many mouse turds furnish only enough to retard definitive speculation. Like other "conclusions" in the trilogy, the notion that self-deception is the key to various quandaries recedes the moment we consider what it can really explain. Self-deception in Nazi Germany is clearly not what it would be in another society, and, in any case, Pilenz's bad faith and equivocation can hardly be said to be perfectly typical of most others of his class. His relation to Mahlke is, obviously, special, and the political background to their relationship only makes us wonder why it should seem to play so small a role in what actually develops.

As to any other conclusions that may be provisionally recommended, we may say simply that they do not persuade. Resonant statements of the sort that Reddick indulges unfortunately betray the terse stringencies of the novel. Nothing in *Cat and Mouse* can warrant Reddick's asking, as if he were formulating what Grass clearly intended: "What good is a humanitarian spirit in an era in which destruction is at a premium?" Things are not so clear in *Cat and Mouse* as Reddick and others would have them be.[39] In a way, Grass would seem to have included *Cat and Mouse* in the trilogy precisely because in it he could try out materials that would in time become potent only by being subjected to political analysis. In effect, the short novel asks us to consider what is to be made of such materials in the absence of the explicit political focus so prodigally elaborated in the final work of the trilogy.

IV

In *Dog Years* the possibility of a collective action is present from the first, insofar as an authors' *collective* is said to conduct an inquiry into the German experience from the 1920s to the 1950s. This collective approach to critical events and issues is not merely a literary or structural device but a statement on the political task confronting the German people. For if in *The Tin Drum* Grass's object was to reach toward an oppositional revolutionary paradigm that could only be theoretical, in *Dog Years* the object is to launch an exploratory projection of what a vital political culture might be. This Grass accomplishes by installing at the center of his universe a director or impressario figure named Brauchsel whose mission is to remember the past by encouraging others to join him in a procedure that is alternately obsessional and deliberate, repetitious and corrective. What use there is in this procedure for the individual participants it is not always easy to see, but as a model of collective witnessing and stock taking it is most impressive. In political terms, Grass gives us nothing less than a definitive demonstration that freedom can be meaningful only when it has been salvaged, as it were, from a collective struggle with Necessity. No one character in *Dog Years* may emerge as free and capable of living an independent life. But no one who has failed to confront the Necessity in which he is enwombed can begin to project the unforeseeable future forms on behalf of which he might reasonably commit himself to a politics.

Dog Years operates with materials that are familiar to readers of the earlier works of the trilogy; and insofar as negative dialectic may be said to control the narrative discourse in *The Tin Drum*, it is surely central to Grass's presentation in the later novel. But there courses through *Dog Years* a sense of missionary purpose that is distinctive. Digression abounds, to be sure; there are gratuitous flourishes that have little to do with a strict thematic coherence. But Grass is bound in this novel to rub his reader's nose in what he takes to be reality itself: that reality that must be the foundation of any legitimate politics. Parody, ironic subterfuge, and fantastic invention are all abundantly present in *Dog Years,* though now and again one feels that Grass has become more than a little impatient with the obliquity of his own discourse and the evasions that are everywhere possible even to men of good will. There is nothing in *The Tin Drum* to quite match the resolute directness of the passage in which Tulla Pokriefke insists that what she sees is a pile of human bones and, what is more, " 'Everybody knows that.' " Nor is she content with a general statement of a concrete fact. "Tulla demanded greater precision," we are told: " 'I'm telling you they come straight from Stutthof [the local concentration camp], want to bet?' " What is more, anything that Tulla can see or her companions try in vain to refute is part of a collective reality from which no one who lived in their world during the Hitler years can escape. "There was once a city," Tulla's cousin Harry Liebenau hopefully intones again and again in Book Two of *Dog Years*. But it was no mythical or fairy tale realm, no kingdom set apart for childish play or adult forgetfulness, for "it had a suburb named Langfuhr," Harry inevitably reminds himself; and "Langfuhr was so big and so little that whatever happens or could happen in this world, also happened or could have happened in Langfuhr." Worst of all, even those who can bring themselves to remember the relevant facts and who sensitively "stood slightly to one side" while others did the genuinely unforgivable things—those like Harry Liebenau, for example—were likely to have "venerated the Führer" and a variety of other models with whose help they "succeeded in burying a real mound made of human bones under medieval allegories" or other duly distracting devices.

The function of this sort of thing in *Dog Years* is not, of course, to suggest that reality itself is available to anyone who would see what stands before him. The awful things that people do to one another under the auspices of this or that political ideology are not always so unmistakable as a pile of human bones. The function of this material is rather to challenge the ubiquitous domination of the philosophic obliquities associated with the writings of Martin Heidegger. Heidegger is not himself a character in *Dog Years*, but he is ever-present in the monstrous word games and parodies of linguistic inflation that punctuate the narrative. Not all of the parodies are linked to Heidegger, but anything that reads like a pastiche of metaphysical jargon is certainly a response to "the arrogant obscurities of German philosophic speech" associated with the author of *Being and Time*.[40] Not surprisingly, Tulla Pokriefke's precisions are insisted on in the very section of *Dog Years* largely devoted to exploring the effects of philosophic language on the German mind. This is no digressive excursion in the novel, no special approach to material that is elsewhere treated in an entirely different way. Still, the final fifty or sixty pages of Harry Liebenau's narrative are colored by the Heideggerean pastiche in a degree that is unusual, and the alternating insistence on calling things by their rightful names thus has a refreshing and sometimes alarming effect on the discourse. The concluding words of Book Two may be given over to the escape route of the Hitler-dog Prinz, but more impressive by far are the litanies of the things left behind by the fleeing German populations: "mounds of bones, mass graves, card files, flagpoles, party books," etc., not to mention "the debts and guilts." There may be room even in the final moments of panic and disgrace for expressions like "dog-thrownness" or "dog greatness, ontic and scientific," but in the main even "the wrecked tank, romantic against the five-o-clock-in-the-morning sky" is made to seem inconsequential next to the plainer facts brought before our attention.

The Heideggerean pastiche in Grass is of course very largely presented as part of a continuous interior monologue. It is never permitted, even when the narrator himself pauses over his own language, to become a detachable subject suited only for abstract reflection. "Words occur to Harry," he himself confesses: "placedness—instandingness—nihilation"; but the narrative proceeds more or less without interruption, the single words assuming their respective functions in the charged but ongoing recitation of events. Thus we learn subsequently of mechanical devices "nihilating the evasive essent"; or, as the corpses continue to pile up in Stutthof, we read that "the next day the placedness took on a quality of growth." This is ominous insofar as the wielder of words himself has no way of distancing himself from the jargon he has inherited. Indeed, the very effort to speak of distance, let alone establish a cogent idea of intellectual detachment, is itself prone to the difficulties inherent in any other kind of communication. Thus we later read that the lost dog Prinz is "attuned to distantiality" and is therefore subsequently "acknowledged as the Nothing," in spite of the fact that the remaining German forces have been commanded to retrieve him. Everything here is touched by the wand of distortion, and though our impulse is to laugh aloud at the accumulation of inventive absurdities, we are frequently restrained by the relentless emergence of facts. Who can overlook the tender lament, the sense of sheer waste and loss, that are so much a part of the convulsively satiric account of Tulla's miscarriage? Thus:

> the finger-size two-months-old fetus lay there in her panties. Made manifest: there. . . . Through world onset: there. A small handful: unkept, beforelike, partly there. . . . Grounding as taking root, and Tulla's handkerchief as well. Unconcealed into what? By whom attuned? Space-taking never without world disclosure. Therefore: panties off. Ski-pants up, no child, but. What a vision of essence! . . . for higher than reality is potentiality: here manifested: what primarily and ordinarily does not show itself, what is hidden but at the same time is an essential part of what does primarily and ordinarily show itself, namely, its meaning and ground, which is not frozen but loosened with heels of shoes from the Air Force supply room, in order that the baby may come into its there. . . .

To speak of facts in connection with such a passage is to note, simply, that a child was lost; that the mother was herself a child, like her accomplice Harry Liebenau; and that even in mature retrospect Harry does not know what to make of the event recorded or how to interpret the larger significance of the more general indifference to human life everywhere around him. The facts are not themselves political facts, except insofar as one regards language itself as the principal medium of political exchange and thus regards the display of empty metaphysical jargon as a critique of the available political discourse.

Grass had to know, of course, that there is more to the issue of Heidegger's language than may be supposed from a pastiche of its most outlandishly eccentric characteristics. In fact, Heidegger's original emphasis on *experiencing* rather than simply *seeing* facts may be said to coincide exactly with Grass's project. Persistently in his work Grass undercuts and devalues what George Steiner has called "the drive towards objective contemplation, logical analysis, scientific classification, which cuts us off from being," quite as Heidegger himself resisted a view of fact as plainly perceived or observed and thus " 'unthought.' "[41] What distinguishes the one from the other is Grass's sense that there are facts that one can experience only by calling them by their given names and looking at them plainly, *as if* whatever truth abided in them might be reached simply by honoring their unavoidable presentness in that way. Just so, truly to think an important fact is for Grass not to clear a space around it so as patiently to penetrate to its essence. "What Heidegger calls *die Lichtung*, the 'clearing' in which truth is *experienced*,"[42] is for Grass the place at which all that exigently clings to the object is carefully removed so that the object may stand free. In so setting it free, however, one experiences not its truth but at most a conceptually valid essence shorn of contingent fact that alone determines what is and is not the Necessity under the auspices of which the object may truly be known.

It is a vital part of Grass's mission to contend that Necessity itself has long been alien to the German mind, so that in taking on Heidegger as he does the novelist would seem to work through and make untenable one kind of evasion to which his fellow citizens have had steady recourse. In trying to project some version of a tolerable political culture, Grass insists again and again that persons unused to acknowledging simple facts or, more important, speaking truthfully cannot begin to create decent institutions. The importance of Grass's decision to install the Brauchsel impressario-figure at the center of his novel is clear the moment one sees that only Brauchsel in *Dog Years* represents the drive to confront Necessity in all its guises. He it is whose many creative, industrial, and entrepreneurial exertions have as their object the registration of identity for a German constituency routinely in flight from itself. Even as a child, Eddi Amsel—later Brauchsel (as he's also known by other names)—created scarecrow figures that "were never anonymous" but "created in man's image." "Though built for no purpose and with no enemy in view," the earliest scarecrow figures are defiantly representational; they *signify* persons not simply as they appear to others like themselves, but in extravagant or grotesque postures such as are likely to seem cruel or offensive. The closer to nature Amsel's creations—which is to say, the more various and inventive their postures—the more capable they seem "of disorganizing the tranquil rural gait" of ordinary human beings. To confront Necessity is for Amsel-Brauchsel to keep oneself perpetually in touch with the "richly variegated" aspects of persons and things, not predominantly in a spirit of "childlike piety" but in a spirit commensurate with the exigencies of human affairs generally. Even as a child Amsel creates scarecrows not with a view to "divine reward" but for money. As wealthy mine owner, Amsel-Brauchsel in the postwar years industriously contrives to show the German people, *for a price*, what they are. Necessity is the impressario's medium as it is also his vocation and his mission.

Nowhere in *Dog Years* does a tolerable political culture actually take shape. Nowhere does the Heideggerean imperative to transform the merely personal into a national or ethnic vocation seem more than empty posturing or militant trash. But there is all the same a movement toward Necessity that is undertaken as a collective enterprise by great numbers of Germans in *Dog Years*, albeit against their will. What does Brauchsel do, after all, if not mobilize or ignite a process of collective recognition? What is the measure of his success if it is not his capacity to move and disturb and enforce recognition? The receptive apparatus of the average citizen may be blunt, his capacity to act on anything he confronts virtually extinct, and yet react he can and does. To create a true political culture is first to alert ordinary persons to their prospects and to the irremediable significance of their past. This much Grass would seem over and over to stress. To come to terms with the past is not to immobilize it in exemplars or formulas but to live with it as a key to one's present identity. Amsel's earliest creations are compelling because they embody the full range of possibilities to which the imagination can assign any given person. Past and present and future live together in the scarecrow figures that violate all sense of quotidian and temporal limitation.

Are the principal characters in *Dog Years* conscious of themselves as political actors in an unfolding conflict that requires collective action if it is to be brought under control? Insofar as the principals are aware at all of Necessity they are at least intermittently aware of the many ways in which it may be evaded or addressed. To speak of them as political actors would be misleading only in the sense that they do not ordinarily take responsibility for the things of public consequence that they do or fail to do. None has a clear notion of what public advantage there may be in a particular course of action, and none but Amsel-Brauchsel can conceive of a collective action as something that may be created rather than joined or acquiesced in. Grass would seem to suggest that ordinary persons become political actors not by supposing that they are equipped to make or affect public policy, but by acknowledging that they are involved in something larger than themselves. This is not accomplished simply by reflecting, dumbly, that powerful persons have made decisions that may one day implicate every citizen. It is accomplished by feeling that one's attitudes toward those decisions, and the behavior that may issue from those attitudes, are somehow a part of the public record and not merely a matter of private conscience. In this sense, all those who in *Dog Years* take stock of their conduct and of their political attitudes may be said to conceive of themselves as political actors. And insofar as their stock taking leads them to understand the inextricable relation between private and public conduct, particularly in times of great social upheaval, they also regard themselves increasingly as belonging to a collective enterprise for which certain kinds of judgment are particularly appropriate. Even the gifted Harry Liebenau finds that he cannot escape the judgments that emerge willy-nilly from his encounter with materials that had once seemed too slight or personal to be worth extended study.

Of course, there is much in *Dog Years* that is so slight and personal that one would be foolish to think of it as political material in itself. Harry Liebenau's relations with Jenny Brunies have only incidental significance in any political reading of the novel. But Grass eventually turns everything in the novel into weighty political capital, and it is plainly a mistake to suppose that, in allowing Jenny to remain somewhere near the center of Harry's narrative, Grass did not know that her work as a ballerina would figure prominently in the choreographic creations of Herr Haseloff—who is none other than Amsel-Brauchsel, a man still obsessed with scarecrows and the enactment of German identity. In *The Tin Drum,* for all its deeply ingrained political purpose, there was much that interested Grass apart from the ulterior uses to which the details could be put. In *Dog Years,* whatever the seemingly digressive surfaces and inspired tours de force, all is finally harnessed to larger and more philosophically patent purposes. Jenny Brunies may often sound like a naive and ineffectual young girl, but she is for a while an integral part of Amsel-Brauchsel-Haseloff's political design. And it is Jenny's letter to Harry, after all, that describes her mentor's terrifying mock-apocalyptic scarecrow ballet on which much of the novel's prophecy devolves.

But we have not said in what degree it is useful to speak of politics as a collective enterprise in the context of *Dog Years*. If characters do not in the main conceive of themselves as launching or deliberately participating in a collective struggle, what point can there be in insisting that a collective action is indeed at the heart of the novel? Consider, for example, Walter Matern's experience in Book Three of the novel with the mysterious eyeglasses manufactured and distributed by Brauchsel's firm, Brauxel and Co. The "recognition glasses" are said to show "youthful wearers varied images of their parents' past," particularly "acts of violence performed tolerated instigated. . . . Aiding and abetting. Smoking cigarettes and looking on while. Certified decorated applauded murderers." And so on. Matern, of course, is no youngster at the time (1957) when the "miracle glasses" have become all the rage, but he is nonetheless deeply affected by them as by other agencies of exposure and revelation by which he is subsequently touched. He is affected by his daughter Wolli's fleeing from him at the moment she puts on the glasses and sees what he is, or what he *was* and *did* when fat Eddi Amsel lay in the snow years earlier, his face beaten to a pulp by his friend and eight accomplices. Matern's immediate response is fear and confusion, though he regains his composure soon after by retreating to "the cozy warmth of the kitchen-living room" and permitting himself to "push halfhearted feelings of guilt back and forth on the kitchen table" with a drinking buddy. The past blurs, as the friends remember their SA *sturm* as "a kind of a hideout for the inner emikrashun" and dwell on "the way we slung the philosophy at the bar." Eventually, the need to help the child forget what has made her so miserable is absorbed into the more comprehensive goal of thinking positively ("beauty, progress, the good in man, etcetera") and becoming an active citizen. "And what activity is more productive than forgetting?"

The collective dimension in all of this is unmistakable in the fact that each man who has been touched, like Walter, finds it necessary under the pressure of a continuously potential susceptibility to guilt to join with others in dealing with it. Nothing will suffice, no wisdom offered by any former foe or accomplice can release the pressure. But the fact that individual initiatives cannot stem the tide of guilt and that even workable solutions are transparently hollow and unreliable even to those who most rely on them is of critical importance. We misread Grass if we fail to see that the satire in *Dog Years* is directed not simply from without but from within. Walter Matern, who is the ostensive author of the Materniads, the narrator of Book Three of the novel, is at least marginally aware of what he is doing, sickened by his flight from himself, and driven to bear witness to his experience even as he succumbs to the seductions of forgetfulness.[43] The West German Radio Executive who gives Matern a broadcasting job may speak to him of the "Urgent Search for Truth" and "the eternal question of man," but Matern is too much the prey of other voices not to know how fundamentally dishonest are the resonant phrases wafted deftly over him. An opportunist Matern may be—he may never discover a capacity to call things by their rightful names or to be content with that accomplishment more than with any other—but he is also a man caught up in the throes of a collective struggle to reclaim identity and redirect possibility. As much as Harry Liebenau, who stands to the side but knows that he is apt to find a mechanism in his tummy not unlike those that drive the marching SA men created in Amsel's studio, Matern knows that he "tosses and turns, unable to sleep, because names . . . unfit for any dog, are gouging his spine." What chiefly circulates in the gaseous precincts of Danzig are not private thoughts, but the shared thoughts of a community that knows all too well what it wishes to forget. For all Grass's savage invective, for all his loathing of the comfortable evasions in which the average postwar German took refuge, his novel shows how unescapable are the facts, the horrors, without which no German can know what he must overcome.

The driving force behind consciousness itself in *Dog Years* is of course Amsel-Brauchsel. It is he who labors throughout to make others see, who labors also to stay afloat in spite of his suspicion that, as one for whom "absolutely nothing is sacred or inviolable," he himself is nothing. Amsel-Brauchsel it is who struggles with the complex of racialist and pseudo-psychological ideas that inspire his enemies and who, as an object lesson to those very enemies, calls those ideas into question. He it is who makes it possible to speak of a consciousness more or less adequate to the holocaust, of a response that can differentiate between political objectives and simple human requirements.

No one would for a moment describe Amsel-Brauchsel as an ideal character. We know too little of his deepest motives to be sure what he deserves from us. We do know that he is an artist-creator of considerable versatility, that he is a half-Jew who manages nonetheless to avoid the fate of most other Jews, and that he is relentlessly committed both to profitability and the representation of the common experience in all its multiplicity. In an environment that makes it impossible for such a person to move to the center of political power, he learns how to move to the cultural and economic center in his own way and to exercise political influence on a scale that can make his competitors more than a little uneasy. Properly described as an artist, a businessman, a publicist, even a leader, he is all and none of these, a protean figure whose sense of himself as either nothing or everything gives him an advantage over those who would reduce him to ashes. In a novel that insists on the centrality of politics, he is the embodiment of the idea that power belongs to those who know their constituents. Populations that wish to take control of their own destinies must learn who they are and by what means they have been deprived of agency in the past. Amsel-Brauchsel is the dominant figure in *Dog Years* because he knows better than anyone else the secrets of German identity. Those who would exercise political power in Germany without destroying themselves and their constituents have need of his knowledge.

What is the nature of this knowledge that in the perspective of *Dog Years* is at the very root of political understanding and potential political power? The root of this knowledge, perhaps, lies in Amsel's youthful encounter with "a diabolical work," namely, Weininger's *Sex and Character*. There Amsel discovered ideas that are to play an important role in his development, ideas like the following: that "the world-historical significance . . . of Jewry consists . . . in having reminded" the Aryan of "what to guard against: against Jewishness as a possibility in himself "; that "they/the Jews/never identify themselves with any cause or idea"; that "they have no ground under their feet" and "all they can do is undermine"; and so on.

These ideas Amsel never quite believes, though he is clearly shaken by them and moved to doubt his own powers. The ideas serve in the novel not only to focus one prominent source of anti-Semitic thinking in the Nazi period, but to indicate what sort of seductive drivel was sufficient to undermine the confidence even of bright young people. More important than the content of the ideas, though, is the way in which they are presented, as part of a frenzied interior monologue in which they are undercut and ridiculed even as their marketability and insidious attractiveness continue to be emphasized. Amsel's confusion as he tries to understand and to accept Weininger demonstrates as well as any rational argument can how riddled with contradictions are the least of Weininger's ideas.

All the more monstrous, therefore, is Amsel's continued sense that Weininger was on to something, that healthy Germans were best advised to guard against the corrosive skepticism and irony in themselves.[44] Grass wants us to have it both ways, of course: He wants us to reject Weininger's patently idiotic drivel and at the same time to wonder whether there was not in Weininger's version of the rootless cosmopolitan Jewish spirit an element of truth that neither Weininger nor any other anti-Semite could possibly have known what to do with. Is *Dog Years* a Jewish book? In a sense, of course, it is. In a sense it is the quintessence of that bristling negativism and ironic subversiveness that hates all things rooted, orderly, secure. And if *Dog Years* is in spirit what might be called a Jewish book, is not its principal character, Amsel-Brauchsel, confirmation of the Jewish stereotype promoted in Weininger? The anti-Semite is one who fears, and therefore hates, those who remind him of his own proclivities, but Amsel-Brauchsel is, after all, just the sort of dark denier who might indeed represent a plausible threat to the less secure members of a community in turmoil. Does he not hold up to ridicule, or at least to critical scrutiny, their least pleasant characteristics? Does he not insist that they look at what they have made of themselves? The Materns of the world may not be "essentially interested in cleansing the world of Amsel[s]," but only in "purging [themselves] of [Jewish] characteristics."[45] But insofar as an Amsel is driven to make them reflect on the complex of insupportable or socially unacceptable or ethically dubious characteristics they occasionally acknowledge in themselves, he *is* the enemy.

Is Grass, then, the enemy of the German people? Obviously, the question is crudely put, but it is also an apt question in the context of a work that politicizes all it touches. Is it not the case that the knowledge Grass would here convey is the knowledge of ideas, emotions, and moral attitudes as manufactured products? And are not these products routinely tailored to the needs of persons who are thereby controlled by the appetites they are permitted to indulge? It is no accident that Grass relies so heavily on Amsel-Brauchsel to discover and convey this knowledge. What other character has the wit, not to say the justification, to rub the noses of the German people in the very attitudes they had once boasted of and berated others for lacking? Who else but an unforgiving Jew—as Amsel might once have put it—would have the audacity to develop "an enterprise [the Brauxel mine] which produces all the warped values of which he was once a victim," to "become an entrepreneur of total degeneracy in order to mine and undermine it"?[46] Amsel-Brauchsel points the way to an important stage in an emergent revolutionary paradigm by in effect accepting himself as "Jewish" aggressor-figure, the enemy and archreconstructor of the German people. There is a good deal of ambiguity here, but it is clear that in "practicing the art of satire (an art form labeled as degenerate and Jewish by the Nazis)" the proprietor of the Brauxel mine makes himself the enemy of all those who would prefer not to be disturbed in their perpetuation of familiar attitudes. More, Brauxel is at bottom the same person he was when, as Amsel, he created simpler scarecrows and thereby engaged "in a form of art the Nazis hated—modernistic, degenerate, dehumanized, inorganic, materialistic, artificial, parodic, soulless, and therefore 'Jewish' art."[47] He may be an unsavory figure, but he is the kind of subversive Grass adores: ambivalent, in some ways admiring of the very things he is driven to subvert, and given to mock-apocalyptic gestures in a "dangerously productive environment" that will turn anything less vehement into a perfectly idle curiosity. In the absence of a fully embodied revolutionary paradigm—unimaginable in the perspective of the German scene studied by Grass—the most he can come up with is an oppositional paradigm based on the irreconcilable tension between German and Jew, nexal or tribal reality and demythologizing satire.

Does *Dog Years* move beyond the political vision that underwrites *The Tin Drum*? Surely *Dog Years* captures "the whole ambience" of postwar Germany in a way that dwarfs the achievement of Book Three of the earlier novel. What George Steiner calls "the evasions and the outright lies, the cynicism of the little men grown fat on the manure of the dead, and the nervous queries of the young"[48] are brilliantly captured in a way that convinces us of the continuities between Nazi Germany and the German society that succeeded it. But there is no progress beyond the theoretical politics of negative dialectic. How could there be? Grass is as assiduous as ever to make positive thinking untenable. He continues to despise the haute sophistication that wallows in degradation and loss only to surface with an edifying expression of hope pasted on its ravaged face. Matern dismisses Amsel-Brauchsel's art as "too cynical," which is to say, without a "healing" effect. But Matern can never be healed and is in any case not quite suited to evaluating the exigencies of a committed art. The political vision of *Dog Years* is a vision of a world in which there is no redemption outside of the recognition of Necessity. To recognize Necessity is, in Grass's sense, to call things by their rightful names and to struggle to understand how even those names may be used to insulate us from the reality of our own experience. The political activist is in this sense not the individual who takes action on the basis of an entirely unsatisfactory grasp of facts and prospects. He is the one who insists on the conceptual reality of a nonidentity that is everywhere ignored or despised. For what reason does Amsel-Brauchsel persist in his efforts to bring the Materns of the world face to face with themselves? Cruel cynicism and profit motive aside, does he not imagine that even Matern has a concept of himself that is—that must be—different from the degraded reflection he actually casts? And is it not the case that the great artist-entrepreneur himself moves closer to his own as yet merely conceptual nonidentity the more vehemently he serves as the scourge and satirist of the German people to whom he belongs? The politics of negative dialectic in *Dog Years* are the politics of critique and of autocritique, quite as they are in *The Tin Drum*. Together, these novels constitute the most extraordinary instances of authentically visionary politics that our period has produced.

10

Between
East and West:
A Letter
to Milan Kundera

Dear Milan Kundera,

Though we haven't met, I find myself thinking of you more and more as I consider what I have and have not done in my book on the political novel. No doubt it is presumptuous for me to suppose that I know you. Though you do often speak of yourself in your fiction, I believe you when you say that "the novel is not the author's confession."[1] I understand also that the statements you make in published interviews are not always reliable, that they are intended frequently to correct what you take to be gross misreadings of your work, and sometimes overstate an argument so as to make contrary views seem untenable.

Still, there are the obsessions you display so persistently in the novels, and the situations you rehearse with every conviction that there is always more to say about them. These obsessions and the situations out of which they emerge make me feel that I know you, for what is a writer if he is not the obsessions and circumstances that constitute his experience? And what is a writer like Milan Kundera, apparently as much "an inveterate skeptic" as some of his characters, if he cannot make us feel uneasy about the conclusions we reach and the principles we think we serve?

I had thought, in structuring my book, to devote a standard chapter to *The Book of Laughter and Forgetting*, but found myself putting that chapter off as long as I could. There are enough "gaps, discontinuities, unanswered questions"[2] in that book to daunt even the most confident critic. But it was not chiefly as a practical critic that I hesitated to tackle your book. I came increasingly to wonder whether it was appropriate to treat it as a political novel at all. One or two of the novel's seven "stories" after all have very little to do with politics as such, and even the stories with an obvious political dimension seem to resist a straightforward political analysis. The more I thought about what I would say in a chapter devoted to your book, the less confident I was that I could do justice to its ambivalence about the sort of book it wanted to be.

Then, in the spring of 1984, the English translation of *The Unbearable Lightness of Being* appeared. It seemed to me so of a piece with your previous novels that it must have grown out of the impulses and concerns that inspired them. It was also so distinctly *not* a political novel that the misgivings I'd entertained about treating your earlier works as such were exacerbated. On top of this, in several long interviews that marked the publication of the new book you raised questions that are bound to create a crisis of conscience in someone who has invested a great deal in ideas you resist.

You are offended, you say, by political interpretations of your work. Why? Such readings are "bad" readings, since they inevitably ignore "everything you think is important in the book you've written."[3] If *The Joke* is read as an indictment of a Communist regime, then it will not be read as a love story. If *The Book of Laughter and Forgetting* is read as a lament over the political destruction of the Czech nation, then it will not be read as a study of memory and desire. So you contend. Dissident literature as such invites ideological interpretations, and so it is necessary for the writer who respects what you've called the "radical autonomy" of the novel to repudiate the "dissident" label journalists affix to his books. The dissident writer, you suggest, knows all too well what he means to say, and his novel is for him largely a means to an end rather than an end in itself. For you, the novel has its own truth to tell; it is committed to a truth that is always and only "to be discovered."[4] Political novels are by definition committed to another kind of truth. They fall prey to a "stupidity [that] . . . comes from having an answer for everything," whereas for you "the wisdom of the novel comes from having a question for everything."[5]

I would like to think that what I have written in this book might persuade you that the qualities you most admire in fiction are often to be found in works content to be political novels. It is tempting, of course, to assert that it little matters whether your books are referred to as "dissident" or "political" or "metaphysical," that they are what they are, just as *Anna Karenina* will remain a great novel whether it is described as a love story or a novel of manners. But I have argued that successful novels know what they are, and that though ambitious works may set in motion various incompatible discourses, they do achieve a provisional unity that allows us to summarize their "project" in a plausible way. The term *political novel* may be a fiction, but it is a fiction intended to school or direct readings of particular texts. Obviously, no one who cares about literature will assume that a book is properly described as a political novel simply because it encompasses the Czech experience since 1948. But it must also be said that once a book has seemed to invite consideration as a political novel, its reader will not be easily persuaded to abandon that designation. There are dangers in treating an autonomous work as if it belonged to a tradition or a category. The concept of genre often serves to domesticate a book, to make it seem more like other books than it is. And yet I am determined to make you feel that the advantages in this case outweigh the dangers.

Those who have no love for the books they read, who are determined to make them confirm only what they already think, will betray literature no matter what assumptions they carry with them. But those who read novels with the view that "the part of the forest immediately before us is a screen, as it were, behind which the rest of it lies hidden and aloof"[6] will not be overly tempted to abuse the classification in terms of which they conduct their inquiry. In your latest book you speak about "the secret the novel asks about," and there is no doubt that politics is not often regarded as a domain of significant mystery. But why shouldn't politics be the key to a consideration of important secrets? Is it inevitable that persons who address themselves to ideological issues will have only ideological solutions to propose? Isn't it legitimate to suggest that a political novel at its best can do many different things?

As I put these questions to you, I summon to mind lines and images from your books, and I anticipate your responses. Of course, you will say, novels can do many things. And, of course, a book that describes characters caught up in trying political circumstances may very well gesture at important matters that are not reducible to ideological imperatives. But how do these questions answer to my objections? Why do you not consider how readily the dissident writer trades upon his image, his virtue, how shamelessly he panders in his books to the public's appetite for "values" and "correct" ideas? The political novel, you will say, insofar as it is aptly named, is bound to lend itself to journalistic purposes, to the affirmation of positions and the drawing of neat distinctions.

Ultimately, it is not important that you agree to my calling *The Joke* and *The Book of Laughter and Forgetting* political novels. I believe that they are great books and that they know what they are, whatever you may wish to say about your intentions in writing them. The question of genre or classification becomes critical only when a book does not know what it is after and which expectations it has aroused in a reader. My criticism of *The Heart of the Matter,* earlier in this book, dwells on this fatal uncertainty in Greene's novel, and I have elsewhere made a comparable criticism of Saul Bellow's *Mr. Sammler's Planet* as a book that "refuses to work through the problems it posits at the level on which they are originally conceived."[7] Your books, which set themselves so many competing objectives yet seem always to know how one objective is related to another, know also how to avoid the pretense that a metaphysical observation is an adequate elaboration of a political problem. Without aiming at definitive resolutions, you make us feel that you appreciate the difference between one sort of question and another.

Why, then, do I insist on pressing the difference between us? Clearly, I want to argue that even so ambivalent a work as *The Book of Laughter and Forgetting* can most usefully be discussed as a political novel. I want to contend, respectfully but firmly, that you cannot be serious when you describe *The Joke* as a love story, that there you are interested less in how characters fall in love than in the forces that shape their imaginations. I accept that there is nothing in your work to suggest that private relations are any less important to you than public issues, but it is no slander to contend that a given novel has a job of work to do that necessarily prioritizes these concerns rather than those.

Early in *The Joke*, Helena Zemanek recalls that she and her future husband had argued about why they married. "We married out of Party discipline," Pavel had said; what is more, the "new man" created by the party had successfully "abolished the distinction between public and private life." It may be easy to dismiss Pavel as an infatuate opportunist, but what are we to do with Helena's acknowledgment that she has always been what she calls a loyal "Party bloodhound"? She insists that she and her husband married for love, but what can this mean to a person who considers lies told to party inquisitors the equivalent of lies told to a loved one? When, many years after her marriage, she moves that a man be expelled from the party for "having deliberately deceived and misled it," she concludes that she acted "for love": "love of love, love of their house and home, love of their children," and so on. For Helena, we may say, there is no distinction between public and private. When she enters into an extra-marital affair with Ludvik Jahn, she may feel that she is engaging in a private indulgence, but the novel knows better than to pretend that a public dimension is absent from Helena's relations with her lover.

It would indeed be a slander to suggest that you invite us to approve of Helena and therefore to associate your views with hers. In fact, your views are not really at issue here at all. What is at issue is the vision of society that is opened up by your novel. In *The Joke* public and private are no longer distinct in the way that we should like them to be. We don't have to argue that Czechoslovakia in your novels is a full-blown totalitarian society to conclude that it has in common with other such societies the tendency to abolish the distinction that Pavel is so pleased to have transcended.[8] This is a political fact which affects every aspect of every life in the society you consider. You say that *The Joke* is a love story. Why not say instead that even the possibilities of love and its expression are shaped by the intrusive standards of a social order that makes everyone's business a matter of public concern? Some things, you will agree, are more important to say than others. This is not a matter of views. Why argue about views, after all, when no one who reads *The Joke*—including the Prague commissars who eventually "took [it] for a pamphlet against socialism and banned it"[9]—can fail to see that it deplores the corruption of spirit endemic in the "new" society? Does this amount to a "view" of socialism or an attack on the Czech nation? Probably an irrelevant question in this instance. To show, as you do, vividly and authoritatively, that a deplorable state of affairs exists is to do something much more important than mounting a political offensive on behalf of a particular objective.

Often, in writing this book, I have discovered that politics in a given novel is used to organize a narrative, but that it is not what the narrative is about. With *The Joke* I am tempted to say something quite the contrary, namely, that love and its distortions organize the narrative but are finally incidental to the issues that matter. The novel is narrated by an alternating succession of figures deployed over the course of seven parts or chapters. That much is certain. It is also clear that the main character is Ludvik, who speaks more than the others and frequently occupies their thoughts. Ought we to say that Ludvik's activity in the novel is reducible to his relations with women? He does spend considerable time thinking about sex and love, and it is convenient to organize our sense of the novel around the progression of affairs he conducts, first with Marketa, then with Lucie, and finally with Helena. But these relations in themselves do not interest us as much as they interest Ludvik. And even Ludvik, so often in the throes of sexual longing, is moved by more than a desire to conquer targets.

As a student, Ludvik is attracted to Marketa. She is an attractive piece of female flesh, but in no other way is she interesting—to Ludvik or to us—except insofar as she may be said to represent in a pathetically innocent way the spirit of the age in which she lives. Marketa is gullible. She believes what she is told and has no resistance to lies. Her only enemy is cynicism, the subversive spirit that eats away at the heart of every enthusiasm and every loyalty. In Marketa, Ludvik notes, we see a reflection of the "oddity" of the new Czech Communist regime. The dark sobriety, the "gravity" etched on the situation, "took the form of a smile, not a frown . . . anyone who failed to rejoice was immediately suspected of lamenting the victory of the working class." This is a stunning observation and utterly consistent with the portrait of Czech society you have elsewhere given us. But I want here simply to point out that Marketa is present in the novel only to set Ludvik's fate in motion and to allow you to make those observations about Czech society in 1948. Of course, you give us a glimpse of Ludvik fantasizing about Marketa's carnal charms, but no more than is minimally required by the situation you evoke. We are not disappointed by your forgetting Marketa once the consequences of Ludvik's prank—his "joke"—are recorded and absorbed. We know throughout that you are after bigger game than Marketa.

Ludvik's relations with the other women are played out over a great many more pages, and there is no doubt that these characters are more interesting to us as individuals. It is even possible to imagine a novel that would accomplish a great deal by dwelling on the private lives of such persons. For a while it seemed that you intended little else in *The Unbearable Lightness of Being,* where you are obviously fascinated by the relationship of Tomas and Tereza. But in *The Joke* you are assiduous to establish the political and cultural significance of characters and relationships before you allow intimacies to develop. Why be interested in Lucie? Precisely because, as Ludvik observes, she represents "a life outside the issues of cosmopolitanism and internationalism, vigilance and the class struggle." Entrammeled in politics, his life destroyed by what he took to be a harmless adolescent prank, Ludvik is attracted to Lucie as to something that "knew nothing of the *major problems of our times,*" and so offers to her admirer the prospect of a life outside of history and society. He is quite prepared to live with problems that are *"trivial and eternal,"* but not any longer with the wretched corruptions produced by the political order of the day.

Is this a journalist's view of Lucie? I must remind you that *The Joke* furnishes all the "evidence" one would need to argue that Lucie is interesting precisely as a corrective, albeit a temporary and patently inadequate one, to the politics of her time. I know it is misleading to suggest that there is nothing more to Lucie than that. But the novel demands that we think of her novelistically, that is, in terms of her function in forwarding the design of the novel. It was your decision, after all, to move steadily, often abruptly, from tender passages describing Ludvik's feelings for Lucie to others that return us to your characteristic cultural-political obsessions. Are we mistaken to suppose that Ludvik's relations with Lucie are made more poignant and convincing than they would otherwise be by your steady insertion (or reassertion) of the political perspective? At one point Ludvik is reciting poetry to Lucie; on the very next page he is discussing his failure to love in terms of the scar left by his expulsion from the party. Specifically, he tells us that

> the image of that lecture hall with a hundred people raising their hands [unanimously voting to expel him], giving the order to destroy my life, comes back to me again and again. . . . Since then, whenever I make new acquaintances, men or women with the potential of becoming friends or lovers, I project them back into that time, that place, and ask myself whether they would have raised their hands; no one has ever passed the test.

A terrifying thought, to be sure, and one to which Ludvik is surely entitled given what he has been through. We note, though, that Ludvik has never had to think of Lucie as one who might have raised her hand against him. In fact, a Lucie might very well be taught to do what is expected of her in a degradation ceremonial, but she is attractive to Ludvik (and, in a more provisional way, to us) because of her relative "innocence." She seems more an eternal victim, a child of the earth, than a potential agent of historical forces on the move.

To see Lucie in this way is to see how *The Joke* is aware not only of what it is, but of what kind of a world it seeks to study. It knows, and wants us to know, that the experience at issue in the novel involves a relentless politicization of everything, and that a Lucie can be interesting only because she seems to exist outside that procedure. She can be a temporary objective only for a character too caught up in the characteristic experience of his time to understand that there is no way out of it. Lucie's simplicity, so the novel would have us see, is not an answer to the destruction of Czech culture. Its attractiveness is itself a measure of the monstrous deformations that have taken place in a society on the way to making all signs of simplicity and private suffering into fetching anachronisms. Lucie's seeming to exist outside *"the major problems of our times"* only brings home to us how pervasive are the problems which are not less real for the fact that they have been translated into edifying exemplars by the commissars of the new order.

None of this can be surprising to you, I think, and none of it is intended to discount or overlook the strictly human dimension of the characters you develop. I don't have to reduce Lucie to the politics of your novel to make my point. I don't have to say that Ludvik's seduction of Helena is of no interest in itself to argue that its principal interest is in what it represents. It shows us a man who doesn't know how to fight politically and a woman who is "merely" a woman in spite of the political pabulum she has been fed. Does this translate characters into political counters or symbolic objects in a pamphleteering operation? Not at all. It simply recognizes that characters in a novel like *The Joke* cannot be what they would be in another kind of book. More than one commentator has speculated—this you've no doubt heard before—that you would be a very different kind of writer if you did not come from Czechoslovakia. This I consider a ludicrous speculation. What would Milan Kundera be if he had been born in Brooklyn, New York, or Newark, New Jersey, and had decided to write "love stories"? Would he be a Norman Mailer, a James Purdy, or a Philip Roth? It is as useless to wonder in this way as to speculate on the intrinsic value or interest of characters outside the domain of the novels in which they exist. The student who recently informed me that you were more interested in sex than in politics overlooked the fact that a major writer is usually interested in various things. The Czech experience may so color a novel of sex, I told my student, that it will turn out to have almost nothing in common with ostensibly comparable works by American or British authors. This was not an easy paradox to explain to my student, but it cannot be an issue I need to debate with you.

The more difficult issue, I believe, has to do with your politics, or, more properly, with the politics of your novel. I can demonstrate well enough that politics plays an important part in your vision of the Czech experience. But what, I ask myself, do you want? What political goals underlie your critique of the existing order? If I agree not to pose my questions in this way, if I accept your view that the novels are not focused critiques of the existing order and that *as a novelist* you have no concrete political objectives, I may still ask what authentically political vision underlies your fiction. You do, of course, criticize various manifestations of the existing order in Eastern Europe, and it is always legitimate to ask on behalf of what values a critique is mounted. If I conclude that you criticize on behalf of humanity, or life, or a vague idea of freedom, I may as a consequence have to conclude that you do not think politically. Would that be an awful thing for me to say about you? It might be, if I felt that you presumed to engage political issues without being able to think about them politically. But since I take you to be an astute political thinker and take your novels to be politically sophisticated in the best sense, I have to believe that there is a politics in your fiction that I can take hold of and evaluate.[10]

To say that a novelist thinks politically is to say that he has a plausible sense of what does and does not belong to the domain of politics; it is to say that he does not confuse political objectives with other kinds of objectives; and it is to say that he understands how changes are brought to pass in the public realm. In *The Joke*, we may say, you dramatize change by showing how various characters register what has happened to persons like themselves in the period between 1948 and 1965. You indicate what are and are not political objectives by distinguishing, for example, between a love of tradition that might conceivably inform a resistance to the Czech Communist regime and a love of tradition that is aesthetically primitive and vulgarly sentimental. What emerges is nothing like an optimistic projection of the future based on the unforeseen changes that did take place in the first decades of Communist rule. The best that can be said about the situation you evoke is that people trapped within it do often manage to grow in spite of it. Not surprisingly, that growth frequently is made possible by their having to confront political realities, the political facts of life they had once thought to deny. In the same way, characters who fail to grow are often unable to acknowledge the way that politics is implicated in aspects of their lives they take to be strictly personal and under no one's control but their own. Your ability to make us understand growth, change, and failure in these terms is what makes you a political novelist.

But I have still to formulate what I take to be the political goals underlying your fiction. *The Joke*, of course, is limited in its purview to the Czech scene, though already one sees signs of the broader critique you were later to mount in novels like *The Book of Laughter and Forgetting*. That broader critique would encompass not only the Soviet domination of Eastern Europe, but the hollowness of cultural alternatives offered by the West. In *The Joke*, or so it seems to me, you long for various changes in Czech social and cultural life that would require at the very least a major political upheaval. But you do not allow yourself in the novel to address the necessity for that upheaval or to consider what your objectives amount to without a focused political perspective. It may be that you did not think it necessary to spell out the political requirements on the grounds that Czech society clearly was not ready to move into a revolutionary stage. Or it may be that you took the political requirements to be so implicit in everything you presented as to be lost on no one. Either way, you did surely decide that readers would pick up the signs and determine for themselves what were the salient political objectives. The danger in that procedure, obviously, is that we will misread the signs. The great advantage is that we will be provoked to think politically without supposing that a political program is the inevitable outcome of analysis and speculation.

If *The Joke* were a political tract or a no-nonsense analytic study of Communist rule in Czechoslovakia, it might be useful at this point simply to ask what it argues. But it is a novel, and your readers are throughout largely attracted by what they take to be the unfolding of a sensibility. We attend, that is, not only to the object of your study, but to the responsive apparatus. We ask not only what you discover, but how you feel about it. Why do certain things seem more important to you than others? When we refer to "you," of course, we do not suppose that we are talking about the actual person who has opinions of his own on what he intended and what he actually accomplished. We are content to infer an authorial consciousness from the text and to attribute to it whatever we can justify by limiting ourselves to the instructions inscribed in the pages before us. If I conclude, as I must, that the sensibility unfolding before me is deeply ironic, I do not need to seek evidence outside of the text, for as reader I am interested primarily in the mind and spirit that inhabit the text. And I go on from my reading of the operant sensibility to consider which ideas and projections might be plausible to the intelligence dominated by that sensibility.

You will forgive me if I say that no one in *The Joke* seems to me in the end a likable character. The mood of the novel is in the main sour, the sensibility displayed alternately amused and disgusted by the spectacle of human beings humiliated or corrupted by the conditions under which they live. Irony defines the voice of the novel by insisting that no perspective associated with a particular narrator be permitted to seem fully adequate. Ludvik may understand more than the other narrator-characters, but his perspective is undercut by the relentless irony to which he subjects his own observations. It is challenged also by the more generous, less defiantly cynical ruminations of other characters. In the same way, the sincerity or idealism of lesser characters is routinely undercut by an irony that considers everything suspect. We are left with a corrosive bitterness that yet cannot entirely dispel an alternative longing for a suspension of hostilities.

I know that I am postponing—maybe longer than I should—my formulation of those political objectives I hoped to evaluate. But I want to prepare the way, and this I can do only by citing the poles of sensibility within which you operate. On one side, if you will, there is the unabashed cynicism which concludes that a woman in love is simply a woman who wishes to be "a woman in love." Or it concludes that the impulse to brand and expel traitors is simply an impulse to promote a feeling of group solidarity in the absence of other satisfactions denied to persons in a Communist society. This attitude typically empties the ostensive contents of feelings and reduces every human reflex to the level of a predictable mechanism. Irony is the expression of the distance between a character's sense of what he is doing or feeling and our *instructed* sense of what is actually involved. Irony is also, and more elusively, the novel's expression of how easy it is to promote a routine cynicism that can become almost as programmatic as the naive enthusiasms it means to ridicule.

But the irony in your novels always has a difficult job to perform. Why? Because, for all your bitterness, you continue to attach us, however ambivalently, to things, persons, ideas, and traditions that are obviously in need of our love. Even Ludvik, who behaves so badly, comes through to us as one who has reason to be bitter and whose bitterness is in some respects an exemplary response to the Czech reality. Even Kostka, so obviously deluded about himself and the conditions to which he has adjusted, is in his way right to oppose Ludvik's bitterness and foolishly heroic in his efforts to think the best of the Czech experiment. Opposed to the dominating irony of the novel is the steady attempt to introduce another note. This note is neither optimistic nor sentimental. It is an expression of the conviction that things do change and that people sometimes learn from their individual and collective errors.

Is this too vague? At one point in Part Three of *The Joke*, Ludvik determines to "fight for my right 'not to be an enemy' " of the people, not to think of himself as defined by those who had raised their hands against him. Then he confronts a kindly, mild-mannered Slovak corporal in charge of a work detail to which Ludvik had been assigned. The utterly matter-of-fact way in which this corporal regards Ludvik as the enemy, in no respect different from the "imperialist" enemies of the socialist state, convinces Ludvik that "the bonds tying me to the Party and the Comrades had been irrevocably broken." Why? Because the Slovak corporal had no particular animus towards Ludvik; his antipathy was categorical and could not be dislodged by any persuasive argument Ludvik might have made. There is no satiric irony here, no attempt to ridicule the corporal or mock the futility of Ludvik's desire to clear his good name with the Comrades. Things are as they are and there is nothing and no one to blame. Even "the system" doesn't seem so much at issue here as it does elsewhere, for what would "the system" at this level be were it not for the dumb complicity of corporals and other functionaries? But how can one seriously blame functionaries who believe they are doing their duty and behave with no sadistic ill will toward outcasts in their power? The sadists among the NCOs Ludvik had been able to deal with; sadists, after all, are . . . sadists. Only the mild-mannered corporal convinces him that the situation is quietly awful beyond repair.

This modest passage in the novel marks a point of recognition for Ludvik, and in a sense it enables us to see more clearly what had been at stake for him and what his future course must be. It signifies what is to be the fate of a man who henceforth must live without hope of vindication or accommodation. Having understood that the Slovak corporal cannot but regard him as he does, he sees now that to survive at all he must set himself goals that have nothing to do with rejoining the community as a citizen in good standing. Irony henceforth can serve only to reenforce his sense of alienation. He is fated, as it were, to identifying with his own despair, to regarding the gap between his own goals and the goals of the community as a sign not of his superiority, but of his hopeless disaffection and insignificance.

Is there a political insight embedded in this? There is the obvious suggestion that the system spoils and degrades everything it touches. There is the further suggestion, elaborated throughout the novel, that if there is to be resistance, it will come not from those who have a purpose, but from those who have given up hope of living in the bosom of the community. These insights are related, in the sense that the system is shown to breed attitudes that make all serious thought of collective resistance impossible. Ludvik's alienation is spiritually not much more edifying than the behavior of those he detests.[11] We tend—most of us, at any rate—to regard cynicism and the refusal to believe in anything as signs of intellectual distinction. Ludvik is thus attractive to us as a superior fellow who feels a little nauseous when he hears the rhetoric of May Day parades. But in allowing ourselves to find him attractive we are likely to overlook his inability to see much value in anything or to perceive the political character of his own cynicism. His friend Kostka tells him, "The general scorn you have for your fellow man is terrifying and sinful." This is not in itself a political insight, but it does lead to one. For it is clear in your novel that the failure to see any hope in the customary behavior of ordinary persons is a refusal of political purpose and, ultimately, of political thinking.

Do you see what I am getting at? Your book engages political issues in a sustained and serious way. More important, it enables us to see why political action is not possible for persons so entirely cynical that they cannot imagine a basis on which to revolt. This is an important political insight. I have said elsewhere in my book that the capacity to imagine alternatives, to project a hypothetically nurturant political culture, is in general essential to successful political novels. What form these projections will take is not possible to dictate or predict. *The Joke* does imagine alternatives in the way I propose. There is, I think, an ideal embodied in the novel. It is not an ideal any of your characters can realize in the space of their lives. The political facts prevent them from making the leap from the hypothetical to the actual. But the novel thinks politically by putting us in mind of the gap between projection and fulfillment, between cynicism as corruption of spirit and irony as a mode of corrective dispassion.

The key to your vision in this novel, to your politics generally, is your handling of the past and of memory. This will come as no surprise. The struggle to remain human, you have insisted again and again, is the struggle to remember. What makes Ludvik more than a cynic, though he cannot escape his bitterness and sense of futility, is his refusal to forget what was done to him, his insistence on evaluating the present in light of the past. Attached, as he says, to "something that no longer was," he is forever separated from those who live in a perpetual present. "My only real home," he acknowledges, "was this descent, this searching eager fall" wherein the lost soul reaches for that which is valuable precisely because it has been abandoned. Ludvik may not know what to do with the fragments of the past he retrieves from oblivion, but he knows that to live "as a man should live, facing forward," is not for him. His determination, his "searching eager fall," never assumes the dimensions of a political quest, but it has the character of a political gesture in a culture that is dedicated to the pursuit of forgetting.

You will perhaps object that I unduly politicize what has little to do with politics as such. Jaroslav, after all, is the character most committed to the past, whose staging of ancient folk rituals and retrieval of Moravian folk song is so central to the idea of the past in your novel. And what, you will ask, does this infatuation with the past do for Jaroslav's political acumen? How does his knowledge of Czech history, his appreciation of "the folk song or rite" as "a tunnel beneath history . . . that keeps alive much of what wars, revolutions and brutal civilizations have long since destroyed aboveground"—how do these accomplishments inform his transactions with present reality? Is it your object to suggest that a reverence for the past has no political component, that it is a value in itself and exists apart from anything that I might wish to make of it? I cannot accept that this is your intention. Jaroslav's addiction to the past does not, it is true, empower him to take arms against the commissars who regard culture only as a potentially useful means of controlling the population. Ludvik's inability to face forward does not lead him to urge others to break ranks. You are not in *The Joke* concerned with political revolution or even with modes of "constructive" dissent. You are evoking a milieu in which constructive dissent has nowhere to go, no constituency to work with, in which Ludvik's contempt for everyone around him is, however corrosive and self-defeating, entirely justifiable. I insist nonetheless that the attempt to hold on to the past has more than sentimental value, and that your novel assigns to it a political value that we cannot ignore.

Consider Jaroslav's remembrance of his own marriage ceremony as the type of a ceremonial dominated by "age-old tradition." Is this a fuzzy-headed, nostalgic recollection? Not if it leads the character, as it does, to reflect that "modern man cheats," which is to say, that he supposes things mean only what he decides at any given moment he wants them to mean. Traditional man, by remembering what things have meant in the past, understands that he cannot have things his way, that a bond is a bond, a lie a lie, and a betrayal wretched no matter what is said in its defense. Can Jaroslav be a traditional man? This, the novel suggests, is not possible. Jaroslav sees too much of the reality around him to behave as if the world had not changed and a rite were designed to effect what it did in the past. In a world committed to controlling every aspect of human development, the rite too becomes a managed affair with a political goal,[12] and Jaroslav's clinging to the spirit of the primitive rite becomes an anachronism. Jaroslav becomes an eccentric because he pretends that things can be even a little what they were, though he knows that the past is gone and even his own son is unwilling to go along with his father's touching pretense.

The political aspect of remembrance has nothing to do with an implicit injunction to act. It asks only that what has not proven useful to the commissars be loved, protected, promoted. Ludvik feels warmly toward Jaroslav and his ritual enactments as soon as he observes the indifference with which his old friend is regarded by the public that has learned all too well to face forward. At the end of the novel he carries the stricken Jaroslav "through the din of the drunken adolescents" who have dropped the "thin thread" of history and succumbed to "the ocean of what has been forgotten." The gesture portends no oppositional confrontation, but it does securely place the two men on "the other side." Whatever hope there is in the novel must lie with them.

This would be a feeble conclusion if nothing more were involved than the determination of two alienated persons to play folk songs and show contempt for the programmed louts around them. Both know that "the magic circle of music" can never be secure against the predators intent on forcing their way in. But the idea of memory in The Joke goes well beyond the folklorist's addiction to "sources." And it goes beyond the wish of a disillusioned skeptic like Ludvik and an ineffectual dreamer like Jaroslav to find solace in retreat. Can memory serve as a basis for an exploratory projection of a hypothetical political culture? The ancient Moravian culture from which folk songs emerged obviously was not a vital culture. Neither is Ludvik's memory of the hands that went up against him the key to a more acceptable culture. The search for a model cannot proceed in either of these directions. Memory is the key not to the recovery of a time past that modern men and women can bring up to date, but to a habit of thought that alone prepares them for living in a decent world. I hope you will agree that your novel teaches us to appreciate the virtue of memory by showing us what is detestable and shallow in the practice of forgetting. To remember and study the past, to preserve it as a living presence within oneself, may not enable anyone to resist what is done in the name of the future, but it is the only hope for those who find the future intolerable.[13]

Late in The Joke you introduce a Miss Broz. An attractive young woman, a student, she is depicted as an exemplar of a specious health in the brave new society struggling to break free of inherited constraints and misgivings. Her lover Zemanek, who is of course Ludvik's bête noir, is proud of her as one who knows nothing of the sour memories he and Ludvik share. To her, as she asserts, all the old words and categories are "alien"; she is "neither dogmatist nor revisionist nor sectarian nor deviationist." She is frankly interested in herself, in her own "development," and even the word egotist has no particular capacity to wound someone so content to be what she is. What makes her so attractive to Zemanek, and, in a sense, promising to us, is her utter lack of fanaticism. As Zemanek says, "We wanted to save the world and with our messianic vision nearly destroyed it." Miss Broz is too "healthy" to want to save the world, and probably too cautious to risk destroying it. She represents a stage of development in Eastern Europe that some have called "totalitarianism with a human face," though clearly you don't for a moment believe in this idea.

Why aren't you more ready to believe in the idea? Why can't you make Miss Broz more appealing? Zemanek is permitted to articulate the main thrust of your objection. "On entrance exams," he says, "when we ask them about the purges, they don't know what we're talking about. Stalin is just a name to them. And most of them have no idea there were political trials in Prague."[14] Free of the "overpoliticized thought" that colors every one of Ludvik's experiences, she is unwilling to be bothered by what she takes to be trifles. She is on her way to becoming the generic *human being* for whom even the immediate past is remote, for whom reality is what lies just ahead. Blissfully unconcerned about her own past or the past she shares with the Czech people, her goal is to travel and venture and feel, not as a person with something to lose, but as one who carries all value within herself. She is our contemporary version of the *luftmensch* who has never had to overcome anything, born to know that whatever came before was not for her. To people of her own generation she is nature itself. To those, like Zemanek, whose former "views" were but a means of getting ahead, she is a model of liberation, the "end of ideology" incarnate. For those like Ludvik and, one supposes, like Milan Kundera, she is the death of culture and a clear indication that political struggle is likely to be hopeless. To live as if the past were not worth remembering is to be without a sense of oneself as belonging to something particular on behalf of which one might summon the will to struggle.

The American writer Philip Rieff, who has understood this better than any of his countrymen, has seen in people like your Miss Broz the triumphant barbarians of the new order, triumphant most especially in the West, but also in the more "advanced" reaches of the Communist satellite cultures. The new "freedom," he writes, entails

> the liveliness with which a human can step aside, as if no particular act represented the responsible I in the middle of his head . . . eternally young and unsettled, we teachers ourselves engage in the most acrobatic hopping from one order to another. . . . To be radically contemporaneous, to be sprung loose from every particular culture, is to achieve a conclusive, unanswerable failure of historical memory.

Finally, Rieff explains, "we moderns shall arrive at barbarism," which is "a playing at being 'Man' or 'Human'; barbarism means the universality of those educated out of membership in the binding particularities of their culture."[15] Is this not what your novels have enabled us to see so clearly? Is this not—this barbarism—more than the intrusion of Soviet power into Czech society, at once the source and the symptom of your conviction that Czech culture is rapidly disappearing?

There is ever so much more I should like to say here about *The Joke*, but this seems a good place to turn to *The Book of Laughter and Forgetting*. For one thing, I have arrived, finally, at what I take to be the heart of your fiction, the issue that dominates your imagination. This issue—the past, forgetting, the new barbarism—is the primary link between *The Joke* and the later work. It is everywhere present in *The Unbearable Lightness of Being*. But in that brilliant work you refuse to give us a political novel. You refuse, that is, to make of politics more than a background against which the characters enact their fates and allow you to pose metaphysical questions. *The Book of Laughter and Forgetting,* by contrast, is a political novel by virtue of its insisting that cultural disorder and political corruption are intimately related phenomena. As in *The Joke*, you are interested in how things come to pass and in how far it is useful to consider political causes as adequate to explain events.

I have argued time and again in my book that political novels put us in touch with an absent cause that the novels cannot themselves designate in so many words. This would seem particularly evident in your novels. Though *The Joke* limits its coverage to the Czech setting, its concern with cultural barbarism, as we have seen, inevitably calls to mind comparable developments in the West.* *The Book of Laughter and Forgetting* more explicitly develops the comparison between East and West, suggesting that the obvious political differences may finally not be so important as the grotesque cultural manifestations discernible in both camps. We may be tempted, in other words, to regard the politics in your novels as a sufficient explanatory cause, but obviously they are not. This we can understand simply by asking ourselves what purges and party shibboleths have to do with the new forgetting at which the emergent generations are apparently so adept. We can explain Miss Broz by stating that she has good reason to forget the shabby record of her predecessors. Miss Broz, like the liberated Western types in *The Book*, did not *decide* to disburden herself. She is weightless because she has no capacity to feel how terrible are the words "It could just as well be otherwise."[16] How she came not to have this capacity the novel cannot (and must not) let us feel we know. We suspect that the cause lies in the political history of her country, but the novel complicates our reading by refusing to embody the ostensive cause in a fully satisfactory way.

The Book seems to me your most wonderful work, for two related reasons. It invokes Necessity as a system of social relations and political constraints without suggesting that the system is all there is to reality. It is also a deeply playful meditation on what it means to be *in reality* and, at the same time, to imagine ways of escape. The pathos of escapism is caught along with the vitality of the will to project and dream. Cause itself is presented as a fabrication subject as much to whim as to unalterable

---

* There is no coincidence in the fact that your Miss Broz is described in terms of her sexual freedom, her love of jazz music, and other qualities that surely call to mind her liberated Western counterparts.

circumstance. The freedom of the novel to be whatever it wishes is celebrated and challenged, supported and undercut. A tissue of contradictions,
The Book is yet always aiming at a coherence and thematic unity it knows
it needs and cannot have. Its greatness is in its effort to encompass more
than it can hold.

If I argue that it is a political novel, I do so because of its structure and
because of what I take to be the central issues. It opens with a reference
to the Czech propaganda section's airbrushing "out of history" a Communist leader once in favor but later "charged with treason and hanged."
True, *The Book* does not spend much time rehearsing the details of such
procedures, but it comes back to them again and again and indicates how
they are implicated in the daily lives of ordinary people. It even goes so
far as to suggest that an individual who erases from his mind a woman he
had loved "is as much a rewriter of history" as the party propagandists. I
am a bit uncomfortable with that suggestion, but it is, after all, yours. You
also suggest that the wildest desires—to rape, to engulf, to laugh without
object or restraint—are distinctly related to, though not caused by, the
combined political and cultural circumstance in which people live. This is
not a matter of my selecting for emphasis occasional statements that someone else might justifiably discount. The political thrust of your novel is
indicated by the way in which you make everything come back to—even
if it does not devolve on—the political.

What is the political content of *The Book*? Obviously, it is a novel about
your country and about those who feel that it is slipping away from them
as it ceases to be an autonomous cultural entity. The frame of reference
is the period between 1948 and the late 1970s, a period in which many
changes occurred in the country's relations with the Soviet Union, but in
which there appeared very little promise of any kind. You do not go over
the various developments as if you considered them individually significant
or as if you were bent on writing a topical work. You note particular
moments simply to dramatize the effects of alien power on persons accustomed to "drowsing" in its "sweet, strong embrace." No one is blamed.
All are complicit in "forgetting," which is to say, in living as if a monstrous
violation were not taking place. Those who refuse to go along with the
public crimes are most often too weak to do anything but bear witness to
their disaffection and speak about their endless fall. Those who fight to
regain their country are forced also to fight against the idea that their
country is an illusion and that they are in the fight simply so as not to stand
utterly alone. Politics in *The Book* is in one sense what it has always been,
namely, "the struggle of man [or men] against power"; but that struggle
is for you "the struggle of memory against forgetting."

No character in your novel seems to believe that the Soviets can be
gotten out of Czechoslovakia. What is worse, you suggest, even if the
Soviets were to be ousted, much that was valuable in Czech culture would
be very hard to recover. One hundred and forty-five historians were dismissed from Czech universities in 1969 by Husak, "*the President of for-*

getting"; monuments have been torn down by one regime after another, street names changed with stunning rapidity as ideological fashions change. Everywhere in your country there is an effort to "lobotomize," to "invent a new history" and "manufacture a new culture." Politics in such a situation can be nothing more than the effort to remember what is being destroyed. The Soviet state is not the dominant issue so long as the Czech people are largely complicitous in the destruction. Soviet tanks are real, but so also are the adjustments in attitude and identity that allow people to feel that life is life no matter what the cultural or political dispensation under which they live.

Your political outlook, which has in it a large quantity of old-fashioned grief, pessimism, and resignation, is best summarized in your treatment of the word *litost*. This you cite as "a Czech word with no exact translation into any other language," and I must say that the various definitions you provide are sometimes contradictory and confusing. Nevertheless, we do have a decent grasp of what *litost* signifies. "It designates a feeling"; one cannot "understand the human soul without it"; it is "characteristic of immaturity"; it manifests itself in the person who "revenges himself by destroying himself," who chooses "the worst of defeats" by "rejecting compromise" when even compromise is more than it is reasonable to expect. Most important, in spite of the various personal and literary applications to which you subject the word in the chapter devoted to the idea, "the history of the Czechs—a history of never-ending revolts against stronger enemies . . . causing the downfall of its own people—is the history of *litost*." To see things in this way is, of course, to remember only defeat and futility, and politics is then little more than the collective instinct to reenact an "immature" fantasy of hopeless revolt.

An activist would complain that in the novels you do not get close enough to those who revolted, that you assimilate them too readily to "the history of *litost*."[17] Your perspective, he would say, is too grimly colored by your intense disappointment over the failure of the 1968 Prague spring. To read back from that experience is to suppose that the history of a small nation over centuries can be reduced to a simple pattern. What is more, your attempt to draw every aspect of private life as tainted by *litost*, or by the effort to deny *litost*, reflects an unhealthy absorption in a political experience that ought not to loom so large in your mind.

Perhaps you would not wish to answer such charges. Or perhaps you would be content to say, flatly, that a writer has his obsessions and that it is no criticism of a novel to cite them. You do not ask to be judged for the validity of your political views; you ask to be understood, not to be followed. Were you to say some such thing, you would not, of course, close the issue, but you would quite properly place it where it belongs. *Litost* does not purport to say once and for all everything there is to say on the subject of Czech history and politics. It is a trope, an idea, a word that empowers a multitude of narrative variations by promising to them a coherence that is neither specious nor wholly persuasive.

If we say that *litost* casts a spell—not a pall—over *The Book*, we say only that *The Book* knows from the first that its variously tormented figures really have nowhere to turn. You do not tell us that the failure of the 1968 Prague spring is the single causal factor shaping your reading of previous and subsequent events. You do not say that the political domain is at the center of every human failure. But the novel does indicate quite plainly that politics is more than the "fashionable issues" that "concerned" intellectuals and journalists discuss. Political events obviously figure in the fate of your country, but it is necessary to move beyond the elementary opposition between good and evil, open and closed, free and unfree, to see what is at stake in the political struggle to remember. We do not have to declare the distinction between freedom and oppression to be of no consequence to accept that the opposition may serve to obscure as much as it reveals.

This is where your combined critique of East and West has most to offer us. We have seen that *litost* seems to you an appropriate perspective from which to understand the Czech experience. But a sense of futility also colors your observations on the West. This may best be understood, I think, by considering what you do with the word *progressive*. In your country the word has come to signify all that is consistent with the official dogma or party line. It contains the implicit demand that worthy citizens think positively, that they overlook what is unsavory or apparently regressive in the public life of their culture—this in the interests of that better future to which every Communist society is by definition committed. In the West, by contrast, *progressive* signifies a commitment to procedural rights and substantive standards that cannot be realized in a Leninist order based on a morality of unabashed opportunism. No one can for a moment believe that for you there is no important difference between the one definition and the other. Yet you do not wish us to see the difference as an elementary opposition or to imagine that the quality of life in the contemporary West is necessarily superior in every way. You despair of us. Our progressivism seems to you empty, dishonest, a poor response to the alternative dispensation available in your country. You talk, or so it seems to me, with "the voice of litost." You know that conditions in the West are much closer to what you want, yet you insist that they are awful and that to accept them is in effect to make a shabby compromise. To accept what passes for progressive in the West is in fact to miss what is most disgraceful in the culture of the Sovietized East.

In Chapter Six of your book you bring your beloved Tamina (the Tamina who is "main character and main audience," whose story is the "theme" on which all the others are "variations") to the island of children. It is "a place where things weigh nothing at all," where nakedness, like the sense of immodesty or remorse, "had lost all meaning." There she is rubbed and fondled and raped and assaulted, all by way of an invitation to leave behind everything she has been and known, to join the children in an "innocence" without past or consequence. Several reviewers spoke of this phantasmal episode as a conclusive assault on the terror of an authoritarian society, but it is not that at all. Tamina allows herself to be taken to the island from a Western country. The thought of returning to the West is apparently as distasteful to her as returning to Prague. She allows herself to drown because, though she has "a great desire for life," she can summon no "idea about the world she wanted to live in." To Tamina, forgetting on the island of children is not an abrupt break with the life she has known before. For all its apparitional strangeness, its polymorphous perversity, life on the island is continuous with life in Prague and in the Western countries, where "mankind is moving more and more in the direction of infancy." Tamina cannot say what she feels, but, then, you make it clear that she belongs to you, is your character alone, and that she feels in her way what you feel in yours. What is so terrible about the movement toward infancy? It is a movement toward an ideal of paradise in which all forget what they are, what they've been, and in which conflicts and distinctions are suspended or abolished.

So you detest the dream of paradise and you detest the "progressive" thought that abolishes primary conflicts and distinctions as if there were really nothing over which enlightened persons had need to differ. You say that "the basic event" of your novel is "the story of totalitarianism, which deprives people of memory and thus retools them into a nation of children," but you go on to speculate that "perhaps our entire technological age does this."[18] Does it not seem to you that your novels focus more upon what you call "the angels" (who are "so exalted by the afflatus of ideological togetherness that they rise into the air")[19] than on the overt horrors we associate with the Gulag universe? But, then, as you say, "it is extremely easy to condemn gulags,"[20] and not so easy to tell people that their pleasures are shallow, their thought the conditioned exposition of "correct" views, their feelings reducible to kitsch. And what is kitsch? It is the form that the dream of paradise takes in an age of mass culture. It is virtue as the demand for progressive views that mask confusion, lust, emptiness. It is "the absolute denial of shit," the expression of a desire to reach "an agreement with being as such."[21] What you call "totalitarian kitsch" is of course possible only in a fully controlled society, where there are no competing influences to limit one another. But you leave no doubt that kitsch is the ideal to which all "advanced" societies are tending. Tamina's sojourn on the island of children is not itself an example of kitsch; it is an apotheosis of the dream of paradise that is ordinarily promoted in our actual societies—East and West—through the cultivation of kitsch. You avoid kitsch by revealing to us the shit, the conflict, the terror masked by the dream of paradise.

Is this a political matter? By now, perhaps, an all too familiar question. Let me return, if only briefly, to your definition of *kitsch* as the denial of shit, or the desire to reach an agreement with being as such. In *The Unbearable Lightness of Being* you leave us in no doubt about your intentions, which are inscribed unmistakably in the pages of the novel. There you wish no longer to entertain political possibilities. Collective activity inevitably entails parades, slogans, and the belief that one is right. So you suggest. To oppose totalitarianism is to ask questions and to refuse to become a model of anything, not even of dissidence.[22] " 'My enemy is kitsch, not Communism,' " the character Sabina says, and she would seem in this novel to speak for you. In *The Book*, however, one finds no such statement. There the desire to reach "an agreement with being as such" is more explicitly identified as a blissful or witless capitulation to the established reality, which is more often than not figured in political terms. The "angels" who dance in a ring "encircling all the socialist countries and all the Communist parties of the world" sing of "joy and brotherhood" as a way of forgetting what is theirs to know: that decent people are jailed and executed for voicing unacceptable ideas, that failure and doubt are themselves forbidden in the best of all possible worlds. Quite as important for our purposes, the angels in your novel also include the "liberated" French and Americans who in the name of feminism or some other advanced ideology promote a progressivism as mindless as that celebrated by the Communist faithful. Again, it is the agreement with being that you make us think about, with its "ecstatic laughter" that banishes memory and promotes an idea of desire as certain satisfaction without thought of loss or discrimination.

Would you object to my saying that *The Book* fears the angels—as a product and manifestation of kitsch—because no serious political opposition can be generated by people so exalted? The prerequisite to a meaningful resistance (a resistance to all establishments and ideologies) is the capacity of the subject populations to think about their historical situation and about the options that are available. Persons inclined to dance in a ring or to congratulate themselves on their progressive views may participate in demonstrations or even on occasion be persuaded to bear arms, but they will not be political actors in a sense acceptable to you. They will not be horrified by the violation of humane motive implicit in the commodification of collective desire that is kitsch. They will not have any possibility, in other words, of making a significantly better world, no matter how successful their "revolutions" may be.

The consequence of this vision is surely an unwillingness to attach oneself to political movements or parties. And how should one attach, when even the best are likely to be carried away with enthusiasm for what is transparently specious? The working class, a class on its way to becoming permanently anesthetized by the pleasure-providing apparatus of the modern state, is of course not an answer to anything. The intellectuals and their fellow travelers offer nothing better, enwombed as they are in the clichés of the progressive order promoted by the media and too often legitimized by a professoriate eager not to be left behind. Is it fair to say that no politics worthy the effort can be created by people who believe they have been given life simply to enjoy it? If this is so, then a primary function of the modern political novel must be to show us why, as everything becomes politicized under the auspices of a pervasive kitsch, the possibilities of significant political thought narrow. This I take to be fundamental to the intention of your work.

May I conclude by citing an extraordinary passage in *The Book*? It occurs at the very end, in the chapter called "The Border," which takes place in a period—our period—when "the beaches of Western Europe were crowded every summer with women who wore no tops," when everyone is a "liberal" with "good progressive ideas" and the best idea of all "is the one which is provocative enough so its supporters can feel proud of being different, but popular enough so the risk of isolation is precluded by cheering crowds confident of victory." At one point in this remarkable chapter your character Jan is taken to a nude beach, where he studies the varieties of shapes on display and notes that "all of them together were equally bizarre and meaningless." More strangely, he is "overwhelmed by a strange feeling of affliction, and from the haze of that affliction came an even stronger thought: that the Jews had filed into Hitler's gas chambers naked and en masse." Jan can't quite "understand why that image kept coming back to him or what it was trying to tell him," but we take it to be critical to the shape of your narrative. For what would justify the attention you lavish on nudity and bra burning, on liberationist fetishism, in the concluding chapter of your book if the chapter were not informed by the larger vision? That vision has to do with the massification of the individual under the auspices of the modern bureaucratic state, East and West. That your novel should conclude with an examination of a Western society suggests that no satisfactory solutions are to be found in the West. Those who prattle confidently about their freedom from "Judeo-Christian thought" seem in your works the victims of a repressive desublimation as unpromising as the reeducation programs organized by the commissars in the name of socialist brotherhood. The image of Jews filing into gas chambers is a bit lurid and exaggerated in this context, but it does surely serve to underline the gravity of the cultural circumstance you depict.

A function of this circumstance is the despair of politics that grows steadily in your work. How, you seem to ask, are serious political objectives to be formulated by persons for whom politics is at best a means of self-expression and a cultureless (rather than a cultured) society the final goal? To be serious about politics is after all to believe that there is such a thing as legitimate authority, which owes its legitimacy to binding truths on which it can take its stand. Philip Rieff reminds us that "serious attacks on authority must breed new authority," not the sense that authority itself is corrupt and that all discriminations and interdictions serve only the interests of those in power. In the West, as in the Sovietized societies of Eastern Europe, "we shall be dominated by anti-creeds and think ourselves free."[23] Politics—this I take you to suggest—cannot be serious or effective if it is nothing more than a mobilization of anti-credal, promiscuously "open," deconstructive enthusiasms. Neither can it hope to succeed as a call to reason or order. To enlist the participation of capable persons, politics must be made to do more than empty the contents and demythologize the forms of existing institutions. It must help us to imagine binding alternative institutions. This in the present state of things you do not consider a possibility. *The Book* is thus a grimly bracing testimony to the disaffection of the political imagination from the assumptions that make political action a plausible response to present discontents. Because you have little faith in the men and women created by mass society, you have no faith in the institutions such persons might create to promote their diversity and their capacity to think for themselves. Is this "reading" too simple? Does it betray too great an emphasis on politics? If so, I hope that you will let me know.

Yours very truly,
Robert Boyers

Notes

CHAPTER 1

1. Fredric Jameson, *The Political Unconscious* (Ithaca: Cornell University Press, 1980), pp. 107–108. This is a book of central importance to anyone studying the novel. In fact, much of what I say in the opening chapters of my book may rightly be read as a reply to Jameson, while the chapters that follow elaborate a view of the novel that would restore to it much that Jameson tries to take away. But nowhere in this book do I lose sight of the arguments Jameson has mounted.
2. One thinks, for example, of René Girard's brilliant efforts to construct a theory of the novel in *Deceit, Desire, and the Novel* (Baltimore: Johns Hopkins University Press, 1965).
3. See Milan Kundera, *The Book of Laughter and Forgetting* (New York: Penguin Books, 1981), pp. 232 and 165.
4. Irving Howe, *Politics and the Novel* (New York: Horizon Press, 1957), pp. 16–23.
5. E. D. Hirsch, *Validity In Interpretation* (New Haven: Yale University Press, 1967), p. 82.
6. A. Walton Litz, "The Genre of *Ulysses*," in John Halperin, ed., *The Theory of the Novel* (New York: Oxford University Press, 1974), p. 118.
7. Ibid., p. 112.
8. S. L. Goldberg, quoted in Litz, op. cit., p. 112.
9. See "A Fresh Approach to *Wuthering Heights*," in F. R. Leavis and Q. D. Leavis, *Lectures In America* (New York: Pantheon, 1969), pp. 84–152.
10. See my discussion of the Leavises' revisionary efforts in *F. R. Leavis* (Columbia, Missouri: University of Missouri Press, 1978), pp. 72–86.
11. Howe, op. cit., p. 24.
12. Ibid., p. 17.
13. Robert Boyers, "V. S. Naipaul," *The American Scholar* 50, 3, Summer 1981, p. 366.
14. It is customary, in speaking of novels, to distinguish first of all between our sense of the parts and our understanding of the whole. No passage taken in

isolation may be said finally to represent anything with unmistakable authority. No matter how persuasive the declaration of a view may be in a given passage, no matter how sympathetic or central the character who expresses it, no definitive conclusion may be drawn on the basis of that passage, for the novel operates very largely on the basis of tension, contradiction, and correction. More than any other literary form, it proposes questions to which there are *always* various answers. Its ideas are impressive, or tawdry, or familiar, or challenging, but inevitably they are ideas associated with circumstances or with characters whose reliability may never be taken for granted. Though critics select for quotation isolated passages of a novel in order to support this contention or that, all must know that even very careful selections are apt to be challenged by readers who wish to see a text in another way. It is not hard to select passages that will demonstrate a book's sense of itself as a political fiction, but it is very difficult to identify the generic constraints operating in such passages. It is also difficult to see what special advantages there are in paying attention to these constraints rather than to others that belong to our experience of *any* kind of novel. In the end one attends hopefully to the parts precisely because they are our only viable access to the whole. If there are generic constraints, one feels, they ought to be more discernible in their local manifestations than in the form of the fiction as a whole, where the constraints may not seem so important. The *anticipated* sense of the whole is more specifically dependent on our reading of generic constraints than our ultimate and continuing sense of the whole is likely to be.

15. Doris Lessing, "The Temptation of Jack Orkney," in *The Temptation of Jack Orkney and Other Stories* (New York: Knopf, 1972), pp. 237–238.
16. Ibid., pp. 270–271.
17. Ibid., p. 275.
18. Ibid., p. 285.
19. Ibid., p. 278.
20. See Susan Kress's discussion of these matters in "Lessing's Responsibility," *Salmagundi* 47–48, Winter–Spring 1980, pp. 115–131.

CHAPTER 2

1. Fredric Jameson, "On Politics and Literature," *Salmagundi* 7, Spring–Summer 1968, p. 17.
2. Saul Bellow, *The Dean's December* (N.Y.: Harper & Row, 1982), pp. 264 and 161.
3. Ibid., p. 193.
4. Fredric Jameson, *The Political Unconscious* (Ithaca: Cornell University Press, 1980), p. 19.
5. Ibid., p. 36.
6. Ibid., p. 25.
7. The Marxists deny that these master codes are narratives in any ordinary sense or that they conform to customary standards. Althusser's statement that "history [read "narrative"] is a process without a *telos* or a subject" ("Réponse à John Lewis" [Paris: Maspero, 1973], pp. 91–98) may be taken to summarize this position. See also Jameson, *The Political Unconscious*, p. 29. But without a *telos* or a subject the very notion of narrativization seems empty.
8. Jane Austen comes to mind as an instance of this sort of thing, though she is,

to be sure, a special case. No doubt some readers will object to any such view of Austen on the grounds that things are not as simple in her novels as they may once have seemed. Critics like George Levine have made us aware of the parodic elements in a novel like *Northanger Abbey*, aware that it implicitly invokes competing paradigms. But Austen subscribes so entirely to the view that "human relations can be understood rationally" that the competing versions of reality she invokes never have the force they assume in the hands of other writers. The commitment to a firmly "ordered and sensible world" may be ever so slightly compromised by Austen's "secret sympathy with aspirations to break from the quotidian," but no one doubts for a moment what it is Austen means to affirm. She knows precisely what is real and what is not, and she is ever determined to assert the priority of social norms as they are characteristically expressed in the common realistic code of her society. But, for a discriminating account of Austen's realism, see George Levine's *The Realistic Imagination* (Chicago: University of Chicago Press, 1981), esp. pp. 69–77.

9. Jameson, *The Political Unconscious*, pp. 28–29.
10. Ibid., p. 59.
11. Ibid., p. 117.
12. Ibid., p. 58.
13. See Kenneth Burke, "Literature As Equipment for Living," in *The Philosophy of Literary Form* (Berkeley: University of California Press, 1974).
14. William H. Gass, "Representation and the War for Reality," *Salmagundi* 55, Winter 1982, p. 101.

CHAPTER 3

1. In V. S. Naipaul, *The Return of Eva Peron* (N.Y.: Knopf, 1980).
2. Ibid., pp. 202, 198, and 195.
3. Clark Blaise, "Ideas Suggested By Nerves," unpublished paper delivered at a Modern Language Association meeting, Dec. 28, 1981, N.Y.
4. Ibid.
5. Naipaul, op. cit., pp. 201 and 202.
6. In *The Political Unconscious* (Ithaca: Cornell University Press, 1980), Fredric Jameson uses the vocabulary employed in this sentence to indict the characteristic Hegelian strategy of containment. Confronted with Naipaul's novel, Jameson would no doubt argue that a comparable strategy is employed by Naipaul in an effort to demystify the revolutionary promise associated with third world independence movements. But demystification does not always arise from a desire to undercut or abolish. It may also stem from a desire to see things as they are and insist that the revolution be taken in hand not by mimic men, but by those without the standard illusions and simplifications.
7. Would Raymond be one of those "advanced" critics of neocolonialism, for example, who find unacceptable the accommodations promoted by leaders like Felix Houphouet-Boigny of the Ivory Coast? Houphouet-Boigny has for more than twenty years of stability and relative prosperity steered a viable course for his country while refusing to compromise its very close relations with the former colonialist power, France. Would the fact that political control has been maintained without turning the country into a police state seem as important to Raymond as the fact that the president may well find it useful on occasion to "posture for Europeans"?

8. Jameson, op. cit., p. 58.
9. Jameson, op. cit., pp. 36–38, usefully describes Althusser's correction of the classical Marxist version of the state as epiphenomenon of the economic. What Jameson does not see is that to speak of the semiautonomous dynamics of the state apparatus is not necessarily to overlook the dimension of personal responsibility in the crimes of the state. Neither is it to refuse to invoke an implicit ethical standard by which it is possible to evaluate and refer to *corruption* or *betrayal*. Such "naive" concepts are largely absent from the discourse even of revisionist Marxist works, which are in consequence not equipped to deal effectively with the political vision of a Naipaul.
10. For more statistically detailed confirmation of a state of affairs amply set forth in Naipaul's novel, see a three-part article by Charles William Maynes, editor of *Foreign Policy* magazine, entitled "The Third World Crisis: Backward Towards Chaos," in *International Herald Tribune*, Sept. 20, 21, 22, 1983. Quotations in this paragraph are taken from the installments printed on September 20 and 21.

CHAPTER 4

1. Graham Greene, *Ways of Escape* (N.Y.: Penguin Books, 1981), p. 60.
2. John Atkins, *Graham Greene*, new rev. 2nd ed. (London: Calder and Boyars, 1966), p. 125.
3. Quoted by John Atkins, op. cit., p. 167. Atkins totally misunderstands Hardwick's criticism, contending that the Catholic avoids snobbishness simply by conceding now and again that the church and its spokesmen are fallible.
4. In *Ways of Escape*, p. 94, Greene labors to separate himself from Scobie and expresses surprise that readers should have found the character at bottom "a good man." But the Scobie who, Greene says, "was based on nothing but my own unconscious"—whatever that may mean—was not likely to impress readers precisely as he impressed the novelist. In any case, Greene obscures the critical point, that virtue is not finally at issue, and that a peculiar admiration can attend even so perverse a figure as Scobie.
5. In *The Political Unconscious* (Ithaca: Cornell University Press, 1980), Fredric Jameson treats the historical development of the closed monad as a stage in the evolution of narrative. But there is little point in applying the historical schema to the novels of Greene, which may hardly be said to mark an era in the art of the novel or in the extension of political intelligence. See Jameson, pp. 156–159, for a discussion of the monadized subject in writers like Flaubert and Dreiser.
6. Doctor Eduardo Plarr, surely the central character in Greene's *The Honorary Consul*, is a prime instance of the uncommitted though occasionally admirable figure we find in late Greene: the diagnostician reluctant to admit he can be moved, but all the more impressive when he allows himself to be tempted to a sentiment bordering on engagement.
7. Greene, *Ways of Escape*, p. 228.
8. For a thoroughly mechanical discussion of the novel, and of Greene's other works, that invariably accepts Greene's stated intentions as the unfailing key to all novelistic meanings, see J. P. Kulshrestha, *Graham Greene the Novelist* (New Delhi: Macmillan India, 1977). Reference on pp. 170–171.
9. Greene, *Ways of Escape*, p. 204. Greene goes on in the memoir to report that

Papa Doc personally attacked *The Comedians* "in an interview he gave in *Le Matin*, the paper he owned in Port-au-Prince—the only review I have ever received from a Chief of State." "Was it possible", Greene goes on, "that I disturbed his dreams as he had disturbed mine? . . . For five long years after my visit his Ministry of Foreign Affairs published an elaborate and elegant brochure . . . dealing with my case." The novelist concludes that "a writer is not so powerless as he actually feels," though what the power wielded by *The Comedians* amounted to is hard to say. See Greene, op. cit., pp. 206–207.

10. Edmund Wilson, *To The Finland Station* (N.Y.: Doubleday and Co., 1940; Anchor Books ed., 1953), p. 63. The words refer to the novels of Anatole France.

11. One might further speculate that Greene thought to answer the charge that he was irrationally anti-American by drawing in *The Comedians* two American innocents who are at once likeable and positively incapable of doing significant harm to anyone. But, then, as we have argued, Greene's intentions in respect of Mr. and Mrs. Smith remain obscure and lead us to feel that we are not meant to take them seriously as instances of anything.

CHAPTER 5

1. Gerald Martin, *"Yo El Supremo:* The Dictator and His Script," in *Contemporary Latin American Fiction*, Salvador Bacarisse, ed. (Edinburgh: Scottish Academic Press, 1980), p. 78. Martin's contention is supported by, perhaps even derived from, Asturias's statement that the dictators pictured in novels like his "belonged to the days before fascism." He goes on to say, "A dictatorship cannot isolate a country now as it did then, because people can turn on their radios in secret." See the interview with Asturias in *Seven Voices*, Rita Guibert, ed. (New York: Alfred A. Knopf, 1973), p. 134. The distinction at issue seems to me greatly overstated.

2. Martin, op. cit., p. 79.

3. Ibid., p. 77.

4. Regina Janes, *Gabriel García Márquez* (Columbia, Mo.: University of Missouri Press, 1981), p. 103.

5. Martin, op. cit., p. 77.

6. Janes, op. cit., p. 114.

7. García Márquez, quoted by Ernesto Gonzalez Bermejo in the journal *Triunfo* 654, April 12, 1975. See Janes, op. cit., p. 106.

8. Richard J. Callan, *Miguel Angél Asturias* (New York: Twayne Publishers, 1970), p. 22.

9. Gordon Brotherston, "García Márquez and the Secrets of Saturno Santos," in *Contemporary Latin American Fiction*, op. cit., p. 51.

10. Asturias, quoted by Guiseppe Bellini in *La narrativa di Miguel Angél Asturias* (Milan: Storia, 1966), p. 36.

11. Brotherston, op. cit., p. 48.

12. All of these writers are necessarily ambivalent about such matters. Asturias has said: "I esteem France for many reasons and consider her to some extent as my spiritual home." See *Seven Voices*, op. cit., p. 178.

13. Roberto Gonzalez Echevarría, *Alejo Carpentier: The Pilgrim At Home* (Ithaca: Cornell University Press, 1977), p. 260.

14. Michael Wood, "Unhappy Dictators," *New York Review of Books*, December 9, 1976, p. 57.
15. Gonzalez Echevarría, op. cit., p. 259.

CHAPTER 6

1. Walter Benjamin, "The Author As Producer," *Reflections* (N.Y.: Harcourt Brace Jovanovich, 1978), p. 223.
2. The novelist Jorge Semprun, in *What A Beautiful Sunday!* (N.Y.: Harcourt Brace Jovanovich, 1982), argues that before the 1960s even Solzhenitsyn would not have gotten through: "We would probably not have listened to him. I, at least, would not have heard his voice. I was deaf at the time." See p. 229. But the degree to which Semprun's present reflections are influenced by Solzhenitsyn leads one to wonder whether Solzhenitsyn might not have succeeded with him years earlier.
3. Alan Swingewood, *The Novel and Revolution* (N.Y.: Barnes & Noble, 1975), p. 184.
4. See George Lukács's discussion of *One Day* in his *Solzhenitsyn* (London: Merlin Press, 1970), p. 15.
5. Ibid., p. 11.
6. Ibid., pp. 37, 38.
7. Ibid., p. 47.
8. Ibid., p. 48.
9. Ibid., p. 43.
10. Erich Heller, *Thomas Mann: The Ironic German* (South Bend, Ind.: Regnery/Gateway Reprint ed., 1979), pp. 199, 204.
11. As in other instances, Fredric Jameson's *The Political Unconscious* (Ithaca: Cornell University Press, 1980) provides some of the key terms of an appropriate critical discourse without furnishing a corresponding argument that can usefully address the political novel. See p. 148.
12. Solzhenitsyn's regard for facts and his conviction that he can successfully embody in language a reality that is thought actually to exist outside of language will seem intolerably naive to readers whose critical views are taken from the writings of Jacques Derrida. But what can Derrida's resonant objections to the idea of representation mean to a Solzhenitsyn or to any reader who has been moved to accept the terms of his discourse? Is it true, as Edward Said has it, that "so long as we believe that language is mainly a representation of something else, we cannot see what language does"? If "language means not only representation but, paradoxically, the end or permanent deferring of representation," does this disestablish the narrative's claim to fact? Our further discussion of fact and reality in Solzhenitsyn should serve to indicate how trivial are Derrida's customary objections, the interesting account of which is to be found in Said's "Criticism Between Culture and System," in his *The World, The Text, and the Critic* (Cambridge: Harvard University Press, 1983). Quotations from p. 201.
13. Lukács accurately describes Soviet institutions as resting on "the daily mobilization" of hope and fear, with primary emphasis on fear and the need to "educate" people to "inner passivity and thus to the loss of their humanity." Terror is thus an ideological principle in the sense that it is thought to uphold the system as no other idea can, and that one will need to defend it in principle

if one is to defend the regime in practice. But Lukács's argument is not unambiguous on this point. See Lukács, op. cit., p. 55.

14. See Francis Barker, *Solzhenitsyn: Politics and Form* (N.Y.: Barnes and Noble, 1977), p. 35.

15. It is worth recalling in this regard the incisive cautionary remarks of Czeslaw Milosz, reflecting on the "reactionary" moral posture of a Solzhenitsyn. If "truth is an escape from the camp of the victors," he writes, then

> it often happens that truth is on the side of the reactionaries. . . . But it would be wrong to forget that we live in a Tower of Babel under construction and that the signs we use do not signify the same things in different parts of the building. . . . In one country a reactionary is a man who praises decency, while in another country the very appeal to decency is subversive and nearly a call for revolution.

See Milosz's "Questions," in *Aleksandr Solzhenitsyn: Critical Essays and Documentary Materials*, J. B. Dunlop, R. Haugh, and Alexis Klimoff, eds. (Belmont, Mass: Norland Pub. Co., 1973), p. 455.

16. See Victor Erlich, "The Writer as Witness," in Dunlop, Haugh, and Klimoff, op. cit., p. 25.

17. Terrence Des Pres, "The Heroism of Survival," in ibid., p. 59.

18. See Kathryn B. Feuer, "Solzhenitsyn & The Legacy of Tolstoy," in ibid., pp. 129–146.

19. Lukács, op. cit., p. 58.

20. The major study of polyphony in Solzhenitsyn is Vladislav Krasnov, *Solzhenitsyn and Dostoyevski* (Athens, Ga.: University of Georgia Press, 1980), to which we shall refer again. Whatever the limitations of its very instructive approach, it is an indispensable work. For the present citation, see p. 3, which quotes from a little-known interview with Solzhenitsyn.

21. Ibid., p. 5.

22. Ibid., p. 15.

23. Ibid., p. 22.

24. Edward J. Brown, "Solzhenitsyn's Cast of Characters," *Slavic and East European Journal* 15, 2, Summer 1971, pp. 162–163.

25. Lukács's statement that Solzhenitsyn proved himself a "significant artist by never dwelling on petty psychological considerations of Stalin, whether of an accusing or excusing character" will seem incredible to most readers of the novel. See Lukács, op. cit., p. 52.

26. Roy A. Medvedev and others have in recent years argued that in spite of constant opposition even within the ruling elites, Stalin had a good deal of popular support in Soviet society, a fact that Solzhenitsyn does little to show in *The First Circle*. Rubin's support, after all, is hardly typical, reflecting as it does the self-deluding intricacy of a trained dialectical mind. And other Stalinists in the novel cannot, perhaps, really represent the extent of Stalin's popularity either. Even the 1936–1939 purges were supported by many workers who saw in the elimination of bureaucrats and bosses "the underdog's dream of retribution with the aid of a higher justice. . . . Impotence seeks the protection of supreme avenging power." See Medvedev, *On Socialist Democracy* (N.Y.: Knopf, 1975), p. 346.

27. To claim that "the object of power is power" is not to contradict the somewhat

different claim that anything is justified in the service of the state. At one point in the novel Rubin protests against imprisoning two suspects when only one can be charged. What of the one who is innocent? But Oskolupov calmly corrects him: " 'Innocent? What d'you mean? . . . Not guilty of anything at all? The Security Service will sort that one out.' " The critic Stephen Carter concludes that the people are imprisoned—and this is consistent with Solzhenitsyn's view—"simply as a means of imposing arbitrary rule, of crushing and annihilating people who might think of dissension. . . . The message seems to be that the regime aimed in fact to crush or dehumanize the personality." See Carter, *The Politics of Solzhenitsyn* (N.Y.: Holmes and Meier, 1977), p. 17. We see here how the "bourgeois concept" of individual guilt is replaced by the idea of the "inexpediency of the accused to the state." Legality is equated with "the strength required to obtain political power and to maintain it." See Carter, op. cit., p. 32.

28. Mikhail Bakhtin, *Problems of Dostoyevski's Poetics* (Ann Arbor, Mich.: Ardis, 1973), p. 36.
29. For a valuable study of continuity and discontinuity in the evolution of the Soviet system, see Robert Tucker, *The Soviet Political Mind*, rev. ed. (N.Y.: W. W. Norton, 1971).
30. Lukács, op. cit., p. 86.
31. Ibid., p. 61.
32. Ibid., pp. 63–64.
33. The quintessential expression of these Christian virtues is Solzhenitsyn's story "Matryona's House." But the "true, legendary Russia" discovered there is hardly a perfect or fully consoling place.
34. For a convincing account of some of these chapters—there are nine in all— see Carter, op. cit., pp. 78–82. Carter indicates that the chapters were published in numbers of *The Herald of the Russian Christian Movement* (1974) and in *Kontinent* (1974 and following). No doubt, future editions of *The First Circle* will have to renumber chapters to make room for the missing chapters that will be inserted in accordance with Solzhenitsyn's original intentions.

CHAPTER 7

1. "An Interview with Nadine Gordimer," *Contemporary Literature* XXII, 3, 1981.
2. Quoted in Harvey Gross, *The Contrived Corridor* (Ann Arbor: University of Michigan Press, 1971), p. 126.
3. Nadine Gordimer, "A Writer In South Africa," *London Magazine* 5, 2, May 1965.
4. Judie Newman, "Gordimer's *The Conservationist*: 'That Book Of Unknown Signs,' " *Critique* XXII, 3, 1981, p. 33.
5. For a discussion of the competing principles of social order, see Edward Shils, "Charisma, Order, and Status," in *The Constitution of Society* (Chicago: University of Chicago Press, 1982), p. 142.
6. Ibid., p. 133.
7. In Philip Rahv's essay, "Dostoyevski in *The Possessed*," he reminds us of how many competing versions of the Marxist, or "the revolutionary," there may be. But the classic type seems almost invariably distinguished by "the deadly seriousness of its approach to theoretical and ideological issues, . . . its fanat-

icism and tendencies to schism and heresy-hunting." Rahv is, of course, describing in such terms the qualities of the nineteenth-century Russian radical
intelligentsia, but the terms I have singled out go well beyond those intended
parameters. See Rahv, *Essays On Literature and Politics, 1932-1972* (Boston:
Houghton Mifflin, 1978), p. 111. The crucial point here is that Lionel Burger
in no way resembles the figure Rahv describes.

8. See Hannah Arendt, *The Human Condition* (Chicago: University of Chicago
Press, 1958), pp. 213–215.

9. Roland Barthes, *Mythologies*, tr. by Annette Lavers (N.Y.: Hill and Wang,
1972), p. 143. Cited by Sheldon Wolin in an important paper, "Hannah Arendt:
Democracy & The Political," *Salmagundi* 60, Spring–Summer 1983.

10. See Wolin, op. cit.

11. René Girard, *Deceit, Desire and the Novel* (Baltimore: Johns Hopkins University Press, 1965), esp. pp. 194–202.

12. Arendt, quoted in Melvyn A. Hill, ed. *Hannah Arendt: The Recovery of the
Public World* (N.Y.: St. Martin's Press, 1979), p. 317.

13. The 1959–1960 volume of *A Survey of Race Relations in South Africa,* compiled
by Muriel Horrell (South African Institute of Race Relations), reports that
"of the bullet wounds that could be classified, 30 shots had entered the wounded
or killed persons from the front and 155 from the back." See p. 58.

14. Though at first there were signs that laws requiring "Bantus" to carry pass or
reference books might be dropped, this was in fact only a temporary development. See Horrell, op. cit., pp. 66–69. The 1961 volume in the race relations
series nicely indicates the steps taken by the government to exempt itself and
its officers from proceedings "brought in any court of law . . . in respect of
any acts or statements" involved in the Sharpeville disturbances. See pp. 54–
56 of the 1961 volume.

15. Franz Fanon, *The Wretched of the Earth* (N.Y.: Grove Press, 1963).

16. "An Interview With Nadine Gordimer," op. cit., p. 269.

17. Accounts of the Soweto race riots range from the more or less factual report
issued by the South African Institute of Race Relations in its 1976 volume (pp.
51–87) to the more elaborate reports and analyses contained in such works as
Denis Herbstein's *White Man, We Want To Talk To You* (N.Y.: Africana
Publishing Co., 1979). A key point in these various reports is that "violence
on such a vast scale could not have resulted from one issue alone" (*A Survey
of Race Relations in South Africa,* 1976, p. 51) and had to be the culmination
of a long and terrible distress. In addition, the unrest was not limited to a
period of days or weeks, but extended over several months and showed that
the racial situation in the country had reached a new level of conflict out of
which unforeseeable changes would surely emerge.

18. Indeed, the Marxist contempt for the so-called bourgeois or liberal virtues has
made one hesitate even to mention such virtues with anything less than sneering
condescension.

19. Daniel Bell, "Reflections on Jewish Identity," *The Winding Passage* (Cambridge, Mass.: ABT Books, 1980), p. 318.

CHAPTER 8

1. Alvin Rosenfeld, *A Double Dying* (Bloomington: University of Indiana Press,
1980), pp. 5, 8, 10, and 27.

2. Jean Amery, *At The Mind's Limits* (Bloomington: University of Indiana Press, 1980; 1st ed. 1966), p. 79.
3. Librairie Gallimard, 1963; English translation by Grove Press, 1964.
4. Anthony West, "Books", The New Yorker, August 8, 1964.
5. Editions Grasset et Fasquelle, 1980; English translation by Harcourt Brace Jovanovich, 1982.
6. Lawrence L. Langer, *The Holocaust & The Literary Imagination* (New Haven: Yale University Press, 1975), p. 285.
7. Editions du Seuil, 1977; English translation by Karz Publishers, N.Y. 1979. Among the special features to be noted in this work of nonfiction is the almost obscenely candid recantation. This includes the quoting of an old poem— actually Semprun's childish homage to the inspiring perfection and wisdom of the party—so grotesque in its unselfconscious piety as almost to make one doubt Semprun's intelligence. The inclusion of such material in the novel would have disastrously undercut the complexly ironic self-deprecation that converts sterile pessimism to the drama of determined unmasking.
8. H. Stuart Hughes, *The Sea Change* (N.Y.: Harper & Row, 1975), p. 125.
9. There are frequent allusions to Shalamov in the pages of Semprun's novel. Shalamov's stories are available in English translations by John Glad, published by W. W. Norton and entitled *Kolyma Tales* and *Graphite*.
10. Robert Boyers, "The Ideology of Rejection," *London Times Literary Supplement*, January 15, 1982, p. 45.
11. George Lukács, *Theory of the Novel* (Cambridge, Mass.: M.I.T. Press, 1971; original ed. 1920), p. 90.
12. Jonathan Culler, following Roland Barthes, writes, "Literature should attempt . . . 'to unexpress the expressible,' to problematize the meanings we automatically confer or assume." The stress here is on the writer's effort " 'to detach a [presumably chaste] secondary language from the slime of primary languages afforded him by the world.' " Semprun obviously has no sympathy with the enterprise of emptying language even of inherited meaning, and is finally more interested in problematizing particular analyses or interpretations than in challenging the idea of discourse or meaning itself. See Culler, *Roland Barthes* (N.Y.: Oxford University Press, 1983), p. 57.
13. In *Memoirs of a Revolutionist* (N.Y.: Farrar Straus, 1957; original ed. 1945), responding to news of the concentration camps, Dwight MacDonald pointed out that we must now fear persons who obey the law more than those who break it.
14. Lucy Dawidowicz, "Blaming The Jews: The Charge of Perfidy," *The Jewish Presence* (N.Y.: Holt Rinehart and Winston, 1977), p. 269.
15. See Randolph L. Braham, *The Politics of Genocide: The Holocaust in Hungary* (N.Y.: Columbia University Press, 1982), for a detailed examination of a most peculiar and terrifying story.
16. See Michael Checinski, *Poland, Communism, Nationalism, Anti-Semitism* (N.Y.: Karz-Cohl Pub. Co., 1983), for a complex account of the Polish obsession with Jews, among other subjects, and a response to the contention that "real" Catholics had nothing to apologize for in the holocaust years. For a particularly vile example of Catholic apologetics, see Michael Schwartz, "Are Christians Responsible?" *National Review*, August 8, 1980, pp. 956–958.
17. See Abraham Brumberg, "The Ghost in Poland," *The New York Review of Books*, June 2, 1983. Brumberg quotes a Polish Catholic writer who wrote:

"Polish anti-Semitism . . . succeeded in achieving something difficult as well as appalling: it outlived the Polish Jews themselves."

18. George Steiner, "A Kind of Survivor," in *Language And Silence* (N.Y.: Atheneum, 1967), p. 140.

19. See Hyam Maccoby, "George Steiner's Hitler," *Encounter*, May 1982, pp. 27–34.

20. Maccoby, op. cit., pp. 29–30.

21. That Röthling is no typical German is clear even in his view of the law, which has very little to do with the proclivity to follow orders cited by ordinary German citizens who justified what they did on the grounds that they were "law-abiding" and ordinary. Röthling has no interest in excusing what he did, and his confidence in the law is really quite extraordinary given the decline in the authority of the law that set in as early as the late years of the nineteenth century, when Georg Simmel and other reputable philosophers argued that value judgments cast in legal terms were invariably arbitrary. See, on this issue, Arnold Brecht, *Political Theory* (Princeton: Princeton University Press, 1959), which quotes G. Rudbruch to the effect that "philosophy of law is necessarily political philosophy, and vice versa" (p. 138), so that all concepts of law and justice are reducible to political exigency.

22. The competing portrayals of key Nazis provided by various well-known studies are such as to leave one in permanent doubt about what lay behind them all. The most famous—some would say notorious—work on the Nazi mind is surely Hannah Arendt's *Eichmann in Jerusalem* (N.Y.: Viking Press, 1964), but the central thesis of that book is challenged in a great variety of works focused on other figures. The autobiography of Rudolf Hess, entitled *Commandant of Auschwitz* (Cleveland and N.Y.: World Pub. Co., 1959), shows Hess to have been rather an average fellow, not at all a clinical type or a monster of depravity. His failure to understand what he had done, long after the smoke had cleared, makes what he did seem almost more terrible than it would have seemed had he understood. More instructive is Gitta Sereny's biography of Treblinka Commandant Franz Stangl, entitled *Into That Darkness: From Mercy Killing to Mass Murder* (N.Y.: McGraw Hill, 1974). Like so many of the others, Stangl clearly acted without feeling that he was responsible for the orders he carried out, and reminded himself now and again that he bore no special animus toward Jews. He was, so far as we can tell, not a sadist.

Steiner's Röthling has a little more in common with some other camp commandants interviewed by a young Israeli historian whose Ph.D. dissertation is summarized by George Kren and Leon Rappoport in their useful book, *The Holocaust and the Crisis of Human Behavior* (N.Y.: Holmes and Meier, 1980). In Tom Segev, *The Commanders of the Nazi Concentration Camps* (Boston: University Press, 1977), we are told that "the image of . . . personality that emerges is that of individuals who show little sign of pathology . . . , who were tremendously enthusiastic about their being chosen to participate in a new order, swept away by a euphoria that led them to do whatever was necessary, and who still look back nostalgically to 'the good old days.' " (See Kren and Rappoport, op. cit., p. 168). It is hard to see Röthling as ever having been euphoric, but he was surely swept away for a while.

23. See Alvin Rosenfeld, "Steiner's Hitler," *Salmagundi* 52–53, Spring–Summer 1981, pp. 160–174.

24. Maccoby, op. cit., p. 30.

25. Ibid., p. 32.
26. Rosenfeld, op. cit., p. 172.
27. Maccoby usefully argues that "the Israelites fought against the Canaanites with sword in hand, a band of outlaw slaves fighting against the entrenched great ones of the earth for a right to freedom and a place of their own. . . . How can this be compared with the Nazis' cowardly destruction of helpless, unarmed and loyal citizens, on psychotic grounds . . . ?" More, as Maccoby contends, "the Jews have never condemned people outside their church to 'damnation,' or regarded them as being 'sinful' for not being Jews." See Maccoby, op. cit., pp. 30–31. But in spite of Maccoby's instructive reminders, he cannot see that he is arguing not with Steiner, but with Steiner's Hitler, and that this Hitler, as a character, needs to be engaged in other ways.
28. Rosenfeld, op. cit., p. 172.
29. Ibid., p. 167.
30. Maccoby, op. cit., p. 34.
31. Rosenfeld, op. cit., p. 173.
32. Maccoby, op. cit., p. 32.
33. Steiner, "A Kind of Survivor," p. 150.
34. See Bernard Wasserstein, *Britain and The Jews of Europe 1939–1945* (N.Y.: Oxford University Press, 1979). The historian Telford Taylor, in a strangely "even-handed" review of the Wasserstein book ("Quantity Was Not The Point," *New York Times Book Review*, Oct. 7, 1979, p. 7), writes that "a long and bloody road to allied victory remained to be traversed. Should precious shipping have been committed to this evacuation? Should Arab good will have been jeopardized? . . ." Wasserstein's powerful study inspires in Taylor some nice sentiments, but this political 'good sense' remains intact, as therefore does his conviction that the "quantitative impact" of more strenuous allied intervention on behalf of the Jews would have been slight, whatever the hard evidence to the contrary Wasserstein provides.
35. See Gershom Scholem, "Israel and the Diaspora," *On Jews and Judaism in Crisis* (N.Y.: Schocken Books, 1976), p. 251.

CHAPTER 9

1. Philip Stevick, *Alternative Pleasures* (Chicago: University of Illinois Press, 1981), pp. 150, 116, 117, and 118.
2. See Jean Baudrillard, "The Ecstasy of Communication," in Hal Foster, ed., *The Anti-Aesthetic* (Pt. Townsend, Wash.: Bay Press, 1983) p. 142.
3. Ibid.
4. Quoted by Hugh Kenner in *Dublin's Joyce* (Bloomington, Ind.: Indiana University Press, 1956), p. 12.
5. Ibid., p. 10.
6. Ibid., p. 12.
7. Ibid., p. 10.
8. See Otis C. Mitchell, *Hitler Over Germany* (Philadelphia: Institute for Study of Human Issues, 1983), p. 258.
9. David Schoenbaum argues that if any society deserves to be called "sick," Nazi Germany is surely it. See *Hitler's Social Revolution* (N.Y.: Doubleday, 1966), p. 1.
10. For interesting insights into the idea of *Verwandlung*, see Walter H. Sokel,

The Writer In Extremis (Stanford: Stanford University Press, 1959), pp. 141 ff.

11. Hamida Bosmajian, *Metaphors of Evil* (Iowa City: University of Iowa Press, 1979), p. 84.

12. Fritz Stern, *The Politics of Cultural Despair* (Berkeley: University of California Press, 1963), p. 132.

13. For information on the controversy surrounding the term *inner emigration* (or *inward migration*), see H. R. Kleineberger, "The 'Innere Emigration': A Disputed Issue in 20th century German Literature," *Monatshefte* LVII, 1965, pp. 171–180.

14. See Michael Hollington, *Günter Grass* (London: Marion Boyars, 1980), p. 31.

15. Fredric Jameson, *The Political Unconscious* (Ithaca: Cornell University Press, 1980), p. 54.

16. The argument here developed owes much to the writings of J. G. A. Pocock. See his *Politics, Language and Time* (N.Y.: Atheneum, 1971), particularly "On the Non-Revolutionary Character of Paradigms," pp. 273–291, which is exceedingly instructive without addressing itself either to novels or to specific modern societies.

17. Ibid., p. 275.

18. Ibid., p. 274.

19. Ibid., p. 275.

20. John Reddick, in *The Danzig Trilogy of Günter Grass* (N.Y.: Harcourt Brace Jovanovich, 1974), p. 273, among others, has spoken of "Oskar's proteanism," but this dimension of a novelistic "picaresque persona" has little to do with serious growth or transformation. Even Oskar's efforts "to integrate himself in the same bourgeois social structure which he claimed to have rejected so utterly at birth" Reddick rightly describes as "bound to fail since Oskar remains irrevocably an outsider." His changes have to do with image, with masks and disguises. They proceed from no stable and expanding sense of self.

21. Pocock, op. cit., p. 280.

22. Opinions on this sort of thing differ drastically. Reddick, for example, stresses Grass's irreverent, even savage unmasking of Christian conventions and pious sentiments (see Reddick, op. cit., p. 17), while others speak of his commitment to the possibility of Christian redemption. Acknowledging Grass's interest, as a novelist, in the literary possibilities inherent in these issues and their associated motifs, I nonetheless reject the view that Christianity itself was of particular interest to Grass in *The Tin Drum*. But others may wish to argue with my contentions as to Grass's interest in political issues and will surely have much to substantiate their claims given the relative impoverishment or absence of actual political discourse in the surfaces of the novel.

23. Quoted in Marlis G. Steinert, *Hitler's War and the Germans* (Athens: Ohio University Press, 1977), p. 9. This very useful volume furnishes important information on the mood of the German people during the war.

24. In this regard it is instructive to note the debates on the subject of resistance carried on for decades by holocaust scholars interested in the resistance or passivity of the Jewish victims. Raul Hilberg, for example, rejects the idea that resistance is simply a matter of good deeds and humane deportment, arguing that resistance is "opposition to the perpetrator" and that therefore "Jews were not oriented to resistance"—no more than the German masses were, we might add. See Hilberg, *The Destruction of the European Jews* (N.Y.: Harper & Row, 1979), pp. 662–665. For an opposing view, see Meir Dworzecki, "The

Day to Day Stand of the Jews," *Jewish Reistance During the Holocaust* (Jerusalem: Yad Vashem, 1971).

25. See Roger S. Gottlieb, "The Concept of Resistance," *Social Theory & Practice* 9, 1, Spring 1983, p. 35.
26. Reddick, op. cit., pp. 52–53.
27. See Martin Mayer, *They Thought They Were Free* (Chicago: University of Chicago Press, 1955), esp. "Collective Shame," pp. 174–186.
28. It should be obvious here that I have taken over for my own purposes the argument conducted by Herbert Marcuse in *Eros and Civilization* (Boston: Beacon Press, 1955). See, especially, "Critique of Neo-Freudian Revisionism," pp. 238–274.
29. See Herbert Marcuse, *Counterrevolution and Revolt* (Boston: Beacon Press, 1972), p. 50.
30. Ibid., p. 103.
31. The words are Adorno's, as quoted by Gillian Rose in *The Melancholy Science* (N.Y.: Columbia University Press, 1978), p. 44. See Rose's discussion through p. 45 and, for a thorough presentation, Adorno's *Negative Dialectics* (London: Routledge and Kegan Paul, 1973).
32. Rose, op. cit., p. 45.
33. Adorno, quoted in ibid., p. 44.
34. Reddick, op. cit., pp. 159, 167.
35. Ibid., p. 169.
36. Ibid., p. 154.
37. Ibid., p. 165.
38. See James C. Bruce, "The Equivocating Narrator in Günter Grass's *Cat and Mouse*," *Monatschefte* LVIII, 2, 1966.
39. Grass's statement that he aimed to show "the fabrication of a military hero by society" is interesting, but it does not describe the character or the main thrust of the completed work. See Grass, quoted in Hollington, op. cit., p. 64.
40. See George Steiner, "A Note on Günter Grass," in his *Language and Silence* (N.Y.: Atheneum, 1967), p. 116.
41. See George Steiner's *Heidegger* (London: Fontana Modern Masters, 1978), pp. 77–78.
42. Ibid., p. 78.
43. That this reading of *Dog Years* goes against the grain of the enlightened criticism recently directed at the novel will be clear to anyone who has studied, say, Hamida Bosmajian's *Metaphors of Evil* (pp. 113 ff.). There, in the chapter on *Dog Years*, Bosmajian concludes that "the journey underground [at the end of Grass's novel] could be an education for Matern, but he is no pupil, just as Amsel is no teacher. . . . Both simply confirm their damnation, their paralysis in the *status quo*. . . . [U]nable to make analogies and see relationships, the whole experience is wasted on [Matern]." Bosmajian fails to consider that, in having their damnation confirmed, these characters are coming to terms with the very substance of their identity and with whatever prospects for growth they may have. Matern's statement that "this is hell indeed," repeated over and over again in the journey through Amsel's mechanical underground, expresses not a failure "to make analogies and see relationships," but a recognition that nothing could be more terrible than the vivid reminders of Matern's Everyman experience that Amsel has set before him. Bosmajian's conclusion, that "evil is banal" and Matern the pure embodiment of this hopeless banality,

is too easy and one-dimensional; and it is typical of the nihilist readings the novel has frequently inspired.

44. In a remarkable essay entitled "Jews and Germans," originally a lecture delivered in 1966, Gershom Scholem shows how, "in the name of progress," many postholocaust Jews agree that "a resolute disavowal of Jewish nationality" is not a high price to pay for acceptance by those who had recently sought to exterminate them. At the same time, Scholem goes on, in Germany as elsewhere, the inveterate "self-abnegation of the Jews, although welcomed and indeed demanded, was often seen as evidence of their lack of moral substance." Weininger found, apparently, a good deal of support for his proposals among those in routine flight from their own Jewishness and not yet modern enough to regard either their own ancient religion or their alienation from it as particularly valuable. As late as 1935, Scholem points out, articulate Jews like Margarete Susman could write, " 'The vocation of Israel as a people is not self-realization, but self-surrender for the sake of a higher, transhistorical goal.' " This sort of "delusion," Scholem concludes, is the reflection of a perverse thinking that in turn must bespeak "a great inner demoralization, an enthusiasm for self-sacrifice." Such demoralization surely contributed to the ease with which the Nazis carted off and put to death most of their Jewish victims, a point that Grass does not much concern himself with in *Dog Years*, but is critical to our sense of Eddi Amsel's specialness, in spite of his attraction to Weininger. For fuller discussion of the idea of Jewish self-surrender, see Gershom Scholem's essay in *On Jews and Judaism In Crisis* (N.Y.: Schocken Books, 1976), pp. 71–92.

45. See Wesley V. Blomster, "The Documentation of a Novel: Otto Weininger and the 'Hundejahre,' " *Monatschefte* LXI 2, 1969, pp. 136–137.

46. The description provided by Keith Miles in his *Günter Grass* (N.Y.: Barnes and Noble, 1975), p. 133, seems to me particularly good.

47. See Ann L. Mason, *The Skeptical Muse: A Study of Günter Grass's Conception of the Artist* (Bern and Frankfurt/M.: Verlag Herbert Lang, 1974; reprt. in Stanford German Studies, 1974), pp. 51 and 53. Mason stresses too emphatically Amsel's desire "to participate in the spirit of the Nazi movement," but her insights on Amsel as Jewish aggressor-figure are quite helpful.

48. Steiner, "A Note on Günter Grass," p. 114.

CHAPTER 10

1. The words are spoken by the authorial narrator in *The Unbearable Lightness of Being* (N.Y.: Harper & Row, 1984), p. 221.

2. David Lodge handles some of the unanswered questions very tactfully in his piece, "From Don Juan To Tristan," *TLS*, May 25, 1984, p. 567.

3. "An Interview with Milan Kundera" (interviewer: Ian McEwan), *Granta* 11, 1984, p. 25.

4. Milan Kundera, "Somewhere Behind," *Granta* 11, 1984, p. 91.

5. Milan Kundera, "Afterword: A Talk With The Author," in *The Book of Laughter and Forgetting* (N.Y.: Penguin, 1981), p. 237.

6. José Ortega y Gassett, *Meditations on Quixote* (N.Y.: W.W. Norton & Co., 1961), p. 60.

7. Robert Boyers, "Nature and Social Reality in Bellow's *Sammler*," in R. Boyers, *Excursions* (Pt. Washington, N.Y.: Kennikat Press, 1977), p. 34.

8. Robert Nisbet, "*1984* and the Conservative Imagination," in *1984 Revisited*, Irving Howe, ed. (N.Y.: Harper & Row, 1983), associates totalitarianism "in the first instance" with "the rage to politicize" and "the expansion of the state's sovereign authority to all areas of society." This is by now a familiar and persuasive view. See Nisbet, esp. pp. 188–198.

9. Milan Kundera, Author's Preface to *The Joke* (N.Y.: Penguin, 1982), p. xvi.

10. For a model critique of a would-be political novel that fails to think politically and know its own limitations, see Isaac Deutscher's essay on *Dr. Zhivago* entitled "Pasternak and the Revolution," in *Ironies of History* (N.Y.: Oxford University Press, 1966), pp. 248–266.

11. The spiritual status of cynicism, even of contempt for the created universe—including man—has been argued for many centuries. Pascal argued, after all, that we should love only God, "that self-hatred is the true and unique virtue," and went on from this to devalue also the virtuous works of humans as inevitably competing with any proper conception of true good. In this sense it might be argued that Ludvik's contempt for others and for himself is an attitude eminently worthy of respect, though of course it would then have in it nothing that might be called a political virtue. Politics, for Pascal and others like him, "can only be evil," and though a novel like *The Joke* may lead us to attribute to you some such view, finally I think this would be a mistake. See, for an elaboration of Pascal's view, Erich Auerbach, "On The Political Theory of Pascal," in Auerbach, *Scenes From The Drama of European Literature* (N.Y.: Meridian Books, 1959; reprint ed. 1984 by University of Minnesota Press: Minneapolis). See esp. pp. 110–114.

12. The debasement of ritual and its conversion to agitprop is beautifully evoked in Part Five of *The Joke*, when Ludvik happens upon a ceremony called "*a welcoming of new citizens to life*" and is told that attendance is used "as a touchstone for evaluating people's sense of citizenship." It is a mistake to suppose that such ceremonial requirements were initiated by the the the Communist commissars. They have in fact been a part of other "totalitarian democracies" from the time of the French Revolution. J. L. Talmon has written most persuasively of these ceremonial procedures and all they imply, particularly the fact that in such societies "no one would be automatically born into the National Community," but would have to join "a confraternity of faith." Talmon notes the requirements for ceremonially inscribing the names of the faithful "citizens" on a register and taking their public declarations of commitment, quite in the way that Ludvik witnesses in your book. See Talmon, *The Origins of Totalitarian Democracy* (N.Y.: Frederick A. Praeger, 1960), p. 234.

13. Hans Morgenthau, a thinker always associated with political "realism," often nonetheless found it necessary to caution against collective action as an antidote to doubt or a sense of futility. Frequently, he contended, one must register "the absurdity of action" and accept one's "destiny, which is to think and feel." In this sense, the act of remembering in your novels ought not to be viewed as an evasion of action or even as preliminary to acts of resistance. In Morgenthau's words, "It is a distortion of the hierarchy of human values to assign to political action, especially in its collective form, the highest rank." I hope that nothing I have said in this book will lead you to conclude that I am guilty of this distortion. See Morgenthau, "Thought and Action," *Social Research* 38, 4, Winter 1971; reprinted in 51, 1, Spring 1984. Quotations from p. 160.

14. I have no need to explain to you what happened in your country in the course of its history, but there is a book I should mention that does very well cover the period that figures in your novels. Have you seen A. French's *Czech Writers and Politics, 1945–1969* (East European Monographs, Boulder; distributed by Columbia University Press in N.Y., 1982)? It is an orderly and lucid account of the various purges and conflicts to which your works insistently refer.

15. May I recommend to you the writings of Philip Rieff, particularly *The Triumph of the Therapeutic* (N.Y.: Harper and Row, 1966) and *Fellow Teachers* (N.Y.: Harper and Row, 1973)? The quotations included here are taken from a first periodical version of "Fellow Teachers," which appeared in *Salmagundi*, 20, Summer–Fall 1972, reprinted in *The Salmagundi Reader* (Bloomington: Indiana University Press, 1983), p. 30.

16. You will, of course, recognize this resonant formulation from *The Unbearable Lightness of Being*, p. 35.

17. Even those who regard themselves as dissidents would seem in the main to describe their resistance in terms that encourage skepticism. The opposition in Czechoslovakia is "unified," we are often told, but only "on the things they do not want, on sort of a negation of the system they now live in." The opposition doesn't know what it wants or how to attain what it wants, and though "cultural genocide" is occurring, attempts at resistance increasingly assume "the same counter-cultural, extra-political character [that] the Western counterculture did in the 1960s." See Jan Kavan, "Dissidence in Czechoslovakia: An Interview," *Partisan Review* XLIX, 1, 1982, pp. 124 and 125.

18. Milan Kundera, Afterword, *The Book of Laughter and Forgetting*, p. 235.

19. Lodge, op. cit., p. 567.

20. Kundera, "Afterword," p. 234.

21. Kundera, *The Unbearable Lightness of Being*, pp. 248 and 249.

22. The Hungarian novelist George Konrad has written that "those who desire to be discerning rather than virtuous in Eastern Europe today ought to make sure that, having wriggled out of the web of state socialist romanticism, they do not fabricate a new kind of dissident romanticism whose major flaw is that it enjoys no clear autonomy vis a vis Western culture." See Konrad, "Face and Mask," Dissent, Summer 1979, p. 299.

23. Rieff, op. cit., pp. 25 and 27.

Index